Contents

Preface

Philosophy is intriguing even to those who know little of it. But the sort of philosophy studied at universities is difficult to enter into on one's own. The reactions we had to a previous, shorter version of the present material convinced us that we had hit upon a particularly useful way of taking people into the subject – one that preserves what is most fascinating about it while facilitating serious study. We became convinced that there would be a wider audience for a book with these aims. Samuel Guttenplan was responsible for preparing chapters 4, 5 and 6, Jennifer Hornsby for chapter 2, 8 and 9, and Christopher Janaway for chapters 1, 3 and 7.

Reading Philosophy will have appeal both to those beginning their study of philosophy at a conventional university and to those who want to engage with the subject on their own. Unlike introductory books which confine themselves to *telling* you about the subject, this one requires you to *do* philosophy. We think that its direct approach makes the book valuable for both students and other readers. It can be used as the set reading in seminars in introductory courses: it is based on material that has served this purpose at our own Birkbeck College. But the book is also suitable for individuals working without a teacher. Whoever uses it will be well prepared for further study in philosophy, and, we hope, will be encouraged to pursue it.

S. G.
J. H.
C. J.

University of London External Programme

This book is the text for the Introduction to Philosophy course in the Diploma in Philosophy run by the University of London External Programme. The diploma meets the needs of those who are keenly interested in philosophy but uncertain yet whether they can make the commitment required to enrol for the BA degree. It aims to introduce philosophy to those who may have only an inkling of what it is about, and it offers enough of the subject to make possible an easy transition to study at degree level.

The University of London was founded in 1836, and its External Programme was established in 1858. There are currently 28,000 students registered on the programme living in over 180 different countries. The programme's various courses, leading to diplomas and degrees, are designed for those who study either on their own or in tutorial groups in their locality. Course contents and standards are maintained at the same high level as for internal degrees in the University of London. The university sets the syllabuses, provides study materials and guidance, and examines students at the end of the academic year (for further information about the programme consult: http://www.londonexternal.ac.uk).

Sources and Acknowledgements

The publisher gratefully acknowledge the following for permission to reproduce copyright material.

Anscombe, G. E. M., 'Causality and Determination', from an inaugural lecture published by Cambridge University Press in 1971, reprinted by permission of the publishers and author.

Boyle, Robert, 'The Origin of Forms and Qualities' from *Selected Philosophical Papers of Robert Boyle*, ed. M. A. Stewart (Manchester University Press, Manchester, 1979).

Descartes, René, 'Meditations' from *Descartes: Meditations on First Philosophy: with Selections from Objections and Replies*, trans. John Cottingham (Cambridge University Press, Cambridge, 1987).

Feagin, Susan L., 'The Pleasures of Tragedy' from *American Philosophical Quarterly*, 20 (1983), pp. 95–104.

Lemmon, E. J., 'Moral Dilemmas', *Philosophical Review*, 71 (1962), pp. 139–58, copyright 1962 Cornell University. Reprinted by permission of the publisher.

Nozick, Robert, *Anarchy, State and Utopia* (Basic Books, New York, 1977).

Schopenhauer, Arthur, *Prize Essay on the Freedom of the Will*, ed. Günter Zöller, trans. F. J. Payne (Cambridge University Press, Cambridge, 1999).

Strawson, P. F., 'Freedom and Resentment' from *Freedom and Resentment and Other Essays* (Methuen & Co. Ltd, London, 1974), copyright P. F. Strawson.

Strawson, P. F., 'Self, Mind and Body' from *Freedom and Resentment and Other Essays* (Methuen & Co. Ltd, London, 1974), copyright P. F. Strawson.

Williams, Bernard, 'The Idea of Equality' from *Problems of the Self* (Cambridge University Press, Cambridge, 1973), copyright Bernard Williams.

Williams, Bernard, 'The Self and its Future' from *Problems of the Self* (Cambridge University Press, Cambridge, 1973), copyright Bernard Williams.

Every effort has been made to trace all the copyright holders, but if any has been inadvertently overlooked, the publishers will be pleased to make the necessary arrangement at the first opportunity.

Primary Sources

Berkeley, George, *Three Dialogues Between Hylas and Philonous* (1713).

Berkeley, George, *A Treatise Concerning the Principles of Human Knowledge* (1710).

Hume, David, 'Of Tragedy' (1757).

Hume, David, *A Treatise of Human Nature, Book I: Of the Understanding* (1739–40).

Locke, John, *An Essay Concerning Human Understanding* (1690).

Mill, John Stuart, *Utilitarianism* (1863).

Introduction

Central to the study of philosophy are certain persistent, sometimes elusive, and always puzzling questions. Anyone who thinks at all is likely to have reflected on at least some of the following: the contingency of our birth and the inevitability of death; the nature of consciousness; our propensity to find moral value in various kinds of action and character; our tendency to create political and social institutions; our sense of choosing freely; our appreciation of those objects we classify as art; our capacity to construe sounds and marks as meaningful, communicatively useful elements in languages. Reflection on such aspects of human existence leads to many questions. Does human life have a purpose? Is the world essentially material? What is value? Can we define art and beauty? Do we owe special kinds of obligation to societies or governments? What is human freedom? How can sounds possess meaning? These are a small sample of the sort of questions characteristic of philosophy.

It is one thing to be puzzled, another to formulate clear questions which both capture the puzzlement and are precise enough to offer hope of resolution. Throughout the recorded history of human reflection, enormous effort and intelligence have been devoted to sharpening and answering such questions – in the attempt, one might say, to reduce the giddying wonder of it all. Some of these efforts have produced large-scale theories about human life and knowledge, some have been devoted only to quite specific issues. And attempts to answer questions have generated new questions.

The consideration of philosophical questions has produced a written record going back more than twenty-five hundred years, which has contributors from every age and culture. With a little imagination, one can conceive these contributors as participants in an enormously complex polyglot conversation. Think of those now joining this discussion – a position that you might well be in. What is the likelihood of being able to pick up its thread without some kind of guidance? 'Close to nil' would seem to be the answer. It is difficult enough to pick up the thread even of ordinary conversations that have been going on for some time in your absence.

Of course it is fanciful to think of the whole of philosophy as literally a conversation. Many of the supposed participants know nothing of one another, and do not even speak or read one another's languages. And different participants have been occupied with different questions. It might be more realistic to think of philosophy as made up of a great number of more circumscribed conversations, in which the participants have actually communicated, directly or indirectly. There would then be a range of discussions to join. But the point would remain: newcomers to each discussion need some guidance.

Participants in philosophy's conversations will constantly assess the answers others offer to questions, and refine the questions asked. Ideas proposed and conclusions reached are not the property of any one participant. The project is a shared one and has truth as the common goal. Moreover, in order to persuade one another that genuine questions receive true answers, participants will at least implicitly have to agree on what counts as a good argument. This means that the conversations of philosophy have the form of reasoned debates with a logical structure.

The image of philosophy as a conversation of this kind makes a further useful point. Joining in a reasoned debate requires more of you than knowing what others have said: you must be prepared to contribute something of your own. You count as having joined in this or that stretch of philosophical discussion only if you participate actively.

Reading Philosophy is designed not only to help you pick up some threads, but also to encourage you to find your own voice. It is a book for beginners – for those newly joining in philosophical conversations. There is nothing special that we expect readers to know before coming to the book: all we assume is some interest in the subject. The book is distinctive in that it teaches you a technique for reading and analysing philosophical texts, and gives you the opportunity to practise and refine the technique as you go. From the start you will be learning actively, and acquiring the skills which experienced philosophers use in reading and in generating thoughts in response to them.

You might wonder why there would be any question about how to read philosophy. Unless it contains technical jargon (which we have tried to keep to a minimum here), a page of philosophical writing usually looks like ordinary prose. If you can read a newspaper article or a short story, surely you can read philosophy too? The answer is that you can, but that you will most likely need some practice before you can get the most out of it. One way to acquire such practice might be to read and keep reading and hope that you will gradually see how philosophers go about their work. Many introductions take that approach, and it can be effective. But our aim is to instruct you from the start on how to read philosophy well. This is why we have included inter-active commentaries in this book.

By using our commentaries, you will be able to reflect on the process of your own reading, and, we hope, acquire some of the basic skills of phil-osophy more quickly and in a more structured manner. Structure is everything in reading philosophy. A piece of philosophy is never a mere list of points. As you read and take notes, you should always be making connections between premises and conclusions. (An author's premises are the assumptions on which his or her reasoning is based. The conclusion of a piece of reasoning is its endpoint or destination – a destination which the author intends you to reach from the premises.) We try to help you to make such connections. We involve you actively in reading, by making explicit what sort of questions you should be asking, and where to look in the texts for answers.

The eighteen texts in this book provide samples of high-quality philosoph-ical writing spread over nine philosophical topics. Our selection has been made so that:

1   Each text presents a clear, well-argued answer to a central philosophical question.
2   They are accessible to the beginner without being over-simple. None of the pieces was originally written to be introductory – they all take you straight into serious philosophical work 'at the deep end' – but in most cases we have edited them with an eye to the needs of the newcomer to philosophy.
3   Each text gives the reader plenty of scope for discussion and argument.
4   Taken together, they cover a wide range of topics drawn from different areas of philosophical enquiry: ethics, philosophy of mind, aesthetics, political philosophy, metaphysics, and epistemology (or theory of knowledge).
5   They acquaint the reader with philosophical writings from different his-torical periods. Philosophy is a subject in which there is no prejudice concerning the age in which something was written. So here we have pieces from the twentieth century, pieces from the seventeenth century (when the label 'modern' as opposed to 'ancient' or 'medieval' philosophy applies), and pieces from the two intervening centuries.

As currently practised, philosophy has much greater diversity than could be represented in a single book. We believe that the historical range of *Reading Philosophy* gives a rich sense of what philosophy is, and prepares the reader well for different approaches to the subject. The twentieth-century writers we have selected might be described as belonging in a tradition of *analytical philosophy*. Analytical philosophy started as a movement concerned with specific issues in logic and the sciences, and it has probably been the dominant approach to the subject in the English-speaking world in the twentieth cen-tury. But the recent writers we have chosen are analytic philosophers only in a very broad sense: they attach especial importance to argument and clarity of expression and try to avoid dogmatic pronouncements. In this respect you should find the texts by analytic philosophers little different from those by earlier philosophers such as Descartes, Hume or Schopenhauer. So while it is fair to say that we concentrate on a certain style of reading philosophy, the skill we want you to acquire should enable you to read any philosophical material with greater confidence and fulfilment.

A typical chapter in the book has the following pattern:

1   A general introduction to the problem.
2   The first text, with arrow markers, preceded by a brief introduction and followed by an interactive commentary using the text's arrow markers.
3   The second text presented in the same way.

Our system of arrow markers – $\boxed{a}\!\mapsto$, $\boxed{b}\!\mapsto$ and so on – will enable you to link our commentaries with detailed portions of the relevant text. The texts include the markers clearly in the margin, and commentaries invite you to study selected parts of a text rather than skimming through the whole.

We envisage the reader using a chapter in something like the following way. Start with the chapter's introduction. Tackle one text at a time. First read it through to gain a general idea of the argument, then read it a second time more carefully, pausing and taking a few notes, if that is helpful. Then read the commentary on that text slowly, stopping at the boxed questions or tasks. 'Zoom in' on each question or task in its own right, and work on it before moving on. If you use the commentary in this way, you will find yourself continually going back to specific passages in the original text, taking your guidance from the arrow-marker system.

The commentaries can be described as interactive because they do not simply explain and comment, but give the reader tasks to carry out. Here are some examples:

> In your own words, explain the distinction between need and merit, and its relevance to Williams's argument.

> Re-read the paragraph which starts at $\boxed{h}\!\mapsto$. Now see whether you can say what Strawson's argument in this paragraph is using three or four sentences of your own.

> Read from $\boxed{a}\!\mapsto$ to $\boxed{c}\!\mapsto$ in the text, and formulate your answer to these questions: (1) What is the definition of freedom Schopenhauer starts with? (2) What is the revised definition he reaches? (3) Why does he need the revised definition?

In all these cases the material in the boxes prompts you to think through a specific question for yourself. In the last two examples the boxes guide you to parts of the text that are most important to re-read; you will find these parts of the text easily using the marginal arrow markers. We believe that the method of boxed questions and tasks, combined with the system of arrow markers, is a novel and effective way of leading the reader through the experience of active, engaged philosophical reading.

We have arranged the chapters so that material we regard as less demanding comes at the beginning, with the harder discussions towards the end of the book. It is not essential to read every chapter. You may be on a course which emphasizes metaphysics, in which case the most relevant chapters will be those on self, mind and body, personal identity, free will, causality, and the qualities of material things. You may be mainly interested in thinking about topics in ethics, political philosophy or aesthetics, in which case other chapters will be more obvious choices. But whatever else you read, it is advisable to start by working through chapter 1, which contains a single short extract from Descartes, and a commentary which is particularly detailed and gives general advice on how to read – advice that you can apply to the remaining texts. Chapter 2 follows on naturally from chapter 1, but the reader (or course organizer) can use the remaining chapters selectively.

Philosophy is a challenging and exciting activity, but not all philosophical questions fascinate everyone equally. Sometimes a topic has to get under your skin and perplex you somewhat before you can work on it for any length of time. For any given reader this may happen with only a few of the topics in this book. For this reason, it is good advice to devote your time to those topics that most attract you. Doing so will improve your philosophical abilities more effectively than trying to spread your attention evenly over everything in the book. When you find some particular topic fascinating, you can use the Further Reading listed at the end of the book to take you more deeply into it. Also at the end of the book, there are Essay/Examination Questions covering all of the chapters. You can use these as the bases for essays you might want to write.

If you find yourself wanting to re-read a particular piece several times, if you feel impelled to write a couple of pages giving reasons why one of our authors is wrong, if you become keen to discuss and discover more about one of the issues we present here – then you are really doing philosophy.

1

Doubt

Introduction to the Problem

A question raised by many philosophers in recent centuries has been: 'What can I know?' Other versions of the same basic question might be: 'What can I be certain of?' or 'What cannot be called into doubt?' If a philosopher thinks we cannot know something – or that we cannot be certain of it, or that it must be called into doubt – then that philosopher is known as a *sceptic* about that thing. A sceptic is a doubter of something. *Scepticism* is a view that says things are in doubt.

A traditional example would be scepticism about whether there is a world of ordinary objects 'out there'. We usually think we know there are such objects around us, and that we are not just experiencing the contents of our own minds. A sceptic about ordinary external objects would be someone who argued that we do not know this, that we cannot be certain of this, that this should be called into doubt. The kind of conversation which is the butt of jokes about philosophy, the 'Can I know there is a glass of water here on the table?' kind, is a conversation you might have with a sceptic about ordinary external objects.

Often a philosophical writer will use scepticism as a tool, in order to discover just what *can* be known, or what we *can* be certain about. Then the aim is to strengthen our confidence in knowledge by challenging it to beat the arguments of a sceptic. The sceptic need not be a real person. Rather one may simply *imagine* debating with a person who is determined to show that little or no knowledge is possible.

Debating with an imaginary sceptical opponent is an instance of a common technique used in philosophical writing: the technique of conducting a dialogue. Some philosophers have actually written dialogue between two or more characters, Plato being the unparalleled master of this style. But there can be dialogue in more disguised forms in a piece of writing.

Very frequently a philosopher will make a point, then follow it with 'But someone might object . . .' or 'Suppose someone were to say . . .'. An opponent pops up in the text in order that the author can 'reply', advancing his or her own case by answering an objection he or she has thought of. A still more disguised form is what we could call the 'dialogue in a single voice' an example of which we find in our first passage.

Introduction to Descartes

This short piece is one of the most famous pieces of philosophical writing. There can scarcely be a student of Western philosophy anywhere who has not read and puzzled over the First Meditation, written by the French philosopher René Descartes in 1641.

René Descartes (1596–1650) was one of the greatest thinkers of his day and is often called the father of modern philosophy. He did important work in physics and mathematics, and in philosophy was most influential for his views about the foundations of knowledge, and his distinction between mind (or soul) and body. He was in search of a complete system of knowledge, in which he would prove the existence of God, understand the nature of the human mind, and establish the principles on which the material universe can be studied. The *Meditations on First Philosophy* was published originally in Latin and in French. It is a masterpiece of compressed argument from the period of Descartes's mature philosophy.

Descartes gives his First Meditation the title 'What Can be Called into Doubt'. He tries here to press doubt to its limit. The basic pattern is this: the author argues that something or other can be doubted, finds a reason for resisting that doubt, then invents a new reason for pushing the doubt further, then finds another reason for resisting, then invents a new reason for doubting. That is why I called this a 'dialogue in a single voice'.

Descartes is not a sceptic: he is using a dialogue with scepticism in pursuit of knowledge. But he is trying in the First Meditation to give the sceptical line of thought the strongest argument he can find. The aim is to discover certainty, but to do so only after making doubt as thorough as possible.

There are six Meditations altogether, and, although they form a relatively short work, Descartes announced large ambitions in its subtitle: he wanted to demonstrate the existence of God and the distinction between the body and the soul (the distinction known as dualism). But for now the reader should concentrate simply on the selected passage, which consists of the whole of the First Meditation in an English translation.

René Descartes, 'First Meditation: What Can be Called into Doubt'

Some years ago I was struck by the large number of falsehoods that I had accepted as true in my childhood, and by the highly doubtful nature of the whole edifice that I had subsequently based on them. I realized that it was necessary, once in the course of my life, to demolish everything completely and start again right from the foundations if I wanted to establish anything at all in the sciences that was stable and likely to last. But the task looked an enormous one, and I began to wait until I should reach a mature enough age to ensure that no subsequent time of life would be more suitable for tackling such inquiries. This led me to put the project off for so long that I would now be to blame if by pondering over it any further I wasted the time still left for carrying it out. So today I have expressly rid my mind of all worries and arranged for myself a clear stretch of free time. I am here quite alone, and at last I will devote myself sincerely and without reservation, to the general demolition of my opinions.

But to accomplish this, it will not be necessary for me to show that all my opinions are false, which is something I could perhaps never manage. Reason now leads me to think that I should hold back my assent from opinions which are not completely certain and indubitable just as carefully as I do from those which are patently false. So, for the purpose of rejecting all my opinions, it will be enough if I find in each of them at least some reason for doubt. And to do this I will not need to run through them all individually, which would be an endless task. Once the foundations of a building are undermined, anything built on them collapses of its own accord; so I will go straight for the basic principles on which all my former beliefs rested.

[a]→ Whatever I have up till now accepted as most true I have acquired either from the senses or through the senses. But from time to time I have found that the senses deceive, and it is prudent never to trust completely those who have deceived us even once.

Yet although the senses occasionally deceive us with respect to objects which are very small or in the distance, there are many other beliefs about which doubt is quite impossible, even though they are derived from the senses – for example, that I am here, sitting by the fire, wearing a winter dressing-gown, holding this piece of paper in my hands, and so on. Again, how could it be denied that these hands or this whole body are mine? Unless perhaps I were to liken myself to madmen, whose brains are so damaged by the persistent vapours of melancholia that they firmly maintain they are kings when they are paupers, or say they are dressed in purple when they are naked, or that their heads are made of earthenware, or that they are pumpkins, or made of glass. But such people are insane, and I would be thought equally mad if I took anything from them as a model for myself.

b→ A brilliant piece of reasoning! As if I were not a man who sleeps at night, and regularly has all the same experiences while asleep as madmen do when awake – indeed sometimes even more improbable ones. How often, asleep at night, am I convinced of just such familiar events – that I am here in my dressing-gown, sitting by the fire – when, in fact I am lying undressed in bed! Yet at the moment my eyes are certainly wide awake when I look at this piece of paper: I shake my head and it is not asleep; as I stretch out and feel my hand I do so deliberately, and I know what I am doing. All this would not happen with such distinctness to someone asleep. Indeed! As if I did not remember other occasions when I have been tricked by exactly similar thoughts while asleep! As I think about this more carefully, I see plainly that there are never any sure signs by means of which being awake can be distinguished from being asleep. The result is that I begin to feel dazed, and this very feeling only reinforces the notion that I may be asleep.

Suppose then that I am dreaming, and that these particulars – that my eyes are open, that I am moving my head and stretching out my hands – are not true. Perhaps, indeed, I do not even have such hands or such a body at all. Nonetheless, it must surely be admitted that the

c→ visions which come in sleep are like paintings, which must have been fashioned in the likeness of things that are real, and hence that at least these general kinds of things – eyes, head, hands and the body as a whole – are things which are not imaginary but are real and exist. For even when painters try to create sirens and satyrs with the most extraordinary bodies, they cannot give them natures which are new in all respects; they simply jumble up the limbs of different animals. Or if perhaps they manage to think up something so new that nothing remotely similar has ever been seen before – something which is therefore completely fictitious and unreal – at least the colours used in the composition must

d→ be real. By similar reasoning, although these general kinds of things – eyes, head, hands and so on – could be imaginary, it must at least be admitted that certain other even simpler and more universal things are real. These are as it were the real colours from which we form all the images of things, whether true or false, that occur in our thought.

This class appears to include corporeal nature in general, and its extension; the shape of extended things; the quantity, or size and number of these things; the place in which they may exist, the time through which they may endure, and so on.

⟨e⟩→ So a reasonable conclusion from this might be that physics, astronomy, medicine, and all other disciplines which depend on the study of composite things, are doubtful; while arithmetic, geometry and other subjects of this kind, which deal only with the simplest and most general things, regardless of whether they really exist in nature or not, contain something certain and indubitable. For whether I am awake or asleep, two and three added together are five, and a square has no more than four sides. It seems impossible that such transparent truths should incur any suspicion of being false.

And yet firmly rooted in my mind is the long-standing opinion that there is an omnipotent God who made me the kind of creature that I am. How do I know that he has not brought it about that there is no earth, no sky, no extended thing, no shape, no size, no place, while at the same time ensuring that all these things appear to me to exist just as they do now? What is more, since I sometimes believe that others go astray in cases where they think they have the most perfect knowledge, may I not similarly go wrong every time I add two and three or count the sides of a square, or in some even simpler matter, if that is imaginable? But perhaps God would not have allowed me to be deceived in this way, since he is said to be supremely good. But if it were inconsistent with his goodness to have created me such that I am deceived all the time, it would seem equally foreign to his goodness to allow me to be deceived even occasionally; yet this last assertion cannot be made.

Perhaps there may be some who would prefer to deny the existence of so powerful a God rather than believe that everything else is uncertain. Let us not argue with them, but grant them that everything said about God is a fiction. According to their supposition, then, I have arrived at my present state by fate or chance or a continuous chain of events, or by some other means; yet since deception and error seem to be imperfections, the less powerful they make my original cause, the
⟨f⟩→ more likely it is that I am so imperfect as to be deceived all the time. I have no answer to these arguments, but am finally compelled to admit that there is not one of my former beliefs about which a doubt may not properly be raised; and this is not a flippant or ill-considered conclusion, but is based on powerful and well thought-out reasons. So in future I must withhold my assent from these former beliefs just as carefully as I would from obvious falsehoods, if I want to discover any certainty.

But it is not enough merely to have noticed this; I must make an effort to remember it. My habitual opinions keep coming back, and, despite my wishes, they capture my belief, which is as it were bound over to them as a result of long occupation and the law of custom. I shall never get out of the habit of confidently assenting to these opinions, so long as I suppose them to be what in fact they are, namely highly probable opinions – opinions which, despite the fact that they are in a sense doubtful, as has just been shown, it is still much more reasonable to believe than to deny. In view of this, I think it will be a good plan to turn my will in completely the opposite direction and deceive myself, by pretending for a time that these former opinions are utterly false and imaginary. I shall do this until the weight of preconceived opinion is counter-balanced and the distorting influence of habit no longer prevents my judgement from perceiving things correctly. In the meantime, I know that no danger or error will result from my plan, and that I cannot possibly go too far in my distrustful attitude. This is because the task now in hand does not involve action but merely the acquisition of knowledge.

g→   I will suppose therefore that not God, who is supremely good and the source of truth, but rather some malicious demon of the utmost power and cunning has employed all his energies in order to deceive me. I shall think that the sky, the air, the earth, colours, shapes, sounds and all external things are merely the delusions of dreams which he has devised to ensnare my judgement. I shall consider myself as not having hands or eyes, or flesh, or blood or senses, but as falsely believing that I have all these things. I shall stubbornly and firmly persist in this meditation; and, even if it is not in my power to know any truth, I shall at least do what is in my power, that is, resolutely guard against assenting to any falsehoods, so that the deceiver, however powerful and cunning he may

h→ be, will be unable to impose on me in the slightest degree. But this is an arduous undertaking, and a kind of laziness brings me back to normal life. I am like a prisoner who is enjoying an imaginary freedom while asleep; as he begins to suspect that he is asleep, he dreads being woken up, and goes along with the pleasant illusion as long as he can. In the same way, I happily slide back into my old opinions and dread being shaken out of them, for fear that my peaceful sleep may be followed by hard labour when I wake, and that I shall have to toil not in the light, but amid the inextricable darkness of the problems I have now raised.

Commentary on Descartes

When we read a piece of philosophical writing, we are in most cases looking for a conclusion, and an argument which carries us to that conclusion. The conclusion is what the author is trying to convince you of. So to locate the conclusion you should ask, as you read: What am I supposed to believe, according to the author?

Then you should ask: What does the author do to make me believe that? In other words, try to locate the argument the author uses to reach that conclusion. So let us apply this approach to the First Meditation.

Before continuing with the commentary, go back to the text of the First Meditation, and try to answer this question: What is the conclusion that Descartes is trying to persuade the reader of by the end of the Meditation?

Descartes's first two paragraphs are introductory. He tells us what the argument is going to be about (doubting his former beliefs) and what motivates it (the need to find some certainty). In these first two paragraphs Descartes states his *aims* quite clearly. He speaks of 'the general demolition of my opinions' and says that 'for the purpose of rejecting all my opinions, it will be enough if I find in each of them at least some reason for doubt'. If he carries out these aims, the conclusion of his argument will be:

There is reason to doubt everything I believe.

You will not find these exact words in the text – this is my formulation of what I think Descartes's conclusion should be.

It is vital in reading philosophy that you take time to formulate in your own words the proposition that you think is at issue in a text. A good method is to write down your formulation and have it in front of you as you read. Sometimes a great part of your work will be directed towards finding the author's precise conclusion, so you should be prepared to revise your formulation as you read. Attempting to state the conclusion in writing, if necessary deleting it and re-stating it a few times, would be a good use of your time, and note paper, while reading. This kind of active reading is usually more fruitful than waiting passively for something in the text to strike you.

The above proposition 'There is reason to doubt everything I believe' should be the overall or final conclusion of Descartes's train of thought, if he carries out what he says he aims to do. The argument to show what can be called into doubt begins in earnest in the third paragraph. Reading on from here, we should next ask: Where in Descartes's text is the overall conclusion actually reached?

It can be easy to locate an author's conclusions if they are clearly signposted. An author may say: 'So we can conclude...' or 'So a reasonable conclusion from this might be...'. But sometimes a conclusion might simply be signalled by 'Therefore...' or 'So...'. Or it may be more hidden, or even merely implied.

Read from the third paragraph of the First Meditation, and answer this question: Where does Descartes state his overall conclusion that there is reason to doubt everything he believes?

There is an explicit conclusion at the place marked $\boxed{e}\!\!\rightarrow$ in the text: 'So a reasonable conclusion from this might be...' But is this the conclusion we are looking for?

No, because here Descartes is concluding that only *some* branches of knowledge are in doubt, while others are 'certain and indubitable' – there is no reason, so far, for him to doubt everything. It takes more argument before we arrive at the overall conclusion.

> Make sure you understand the difference between the conclusion at
> $\boxed{e}\mapsto$and the stated overall conclusion. If you have not found the statement
> of the overall conclusion in the text, keep looking.

Look carefully at the passage starting at $\boxed{f}\mapsto$. It is in these two sentences, 'I have no answer to these arguments...' and 'So in future I must withhold...' that Descartes states his overall conclusion. 'I...am finally compelled to admit that...' means effectively 'I conclude that...'; and *what* Descartes is compelled to admit is 'that there is not one of my former beliefs about which a doubt may not properly be raised'. For our purposes this says the same as 'There is reason to doubt everything I believe.'

Two long paragraphs follow this conclusion. In them Descartes comments on the difficulty of remembering that every belief is doubtful, and invents a scenario (that a malicious demon might be deceiving him) as a means of counteracting his habitual confidence in his beliefs. The very last sentences, from $\boxed{h}\mapsto$ to the end, do not really seek to convince us of anything more than the overall conclusion already stated, but rather make clear in dramatic fashion just how difficult it is to remain convinced of that conclusion. 'Normal life', in which we happily believe many things without asking whether we should doubt them, exerts a strong pull on the thinker.

Now we are in a position to look at the arguments which Descartes hopes will carry us to the sceptical overall conclusion.

I remarked earlier that Descartes's method here could be called a 'dialogue in a single voice'. From the third paragraph the argument advances in a series of ebbs and flows: the author adopts the point of view of sceptical doubt, then resists it, then gives more reasons for doubt, and so on.

So once again analysing the *structure* of the piece may help the reader to follow it. At $\boxed{a}\mapsto$ the word 'But' introduces the first reason for doubt: the senses have been unreliable, so we should call into doubt beliefs we acquire from or through the senses. But the very next sentence ('Yet...') is from the point of view of someone resisting doubt; some things the senses tell us cannot be denied, or doubted. The voice of doubt replies straightaway ('Unless perhaps I were to liken myself to madmen...'), only to receive the objection 'But such people are insane...' And so on.

> Starting at $\boxed{a}\mapsto$ mark out for yourself those passages (one or more sentences)
> which you think are advancing reasons for doubt, and those which you think
> are objections to the doubt. Proceed to the overall conclusion at $\boxed{f}\mapsto$.

You will find it helps to pay attention to connecting words such as 'But', 'Yet', 'And yet', 'Unless', 'Nonetheless'. But in the paragraph marked ⌐b⌐→ Descartes uses the ironic expressions 'A brilliant piece of reasoning!' and later 'Indeed!' for similar purposes.

If you can see clearly where doubt is being advanced and where it is being resisted, you can now follow the separate arguments for doubt in the First Meditation.

The first argument for doubt is based on the idea that the senses have deceived us in the past, and so should not be trusted.

> About this first argument. (1) Ask yourself: What would be some examples of the senses deceiving us? (2) Evaluate the argument: Does the fact of the senses sometimes deceiving us really give us reason not to believe in anything they seem to be telling us?

The second argument centres on the thought that some people have mad beliefs: if Descartes were like these people, then beliefs of his which seem undeniable to him could be completely wrong. But Descartes's line in response to this doubt is that he cannot proceed with his philosophical argument at all on the basis that he might be insane. He must take it for granted that he is sane.

The next argument, contained in the paragraph marked ⌐b⌐→, is the argument about dreaming, which is generally rated as one of Descartes's most powerful sceptical moves.

> Read just the paragraph marked ⌐b⌐→, preferably more than once. Ask yourself: (1) Is Descartes right in saying 'there are never any sure signs by means of which being awake can be distinguished from being asleep'? (2) If he is right about that, why exactly does it call his beliefs into doubt?

In this argument Descartes first makes the point that for any ordinary belief he has – for example 'that I am here in my dressing-gown, sitting by the fire' – the very same could merely seem to be the case in a dream. However, that point itself is not sufficient to advance the doubt. The anti-sceptical voice points out that 'I know what I am doing' right now when I am awake and looking at things, touching them, and so on. The sheer fact that I *could* have the same experiences when asleep does not remove certainty from my present beliefs.

But by the end of the paragraph Descartes realizes that unless he can *know that he is not dreaming now*, the possibility of there being a dream exactly like waking life is a threat to his knowledge. If he cannot know that he is not dreaming now, then for everything he now thinks he knows, it is possible that he is merely dreaming that he knows it. To dream that he knows something is not to know it. The result would be that he cannot know anything.

Before continuing, stop reading Descartes and think for yourself about these two questions: (1) Can you know that you are not dreaming now? (2) If you cannot know that you are not dreaming now, does it mean that you cannot know anything?

Both are rather hard questions. For now, note that *if* you answer No to question (1) *and* answer Yes to question (2), then you seem to have reached a sceptical predicament, where indeed you cannot really know anything.

However, Descartes does not see the Dreaming Argument as completely settling the issue of doubt. Total doubt is resisted in the passage that begins with the sentence 'Nonetheless...' (c⟩→), leading on to the conclusion at e⟩→ that some things are certain. Notice that in this paragraph Descartes argues *by analogy*. The distinction between what can be doubted by the Dreaming Argument and what cannot is *like* a distinction familiar in paintings. The text makes the analogy crystal clear. The expression 'like paintings' at c⟩→ marks the entrance into the analogy; the phrase 'By similar reasoning' at d⟩→ the exit from it.

In other words, Descartes is not really talking about the distinction between real and imaginary things in paintings. He is interested in mathematical knowledge and knowledge of the basic nature of the material world: there are basic truths here we can know with certainty, even if our beliefs about more specific kinds of things are doubtful. (It is worth wondering if Descartes is right here: might not the Dreaming Argument be more powerful than he realizes? For instance, why couldn't he just be dreaming that it is certain that two and three added together are five?)

This position of relative certainty does not last long, however. The voice of doubt returns, to argue that an all-powerful God could bring it about that *everything* I believe is false. This would be inconsistent with God's being supremely good (says the voice of the objector) – but (replies the voice of doubt) you might as well say it would be inconsistent with God's goodness if he let me be deceived 'even occasionally'. But he does let me be deceived occasionally, so it cannot be inconsistent with his nature. Therefore total deception cannot be inconsistent with his nature.

I have re-arranged the argument here, to try to make it a little clearer. That is often a useful device as you read. Step back from the text, re-order the steps of the argument, and add steps (premises or conclusions) that seem to be missing.

Finally Descartes poses a dilemma: if *there is* an all-powerful God, he could have deceived me about everything; if *there is no* God, there is nothing to guarantee that I am, as it were, well enough made to be safe from constant error. Either way, I could be going wrong in all my beliefs.

Ask yourself: how persuasive is this argument? In particular: (1) Is it not easier to think that a perfect God would allow me to go wrong sometimes than that he would allow me to be totally in error? (2) Is it clear why my beliefs are all in doubt if there is no God?

If his overall conclusion is right, then Descartes ought to stop trusting any of his existing beliefs, if he is serious about avoiding error. In order to suspend his trust in his beliefs, he invents an extreme and fantastical picture (at $\boxed{g} \rightarrow$): 'some malicious demon of the utmost power and cunning has employed all his energies in order to deceive me.'

To spell things out a bit more, we might construct a sceptical Malicious Demon Argument which runs:

1   For all I know, a malicious demon could be systematically making me believe only things that are false.
2   So, for all I know, all my beliefs could be false.
3   So I have reason to doubt all my beliefs.

It is quite legitimate, as part of your reading of Descartes's text, to set out an argument in this way, and begin to explore whether it is convincing.

When you have looked at the different parts of Descartes's argument in something like the above manner, you have asked: What is the author trying to convince me of? (What is the conclusion?) and How does the author try to convince me? (What are the arguments?) Now you are in a good position to ask yourself: Am I convinced? Do you think the conclusion is true? Do you think the arguments are good ones?

Considering the whole of the First Meditation, write down in your own words the argument for Descartes's overall conclusion which you think is the most persuasive.

It must be said that among philosophers reflecting on the First Meditation recently the Dreaming Argument and the Malicious Demon Argument are the two often thought to be most persuasive. But that is by no means the end of the story.

We can criticize even apparently strong arguments: they may contain false steps, or the steps may not hold together properly, or they may remain stubbornly puzzling. To show that an argument has any of these features is to begin to do philosophy oneself. Good philosophical reading generates philosophical writing.

Good philosophical reading is active, interrogative, and open-minded. Actively divide up the text to find its structure, and make your own formulations of conclusions and arguments. Ask what the author is trying to do and whether it convinces you. Listen to the author's case impartially before making up your mind whether you agree, and use your imagination to think of examples, consequences, and objections.

Descartes's First Meditation raises wider philosophical issues which you can debate at any level. Is he right to be looking for certainty in the first place? Is knowing something a matter of being certain about it? Must knowledge be founded on something absolutely beyond doubt? Does it make sense to think of calling all one's beliefs into doubt at the same time? Can we understand knowledge by considering Descartes's highly artificial scenario of a single mind all by itself scrutinizing its own thoughts? Descartes paints such a vivid picture of his initial sceptical situation that we may be beguiled into thinking that this is the only philosophical approach to the topic of knowledge.

The reader who reads with an open mind, slowly and actively, looking for structure, interrogating the text in detail, is likely to acquire eventually the power to debate these larger questions competently.

Reading philosophy, then, is a skill (or perhaps a set of many skills). The commentary in this chapter has tried to show the beginner something of the kind of work needed to help this skill develop. You should expect such development to be a slow, cumulative process. The more you work at your reading, the more you will be engaged in doing philosophy yourself. The more you are engaged with philosophy, the more acute your reading abilities will become.

The remaining commentaries in this book are designed to guide the reader in developing the skill of reading philosophy, by providing the opportunity to think about further philosophical questions in more or less the manner suggested in this chapter.

2

Self

Introduction to the Problem

When I think about myself, am I thinking just about something physical? Are mental phenomena such as thinking and feeling part of the physical world? Questions like these make up what is generally referred to as the mind–body problem. The problem is a central concern of present-day philosophy of mind, and at the core of philosophy itself.

Descartes has a special role in the history of the mind–body problem. He gave an answer to these questions which has set the terms of many debates, and which philosophers have continued to argue for and against. Descartes claimed that so far from thinking just about something physical when he thought about himself, he was thinking about a mental thing – a mind or soul. According to Descartes, a person's mind and a person's body are things of totally different sorts. Minds, Descartes said, are immaterial (i.e. not material, not physical); they are connected with people's bodies and brains (which are material) through causal interactions. Descartes's position is known as 'Cartesian dualism'. To hold, as Descartes did, that minds and bodies causally interact is to hold that minds or happenings in minds may cause effects on bodies, and that bodies or happenings in bodies may cause effects on minds. (There are forms of dualism different from Descartes's that do not subscribe to such causal interactionism between the mental and the physical.)

Nowadays most philosophers reject Cartesian dualism. Some of them say that advances in physical science have shown the position to be untenable. These people may still find a problem about mental/physical relations. Indeed some may think that rejection of Cartesian dualism creates the mind–body problem as it is faced today. Descartes believed that conscious experience is present in the world so long as immaterial, non-physical minds are there, as well as physical things. But if, as today's materialists say, everything is physical, then there is a problem about how conscious experience or meaning or rationality could be present in the world. Self-awareness, for example, doesn't seem to be a property of the world of mere matter: it isn't at all obvious how someone's being aware of themselves could be an arrangement of molecules or be the firings of neurons in their brain. How could conscious experience, or meaning, or rationality, arise in a physical world which in itself is devoid of these characteristics?

There has been a growing revival of interest in consciousness, not only in philosophy but also among psychologists and neuroscientists. In recent years, such scientists have been concerned with the mind–body problem in one of its guises; and the problem of consciousness has even been called 'science's last great frontier'. Here 'consciousness' is used as a general name for experiential phenomena, so that one encounters consciousness when a person experiences anything – the greenness of the grass, or the smell of coffee, or another person speaking to them. Descartes typically used the term 'consciousness' more restrictively than this. When Descartes spoke of being 'conscious' he alluded to an intimate source of knowledge which every person has about *their own* mental occurrences. His focus – at least in the reading that we shall be concerned with – is on what *he himself* is. A problem about the self is one aspect of the more general mind–body problem.

A problem about the self is raised in the first of the questions we began with above: 'When I think about myself, am I thinking just about something physical?'. The word 'I' occurs essentially in this question; the question is one that each person has to ask for himself or herself. The second question we set out from, by contrast – 'Are mental phenomena such as thinking and feeling part of the physical world?' – is posed without using the word 'I'. The two questions are evidently related, as we see from Descartes's answers to them both. But the first question, which approaches problems about mind from the first-person perspective, can seem to be the more fundamental. Certainly it is a starting-point in much philosophical reflection.

When you realize that other people cannot observe your own thoughts, you may have an experience of being 'alone in your head', and a feeling that your body is just a vessel for the mental thing that you really or most essentially are. Such experiences and feelings have been called 'the sense of the mental self'. For many people the sense of the self can appear to be among the deepest certainties of human life. But even if the sense of self is genuine, it cannot be taken for granted that it is genuinely a sense of some mental thing. As you will see from reading Strawson alongside Descartes, it is a question for philosophical debate whether there really are such things as mental selves, or souls, or minds, or consciousnesses.

The terms 'mind', 'soul', 'consciousness' are all of them used to apply to the mental things whose existence Descartes thought he had established. When the word 'consciousness' is used in this way – as it is by Strawson for example – it has a plural. This is a different use from that which we find in 'the problem of consciousness'. A philosopher who holds that there are no such things as minds may still want to allow that there is a problem about consciousness. She thinks that there are no immaterial things (minds, consciousness*es*) from which human beings are made up, but that we still need to say something about how it can be that human beings are conscious beings (or have the property of consciousness).

Introduction to Descartes

Descartes needs no introduction because you have already encountered him and read the First Meditation. In the Second, Descartes begins on one of his *Meditations*' overall tasks – to 'demonstrate the . . . distinction between mind and body'. Reprinted here is the first half of this Second Meditation, in which Descartes establishes that he exists and that he is a thinking thing.

'I think, therefore I am' is perhaps the most famous statement in the history of philosophy. It is often called 'the cogito', after its Latin original 'cogito, ergo sum'. The claim advanced by the cogito is pivotal in this extract from the Second Meditation. Descartes discovers that he can use the cogito to rescue himself from the doubt he has brought upon himself in the First Meditation; and that he can use it in turn in a proof of his existence as a thinking thing, and consequently as a basis for his distinction between mind and body. Thus Descartes's mind–body dualism emerges from his pursuit of the sceptical method. (You won't find the actual words 'I think, therefore I am' here. The statement appears in other works of Descartes, in his *Principles of Philosophy* and his *Discourse on the Method*.)

René Descartes, 'Second Meditation: Of the Nature of the Human Mind . . .' (extract)

So serious are the doubts into which I have been thrown as a result of yesterday's meditation that I can neither put them out of my mind nor see any way of resolving them. It feels as if I have fallen unexpectedly into a deep whirlpool which tumbles me around so that I can neither stand on the bottom nor swim up to the top. Nevertheless I will make an effort and once more attempt the same path which I started on yesterday. Anything which admits of the slightest doubt I will set aside just as if I had found it to be wholly false; and I will proceed in this way until I recognize something certain, or, if nothing else, until I at least recognize for certain that there is no certainty. Archimedes used to demand just one firm and immovable point in order to shift the entire earth; so I too can hope for great things if I manage to find just one thing, however slight, that is certain and unshakeable.

I will suppose then, that everything I see is spurious. I will believe that my memory tells me lies, and that none of the things that it reports ever happened. I have no senses. Body, shape, extension, movement and place are chimeras. So what remains true? Perhaps just the one fact that nothing is certain.

[a] → Yet apart from everything I have just listed, how do I know that there is not something else which does not allow even the slightest occasion for doubt? Is there not a God, or whatever I may call him, who puts into me the thoughts I am now having? But why do I think this, since I myself may perhaps be the author of these thoughts? In that case am not I, at least, something? But I have just said that I have no senses and no body. This is the sticking point: what follows from this? Am I not so bound up with a body and with senses that I cannot exist without them? But I have convinced myself that there is absolutely nothing in the world, no sky, no earth, no minds, no bodies. Does it now follow that I too do not exist? No: if I convinced myself of something then I certainly existed. But there is a deceiver of supreme power and cunning who is deliberately and constantly deceiving me. In that case I too undoubtedly exist, if he is deceiving me; and let him deceive me as much as he can, he will never bring it about that I am nothing so long as I think that I am something. So after considering everything very thoroughly, I must finally conclude that this proposition, *I am, I exist*, is necessarily true whenever it is put forward by me or conceived in my mind.

[b] → But I do not yet have a sufficient understanding of what this 'I' is, that now necessarily exists. So I must be on my guard against carelessly taking something else to be this 'I', and so making a mistake in the very item of knowledge that I maintain is the most certain and evident of all. I will therefore go back and meditate on what I originally believed myself to be, before I embarked on this present train of thought. I will then subtract anything capable of being weakened, even minimally, by the arguments now introduced, so that what is left at the end may be exactly and only what is certain and unshakeable.

c→   What then did I formerly think I was? A man. But what is a man? Shall I say 'a rational animal'? No; for then I should have to inquire what an animal is, what rationality is, and in this way one question would lead me down the slope to other harder ones, and I do not now have the time to waste on subtleties of this kind. Instead I propose to concentrate on what came into my thoughts spontaneously and quite naturally whenever I used to consider what I was. Well, the first thought to come to mind was that I had a face, hands, arms and the whole mechanical structure of limbs which can be seen in a corpse, and which I called the body. The next thought was that I was nourished, that I moved about, and that I engaged in sense-perception and thinking; and these actions I attributed to the soul. But as to the nature of this soul, either I did not think about this or else I imagined it to be something tenuous, like a wind or fire or ether, which permeated my more solid parts. As to the body, however, I had no doubts about it, but thought I knew its nature distinctly. If I had tried to describe the mental conception I had of it, I would have expressed it as follows: by a body I understand whatever has a determinable shape and a definable location and can occupy a space in such a way as to exclude any other body; it can be perceived by touch, sight, hearing, taste or smell, and can be moved in various ways, not by itself but by whatever else comes into contact with it. For, according to my judgement, the power of self-movement, like the power of sensation or of thought, was quite foreign to the nature of a body; indeed, it was a source of wonder to me that certain bodies were found to contain faculties of this kind.

d→   But what shall I now say that I am, when I am supposing that there is some supremely powerful and, if it is permissible to say so, malicious deceiver, who is deliberately trying to trick me in every way he can? Can I now assert that I possess even the most insignificant of all the attributes which I have just said belong to the nature of a body? I scrutinize them, think about them, go over them again, but nothing suggests itself; it is tiresome and pointless to go through the list once more. But what about the attributes I assigned to the soul? Nutrition or movement? Since now I do not have a body, these are mere fabrications. Sense-perception? This surely does not occur without a body, and besides, when asleep I have appeared to perceive through the senses many things which I afterwards realized I did not perceive through the senses at all. Thinking? At last I have discovered it – thought; this alone is inseparable from me. I am, I exist – that is certain. But for how long? For as long as I am thinking. For it could be that were I totally to cease from thinking, I should totally cease to exist. At present I am not admitting anything except what is necessarily true. I am, then, in the strict sense only a thing that thinks; that is, I am a mind, or intelligence, or intellect, or reason – words whose meaning I have been ignorant of until now. But for all that I am a thing which is real and which truly exists. But what kind of a thing? As I have just said – a thinking thing.

e→   What else am I? I will use my imagination. I am not that structure of limbs which is called a human body. I am not even some thin vapour which permeates the limbs – a wind, fire, air, breath, or whatever I depict in my imagination; for these are things which I have supposed to be nothing. Let this supposition stand; for all that I am still

f→ something. And yet may it not perhaps be the case that these very things which I am supposing to be nothing, because they are unknown to me, are in reality identical with the 'I' of which I am aware? I do not know, and for the moment I shall not argue the point, since I can make judgements only about things which are known to me. I know that I exist; the question is, what is this 'I' that I know? If the 'I' is understood strictly as we have been taking it, then it is quite certain that knowledge of it does not depend on things of whose existence I am as yet unaware; so it cannot depend on any of the things which I invent in my imagination. And this very word 'invent' shows me my mistake. It would indeed be a case of fictitious invention if I used my imagination to establish that I was something or other; for imagining is simply contemplating the shape or image of a corporeal thing. Yet now I know for certain both that I exist and at the same time that all such images and, in general, everything relating to the nature of body, could be mere dreams and chimeras. Once this point has been grasped, to say 'I will use my imagination to get to know more distinctly what I am' would seem to be as silly as saying 'I am now awake, and see some truth; but since my vision is not yet clear enough, I will deliberately fall asleep so that my dreams may provide a truer and clearer representation.' I thus realize that none of the things that the imagination enables me to grasp is at all relevant to this knowledge of myself which I possess, and that the mind must therefore be most carefully diverted from such things if it is to perceive its own nature as distinctly as possible.

g→   But what then am I? A thing that thinks. What is that? A thing that doubts, understands, affirms, denies, is willing, is unwilling, and also imagines and has sensory perceptions.

This is a considerable list, if everything on it belongs to me. But does it? Is it not one and the same 'I' who is now doubting almost everything, who nonetheless understands some things, who affirms that this one thing is true, denies everything else, desires to know more, is unwilling to be deceived, imagines many things even involuntarily, and is aware of many things which apparently come from the senses?

Are not all these things just as true as the fact that I exist, even if I am asleep all the time, and even if he who created me is doing all he can to deceive me? Which of all these activities is distinct from my thinking?

[h]→ Which of them can be said to be separate from myself? The fact that it is I who am doubting and understanding and willing is so evident that I see no way of making it any clearer. But it is also the case that the 'I' who imagines is the same 'I'. For even if, as I have supposed, none of the objects of imagination are real, the power of imagination is something which really exists and is part of my thinking. Lastly, it is also the same 'I' who has sensory perceptions, or is aware of bodily things

[i]→ as it were through the senses. For example, I am now seeing light, hearing a noise, feeling heat. But I am asleep, so all this is false. Yet I certainly *seem* to see, to hear, and to be warmed. This cannot be false; what is called 'having a sensory perception' is strictly just this, and in this restricted sense of the term it is simply thinking.[...]

Commentary on Descartes

At the beginning of his Second Meditation, Descartes thinks himself back into the state of mind he got into as a result of his project of doubting everything that he could. He announces his intention of pursuing this project to its ultimate limit.

At the end of the first paragraph, Descartes registers a hope: perhaps instead of reaching the conclusion that *nothing* is certain and unshakeable, he may find that there is just one thing that is. It is this one, unshakeable certainty which Descartes arrives at at the end of the paragraph marked [a]→. Notice the words 'I must finally conclude' which introduces his conviction that it must be true that he exists so long as he is thinking that he does.

> Try to reconstruct the argument of the paragraph starting at [a]→. Ask yourself how Descartes decides that he cannot be deceived about his own existence.

Descartes says that the very fact of his entertaining doubts ensures that he exists. His existence – at least as long as he is engaged in the process of thinking – is not something that he could be deceived about.

Descartes's 'But' at [b]→ introduces a shift of focus. He turns his attention to the question of what it is whose indubitable existence he has established. Granted that it is certain he exists, what sort of thing is he? Descartes explains what his strategy will be for settling this new question with certainty. And he embarks on the strategy by asking himself first the question what it is that he used to take himself to be. He gives an account of the thinking he used to undertake, before he engaged in the doubt, if he considered what he was.

Examine the account that Descartes gives in the paragraph marked ⟨c⟩↦. Would you give this sort of account yourself if asked to consider what you are?

Descartes acknowledges that in his former thinking he assigned some of his properties (or attributes) to a body and some to a soul. At ⟨d⟩↦, he raises the question of which of these properties survives the doubt – which of them escape the clutches of a sceptical Malicious Demon Argument (see 'Commentary on Descartes' in chapter 1). He realizes that in taking himself to have some of his properties he had relied on the belief that he had a body, and this is a belief which a demon might have tricked him into having.

Which of his properties does Descartes think he would not have if he did not have a body?

Descartes mentions 'nutrition', 'movement' and 'sense perception' as properties that he doesn't have if he has no body. The property of thinking, by contrast, is one that he cannot suppose he lacks – not even on the hypothesis of a Malicious Demon. He is thus led to a view about what he is: something whose properties survive the doubt – a thinking thing.

With the words 'What *else* am I', at the start of the paragraph at ⟨e⟩↦, Descartes for a moment introduces the possibility that he might be something with properties other than those that survive the doubt. He points out immediately that, making the suppositions that his Method of Doubt requires him to make, he can rule it out that he is a human body, or a thin vapour. But with 'And yet' at ⟨f⟩↦, he considers that he might be wrong to rule them out. Descartes goes on to satisfy himself that, if he wants to find out what he is, he need not take into account ideas about himself that his imagination introduces.

Why does Descartes think that his imagination doesn't really have any role to play in finding out what he is?

Descartes appears to have two (related) reasons for not allowing imagination a role here. (1) He can have knowledge of himself without using his imagination. (2) Imagination involves 'corporeal' (bodily) things, and is not an appropriate source of knowledge for someone engaged in the project of doubting everything he can: if one wants certain knowledge, then there is no more reason to turn to one's imagination than to decide to fall asleep.

At ⟨g⟩↦ Descartes lists the properties/attributes that make him a thinking thing. The list is important. In the end Descartes will believe that there are two fundamental kinds of substances in the world, souls and matter. Thinking is the essence of soul for him, and his list here defines the properties of souls.

> Consider the list at [g]→ of attributes that comprise 'thinking'. Do you think this list defines what *you* are?
> Compare your answer to the answer you gave to the question (in the box above) relating to the paragraph marked [c]→

   With his next 'But' (second sentence of next paragraph after [g]→), Descartes appears to question whether the list should be so long. But the four rhetorical questions that follow are all designed to convince him and his reader that indeed the properties in his list do belong to him.
   At [h]→ Descartes indicates that he finds the fact that he doubts, understands and wills more evident than the fact that he imagines. He needs to reassure himself that the 'I' who imagines is the same as the 'I' who doubts. The context is one in which he has recently pointed out that the imagination involves bodily things. Descartes's point is that even though he can doubt *what* he imagines he cannot doubt that it is *he* who imagines.
   Descartes thinks that the case of sense perception is similar to the case of imagination. He wants to distinguish between something which is sensed (whose existence can be doubted) and a sensory experience belonging to him (which he cannot doubt). At [i]→ the distinction Descartes makes is between having a sensory perception (on the one hand) and seeing the light for instance (on the other hand). What Descartes means by a sensory perception is someone's having an experience in which it seems to them as if things are some way, in which, for instance, it seems to them as if there is light.

> Why do you think the distinction at [i]→ is important to Descartes? Do you think the distinction is sustainable? Are you able to separate your sensory perception of these words from the fact that you are seeing these words?

When Descartes separates sensory perception from seeing, he takes seeing to be made up of distinguishable components. Take the case of seeing a book. Descartes would say that this requires not only a component experience – 'a sensory perception', or its seeming as if there were a book – but also the presence of a physical book causing the experience. (We saw earlier that Descartes mentions 'sense perception' as a property that he doesn't have if he has no body. But he now introduces a 'restricted sense of the term "having a sensory perception"'. In this restricted sense, he does not need a body in order to have a sense perception.) The distinction between the experience ('the sensory perception' in Descartes's restricted sense), which is purely mental, and the seeing, which is partly physical, can be based in the possibility of doubt. According to Descartes, you can doubt whether there is really a book and whether you have eyes (and thus whether you are truly seeing anything), but you cannot doubt that you are having an experience in which it seems to you as if there is a book in front of your eyes. Here we appreciate how Descartes's mind–body dualism emerges from his pursuit of the sceptical method: the use of doubt makes him drive a wedge between mental and physical.

You will find that Strawson questions whether Descartes is entitled to drive such a wedge. Strawson is very suspicious of the idea that someone's seeing a book might be a matter of their soul's being some way on the one hand and of physical things' being some way on the other hand.

Introduction to Strawson

Professor Sir Peter Strawson (born 1919) studied at the University of Oxford, where he became a Fellow of University College in 1948 and was Waynflete Professor of Metaphysics from 1968 until his retirement from the post (but not from philosophy). Strawson's predecessor in the Waynflete Chair was Gilbert Ryle, whose *Concept of Mind* (1949) Strawson refers to in the text below. Strawson also refers there to Wittgenstein's *Philosophical Investigations* (1953) of which he wrote an instructive review at the time of its first publication.

Strawson's 1959 book *Individuals* has been extremely influential. Many of its themes run through his work, and some are to be found in the text, 'Self, Mind and Body'. Those themes include: the problem of individuation, the distinction between subject and predicate, the nature of persons, and the possibility of objective knowledge. Strawson's many books and collections of papers include an introduction to philosophy: *Analysis and Metaphysics* (1992).

In 'Self, Mind and Body', Strawson argues against Descartes's distinction between mind and body, and in favour of a unitary view of human beings – a view of them as not made up of things of two different sorts. Strawson wants his readers to reflect carefully upon exactly what we are saying when we talk about one another in an everyday way, and upon exactly what Descartes purports to be speaking about when he uses the word 'I' and takes it to refer to a mind (or a soul or a consciousness).

Terminological note

You were invited to consider which of his properties Descartes assigns to his soul, which to his body. One of Strawson's points is that it is often not straightforward to separate out properties of souls from properties of bodies. Strawson puts this point using the vocabulary of 'subject', 'predicate' and 'ascribing'. To understand how this vocabulary works, consider the sentences 'That book is red' and 'Descartes is playing chess.' These are both subject–predicate sentences. In them, a subject – that book, Descartes – is said to be some way. In other words, some predicate or property is ascribed to a subject: the predicate 'is red' is ascribed to that book; the predicate 'is playing chess' is ascribed to Descartes. The words 'that book' and 'Descartes' designate the items that are the subjects of these sentences. A designator of something is a term which refers to the thing, which one uses to mention the thing.

P. F. Strawson, 'Self, Mind and Body'

One of the marks, though not a necessary mark, of a really great philosopher is to make a really great mistake: that is to say, to give a persuasive and lastingly influential form to one of those fundamental misconceptions to which the human intellect is prone when it concerns itself with the ultimate categories of thought. So today, more than three hundred years after the death of René Descartes, philosophers struggling with one of these fundamental misconceptions think of it under the name of Cartesian dualism. Not that they all think of the doctrine in question as a misconception. The doctrine has its defenders. Indeed if it did not represent a way of thinking about mind and body which has a powerful intellectual appeal, it would not be worth struggling against. There is little point in refuting errors which no one is inclined to make.

In this article I want to try to bring out the force of one way, which has received some attention in recent English philosophy, of demonstrating the, or a, central error in Cartesian dualism. First, we need a reasonably clear statement of the dualist position to work on.

It seems an obvious and uncontentious point that the sorts of things which we can truthfully say about ourselves and other human beings are very various, that they form a very mixed bag indeed. Thus we can and do ascribe to one and the same individual human being things as various as actions, intentions, sensations, thoughts, feelings, perceptions, memories, physical position, corporeal characteristics, skills or abilities, traits of character and so on. A person or human being, as a subject of discourse, typically collects predicates of all these kinds. Now a Cartesian dualist is one who holds that this way of talking about people, though convenient and perhaps essential for practical purposes, tends to disguise rather than display the real nature of a human individual. We should first recognize, he thinks, that of these various predicates some refer directly to the states of consciousness of a person, some refer directly to his bodily condition and some refer in a more or less indirect and complicated way to both at once. But recognizing this is no more than a step in the right direction. It is not enough to acknowledge that a person has two sides to his nature and his history, a mental or conscious side and a material or corporeal side. For really the history of a human being is not the history of one two-sided thing, it is the history of two one-sided things. One of these things is a material object, a body; the other is an immaterial object, a soul or mind or spirit or individual consciousness. These are totally distinct kinds of thing, with totally distinct kinds of properties and states. None of the predicates which properly apply to bodies (like having a certain weight or size or colouring) properly apply to minds; and none of the predicates which properly apply to consciousnesses (like having a certain thought or experiencing a certain sensation) properly apply to bodies. During the lifetime of a human being, two of these things, one of each kind, are peculiarly intimately related; but the intimacy of their union does not count against or diminish the essential independence of their nature.

b→ Now if the Cartesian were right in this, it seems that it should be possible in principle to lay down at least the general outlines of a new and more metaphysically revealing way of talking about people than that which we find practically convenient. This new way of talking would reflect, in a dualism of grammatical or linguistic subjects the dualism of real or metaphysical subjects which the Cartesian finds conjoined in the human individual. If we assembled all the statements which in our ordinary way of talking have the name of one man as their grammatical subject, and reconstructed them in a Cartesian grammar, then for each statement there would be three possibilities of reconstruction: either the grammatical subject of the new statement would be the designation of a body or part of a body or it would be the designation of a mind or consciousness or the original statement would be analysed into two separate statements, one of them about a mind and one of them about a body.

It might seem at first that the germs of an 'improved' or Cartesian style of speech about people were already present in our ordinary style of speech about people. For included in our ordinary style of speech is a lot of perfectly intelligible talk in which we explicitly ascribe predicates to people's bodies (or parts of them) and also a lot of perfectly intelligible talk in which we explicitly ascribe predicates to people's minds or even consciousnesses. So it might look as if our ordinary habits of thought and speech already contained an implicit, though incomplete, acknowledgement of the truth of Cartesianism.

However, it is clearly not enough for the Cartesian to point to our habit of talking about people's minds and bodies as well as about people, as if this were conclusive evidence for his thesis. The difference between the Cartesian and his opponent is a difference of view about the relation between the concept of a person on the one hand and the concept of a person's mind on the other. The anti-Cartesian holds that the concept of a person's mind has a secondary or dependent status. The fundamental concept, for him, is that of a human being, a man, a type of thing to which predicates of *all* those various classes I distinguished earlier can be ascribed. To talk about the mind of a man is just a way of talking about a man, in respect of certain sorts of things that are true of him. Just so we can talk of the *surfaces* of tables as well as of tables, of the score in a football match as well as of a football match. But we recognize that the concept of a surface is dependent on the concept of a material object, that the concept of a score is dependent on the concept of a game. Similarly, the anti-Cartesian holds, the concept of a mind or consciousness is dependent on the concept of a living person.

c⟶   But the Cartesian cannot admit this dependence. He must hold that the notion of an individual consciousness or mind is perfectly intelligible apart from the notion of a person whose mind or individual consciousness it is. He cannot admit that the idea of a mind presupposes that of a person; he must hold, on the contrary, that a dualistic *reduction* or *analysis* of the idea of a person is in principle possible or intelligible.

d⟶   Let us consider more carefully what would be necessary in order for a Cartesian reduction to be successfully carried through. We begin with statements of which the subjects are the designations of people and the predicates are of the various kinds already mentioned. The Cartesian thesis requires that these be replaceable in principle with sentences of which the subjects are either the designations of minds (consciousnesses) or the designations of bodies. Hence it seems to require too that the predicates of our original sentences should either be already equivalent to consciousness-predicates or to body-predicates or be capable of being analysed into a body-predicate component and a consciousness-predicate component. Moreover the Cartesian reduction-sentences, it seems, must be genuinely, and not merely apparently, reductive. Consider, for example, the statement that John is writing a letter. 'Writing a letter' seems to be one of those predicates which must be split up into a mental component and a bodily component; but it would seem unsatisfactory to try to isolate the mental component by means of some such a sentence as 'His mind was going through the mental processes involved in writing a letter'. For this leaves it open to the anti-Cartesian to say that the concept of such a mental process is dependent on the concept of writing a letter; and that writing a letter is essentially not something that a mind does or something that a body does, but something that a person does.

It seems, then, that there might be very considerable difficulties in effecting a genuine reduction of person-predicates to a mental component and a bodily component. And many of these difficulties are very clearly indicated in some work in recent British philosophy, notably in Professor Ryle's book, *The Concept of Mind*, and in Wittgenstein's posthumous *Philosophical Investigations*. Yet I think that a convinced Cartesian might be comparatively unmoved by this kind of

e ⊢→ difficulty. He might agree that there were good reasons why our language was unequipped with, and perhaps was bound to remain unequipped with, the resources necessary for a genuine reduction of all such predicates as these to a mental component and a bodily component, and yet maintain that it was really quite obvious that all such activities as writing a letter really did involve both mental processes and bodily processes; and it would be hard to deny that on this point he was right in some sense, even if not in quite the sense he supposed.

f ⊢→ What would move the Cartesian much more, I think, would be a clear demonstration that there was something wrong, not on the predicate side, but on the subject side, with the idea of a Cartesian reduction. We have already remarked that it is not sufficient for the Cartesian to appeal to the fact that we do intelligibly talk about people's minds and people's bodies. The anti-Cartesian thesis is not the thesis that there are no such things as minds, but that the concept of an individual mind or consciousness is only to be understood as logically derivative from the concept of an individual person. It is up to the Cartesian to show that this is not so, to show that we can make perfectly good sense of the idea of an individual mind without making that very idea dependent upon the idea of an individual person. Hence it is a prima facie awkwardness for the Cartesian that when we ordinarily talk about people's minds or consciousnesses, we do so by way of referring to the people whose minds or consciousnesses they are. Thus if we say 'Mary's consciousness was entirely occupied by the thought of how becoming her dress was', the grammatical subject of our statement is certainly the designation of an individual mind or consciousness. But we succeed in designating the consciousness only by way of designating Mary; and Mary, happily, is not simply a consciousness; she is not only *thinking* about the dress, she is *wearing* it.

g ⊢→ It is easy enough for the Cartesian to meet this difficulty in a formal way: that is, to give examples of expressions designating consciousnesses which don't formally depend on designating people. One general form of substitute-designation might go something like this: 'The consciousness which stands in a peculiarly intimate relation with the body in such-and-such a place'. Another general form might run something like this: 'The mind which is at such-and-such a time occupied by such-and-such thoughts and feelings'. But we simply don't know whether, by the use of such forms, we achieve a reference to a mind which is genuinely independent of reference to a person, until we know the answer to a further and most important question: viz., what justifies us in using the little word 'the' – implying reference to a single one – before 'mind' or 'consciousness'.

[h]→ It is here that we come – at last – to the central difficulty in Cartesianism. If we are to talk coherently about individual consciousnesses or minds, or about individual items of any kind whatever, there is one thing at least which we must know. We must know the difference between one such item and two such items. We must know, that is, on what principle such items are to be counted. And this means further – if they are supposed to be items capable of lasting through a period of time – that we must know how to identify the *same* item at different times. In general we have no idea what a *so-and-so* is unless we have some idea what *a* so-and-so is. If we have no idea of how the notions of numerical identity and difference apply to individual consciousnesses then we really have no clear concept at all of such items.

[i]→ Now the anti-Cartesian is able to satisfy this requirement for having a coherent concept of an individual mind or consciousness. Since he regards this concept as secondary to, or derivative from, that of an individual person, he can advance the following simple rule: one person, one consciousness; *same* person, *same* consciousness. His recipe for counting individual minds is to count people; for him the identification of a mind presents no greater (and no less) a problem than the identification of a person. He does not have to pretend that the question as to what the criteria of personal identity are is an easy or straightforward question. But he can properly point out that we have, and know how to use, adequate criteria for ordinary cases; and that we can perfectly intelligibly discuss how our criteria should be interpreted or adapted for any extraordinary cases which we might encounter or imagine.

[j]→ But how does the matter stand on the Cartesian philosopher's view? It is essential to his view that the application of the notions of identity and numerability to souls (consciousnesses) should not be determined by their application to persons. (The determining must be the other way about.) But then how is the application of these notions to souls or consciousnesses to be determined? Suppose I were in debate with a Cartesian philosopher, say Professor X. If I were to suggest that when *the man*, Professor X, speaks, there are a thousand souls simultaneously thinking the thoughts his words express, having qualitatively

indistinguishable experiences such as he, the man, would currently claim, how would he persuade me that there was only one such soul? (How would each indignant soul, once the doubt has entered, persuade itself of its uniqueness?) There is another, more familiar difficulty, about the identity of a soul from one time to another. If the concept of the identity of a soul or consciousness over time is not derivative from, dependent upon, the concept of the identity of a person over time, then how is it determined? What do we mean by 'the same consciousness' if not 'the same person's consciousness'? Some philosophers, like the British empiricist, Locke, used to suppose that an adequate account of the identity of a consciousness through time could be given in terms of memory alone; but the failure of such accounts is a commonplace of philosophical criticism which I will not repeat. Other philosophers refer, or used to refer, to a Pure Ego or soul-substance, as if this exempted them from having any idea what it *meant* to speak of *the same one* from one time to another. To them one may reply, in a rough paraphrase of Kant: if you're allowed to invoke that hypothesis whenever you like, without being required to elucidate the principle of its application, what is to prevent me from introducing a rival hypothesis, also unelucidated: wherever you say there's one continuing soul-substance, I say there's whole series of them each of which transmits its states and the consciousness of them, to its successor, as motion might be transmitted from one to another of a whole series of elastic balls.

k ⊢→   The dilemma is roughly, this. Either the concepts of identity and difference of individual human consciousnesses are derivative from the concepts of identity and difference of individual people (human beings, men and women) or they are not. If they are, then our ordinary style of talking about human beings is not even in principle reducible in the way in which the Cartesian must hold that it is. If they are not, if a Cartesian reduction is in principle possible, then it must also be possible to make *independently* intelligible what is meant by identity and difference of human consciousness. But there is not the slightest reason for thinking that this can be done.

l ⊢→   What, then, is the source of the Cartesian delusion? Well, no doubt it has several sources. But I think a particularly important one is a certain experience of intense looking within, or introspective concentration, of which most of us are capable and which certainly seems to have been characteristic of Descartes' own meditations. One is tempted to say in such moments that one has direct experience of oneself as a conscious being. And this may be a harmless thing to say. But it may put us on the path of illusion. Let us see how it can do so.

The ordinary personal pronouns and possessives, including 'I' and 'my', are used in ordinary interpersonal communication for the purposes of personal reference. If the speaker says 'I', his or her hearers know what man or woman is meant. But when we reflect philosophically on the type of introspective experience I have just described, we can quite easily get into a kind of daze about the meaning of 'I' and '*my*'. We can say to ourselves things like '*I* am aware of *myself* now' or 'This is how it is with *me* now' and say such things with the conviction of their expressing absolutely indubitable fact. And then perhaps we may begin to feel that we don't have to *explain* the notions of identity and difference as applied to the soul, for we have *direct experience* of the individuality and identity of the soul, experience which might be expressed in remarks like these. And no doubt an experience of some kind is expressed in such a remark. But, really, if we make this kind of claim about it (i.e. that it is direct experience of the individuality and identity of the human soul), then we are trying to have things both ways: we are trying to keep the immediacy and indubitability of the experience and at the same time to keep the ordinary referential force of 'I', the word that the individual *man* uses to refer to himself. We are tricking ourselves by simultaneously withdrawing the pronoun from the ordinary game and yet preserving the illusion that we're still using it to play the ordinary game. And it should be easy to see this, since Kant exposed the illusion; yet, as Kant also remarked, the illusion is powerful. Perhaps a way to get at it is this. All the immediacy and indubitability of experience which seem to go with the use of 'I' and 'me' in such remarks as I've just quoted could be preserved while re-expressing the remarks in some such form as '*This* is a conscious experience' or 'The soul having *this* experience is conscious of itself as having this experience'. Then it would be apparent where the limits of immediacy and indubitability fall; it would be apparent that there is nothing in the experience itself to rule out the suggestion that there might be a thousand exactly similar experiences occurring in association with the same body – hence a thousand souls simultaneously associated with that body – and equally nothing to rule out the suggestion that the, or each, soul having such an experience is just one evanescent member of such a temporal series as Kant spoke of – hence, perhaps, a thousand souls the next moment. If this suggestion is to be ruled out, it must be on grounds extraneous to the experience itself. But the fact that this is so is masked by the use of 'I' and 'me' – expressions which, even while they seem in this context to shake off, yet surreptitiously invoke, the ordinary criteria of distinctness and identity of persons. For when *a man says* 'I', then there speaks *one* identifiable man: he can be *distinguished* as one by ordinary criteria and *identified* by ordinary criteria as, perhaps, Professor X, the Cartesian.

[m]→ The fact is that a Cartesian and an anti-Cartesian alike, and anyone else who wants to be taken seriously on the subject of the soul, wants his doctrine to have the consequence that a perfectly ordinary man, in the course of a perfectly ordinary life, has just one soul or consciousness which lasts him throughout. There is only one way of guaranteeing this consequence; and that is to allow that the notions of singularity and identity of souls or consciousnesses are conceptually dependent on those of singularity and identity of men or people. But if we allow this, we must reject a Cartesian conception of the soul.

[n]→ The arguments I have used to bring out a central incoherence in the doctrine of Cartesian dualism are arguments of a partly logical, and partly epistemological, character. They turn essentially on the notions of the identity, and of the identification, of particular things. The importance of these notions, both in the present connection and in others, has recently received a fair measure of acknowledgement in English philosophy. But, as my references to Kant have shown, these arguments are not essentially novelties, any more than is the recognition of the importance of these notions. The progress of philosophy, at least, is dialectical: we return to old insights in new and, we hope, improved forms.

Commentary on Strawson

Some of the arrow markers in the text have been used to bring out the overall structure of Strawson's essay. There isn't only one way of marking its structure, however, because Strawson weaves the different strands in his essay together. For instance, there is no precise cut-off point between Strawson's characterization of Descartes's position at the beginning of his essay and Strawson's first starting to argue against Descartes. For ease of reference it is suggested that you follow the essay according to the structure sketched below.

> Check that the structure sketched below corresponds to a way of understanding Strawson's essay that you can follow.

Until [a]→	Strawson sets out his pitch.
Between [a]→ and [b]→	We have Strawson's characterization of Cartesian dualism.
Between [b]→ and [f]→	Strawson expounds a difficulty for the dualist, which we'll call *the predication difficulty*.

Between ⬚f⬚↦ and ⬚I⬚↦   Strawson gives his main argument against the dualist, which we'll call *the identity and numerability argument.*

Between ⬚I⬚↦ and ⬚n⬚↦   Strawson provides an explanation of why people have accepted Cartesian dualism despite its errors. We'll call this *the diagnosis.*

From ⬚n⬚↦   Strawson comments on his arguments and places them in historical context.

In the remainder of this commentary, we'll focus on ⬚a⬚↦ to ⬚n⬚↦, taking in turn the four main sections into which the essay falls according to the sketch above.

1   Strawson's characterization of Cartesian dualism (*from* ⬚a⬚↦ *to* ⬚b⬚↦)

Strawson's starting-point is very different from Descartes's. Although Strawson refers to *The Meditations*, he gives no hint of how Descartes himself arrived at his position. It is evidently a conclusion of Descartes's, not his arguments, which Strawson wishes initially to challenge.

> Ask yourself whether the account of 'what a Cartesian dualist holds' that Strawson gives is accurate so far as you can tell from the Descartes you have read so far.

In reading the Second Meditation, one starts to see how mind–body dualism may emerge from the pursuit of Descartes's sceptical method. (In reading the Descartes and Strawson together, you might bear in mind that Descartes's arguments for what Strawson calls 'the Cartesian position' are not completed at the end of the passages you have read. In the Sixth Meditation Descartes presents an argument for mind–body distinctness, and he prepares some of the ground for this in a part of the Second Meditation which is not included in the extract above.)

Before moving towards difficulties with the position of his Cartesian opponent, Strawson begins to draw out claims that his opponent is committed to. Naturally enough, since Strawson is preparing to show that Descartes is wrong, the aspect of the Cartesian view that Strawson wants to bring out is one that he intends to argue against.

2   The predication difficulty (*from* ⬚b⬚↦ *to* ⬚f⬚↦)

Strawson starts his account of the difficulty by setting up his target – a commitment of the Cartesian dualist that he thinks we should question.

When Strawson uses the words 'it seems that it should be possible in principle' he tentatively suggests that the Cartesian dualist is committed to thinking that there is a philosophically more revealing way of talking about people than our everyday way. Strawson's suggestion is this: that if a human being was really 'two one-sided things' then what would really be said, when a predicate is ascribed to a human being, might be best expressed with *two* subject–predicate sentences – one of them having a soul as subject, the other having a body as subject.

Strawson speaks of his Cartesian opponent as committed to thinking that a dualist *reduction* or *analysis* of the idea of a person is possible. In order to understand what Strawson means, it may be helpful to look at a rather different case. Consider the sentence 'The average man is less than two metres tall.' We know this to be true, and we know that there isn't *really* any such *thing* as the average man. Thus there ought to be a way of saying what the sentence means which speaks only about ordinary actual men. Well, 'the average man is less than two metres tall' can presumably be re-expressed in some very long statement which gives the height of each individual man along with something about what 'average' means. To put this another way: the statement that the average man is less than two metres tall can be analysed into a statement about actual individual men. Believing in the possibility of such analysis goes hand in hand with thinking that there isn't really any such thing as the average man – that 'the average man' is not the subject of what Strawson calls a 'metaphysically revealing' sentence. Now just as we might want to show that we could analyse statements about 'the average man' into statements about ordinary individual men, so, Strawson thinks, the Cartesian dualist ought to be able to show that they can analyse statements about persons into statements about souls and statements about bodies. A dualistic reduction of the idea of a person would provide, for any predicate ascribed to a person, an analysis of statements containing that predicate into statements which do not speak about persons but only about souls and bodies.

By [c]↦, Strawson takes himself to have brought out the difference between the Cartesian dualist and the anti-Cartesian in their attitudes to the relation between statements about persons (on the one hand) and statements about minds and statements about bodies (on the other hand). At [c]↦ he expands on the claim of Cartesians which he thinks is highly questionable. According to the Cartesian, the concepts of the mind of a person and of the body of a person are fundamental, and the concept of a person dependent upon them.

One might make a comparison here with the example we used above to explain analysis and reduction. Statements about 'the average man' are (to use a phrase that Strawson uses in his own argument) 'logically derivative' from statements about individual men. The concept of 'the average man' depends upon the concept of a man. The Cartesian, then, is committed to saying something about 'person' a bit like what one says about 'the average man'. (Of course the analogy is not exact.)

In the paragraph that starts at $\boxed{d}\!\!\rightarrow$ Strawson focuses on a particular subject–predicate sentence about a person, John. The Cartesian ought to be able to come up with an account of the sentence in which something is predicated of John's mind. Strawson points out that it is not enough for his opponent to find a sentence about John's mind which will be true only if John is writing a letter. The trouble is that such a sentence seems to use concepts that are dependent on the concept of writing a letter, and this is a concept applied to persons rather than to their minds. In other words we cannot understand the Cartesian's sentence about John's mind except by understanding our original sentence about John. But then no reduction of the concept of person has been effected. (Again a comparison may be helpful. We *can* understand statements about individual men without understanding statements that begin: 'The average man . .'. In *this* case, reduction does seem to be possible.)

At $\boxed{e}\!\!\rightarrow$ Strawson envisages a response from his Cartesian opponent.

> Try to express the Cartesian's response at $\boxed{e}\!\!\rightarrow$ in your own words, and ask yourself how forceful you think it is.
> Look back over the text so far, seeking out other points at which Strawson envisages a response from his Cartesian opponent.

3   The identity and numerability argument (from $\boxed{f}\!\!\rightarrow$ to $\boxed{l}\!\!\rightarrow$)

At the start of this argument, Strawson signals that he thinks it is powerful. He said about the difficulty that he has already raised that 'a convinced Cartesian might be comparatively unmoved' by it; but he turns now to considerations which he takes to be more compelling. Strawson wants to know how we are to understand terms which, according to the Cartesian, stand for minds. These are the terms which in a Cartesian reduction of the concept of a person would designate individual minds and ascribe to them 'the mental component' of a predicate ascribed to a person.

> At $\boxed{g}\!\!\rightarrow$ Strawson says that there is a formal way for the Cartesian to meet the difficulty. What exactly is this 'formal' way?

Strawson imagines his opponent constructing descriptions containing 'consciousness' or 'mind'. But he points out that to find a description whose form suggests that it can be used to refer to a particular consciousness or mind is not yet to show that there is some one individual consciousness or mind to which the description actually refers.

At $\boxed{h}\!\!\rightarrow$, with the words 'the central difficulty', Strawson moves into his main argument. He is going to show that the Cartesian's formal way of meeting the difficulty at $\boxed{g}\!\!\rightarrow$ doesn't succeed in showing that we can make reference to individual minds. His underlying claim is that no one really understands the concept of an F (a person, a soul, an apple or whatever) unless they can say what it is for something to be an *individual* F (an individual person, an individual soul, an individual apple). If we can talk about Fs, then there must be something to be said about what makes one F different from all the other things that are also Fs. According to Strawson, Cartesians can give no principled account of how the things they calls souls are identified, unless they help themselves to the concept of an individual human being. (i) The Cartesian doesn't have any principled way of saying what it is for there to be one soul as opposed to two souls, or ten souls, or ten thousand. This is a problem about 'numerability'. (ii) The Cartesian doesn't have any principled way of saying what it is for the same soul to be identified first at one time, then at another time. This is a problem about 're-identification', which Strawson later says is 'more familiar'. (It may not be at all familiar to a beginner in philosophy; it will be the topic of chapter 6.)

In the paragraph at [i]⟩ Strawson shows that the problems about numerability and re-identification do not arise for the anti-Cartesian. And in the paragraph which starts at [j]⟩ he spells out what the problems are for the Cartesian.

> See whether you can say what Strawson's argument is in the paragraph at [j]⟩ using three or four sentences of your own.

Strawson's main argument against the Cartesian is summed up using a dilemma at [k]⟩. This summary has the following form:

> Either *p* or *not-p*.
> If *p*, then the Cartesian cannot agree.
> If *not-p*, then the Cartesian must be able to do something which Strawson has just shown cannot be done.

> Here is a way to try to understand Strawson's argument at [k]⟩ for yourself. Treat the argument as having the form just shown, and ask yourself:
> What is *p*?
> What is it that the Cartesian cannot agree with?
> What is it that Strawson claims that the Cartesian both must be able to do and also cannot do?

4 The diagnosis (from [l]⟩ to [n]⟩)

Strawson believes that the Cartesian suffers a 'delusion', for which a style of thinking, characteristic of Descartes's *Meditations*, is partly responsible. When we think introspectively we are apt to suppose that we just know what 'I' means. But then we deceive ourselves, Strawson says, because we use the word 'I' in thought supposing that the very experience of introspection tells us what it means while actually relying upon its meaning what it ordinarily does. 'I' is ordinarily applied to an individual human being – to the very one who utters the word.

Do you agree with Strawson that adopting the introspective style of thinking that Descartes adopts in his *Meditations* may lead one to deceive oneself about the meaning of 'I'?

At $\boxed{m}$⊢→, before his overall summing up, Strawson reminds us that even a Cartesian philosopher makes use of our ordinary conception of a man or a human being. (When Descartes asked himself the question 'What then did I formerly think I was?', he answered 'A man.') Strawson's point is that his arguments have shown that we cannot recover our ordinary conception of a human being from a Cartesian conception of a soul.

How do you think that Descartes might react to Strawson's claim that his concept of a soul is dependent upon his concept of a human body? This is a hard question, but try at least to get clear about how Strawson's claim relates to claims that Descartes makes.

3
Tragedy

Introduction to the Problem

This can claim to be one of the oldest philosophical issues discussed in the present book. Tragedy began as an art form in Ancient Greece, as a species of theatre involving characters and a chorus, with dialogue, music and dance. Plato, who belonged to the culture which invented tragedy and which valued it extremely highly, already found it strange that the public should come away from seeing a story of horrific suffering and be pleased, even grateful to the playwright who made them feel the pain most intensely. Aristotle's *Poetics* is in many ways a reply to his teacher Plato, and remains a classic analysis of tragedy which associates it with a specific kind of pleasure involving the emotions. Albeit with somewhat different terms of reference, essentially the same debate is carried on today in the branch of the subject known as aesthetics or philosophy of art.

In this debate the term 'tragedy' refers primarily to an invented story of human action in the form of drama, or in a narrative such as a novel, or a film. *Oedipus Rex* and *Medea* are ancient tragedies, *Othello* and *King Lear* Shakespearean examples. But a novel such as *Anna Karenina*, or films such as *Citizen Kane* or *The Godfather II* might be considered equally good examples. The storylines in typical tragic works tend to have the following general features: human beings who are ordinary enough that we can iden-tify with them in their successes and aspirations find themselves in a situa-tion in which their own actions and characters propel them into a life of extreme suffering and destruction from which there is no escape, and which appears to serve no purpose for them. In a successful tragedy the audience, identifying emotionally with the characters, feels the full force of devastation that can be wrought in any life as the result of all-too-possible human circumstances.

Tragic works, if they are well conceived and performed, rank among the most valuable for many audiences. One of the questions this raises is: Why do we like and admire so much these portrayals of what ought to be among the most negative and fearful events? If, as many have thought, the common and appropriate reaction to seeing, reading and taking part in these narratives is one of positive *pleasure*, how can that be? What is sometimes called the paradox of tragedy is just this: how can we take pleasure in, or positively enjoy, the deliberate portrayal of what is extremely negative and painful?

The pieces included in this chapter accept the assumptions that give rise to this paradox: they argue from the position that the audience of a tragedy, when responding appropriately, both experience painful feelings and feel pleasure. But both authors argue, in quite different ways, that this combination of pain and pleasure is not paradoxical.

Introduction to Hume

The Scottish philosopher David Hume (1711–76) is widely regarded as one of the greatest philosophers ever to write in the English language. The works of Hume most studied today are the *Treatise of Human Nature* and *Enquiries concerning Human Understanding and concerning the Principles of Morals*, which deal with many central issues in epistemology, metaphysics, philosophy of mind, and ethics. You will encounter his work on causality in chapter 8. Hume was an erudite and knowledgeable man with many interests in the wider culture around him. He wrote on issues concerning history, politics, religion and the arts. The short essay 'Of Tragedy', first published in 1757, takes up the problem of the supposed paradox in our reaction to tragedy.

Hume's involvement with the arts and his knowledge of many figures in European culture come through clearly in the essay. He discusses the views of the French writers Dubos and Fontenelle, uses examples from the English literature of his day, and makes references to classical Roman writers, Cicero and Ovid, whose works would have been common knowledge to his educated readers. In nearly all these cases, there should be little problem for a modern reader who lacks the benefit of such background knowledge. The examples are *only* examples: Hume is merely seeking to illustrate points he makes along the way, and most are self-explanatory. And you will not need to know anything more about Dubos and Fontenelle in order to pick up the points Hume takes from their writings.

Perhaps the one exception where a little background knowledge is needed is the example of Cicero and Verres, drawn from the time of the Roman Republic. Verres was a corrupt politician guilty of exploitation and atrocities against the people of Sicily. He was prosecuted by the great thinker and orator, Cicero, who later published a collection of his speeches against Verres. These speeches are great works of literature, which at times describe horrific scenes and are emotionally very persuasive – hence Hume's use of them as a parallel to the case of a well-constructed and moving tragic drama.

In the following text of Hume's 'Of Tragedy' a short passage has been omitted, and spelling and punctuation have been modernized to some extent.

David Hume, 'Of Tragedy'

a|→ It seems an unaccountable pleasure, which the spectators of a well-written tragedy receive from sorrow, terror, anxiety, and other passions, that are in themselves disagreeable and uneasy. The more they are touched and affected, the more are they delighted with the spectacle; and as soon as the uneasy passions cease to operate, the piece is at an end. One scene of full joy and contentment and security is the utmost, that any composition of this kind can bear; and it is sure always to be the concluding one. If, in the texture of the piece, there be interwoven any scenes of satisfaction, they afford only faint gleams of pleasure, which are thrown in by way of variety, and in order to plunge the actors into deeper distress, by means of that contrast and disappointment. The whole heart of the poet is employed, in rousing and supporting the compassion and indignation, the anxiety and b|→ resentment of his audience. They are pleased in proportion as they are afflicted, and never are so happy as when they employ tears, sobs, and cries to give vent to their sorrow, and relieve their heart, swollen with the tenderest sympathy and compassion.

c|→ The few critics who have had some tincture of philosophy, have remarked this singular phenomenon, and have endeavoured to account for it.

d|→ L'Abbé Dubos, in his reflections on poetry and painting, asserts, that nothing is in general so disagreeable to the mind as the languid, listless state of indolence, into which it falls upon the removal of all passion and occupation. To get rid of this painful situation, it seeks every amusement and pursuit; business, gaming, shows, executions; whatever will rouse the passions, and take its attention from itself. No matter what the passion is: Let it be disagreeable, afflicting, melancholy, disordered; it is still better than that insipid languor, which arises from perfect tranquillity and repose.[1]

It is impossible not to admit this account, as being, at least in part, satisfactory. You may observe, when there are several tables of

---

[1] [Jean-Baptiste Dubos, *Critical Reflections on Poetry, Painting and Music*, pt 1, ch. 1.]

gaming, that all the company run to those, where the deepest play is, even though they find not there the best players. The view, or, at least, imagination of high passions, arising from great loss or gain, affects the spectator by sympathy, gives him some touches of the same passions, and serves him for a momentary entertainment. It makes the time pass the easier with him, and is some relief to that oppression, under which men commonly labour, when left entirely to their own thoughts and meditations.

We find that common liars always magnify, in their narrations, all kinds of danger, pain, distress, sickness, deaths, murders, and cruelties; as well as joy, beauty, mirth, and magnificence. It is an absurd secret, which they have for pleasing their company, fixing their attention, and attaching them to such marvellous relations, by the passions and emotions, which they excite.

e⟶ There is, however, a difficulty in applying to the present subject, in its full extent, this solution, however ingenious and satisfactory it may appear. It is certain, that the same object of distress, which pleases in a tragedy, were it really set before us, would give the most unfeigned uneasiness; though it be then the most effectual cure to languor and f⟶ indolence. Monsieur Fontenelle seems to have been sensible of this difficulty; and accordingly attempts another solution of the phenomenon; at least makes some addition to the theory above mentioned.[2]

g⟶ 'Pleasure and pain,' says he, 'which are two sentiments so different in themselves, differ not so much in their cause. From the instance of tickling, it appears, that the movement of pleasure, pushed a little too far, becomes pain; and that the movement of pain, a little moderated, becomes pleasure. Hence it proceeds, that there is such a thing as a sorrow, soft and agreeable: it is a pain weakened and diminished. The heart likes naturally to be moved and affected. Melancholy objects suit it, and even disastrous and sorrowful, provided they are softened by some circumstance. It is certain, that, on the theatre, the representation has almost the effect of reality; yet it has not altogether that effect. However we may be hurried away by the spectacle; whatever dominion the senses and imagination may usurp over the reason, there still lurks at the bottom a certain idea of falsehood in the whole of what we see. This idea, though weak and disguised, suffices to diminish the pain which we suffer from the misfortunes of those whom we love, and to reduce that affliction to such a pitch as converts it into a pleasure. We weep for the misfortune of a hero, to whom we are attached. In the same instant we comfort ourselves, by reflecting, that it is nothing but a fiction: And it is precisely that mixture of sentiments, which composes an agreeable sorrow, and tears that

[2]   *Réflexions sur la poetique* [*Reflections on Poetry*], § 36.

delight us. But as that affliction, which is caused by exterior and sensible objects, is stronger than the consolation which arises from an internal reflection, they are the effects and symptoms of sorrow, that ought to predominate in the composition.'

[h]→   This solution seems just and convincing; but perhaps it wants still some new addition, in order to make it answer fully the phenomenon, which we here examine. All the passions, excited by eloquence, are agreeable in the highest degree, as well as those which are moved by painting and the theatre. The epilogues of Cicero are, on this account chiefly, the delight of every reader of taste; and it is difficult to read some of them without the deepest sympathy and sorrow. His merit as an orator, no doubt, depends much on his success in this particular. When he had raised tears in his judges and all his audience, they were then the most highly delighted, and expressed the greatest satisfaction with the pleader. The pathetic description of the butchery, made by Verres of the Sicilian captains,[3] is a masterpiece of this kind: But I believe none will affirm, that the being present at a melancholy scene of that nature would afford any entertainment. Neither is the sorrow here softened by fiction: For the audience were convinced of the reality of every circumstance. What is it then, which in this case raises a pleasure from the bosom of uneasiness, so to speak; and a pleasure, which still retains all the features and outward symptoms of distress and sorrow?

[i]→   I answer: This extraordinary effect proceeds from that very eloquence, with which the melancholy scene is represented. The genius required to paint objects in a lively manner, the art employed in collecting all the pathetic circumstances, the judgment displayed in disposing them: the exercise, I say, of these noble talents, together with the force of expression, and beauty of oratorial numbers,[4] diffuse the highest satisfaction on the audience, and excite the most delightful movements. By this means, the uneasiness of the melancholy passions is not only overpowered and effaced by something stronger of an [j]→ opposite kind; but the whole impulse of those passions is converted into pleasure, and swells the delight which the eloquence raises in us. The same force of oratory, employed on an uninteresting subject, would not please half so much, or rather would appear altogether ridiculous; and the mind, being left in absolute calmness and indifference, would relish none of those beauties of imagination or expression, which, if joined to passion, give it such exquisite entertainment. The impulse or vehemence, arising from sorrow, compassion, indignation,

---

[3]   [Cicero, *The Second Speech against Gaius Verres*, 5.118–38.]
[4]   [Verses; poetry.]

k→ receives a new direction from the sentiments of beauty. The latter, being the predominant emotion, seize the whole mind, and convert the former into themselves, at least tincture them so strongly as totally to alter their nature. And the soul, being, at the same time, roused by passion, and charmed by eloquence, feels on the whole a strong movement, which is altogether delightful.

l→ The same principle takes place in tragedy; with this addition, that tragedy is an imitation; and imitation is always of itself agreeable. This circumstance serves still farther to smooth the motions of passion, and convert the whole feeling into one uniform and strong enjoyment. Objects of the greatest terror and distress please in painting, and please more than the most beautiful objects, that appear calm and indifferent.[5] The affection, rousing the mind, excites a large stock of spirit and

m→ vehemence; which is all transformed into pleasure by the force of the prevailing movement. It is thus the fiction of tragedy softens the passion, by an infusion of a new feeling, not merely by weakening or diminishing the sorrow. You may by degrees weaken a real sorrow, till it totally disappears; yet in none of its graduations will it ever give pleasure; except, perhaps, by accident, to a man sunk under lethargic indolence, whom it rouses from that languid state.

n→ To confirm this theory, it will be sufficient to produce other instances, where the subordinate movement is converted into the predominant, and gives force to it, though of a different, and even sometimes though of a contrary nature.

Novelty naturally rouses the mind, and attracts our attention; and the movements, which it causes, are always converted into any passion, belonging to the object, and join their force to it. Whether an event excite joy or sorrow, pride or shame, anger or goodwill, it is sure to produce a stronger affection, when new or unusual. And though novelty of itself be agreeable, it fortifies the painful, as well as agreeable passions.

Had you any intention to move a person extremely by the narration of any event, the best method of increasing its effect would be artfully to delay informing him of it, and first to excite his curiosity and impatience before you let him into the secret. This is the artifice practised by Iago in the famous scene of Shakespeare; and every

---

[5] Painters make no scruple of representing distress and sorrow as well as any other passion. But they seem not to dwell so much on these melancholy affections as the poets, who, though they copy every emotion of the human breast, yet pass very quickly over the agreeable sentiments. A painter represents only one instant; and if that be passionate enough, it is sure to affect and delight the spectator. But nothing can furnish to the poet a variety of scenes and incidents and sentiments, except distress, terror, or anxiety. Complete joy and satisfaction is attended with security and leaves no farther room for action.

spectator is sensible, that Othello's jealousy acquires additional force from his preceding impatience, and that the subordinate passion is here readily transformed into the predominant one.[6]

Difficulties increase passions of every kind; and by rousing our attention, and exciting our active powers, they produce an emotion, which nourishes the prevailing affection.

Parents commonly love that child most, whose sickly infirm frame of body has occasioned them the greatest pains, trouble, and anxiety in rearing him. The agreeable sentiment of affection here acquires force from sentiments of uneasiness.

Nothing endears so much a friend as sorrow for his death. The pleasure of his company has not so powerful an influence.

Jealousy is a painful passion; yet without some share of it, the agreeable affection of love has difficulty to subsist in its full force and violence. Absence is also a great source of complaint among lovers, and gives them the greatest uneasiness: Yet nothing is more favourable to their mutual passion than short intervals of that kind. And if long intervals often prove fatal, it is only because, through time, men are accustomed to them, and they cease to give uneasiness. [...]

o→ These instances (and many more might be collected) are sufficient to afford us some insight into the analogy of nature, and to show us, that the pleasure, which poets, orators, and musicians give us, by exciting grief, sorrow, indignation, compassion, is not so extraordinary or paradoxical, as it may at first sight appear. The force of imagination, the energy of expression, the power of numbers, the charms of imitation; all these are naturally, of themselves, delightful to the mind.

p→ And when the object presented lays also hold of some affection, the pleasure still rises upon us, by the conversion of this subordinate movement into that which is predominant. The passion, though, perhaps, naturally, and when excited by the simple appearance of a real object, it may be painful; yet is so smoothed, and softened, and mollified, when raised by the finer arts, that it affords the highest entertainment.

q→ To confirm this reasoning, we may observe, that if the movements of the imagination be not predominant above those of the passion, a contrary effect follows; and the former, being now subordinate, is converted into the latter, and still farther increases the pain and affliction of the sufferer.

Who could ever think of it as a good expedient for comforting an afflicted parent, to exaggerate, with all the force of elocution, the irreparable loss, which he has met with by the death of a favourite

---

[6] [Shakespeare, *Othello*, act 3, sc. 3.]

child? The more power of imagination and expression you here employ, the more you increase his despair and affliction.

The shame, confusion, and terror of Verres, no doubt, rose in proportion to the noble eloquence and vehemence of Cicero: so also did his pain and uneasiness. These former passions were too strong for the pleasure arising from the beauties of elocution; and operated, though from the same principle, yet in a contrary manner, to the sympathy, compassion, and indignation of the audience.

Lord Clarendon, when he approaches towards the catastrophe of the royal party, supposes, that his narration must then become infinitely disagreeable; and he hurries over the king's death, without giving us one circumstance of it.[7] He considers it as too horrid a scene to be contemplated with any satisfaction, or even without the utmost pain and aversion. He himself, as well as the readers of that age, were too deeply concerned in the events, and felt a pain from subjects, which an historian and a reader of another age would regard as the most pathetic and most interesting, and, by consequence, the most agreeable.

An action, represented in tragedy, may be too bloody and atrocious. It may excite such movements of horror as will not soften into pleasure; and the greatest energy of expression, bestowed on descriptions of that nature, serves only to augment our uneasiness. Such is that action represented in the *Ambitious Stepmother*,[8] where a venerable old man, raised to the height of fury and despair, rushes against a pillar, and striking his head upon it, besmears it all over with mingled brains and gore. The English theatre abounds too much with such shocking images.

Even the common sentiments of compassion require to be softened by some agreeable affection, in order to give a thorough satisfaction to the audience. The mere suffering of plaintive virtue, under the triumphant tyranny and oppression of vice, forms a disagreeable spectacle, and is carefully avoided by all masters of the drama. In order to dismiss the audience with entire satisfaction and contentment, the virtue must either convert itself into a noble courageous despair, or the vice receive its proper punishment.

Most painters appear in this light to have been very unhappy in their subjects. As they wrought[9] much for churches and convents, they have chiefly represented such horrible subjects as crucifixions and martyrdoms, where nothing appears but tortures, wounds, executions, and

---

[7] [Edward Hyde, First Earl of Clarendon, *The True Historical Narrative of the Rebellion and Civil Wars in England*, describing the events of 1649.]
[8] [A tragedy by Nicholas Rowe, performed and printed in 1700.]
[9] [Produced; worked]

passive suffering, without any action or affection. When they turned their pencil from this ghastly mythology, they had commonly recourse to Ovid, whose fictions, though passionate and agreeable, are scarcely natural or probable enough for painting.

The same inversion of that principle, which is here insisted on, displays itself in common life, as in the effects of oratory and poetry. Raise so the subordinate passion that it becomes the predominant, it swallows up that affection which it before nourished and increased. Too much jealousy extinguishes love: Too much difficulty renders us indifferent: Too much sickness and infirmity disgusts a selfish and unkind parent.

What so disagreeable as the dismal, gloomy, disastrous stories, with which melancholy people entertain their companions? The uneasy passion being there raised alone, unaccompanied with any spirit, genius, or eloquence, conveys a pure uneasiness, and is attended with nothing that can soften it into pleasure or satisfaction.

Commentary on Hume

In his first paragraph Hume sets out what he takes to be a 'singular phenomenon' (see $\boxed{\text{c}}\rightarrow$). He is saying that there is something uniquely strange about the state in which 'the spectators of a well-written tragedy' find themselves.

> Read the first paragraph of 'Of Tragedy'. State in your own words what Hume says is the strange feature of spectators of a tragedy. State also which of Hume's words best make his point.

One way to state Hume's opening point would be to say that negative emotions (or 'passions') are excited in the audience by tragedy. But the most strange or singular point is brought up at $\boxed{\text{a}}\rightarrow$ and $\boxed{\text{b}}\rightarrow$. It is not just that the spectators feel negative emotions, but that their pleasure is the greater the stronger their negative emotions are.

> List the 'negative' emotions Hume mentions in his first paragraph, and explain what about them is negative.

The first three negative emotions are 'sorrow, terror, anxiety', but there seem to be another five in the first paragraph. Hume says that they are all 'disagreeable and uneasy'. This means that it is painful, or at least unpleasant, to be in these states.

So the strange feature of the tragic audience is that they gain more pleasure, the more unpleasant or painful the emotions that are aroused in them.

Next Hume turns to two attempted explanations of this phenomenon, that by Dubos (from $\boxed{d}\!\mapsto$ to $\boxed{f}\!\mapsto$) and that by Fontenelle (from $\boxed{f}\!\mapsto$ to $\boxed{h}\!\mapsto$).

> State in your own words the explanation Hume attributes to Dubos. Then state what Hume's reaction to it is.

Hume starts by being polite about Dubos's view, up until $\boxed{e}\!\mapsto$ where he mentions a difficulty with it. Dubos's view, put simply, is that any powerful emotion, no matter what, is better than the unpleasant state of having nothing to occupy the mind. Hume finds many examples from ordinary life which seem to corroborate this. But there is a difficulty in applying it to the case of tragedy.

> What is the difficulty (at $\boxed{e}\!\mapsto$) in applying Dubos's explanation to tragedy?

It seems the problem is that we have failed to explain the *enjoyment* people derive from tragedy. A real-life scene of disaster and anguish would certainly drive away empty boredom, but that is not at all the same as its positively giving us pleasure. So something else is needed to explain the pleasure taken in tragedy.

> How does the solution offered by Fontenelle (stated from $\boxed{g}\!\mapsto$ to $\boxed{h}\!\mapsto$) improve over the previous attempt?

As you read, notice that everything from $\boxed{g}\!\mapsto$ to $\boxed{h}\!\mapsto$ is a quotation. This is not Hume's own voice, but that of someone else putting forward a point, which Hume will then debate. The Fontenelle view provides a way of differentiating our reactions to fictional tragic drama from our reactions to real-life horrific scenes. An important sentence is 'there still lurks at the bottom a certain idea of falsehood in the whole of what we see.' What we find painful in real life we can find pleasurable in a fiction, because we never lose our sense that it is a fiction.

> What problem does Hume find with this solution?

Once again Hume begins his reply (in the paragraph starting at $\boxed{h}\!\mapsto$) in generous mode ('This solution seems just and convincing'). His very next word ('but') marks the start of an objection, however. Here is the substance of his objection: Cicero and Verres were real people, and Cicero's speeches prosecuting Verres for real atrocities he committed are 'the delight of every reader of taste'. In other words, we enjoy hearing the narration of these awful events. But if Fontenelle's explanation were right, it should be impossible to take pleasure in the narration unless our pain were diminished by a belief that it was not true. So Fontenelle's explanation is not right. Fictionality is not necessary for the reaction of pleasure towards a distressing narrative.

So far Hume has been finding problems, rather than offering a solution. This changes in the paragraph beginning at $\boxed{\text{i}}$→ and the following one marked $\boxed{\text{I}}$→. These passages should be studied very carefully, as Hume here presents his own positive answer to the question he has set himself. In the first of these two paragraphs Hume states his thesis about the way negative emotions can be converted into pleasure – a thesis about the operation of the mind. For 'conversion' see $\boxed{\text{j}}$→ and $\boxed{\text{k}}$→ and in a later re-statement $\boxed{\text{p}}$→. 'Transformed' at $\boxed{\text{m}}$→ is also equivalent to 'converted'.

The 'conversion' theory is hard to interpret, as we shall see. What is converted into what, we shall need to ask, and how does it happen? But before we confront these problems directly, let us see more of Hume's strategy here.

It is only in the paragraph marked $\boxed{\text{I}}$→ that Hume applies his idea about the process of 'conversion' to tragedy as such. The previous paragraph is more general, and is still meant to apply to the case of Cicero's literally true evocation of the horrors committed by Verres. But it is best to read these two paragraphs together.

Hume finds one relevant difference between the case of tragedy and the case of a description such as Cicero's: what is that difference?

The difference is precisely that a tragedy is not an attempt to report real events, but a fictional representation. Hume's word for this is 'imitation'. This is relevant because, as he puts it, 'imitation is of itself agreeable': we take pleasure in seeing a fictional representation of something, almost regardless of what that something is. (The idea that taking satisfaction in inventing pictures, stories and other representations is a basic feature of human beings goes back to Aristotle's account of *mimesis*, for which 'imitation' is a translation.)

So the strategy is roughly this: first show that even a literal narration of horrific events can be pleasurable under certain conditions. Then argue that if a narration meets these conditions and is also a fictional 'imitation' (a further source of pleasure), then the pleasure it gives can be all the greater.

Hume makes use of two important ideas about pleasure in these paragraphs: (1) that pleasures may be taken in a variety of different aspects of a tragedy; (2) that when we are pleased by the different aspects, what we feel may amount to a single sense of enjoyment.

Point (1) can also be put by saying that there are different *objects* of pleasure for us. We take pleasure in beautiful use of language, in the artistry with which the plot is unfolded by the author, and so on. (In the case of a dramatic production we might take pleasure also in the appearance of the actors and their costumes, music, stage design, and so on.) Nowadays we might be inclined to call such aspects or objects of pleasure *aesthetic*, though Hume does not use that term. At any rate, the features we have listed relate to the beauty or pleasingness of what we see and hear, or to the artistry or skill with which something is executed. (See paragraphs marked $\boxed{i} \rightarrow$ and $\boxed{o} \rightarrow$ for Hume's examples.)

Point (2) can be put by saying that, although we may theoretically itemize the various objects of pleasure, such as the storyline, the use of language, the skilled acting, the stage design and so on, what we experience is a single feeling of pleasure, or as Hume puts it, 'one uniform and strong enjoyment'. The pleasure in seeing a fiction or imitation also combines happily with the pleasures we take in beauty and compositional skill, and enhances them. And when these pleasures with different objects enhance one another, we experience not so much several distinguishable feelings of pleasure, but a single, greater pleasure.

But now the crucial question for Hume is whether the *negative* emotions which make tragedy problematic can find a place in this compound enjoyment. His hope is that the distressing negative emotions – sorrow, terror, anxiety – can enhance the pleasure that we have tentatively called aesthetic. But how is this supposed to happen?

> What do you think Hume means by the process of converting (or transforming) our negative emotions into pleasure? Does he mean:
>
> (a)   Our distress is obliterated by aesthetic pleasure, so that in the end only pleasure is felt?
> (b)   Our distress goes on being felt, but is itself a pleasurable feeling because of the predominance of aesthetic pleasures?
> (c)   We feel a strong negative emotion, and as a result our overall pleasure takes on more strength, and becomes more pleasurable?
>
> Which, if any, of these accounts, has any plausibility?

It is genuinely hard to settle on what Hume means. He says that the aesthetic pleasure (as we have called it) is 'predominant' or 'prevailing' in the mind of the audience, and seems to think that this gives it the power to coopt the negative emotions into itself. Yet at the same time the negative emotions still retain such 'vehemence' or 'impulse' that they make the aesthetic pleasure all the greater. This makes (c) look the most likely interpretation. As long as the aesthetic pleasures are the dominant feelings in the mind, an increase in one's feeling of terror or anxiety increases one's pleasure.

Hume ends his piece with a list of examples intended to show the converse.

> What do the examples from $\boxed{q} \rightarrow$ to the end claim to show about the relation of negative emotions to pleasure? Which of the examples, in your view, best serve to show it?

What Hume tries to show here is that if terror or anxiety or grief are dominant in the mind, then intensifying the 'aesthetic' features of one's presentation will not make the pain less, and will not provide any pleasure.

But these cases suggest a problem for the 'conversion' theory. Hume tells us that terror or anxiety or other distressing feelings can be so strong that they will not allow the aesthetic pleasures to become dominant. But what about the cases of terror and anxiety which are not 'predominant' in this way, and allow themselves to be 'transformed' into a positive feeling – are they real terror and anxiety at all? Or take grief: if I am feeling a kind of grief that lends itself quite easily to mingling with aesthetic pleasure, how genuine a grief is it? The suspicion arises that only if I am not really grief-stricken or terrified will my negative feelings yield themselves up readily to incorporation in aesthetic enjoyment. In which case, Hume has not really done what he claims. He claims to tell us why enjoyment of tragedy is greater when our affliction by distress is greater. Now it appears that our distress must be limited to a kind that is tame enough not to interfere with aesthetic pleasure.

Finally, we must question Hume's apparent presumption that a strong state of distress can lend its strength (he says force, vehemence, or impulse) to a state of pleasure. What does that mean? Imagine I have a strong pain in my leg, and at the same time enjoy the taste of some vanilla ice-cream. Could the *strength* of my pain be transmitted to my enjoyment, resulting in my enjoying the ice-cream more strongly than if I lacked the pain? Hume's examples are more subtle – but is what he is proposing really different from this in principle? I have a strong sorrow or anxiety about the situation of Oedipus in the drama, and at the same time enjoy the dramatist's presentation of this in well-crafted verse. Could the strength of my sorrow be transmitted to my enjoyment, resulting in my enjoying the verse more strongly than if I lacked the sorrow?

Hume's essay is fruitful for its understanding of some of the philosophical problems about tragedy. But it can seem to substitute one puzzle for another. We want to know just how such 'conversion' in the mind can work.

We have so far not discussed the earlier list of examples, from ⊡n ⊢→ to ⊡o ⊢→ in the text, where Hume gives a variety of situations which he thinks parallel the case of tragedy because 'the subordinate movement' of the mind is 'converted into the predominant'. Reading through these may help to confront the questions about the nature and possibility of the conversion Hume alleges.

> Read the examples from ⊡n ⊢→ to ⊡o ⊢→. State in your own words what single principle they are all supposed to illustrate. Then answer the question: to what extent do these examples support Hume's claim about the emotions and pleasure in the case of tragedy?

In general Hume makes the task hard for himself by insisting that both distress and pleasure are present in our reactions to tragedy. The task would be easier if he were prepared to deny one of the starting assumptions of the paradox of tragedy – a line some writers in aesthetics have favoured – and say that no pain is essentially involved in the experience, that we simply enjoy the aesthetically pleasing 'vehicle' in which a tragic story is conveyed to us, while merely, as it were, putting up with the horrible content.

But it is arguable that Hume's starting position is psychologically the more plausible, and that Hume is right in his insight that the audience is pleased *because of*, not in spite of, their distress. The 'No Pain' solution, as we might call it, seems too easy a way out of the paradox because it begins to make the content of the tragedy look irrelevant to our pleasure. In that case, why are tragedies not improved by minimizing the horror they contain? And why are not all dramas light romantic comedies or adventure stories with happy endings?

Our next selected piece starts by alleging inadequacy in Hume's account, and proceeds to a clearer solution to the problem Hume posed at the outset, but still retaining his insight that our pleasure has to occur somehow because of our distressing reaction to the events in the tragic story.

Introduction to Feagin

Susan L. Feagin is professor of philosophy at the University of Missouri in Kansas City. She has published numerous articles on aesthetics and its connections with the philosophy of mind. Her *Reading with Feeling: The Aesthetics of Appreciation* was published in 1996. Feagin's article 'The Pleasures of Tragedy' was originally published in the *American Philosophical Quarterly* in 1983. The version printed here was edited by the author herself for publication in Susan L. Feagin and Patrick Maynard (eds), *Aesthetics* (Oxford University Press, 1997). The piece is a good pairing with the previous essay, since it starts from a criticism of Hume's theory of 'conversion' of the passions, but then moves to state an alternative theory, which, like Hume's, seeks to show how, without paradox, painful or unpleasant responses to tragedy can co-exist with pleasure.

Feagin's central notion is that of a meta-response. Although she explains the idea clearly in the first section of her paper, an initial word on this may be appropriate here as well. *Meta* originates in the Greek word meaning 'after' (among other things). In modern philosophy the notion of something's being 'meta-' crops up in many contexts, almost always meaning 'at a higher level than' or 'of a higher order than' something else. Meta-philosophy, for instance, means philosophical thinking *about philosophy itself*. A meta-language is a language used to talk *about another language*. Likewise, Feagin's meta-response is a response that we have *to a response*. By a response here is meant some state of mind such as being pleased or being pained, or feeling an emotion such as shame, pride, anger, or embarrassment. A straightforward or 'direct' response would be a reaction to some event or state of affairs in the world. Imagine you see someone slip over in the street; your direct response to that event might be to feel amused. But suppose that instantaneously you feel ashamed *about being amused*. Then this feeling of shame is a response to your own response. It is, in Feagin's sense, a meta-response. The direct response is your being amused at someone's slipping over. The meta-response is your feeling ashamed at being amused at someone's slipping over.

These meta-responses are in fact remarkably common in our mental lives. We feel angry about feeling afraid in some situations, guilty about feeling attracted to certain things, proud that we feel contempt for other things, and so on. It is worth grasping this structure securely because Feagin's case depends on it. She gives a number of parallel examples, but it might help to construct some for yourself too.

Susan L. Feagin, 'The Pleasures of Tragedy'

David Hume begins his little essay 'Of Tragedy' with the observation: 'It seems an unaccountable pleasure which the spectators of a well-written tragedy receive from sorrow, terror, anxiety, and other passions that are in themselves disagreeable and uneasy.' Here Hume addresses a paradox that has puzzled philosophers of art since Aristotle: tragedies produce, and are designed to produce, pleasure for the audience, without supposing any special callousness or insensitivity on its part (in fact, quite the opposite). I will introduce a distinction which enables us to understand how we can feel pleasure in response to tragedy, and which also sheds some light on the complexity of such responses. The virtues of this approach lie in its straightforward solution to the paradox of tragedy as well as the bridges the approach builds between this and some other traditional problems in aesthetics, and the promising ways in which we are helped to see their relationships. In particular, we are helped to understand the feeling many have had about the greatness of tragedy in comparison to comedy, and provided a new perspective from which to view the relationship between art and morality. The very close connection which is seen to hold here between pleasures from tragedy and moral feelings also gives rise to a potential problem, which is examined later in the paper.

a→   Hume himself alleged that imagination, imitation, and expression are all 'naturally' pleasurable to the mind, and argued that when they 'predominate' over the unpleasant feelings the latter are 'converted' into the former. But it is not clear how the 'dominance' of imagination and expression is to be achieved. It is not insured by the fact that what is depicted is fictional, or even by our knowledge that it is fictional, since Hume discusses a play where the events depicted (even though fictional) are so gory that no amount of expression can 'soften' them into pleasure. More puzzling, however, is the process of 'conversion' which imagination performs on the unplesant feelings (and which those feelings, when dominant, perform on the natural pleasantness of the imagination). Pains are not merely mitigated by the pleasure, but converted or transformed into something different. The mechanics of this conversion are never explained, and as long as they remain obscure, even if we accept other features of Hume's view, many of which are quite insightful, we have merely substituted one puzzle for another. [...]

b⟼   Though my own discussion of the pleasures of tragedy does not utilize such notions as imagination and passion on which Hume depended, it does have its own special presuppositions. I shall speak of two kinds of responses to art: a direct response and a meta-response. A direct response is a response to the qualities and content of the work. A meta-response is a response to the direct responses. The distinction is not one of epistemological or ontological status; I presuppose no view about sense data, epistemologically 'primitive' experiences, or incorrigibility of mental status. A direct response is direct only in the sense that it is a response to the qualities and content of the work of art. Of course, there are complex questions about what is 'in the work' and what constitutes the 'work itself,' but those need not be resolved for the purposes of this discussion. The important contrast is not between a direct response to the work as opposed to a direct response to what is not really in the work. The important contrast is between a direct response and a meta-response which is a response to the direct response: it is how one feels about and what one thinks about one's responding (directly) in the way one does to the qualities and content of the work. The meta-response is what Ryle called a 'higher order' operation: it depends on (and is partly a function of) another mental phenomenon, i.e., a direct response. Ideally, my remarks will be independent of any specific view of the 'logical category' of pleasure itself, and I fear perhaps the term 'response' may cause some unwarranted discomfort in that sphere. Let me therefore make the following caveats: (1) by calling pleasure a response I do not imply that it is not essentially connected to its source (what one finds pleasurable), i.e., it is not distinguishable as a response independently of what the pleasure is a pleasure in; (2) a response is not necessarily a mental episode or occurrence (*a fortiori* it is not necessarily a private mental episode) but it may turn out to be a mood or even a disposition or a change of disposition, or some other type of thing.

c →   Both direct and meta-responses exist in ordinary life as well as in artistic contexts. For example, the remains of a spectacular car crash may titillate our curiosity, and we may feel disgusted with ourselves for being so morbid. On the other hand, we may enjoy the enticement of hawkers outside seamy strip joints, and be pleased with ourselves for having overcome a puritanical upbringing. We can be depressed at our failure to meet a challenge, impressed with our ability to rise to an occasion, disgusted with our lack of sympathy for a friend's bereavement, or pleased with the commitment we are inclined to make to help a neighbor. It should be noted that in ordinary as well as aesthetic contexts the two kinds of responses cannot be distinguished merely by what words are used to describe them. 'Pleasure,' 'shock,' 'melancholy,' and 'delight' may all describe direct or meta-responses, and the two are not always clearly distinguishable from each other. A blush of embarrassment may be intensified by embarrassment over the blush. That two things being distinguished cannot be infallibly distinguished, and that there are unclear cases of how and even whether the two are distinguishable, does not necessarily undermine the utility of the distinction.

A Solution

d →   Direct responses to tragedy are responses to the unpleasantness of the work, and they are hence unpleasant experiences we would expect to have from works having unpleasant subject matter and/or unhappy endings. Direct responses draw on our feelings and sympathies: tearjerkers jerk tears because of our sympathy with persons who are ill-treated or the victims of misfortune. Many people, in fact, dislike attending depressing plays and violent movies, or reading weighty books and poetry, precisely because these experiences are unpleasant and consequently depress and sadden them, making them too well aware of the evil of people and the perils of existence. These works of art, rather than being uplifting and inspiring, often instead produce feelings of torpor and futility as one is overwhelmed by the amount and variety of viciousness in the world. A dose of direct response unpleasantness is a good antidote to creeping misanthropy, as it feeds off of our concern for others. It is also, as John Stuart Mill discovered, a cure for ennui. Mill reported in his *Autobiography* (Sec. v) that it was his crying over the distressed condition of Marmontel as related in his memoirs that initially jogged Mill out of his 'mental crisis' by showing him that he did have feelings, concerns, and cares, and that he was not just 'a logic machine.'

It is the nature of these direct responses to tragedy which we expect and in fact receive which gives rise to the question in the first place, how do we derive pleasure from tragedy? Certainly the typical person who appreciates and enjoys such works of art doesn't feel the direct response any less poignantly than those described above who don't enjoy these works. Lovers of Dostoyevsky, Verdi, and Shakespeare, let us hope, are no more callous than those who find them too hard to e ⊢→ take. But whence the pleasure? It is, I suggest, a meta-response, arising from our awareness of, and in response to, the fact that we do have unpleasant direct responses to unpleasant events as they occur in the performing and literary arts. We find ourselves to be the kind of people who respond negatively to villainy, treachery, and injustice. This discovery, or reminder, is something which, quite justly, yields satisfaction. In a way it shows what we care for, and in showing us we care for the welfare of human beings and that we deplore the immoral forces that defeat them, it reminds us of our common humanity. It reduces one's sense of aloneness in the world, and soothes, psychologically, the pain of solipsism. Perhaps this is something like what Kant had in mind when he spoke in the *Critique of Judgment* of a 'common sense.' We derive pleasure from the communicability or 'shareability' of a response to a work of art: it is something which unites us with other people through feeling something which could, in principle, be felt by anyone. [...]

Tragedy and Comedy

f ⊢→ The observation is often made that tragedies are much more important or significant artworks than comedies. The great works of Shakespeare are *Hamlet, King Lear*, and *Macbeth*, notwithstanding the brilliance of *Twelfth Night* and *As You Like It*. The greatest plays of antiquity are the Oedipus Trilogy and the *Oresteia*, despite the cunning wit of Aristophanes. The greatness of Voltaire's *Candide* is due more to his portrayal of the fate of humankind than his avowedly clever humor. There are great comedies, but the significance of the greatest is not thought to reach the significance of even less great tragedies. Why?

g ⊢→ It is not due, as one might suppose on first blush, to some essential morbidity in the outlook of those who defend this judgment. If it were, the greatness of tragedy would be due to the simple truth of the basic picture drawn by tragedy of the nature of man's lot: doomed to suffer injustice, wage war, suffer defeat, and be overcome by conniving women, conniving men, mistakes in judgment, accidents of birth, ignorance, and foolish advice. Tragedy then would be taken to confirm, or at least to echo, one's solemn conviction in the nastiness of human life. The pleasure from tragedy would then also be a morbid one, like the evil-doer who, in his every act, enjoys providing more evidence against the existence of a benevolent god. Whether or not one does believe in the existence of such a god, the pleasure taken in providing evidence against its existence by performing acts of evil is undoubtedly a morbid one.

But the greatness of tragedy is not due to any supposed truth of 'profound' pictures such as these, and our pleasure in it is not therefore in recognizing this unpleasant truth. Tragedy is anything but morbid, for if people did not feel sympathy with their fellow human beings we would not have the initial negative responses we do to the tragic situation, the unpleasant direct responses. At the foundation of the aesthetic pleasure from tragedy is the same feeling which makes possible moral action: sympathy with, and a concern for, the welfare of human beings *qua* human beings, feelings which are increased if those human beings bear any special relationship to oneself such as friends or family, with an attendant increase in moral commitment to them. I do not wish to argue about the basis of morality, but I do wish to suggest that the basis for our judgments of the aesthetic *significance* of tragedy (as opposed to the lesser significance of comedy) can plausibly be its calling forth feelings which are also at the basis of morality. Judgments about tragedy's greatness derive from a recognition of the importance of morality to human life.

In comedy there must be a 'butt' of the joke. The pleasure from comedy, then, is generally a direct response to the failures, defects, or absurdities of whomever (or whatever) is the object of ridicule or fun. Of course not all laughing is laughing *at* people – there is also laughing *with* people – and the two kinds of responses also provide a means for explaining what this means. One laughs *with* people when one is among those being laughed at. Depending on the joke, one's own emotional reactions to parts of the work may be the object of fun, or perhaps what one remembers having done or imagines one would have done under circumstances presented in the work. The response has then become more complex, requiring a kind of self-awareness, much like the meta-response that pleasure from tragedy requires.

Moreover, responses to comedy are to failures or defects judged to be insignificant. This judgment is important because if the imperfections were thought to be of great significance, the work would then take on the air of tragedy rather than comedy, it would be saddening rather than amusing that people were subject to such flaws. The arrogance and pomposity of Trissotin in Molière's *The Learned Ladies* is comic because he is a parochial poet with little influence outside of an equally insignificant small circle of dotty old ladies. But the arrogance of Jason is of cosmic proportions: it ruins Medea, and she in turn destroys his children, his bride, his future father-in-law, and by that act unstabilizes the very order of society. Human foibles may be minor or major, and it is precisely the latter ones which tear at (rather than tickle) the hearts of an audience. Comedy, one might say, is skin deep: it generally goes no further than direct response, and requires that one's responses be to things which do not play major roles in maintaining the happiness and security of human life. Presuming an imperfection to be insignificant makes it possible to laugh at it, but believing it to be important makes one cry. The person who laughs at tragedy may justifiably be called 'callous,' and one might sensibly harbor serious doubts about that person's morality. [...]

A Potential Problem

Given that, on this analysis, the same feelings are at the base of both morality and aesthetic pleasure from tragedy, it is necessary to explain how, consistently with this, one might respond aesthetically and be, for all intents and purposes, an immoral person, and also how one might be morally very upright but aesthetically insensitive. The first is what John Ruskin calls somewhere the 'selfish sentimentalist.' One can weep, groan, and cringe over a novel or in the theater, but remain blasé if the fictional events were to occur in reality. The pride one feels in one's theater tears is a selfish pride, and has actually very little to do with any concern for human welfare, or, consequently, one's virtue (though it may have a lot to do with one's supposed virtue). Wouldn't such an account as mine have to suppose that the moral feelings exist when one is in the theater, but that they dissolve when one walks outside?

In *The Concept of Mind*, Gilbert Ryle says, 'Sentimentalists are people who indulge in induced feelings without acknowledging the fictitiousness of their agitations'. Their agitations are not real since their concern is not: without a genuine desire for people's welfare there is no opposition between that desire and the fate that eventually befalls them. They pretend a concern for the poor devils, and then feel real distress when they suffer only because their pretense has been so effective. But then one wonders how people can feel real distress over pretended concerns.

There should be another way of explaining the situation which does not involve so much self-delusion. Indeed, there is. One might genuinely care for others but not nearly so much as for oneself. Hence, when there is no risk to oneself all the tears come pouring forth out of compassion: as a casual reader or theater-goer one is merely a witness to, and cannot be a participant in, the proceedings. That is one of the delights of fiction (even tragedy): one is free to feel as one wishes at no risk to oneself, incurring no obligation, requiring no money, time, or dirty fingernails. But once one gets outside, the situation changes, and one's concern for others may just not be strong enough to overcome self-interest. Concern for others does not miraculously disappear when one travels from the theater to the marketplace – it is overpowered by concern for self. And there is still another way to view the phenomenon, consistently with what I have said about sympathetic responses and meta-responses. Perhaps one identifies with the character in the novel, film, or play, and hence one's concern is self-interested in the sense that it exists *only* because of that identification. What one may never have learned to do is to be concerned about others even when one does *not* feel at one with them. In this case there is a genuine sympathetic response, but one's capacity for sympathy is limited. I, at least, would expect such individuals to show rather pronounced patterns of likes and dislikes with respect to fictional material: only characters with certain salient properties (divorced women, perhaps, or aristocrats, or characters plagued by self-doubt, etc.) would excite their compassion, while others (bachelors, immigrants, or the chronically self-assured, etc.) leave them cold. One of the things we generally expect from a good work of art is a capacity to evoke sympathetic feelings in us for some of its characters, and it is a measure of its goodness that it can melt the hearts even of those not disposed to any concern for others. Of course, there are 'cheap' ways of doing this which we all recognize: there are tools for manipulating an audience that practically no one can resist. One such tool is to introduce someone who is young, intelligent, and good, but dies an untimely death (*Love Story, Death Be Not Proud*), and another is to capitalize on adorable youngsters who have been wronged in all their innocence and goodness (Cio-Cio-San's child, Trouble, in *Madame Butterfly*). Both are effective in disturbing even the weakest sense of injustice.

The other side of the potential problem is the unimaginative moralist, whose behavior is always exemplary but who cannot get worked up over a fictional creation. Isn't it even more difficult to explain how such a person will not respond sympathetically to fiction although he or she will do so in reality? We certainly do not have a case here of one's sympathy being overpowered by self-interest. The key to the solution is that this moralist is unimaginative, for it takes *more* effort of imagination to respond to a work of art than it does to respond to real life. In art one has to overcome the conventions of the medium, contemplate counterfactuals, and make the appropriate inferences and elaborations on the basis of them. Perhaps this is why some have thought that developing an appreciation of appropriate works of art is a good ingredient of moral education: if one can learn to respond morally in the imagined case, then it will be even easier to do so in reality. Too little, it seems to me, has been written on the role of imagination in art appreciation. The discussion has instead focused on the role of belief, and how we can respond emotionally without believing (or suspending disbelief) in the reality of the characters and events. If we pursue the suggestion mentioned earlier that our responses to art are from entertaining counterfactuals, which, *qua* counterfactuals are *imagined* characters and events (not believed ones), then the way is opened for examining traits of imagination which are involved in doing this. It seems we *are* at last, led back to Hume and imagination, in a way which has more potential for understanding our responses to art than his notion of imagination did. But this is a matter for separate study. For these purposes, we can explain the unimaginative moralist's failure to respond to art by virtue of that person's being unimaginative in a way which is required in the aesthetic context but not required in the actual moral one.

Meta-responses to Art and to Life

Given the nature of pleasure from tragedy as analyzed here, it is not surprising to find philosophers alleging the existence of special 'aesthetic emotions,' unlike those which exist in real life. Indeed, we don't generally feel pleasure from our sympathetic responses to real tragedies, and there needs to be some explanation of why the pleasurable response is appropriate to fiction and not to reality. The fact about fiction which makes this so is that in it no one *really* suffers; the suffering is fictional, but the fact that perceivers feel genuine sympathy for this imagined suffering enables perceivers to examine their own feelings without regard for other people. In real life, the importance of human compassion is easily overshadowed by the pain of human suffering. It is not possible in real life to respond to the importance of human sympathy as a distinct phenomenon, since that sympathy depends on, one might even say 'feeds on,' human misery. It is not, in life, an unequivocal good. In art, however, one experiences real sympathy without there having been real suffering, and this is why it is appropriate to feel pleasure at our sympathetic responses to a work of art, whereas it is not appropriate to feel pleasure at our sympathetic responses in reality. There the sympathy comes at too great a cost.

In real life, it is more appropriate to feel satisfaction, pride, or even pleasure with what one has done rather than with what one has felt. Though one should have some caution in how one feels about what one has done (because of unforeseen consequences), 'caution' isn't the right word to describe the hesitation one should have in responding to how one felt. Actions can be completed so that one can respond to them in themselves in a way inappropriate with feelings. One can go to a funeral, and be glad, looking back on it, that one had the courage to do so, but sadness over the person's death has no determinate end. Feelings are not the sorts of things which can be completed; they are not tasks to be performed. Feelings reveal one's sensitivities, which can be revealed not only in first-hand experience but also when one simply thinks about or remembers a situation. In real life, to be pleased with the feelings one had reveals a smugness, self-satisfaction, and complacency with what one has already felt. To be pleased that one once was sensitive (though now insensitive), is to be (properly) pleased very little, because one is at best pleased that one *once* was a feeling person (and, as explained above, one is pleased – because one's sympathy exists – at the expense of other people's misfortune). One should be more displeased that one has lost the sensitivity one once had. Pleasurable meta-responses in real life are foreclosed by the continued call for direct (unpleasant) responses, even when one is confronted with just the idea or memory of the event.

But such is not the case with a work of art. The direct response is to the work of art as experienced in its totality, in the integration of all its sensuous elements. The direct response is possible only in the presence of the work; take away the work and one is left merely to memories and meta-responses. In this sense, a direct response to art has 'closure' (unlike feelings in real life and somewhat like actions) so that those responses can, without smugness, self-satisfaction, and complacency, themselves be singled out and responded to.

Though a meta-response of pleasure to sympathy felt in real life would reveal smugness and self-satisfaction, a meta-response of displeasure to one's lack of sympathy is appropriate and even laudable. This shows that it is not the case that meta-responses are always inappropriate (or impossible) in real life, but that it depends on the nature of the situation. Discomfort, disgust, or dissatisfaction with oneself is desirable because it shows that we are aware of defects in our character, which is a first step to self-improvement. It is courting temptation to concentrate on how well one has done, for this makes us inattentive to the ways in which we might do better. It is also true that when one doesn't 'reap the benefits' of, i.e., gain pleasure from one's sympathy, we can be reasonably sure that it is genuine.

The differences between responses and meta-responses to real situations and to art have to do both with (1) the important role actions play in morality but not in our responses to art, and (2) the differing roles which emotions themselves play in the two cases. This latter, at least, turns out to be a very complicated matter, a complete examination of which would require an analysis of the importance of a first person, direct experience of a work of art for an appreciation of it (a phenomenon which I have suggested allows for 'closure' of feelings in response to art which is not present in real life). But, most fundamentally, the meta-response of pleasure to the sympathy we feel for other people is appropriate to art but not in life because in the former there is no real suffering to continue to weigh on our feelings. In the latter case, real suffering easily commands our attention, so that any desirability of sympathy is of minuscule importance in comparison with the perniciousness of the conditions which gave rise to it.

In summary, pleasures from tragedy are meta-responses. They are responses to direct responses to works of art, which are themselves painful or unpleasant. But given the basis for the direct response, sympathy, it gives us pleasure to find ourselves responding in such a manner. That is, it is a recognition that there can be a unity of feeling among members of humanity, that we are not alone, and that these feelings are at the heart of morality itself. [. . .] It is, of course, possible to respond appropriately to art, even when those responses require sympathy, and not with the appropriate sympathy in life, as it is also possible to be morally upstanding in life but insensitive to art. Explanations of these phenomena involve intricacies of their own, but they reinforce rather than resist the analysis given of pleasure from tragedy as a meta-response. The fact that pleasurable meta-responses to our sympathetic responses to tragedy are appropriate to art but not in life suggests one respect in which aesthetic emotions are different from emotions of life, and also has to do with the importance of direct experience of a work for an appreciation of it. The peculiarity of the responses hinges on the fact that what one initially responds to is *not* real, thus making continued sympathy idle, and allowing one to reflect on the sympathy one previously felt.

Commentary on Feagin

Feagin opens with a paragraph which states the problem of tragedy, using Hume's words, and goes on to advertise some of the issues that her own treatment will engage with. In the paragraph marked ⟨a⟩→ she briefly criticizes Hume's view in 'Of Tragedy'.

What two criticisms of Hume does Feagin offer?

The first criticism uses Hume's own example of a violent incident (in the play *The Ambitious Stepmother*) whose sheer unpleasantness no amount of pleasure in fiction, beauty and artistry can compensate for. The critical point is that Hume cannot say why all cases of unpleasantness are not like this – he cannot explain how the aesthetic pleasures can ever become dominant over our distressing emotions. Feagin does not attach much weight to this criticism. How worrying should it be to Hume?

The second and more important criticism is the unclarity of Hume's whole account of 'conversion', a criticism also made at the end of our commentary on Hume: as Feagin puts it, 'The mechanics of this conversion are never explained, and as long as they remain obscure ... we have merely substituted one puzzle for another.'

This sets the stage for Feagin's own contribution, which begins in earnest at ⟨b⟩→. She announces that her central pair of concepts will be *direct response* and *meta-response*. Another vocabulary for the same distinction is *response* and *higher-order response*. This terminology is associated with Gilbert Ryle, whose book *The Concept of Mind* was influential in the 1950s and 1960s. Philosophers sometimes talk also of *first-order* and *second-order* attitudes, meaning essentially the same. What is meant is that there occur or exist in the mind both (1) a response and (2) a response to that very response. The examples in the paragraph labelled ⟨c⟩→ should clarify the point here, if the description does not.

Note two features of the examples Feagin gives. First, all the responses and meta-responses are essentially about or directed towards some object. We are disgusted *with*..., pleased *with* ..., or depressed *at* .... Secondly, all the meta-responses are distinctly positive or negative in tone: *pleased* with, *disgusted* with, and so on. So we are talking about cases where we have some kind of pleasurable or painful reaction concerning the way we ourselves respond directly to events.

Read the paragraph marked ⟨c⟩→. Invent for yourself some new examples where someone has a direct response to something and a positive or negative meta-response.

At this stage Feagin makes no distinction between responses to events in ordinary life and responses to events portrayed in a work of art. Later this distinction will come into play in an important way. The section entitled 'A Solution' homes in on tragedy, and is the core of Feagin's paper. All her other claims depend on what is put forward here.

> Read the section 'A Solution'. What point is established from $\boxed{d}\!\mapsto$ to $\boxed{e}\!\mapsto$? What point is established from $\boxed{e}\!\mapsto$ to the end of the section?

The text from $\boxed{d}\!\mapsto$ to $\boxed{e}\!\mapsto$ contains different observations which tend to show that our ordinary, direct responses to tragic works are genuinely unpleasant or distressing experiences. For example, such experiences are sometimes avoided because of the distress they involve. The distress is real enough to affect one's overall outlook on life, and is not restricted to moments when one is in the theatre or immersed in a book. And finally, even people who enjoy tragedies are as deeply affected by distress as those who avoid them. This last point, which really re-states the whole problematic aspect of tragedy, may be difficult to accept at first sight. If I can bear to watch the violence in *King Lear* and so can enjoy the play, but you cannot, surely it is reasonable to think that you experience it with greater distress. But all that Feagin needs to establish here is that those who seek out and enjoy tragedies genuinely feel some distress too.

From $\boxed{e}\!\mapsto$ to the end of the section Feagin gives her substantial answer to the question 'But whence the pleasure?' The bare-bones answer is that our pleasure can co-exist with our direct feelings of distress because it is a meta-response to those very feelings. We are pleased *at our being distressed* by what happens in the tragedy. The strength of this answer is that, as well as explaining how distress and pleasure can co-exist in our experience, it gives the distress an essential place in the picture: the specific pleasure we take in tragedy could not exist at all unless we felt distress, because the distress is the very thing that pleases us.

But how can a painful or unpleasant feeling be the object of a pleasurable meta-response?

> According to Feagin, *what* is it about our distressing response that pleases us?

There is a great deal of relevant material packed into the passage starting at $\boxed{e}\!\mapsto$. Feagin claims: (1) that we are pleased by recognizing that we are a certain kind of ethically sensitive person, whom certain things distress; (2) that we are pleased by a reduction in the sense of aloneness in the world (solipsism is the philosophical position which states that I alone exist – here used more or less as a synonym for the 'sense of aloneness'); (3) that we are pleased to be feeling something that all human beings can feel.

Many questions might be posed about this suggestion. Is it necessary for someone enjoying a tragedy to be pleased in *all* these ways? Could one not be pleased at one's ethical sensitivity without ever having felt alone in the world, for example? Is it necessary for someone enjoying a tragedy to feel *any* of these specific pleasures? A possible problem is that the account might apply only to a restricted group of people who have these very thoughts and attitudes to themselves and other human beings – having felt a sense of aloneness, realizing that they feel something all human beings can feel – whereas presumably the account is meant to explain why *anyone* might take appropriate pleasure in tragedy. Or is it the case that everyone is prone to think and feel in these specific ways? Feagin's further observations about the profundity of tragedy and its relation to morality seem to rely on that thought.

An interesting question that is sometimes addressed in aesthetics is why tragedies are regarded as greater or more important works than comedies. Feagin states that tragedies are regarded as greater in the paragraph labelled $\boxed{f}\rightarrow$, then rejects one explanation of it, before offering one of her own.

> In the paragraph marked $\boxed{g}\rightarrow$ Feagin rejects an explanation of the greater significance of tragedy. What is that explanation?

Simply put, the rejected explanation is the one which says that tragedy gives a true picture of human life, whereas comedy fails to reflect the same truth. This requires us to believe the pessimistic view that life is bound to be full of suffering and disaster. That is not such an odd view, despite Feagin's apparent reluctance to say so. It has long been thought that one of the points of tragedy is that it reveals what could possibly go wrong for any of us, and there is reason to believe that life is likely to contain a fair amount of suffering and disaster. But Feagin's question is whether this could be the source of *pleasure* in tragedy, and her answer is that it could be the source only of an unacceptably cynical or morbid kind of pleasure.

There can perhaps be a pleasure in simply learning and facing up to the truth. However, those who think, against Feagin, that tragedy is superior to comedy because it presents a truer picture are less likely to insist that the prime reaction to tragedy is in fact pleasure. Tragedy, they might say, has great value for us, but it is the value of an inescapably painful lesson. (A parallel might be made with the value of visiting the site of Auschwitz or learning about the horrors of the slave-trade.)

There might then be a 'No Pleasure' solution to the paradox: another solution that denies one of its founding assumptions. However, to pursue this would take us too far away from Feagin's approach, which, like Hume's, is designed to defend a view in which tragedy is a source of pleasure, but still without giving rise to paradox.

What explanation does Feagin give of tragedy's having greater importance than comedy? (See the three paragraphs after h|→.)

The broad answer is that, for Feagin, the possibility of enjoying tragedy is closely linked to morality. More specifically, unless we were capable of moral feelings and commitments – which, she says, centre around sympathy for the welfare of all human beings – we would not be able to enjoy tragedies. At least, her account of the pleasure we take in tragedy has this consequence. If we could not painfully sympathize with the situation of the characters in the drama, then we could not have the pleasurable meta-response that arises from recognizing the moral nature of our sympathy. Thus Feagin can claim that her account explains tragedy's greater profundity and significance. In tragedy we appreciate our own connectedness with moral values; whereas comedy 'generally goes no further than direct response'.

Having linked our positive responses to tragedy to our understanding of moral value, Feagin spends the rest of her paper examining questions about the relationship between art and real life.

State what the problem is in Feagin's section 'A Potential Problem'. Explain how (1) the 'selfish sentimentalist' (i|→) and (2) the 'unimaginative moralist' (j|→) might be thought to give rise to this problem.

The two imagined people discussed here are mirror-images of one another. One takes pleasure in tragic works of art but shows no sympathy for human beings in real situations. The other is sympathetic and morally aware in real life, but cannot find any enjoyment in seeing people's actions portrayed in a tragic drama. The problem is that, if these two characters are readily conceivable, then the capacity to enjoy a tragic work of art and the capacity to be distressed in sympathy with real human beings look to be unrelated character traits that can exist apart from one another. Having raised this issue, however, Feagin resolves it relatively quickly in both cases.

How convincing is Feagin's claim that the possibility of the 'selfish sentimentalist' and the 'unimaginative moralist' presents no genuine problem for her theory?

Feagin's position leaves us, as she herself asserts, with an asymmetry between our responses to art and our responses to life. See k|→ for this important point. But is Feagin right here? If one wanted to disagree with Feagin's point, there would be two alternative lines to take, both of which would make for *symmetry* between the cases of art and life. One might think that meta-responses of the kind Feagin describes are inappropriate not only in real-life situations, but in reaction to art works as well. Or one might think that satisfaction with one's ability to feel distress for others is not restricted to the case of fictional tragedy but carries over into real life as well. Here are some questions that may help to sharpen up the debate.

At $\boxed{1}\to$ Feagin claims 'a meta-response of pleasure to sympathy felt in real life would reveal smugness and self-satisfaction'. (1) If this is so, is there good reason to think the same is not true of such meta-responses to art works? (2) Is it really so? Is it abnormal or blameworthy in real life to feel pleased that one has been distressed by the suffering of others?

These are not easy questions for anyone to answer. On (1) someone might suggest that it is strangely self-regarding to take satisfaction in one's own capacity to sympathize with suffering, and that to do so in the theatre or cinema is no less 'smug and self-satisfied': should we not be caring less about ourselves and more about the action in the play or film? On (2) someone might find it odd that in real-life events 'a meta-response of displeasure to one's lack of sympathy is appropriate and even laudable' (see $\boxed{1}\to$), while pleasure at one's feeling sympathy is not. If I am allowed to be dissatisfied with myself when I err from a morally good reaction – feeling displeased with my own amusement when someone falls over, for example – why should I not be legitimately satisfied with myself for my morally good reactions?

Feagin's position sets out wanting to place the pleasure of tragedy firmly on a moral basis. Yet she finishes by arguing that the way we react to tragedy would not be a morally proper way to react to people's real suffering. This result might prompt the question: Why then is it so morally significant that we react in that way to tragedy?

Very few people think that moral value and aesthetic (or artistic) value are the same. But the relationship between the two seems to be a highly complex matter. Tragedy provides one set of problems that may help us begin to explore that relationship.

4

Equality

Introduction to the Problem

Some topics in philosophy are well known because they deal with quite specific issues. Thus, the problem of free will (see chapter 7) arises from the tension between our idea of ourselves as agents with free choice and our idea of ourselves as inhabitants of a world in which causality and determinism reign. In contrast, however, the notion of equality raises no single problem or puzzle, though it plays a central role in many. It is a notion fundamental to political philosophy.

Next to the family, political institutions are those with the most palpable effects on every individual human being. Such institutions include: types of government, systems for putting governments in place, methods of establishing and enforcing laws and decisions about economic arrangements and education. As is familiar, these institutions are the subject of sustained study in history, political science, sociology and economics as well as the focus of much journalism. Political philosophy is not so much concerned with the nature and history of these institutions – though these of course must be taken into account – as with what is, in a very broad sense, their justification or legitimacy. Whereas the political scientist will investigate the nature of governments or systems of putting government leaders in place, political philosophers will ask about the justifications that can be given for different types of government and methods of leadership selection.

Given this concern with justification, it is unsurprising to find moral issues at the heart of political philosophy. In order to decide whether some government, or system for selection of a government, is legitimate, the notion of consent is bound to crop up, and with it will come a consideration of individual human worth and dignity. Also, in order to assess arguments for the justification of different economic, social or educational arrangements, we have to have some conception of the nature and extent of human rights.

It is in debates about human worth and human rights that the notion of equality comes onto the scene. To some, it is a fundamental moral and political value that should be at the centre of any decent political system. 'All human beings are equal, and should therefore be treated as such' is a typical claim one finds in the mouths of equality's champions. To others, it as a hopeless ideal which is at best utopian and at worst can lead to the destruction of other more important values in a society – values such as self-reliance and freedom. 'Equality is the enemy of incentive and creativity', might be a slogan for its detractors. Yet, before one can even begin to assess arguments about equality, one must have some clearer idea what the notion involves. And this is notoriously difficult to achieve. Is equality a feature of human beings, or a demand about how individuals should be treated? (As you will see, these are not exclusive options.) Does equal treatment mean just that – treating everyone in exactly the same way – or does it mean something more like treating each person fairly and in accord with his or her differing abilities? These are crucial questions and they are also enormously complicated. Certainly, no selection of two readings could hope to cover them adequately.

For this reason, one of our main tasks will be to narrow the focus, to sift through the complex detail to find one or two issues that can be usefully and argumentatively addressed in the limited space available. Independently of the importance of the topics discussed in this chapter, such a narrowing of focus is an important philosophical skill. Being able to read around an area bristling with different issues and arguments, without becoming confused by this variety, is a useful and necessary philosophical accomplishment. (It is useful outside philosophy too.)

Introduction to Williams

Bernard Williams has been a professor of philosophy in both Cambridge and Oxford, as well as in the University of California at Berkeley. He has also served as chairman of a government committee that produced an influential report on the difficult questions of obscenity, pornography and censorship. He has written many important articles on issues in moral and political philosophy, as well as several books that are widely read and discussed, including *Descartes: The Project of Pure Enquiry* (1978) and *Ethics and the Limits of Philosophy* (1985).

Bernard Williams, 'The Idea of Equality'

The idea of equality is used in political discussion both in statements of fact, or what purport to be statements of fact – that men are equal – and in statements of political principles or aims – that men should be equal, as at present they are not. The two can be, and often are, combined: the aim is then described as that of securing a state of affairs in which men are treated as the equal beings which they in fact already are, but are not already treated as being. In both these uses, the idea of equality notoriously encounters the same difficulty:

a⟶ that on one kind of interpretation the statements in which it figures are much too strong, and on another kind much too weak, and it is hard to find a satisfactory interpretation that lies between the two.[1]

b⟶ To take first the supposed statement of fact: it has only too often been pointed out that to say that all men are equal in all those characteristics in respect of which it makes sense to say that men are equal or unequal, is a patent falsehood; and even if some more re-stricted selection is made of these characteristics, the statement does not look much better. Faced with this obvious objection, the defender of the claim that all men are equal is likely to offer a weaker interpret-ation. It is not, he may say, in their skill, intelligence, strength, or virtue that men are equal, but merely in their being men: it is their common humanity that constitutes their equality. On this interpret-ation, we should not seek for some special characteristics in respect of which men are equal, but merely remind ourselves that they are all

c⟶ men. Now to this it might be objected that being men is not a respect in which men can strictly speaking be said to be equal; but, leaving that aside, there is the more immediate objection that if all that the statement does is to remind us that men are men, it does not do very much, and in particular does less than its proponents in political argument have wanted it to do. What looked like a paradox has turned into a platitude.

I shall suggest in a moment that even in this weak form the state-ment is not so vacuous as this objection makes it seem; but it must be admitted that when the statement of equality ceases to claim more

[1]   For an illuminating discussion of this and related questions, see R. Wollheim and I. Berlin, 'Equality', *Proceedings of the Aristotelian Society*, LVI (1955–6), pp. 281 et seq.

than is warranted, it rather rapidly reaches the point where it claims less than is interesting. A similar discomfiture tends to overcome the

d⟶ practical maxim of equality. It cannot be the aim of this maxim that all men should be treated alike in all circumstances, or even that they should be treated alike as much as possible. Granted that, however, there is no obvious stopping point before the interpretation which makes the maxim claim only that men should be treated alike in similar circumstances; and since 'circumstances' here must clearly include reference to what a man is, as well as to his purely external situation, this comes very much to saying that for every difference in the way men are treated, some general reason or principle of differentiation must be given. This may well be an important principle; some indeed have seen in it, or in something very like it, an essential element of morality itself. But it can hardly be enough to constitute the principle that was advanced in the name of *equality*. It would be in accordance with this principle, for example, to treat black men differently from others just because they were black, or poor men differently just because they were poor, and this cannot accord with anyone's idea of equality.

e⟶ In what follows I shall try to advance a number of considerations that can help to save the political notion of equality from these extremes of absurdity and of triviality. These considerations are in fact often employed in political argument, but are usually bundled together into an unanalysed notion of equality in a manner confusing to the advocates, and encouraging to the enemies, of that ideal. These considerations will not enable us to define a distinct third interpretation of the statements which use the notion of equality; it is rather that they enable us, starting with the weak interpretations, to build up something that in practice can have something of the solidity aspired to by the strong interpretations. In this discussion, it will not be necessary all the time to treat separately the supposedly factual application of the notion of equality, and its application in the maxim of action. Though it is sometimes important to distinguish them, and there are clear grounds for doing so, similar considerations often apply to both. The two go significantly together: on the one hand, the point of the supposedly factual assertion is to back up social ideals and programmes of political action; on the other hand – a rather less obvious point, perhaps – those political proposals have their force because they are regarded not as gratuitously egalitarian, aiming at equal treatment for reasons, for instance, of simplicity or tidiness, but as affirming an equality which is believed in some sense already to exist, and to be obscured or neglected by actual social arrangements.

1   Common Humanity

The factual statement of men's equality was seen, when pressed, to retreat in the direction of merely asserting the equality of men as men; and this was thought to be trivial. It is certainly insufficient, but not, after all, trivial. That all men are human is, if a tautology, a useful one, serving as a reminder that those who belong anatomically to the species *homo sapiens*, and can speak a language, use tools, live in societies, can interbreed despite racial differences, etc., are also alike in certain other respects more likely to be forgotten. These respects are notably the capacity to feel pain, both from immediate physical causes and from various situations represented in perception and in thought; and the capacity to feel affection for others, and the consequences of this, connected with the frustration of this affection, loss of its objects, etc. The assertion that men are alike in the possession of these characteristics is, while indisputable and (it may be) even necessarily true, not trivial. For it is certain that there are political and social arrangements that systematically neglect these characteristics in the case of some groups of men, while being fully aware of them in the case of others; that is to say, they treat certain men as though they did not possess these characteristics, and neglect moral claims that arise from these characteristics and which would be admitted to arise from them.

Here it may he objected that the mere fact that ruling groups in certain societies treat other groups in this way does not mean that they neglect or overlook the characteristics in question. For, it may be suggested, they may well recognise the presence of these characteristics in the worse-treated group, but claim that in the case of that group, the characteristics do not give rise to any moral claim; the group being distinguished from other members of society in virtue of some further characteristic (for instance, by being black), this may be cited as the ground of treating them differently, whether they feel pain, affection, etc., or not.

This objection rests on the assumption, common to much moral philosophy that makes a sharp distinction between fact and value, that the question whether a certain consideration is *relevant* to a moral issue is an evaluative question: to state that a consideration is relevant or irrelevant to a certain moral question is, on this view, itself to commit oneself to a certain kind of moral principle or outlook. Thus, in the case under discussion, to say (as one would naturally say) that the fact that a man is black is, by itself, quite irrelevant to the issue of how he should be treated in respect of welfare, etc., would, on this view, be to commit oneself to a certain sort of moral principle.

This view, taken generally, seems to me quite certainly false. The principle that men should be differentially treated in respect of welfare merely on grounds of their colour is not a special sort of moral principle, but (if anything) a purely arbitrary assertion of will, like that of some Caligulan ruler who decided to execute everyone whose name contained three 'R's.

This point is in fact conceded by those who practise such things as colour discrimination. Few can be found who will explain their practice merely by saying, 'But they're black: and it is my moral principle to treat black men differently from others.' If any reasons are given at all, they will be reasons that seek to correlate the fact of blackness with certain other considerations which are at least candidates for relevance to the question of how a man should be treated: such as insensitivity, brute stupidity, ineducable irresponsibility, etc. Now these reasons are very often rationalisations, and the correlations claimed are either not really believed, or quite irrationally believed, by those who claim them. But this is a different point; the argument concerns what counts as a moral reason, and the rationaliser broadly agrees with others about what counts as such – the trouble with him is that his reasons are dictated by his policies, and not conversely. The Nazis' 'anthropologists' who tried to construct theories of Aryanism were paying, in very poor coin, the homage of irrationality to reason.

The question of relevance in moral reasons will arise again, in a different connexion, in this paper. For the moment its importance is that it gives a force to saying that those who neglect the moral claims of certain men that arise from their human capacity to feel pain, etc., are *overlooking* or *disregarding* those capacities; and are not just operating with a special moral principle, conceding the capacities to these men, but denying the moral claim. Very often, indeed, they have just persuaded themselves that the men in question have those capacities in a lesser degree. Here it is certainly to the point to assert the apparent platitude that these men are also human.

I have discussed this point in connexion with very obvious human characteristics of feeling pain and desiring affection. There are, however, other and less easily definable characteristics universal to humanity, which may all the more be neglected in political and social arrangements. For instance, there seems to be a characteristic which might be called 'a desire for self-respect'; this phrase is perhaps not too happy, in suggesting a particular culturally-limited, bourgeois value, but I mean by it a certain human desire to be identified with what one is doing, to be able to realise purposes of one's own, and not to be the instrument of another's will unless one has willingly accepted such a role. This is a very inadequate and in some ways rather empty specification of a human desire; to a better specification, both philosophical reflexion and the evidences of psychology and anthropology would be relevant. Such investigations enable us to understand more deeply, in respect of the desire I have gestured towards and of similar characteristics, what it is to be human; and of what it is to be human, the apparently trivial statement of men's equality as men can serve as a reminder.

2   Moral Capacities

So far we have considered respects in which men can be counted as all alike, which respects are, in a sense, negative: they concern the capacity to suffer, and certain needs that men have, and these involve men in moral relations as the recipients of certain kinds of treatment. It has certainly been a part, however, of the thought of those who asserted that men were equal, that there were more positive respects in which men were alike; that they were equal in certain things that they could do or achieve, as well as in things that they needed and could suffer. In respect of a whole range of abilities, from weight-lifting to the calculus, the assertion is, as was noted at the beginning, not plausible, and has not often been supposed to be. It has been held, however, that there are certain other abilities, both less open to empirical test and more essential in moral connexions, for which it is true that men are equal. These are certain sorts of moral ability or capacity, the capacity for virtue or achievement of the highest kind of moral worth.

The difficulty with this notion is that of identifying any purely moral capacities. Some human capacities are more relevant to the achievement of a virtuous life than others: intelligence, a capacity for sympathetic understanding, and a measure of resoluteness would generally be agreed to be so. But these capacities can all be displayed in nonmoral connexions as well, and in such connexions would naturally be thought to differ from man to man like other natural capacities. That this is the fact of the matter has been accepted by many thinkers, notably, for instance, by Aristotle. But against this acceptance, there is a powerful strain of thought that centres on a feeling of ultimate and outrageous absurdity in the idea that the achievement of the highest kind of moral worth should depend on natural capacities, unequally and fortuitously distributed as they are; and this feeling is backed up by the observation that these natural capacities are not themselves the bearers of the moral worth, since those that have them are as gifted for vice as for virtue.

This strain of thought has found many types of religious expression; but in philosophy it is to be found in its purest form in Kant. Kant's view not only carries to the limit the notion that moral worth cannot depend on contingencies, but also emphasises, in its picture of the Kingdom of Ends, the idea of *respect* which is owed to each man as a rational moral agent – and, since men are equally such agents, is owed equally to all, unlike admiration and similar attitudes, which are commanded unequally by men in proportion to their unequal possession of different kinds of natural excellence. These ideas are intimately connected in Kant, and it is not possible to understand his moral theory unless as much weight is given to what he says about the Kingdom of Ends as is always given to what he says about duty.

The very considerable consistency of Kant's view is bought at what would generally be agreed to be a very high price. The detachment of moral worth from all contingencies is achieved only by making man's characteristic as a moral or rational agent a transcendental characteristic; man's capacity to will freely as a rational agent is not dependent on any empirical capacities he may have – and, in particular, is not dependent on empirical capacities which men may possess unequally – because, in the Kantian view, the capacity to be a rational agent is not itself an empirical capacity at all. Accordingly, the respect owed equally to each man as a member of the Kingdom of Ends is not owed to him in respect of any empirical characteristics that he may possess, but solely in respect of the transcendental characteristic of being a free and rational will. The ground of the respect owed to each man thus emerges in the Kantian theory as a kind of secular analogue of the Christian conception of the respect owed to all men as equally children of God. Though secular, it is equally metaphysical: in neither case is it anything empirical about men that constitutes the ground of equal respect.

This transcendental, Kantian conception cannot provide any sound foundation for the notions of equality among men, or of equality of respect owed to them. Apart from the general difficulties of such transcendental conceptions, there is the obstinate fact that the concept of 'moral agent', and the concepts allied to it such as that of responsibility, do and must have an empirical basis. It seems empty to say that all men are equal as moral agents, when the question, for instance, of men's responsibility for their actions is one to which empirical considerations are clearly relevant, and one which moreover receives answers in terms of different degrees of responsibility and different degrees of rational control over action. To hold a man responsible for his actions is presumably the central case of treating him as a moral agent, and if

men are not treated as equally responsible, there is not much left to
their equality as moral agents.

h →   If, without its transcendental basis, there is not much left to men's
equality as moral agents, is there anything left to the notion of the
respect owed to all men? This notion of 'respect' is both complex and
unclear, and I think it needs, and would repay, a good deal of investigation. Some content can, however, be attached to it; even if it is some
way away from the ideas of moral agency. There certainly is a distinction, for instance, between regarding a man's life, actions or character
from an aesthetic or technical point of view, and regarding them from
a point of view which is concerned primarily with what it is for him to
live that life and do those actions in that character. Thus from the
technological point of view, a man who has spent his life in trying to
make a certain machine which could not possibly work is merely a
failed inventor, and in compiling a catalogue of those whose efforts
have contributed to the sum of technical achievement, one must 'write
him off': the fact that he devoted himself to this useless task with
constant effort and so on, is merely irrelevant. But from a human point
of view, it is clearly not irrelevant: we are concerned with him, not
merely as 'a failed inventor', but as a man who wanted to be a
successful inventor. Again, in professional relations and the world of
work, a man operates, and his activities come up for criticism, under a
variety of professional or technical titles, such as 'miner' or 'agricul-
tural labourer' or 'junior executive'. The technical or professional
attitude is that which regards the man solely under that title, the
human approach that which regards him as *a man who has* that title
(among others), willingly, unwillingly, through lack of alternatives,
with pride, etc.

That men should be regarded from the human point of view, and not
merely under these sorts of titles, is part of the content that might be
attached to Kant's celebrated injunction 'treat each man as an end in
himself, and never as a means only'. But I do not think that this is all
that should be seen in this injunction, or all that is concerned in the
notion of 'respect'. What is involved in the examples just given could
be explained by saying that each man is owed an effort at identification: that he should not be regarded as the surface to which a certain
label can be applied, but one should try to see the world (including the
label) from his point of view. This injunction will be based on, though
not of course fully explained by, the notion that men are conscious
beings who necessarily have intentions and purposes and see what they
are doing in a certain light. But there seem to be further injunctions
connected with the Kantian maxim, and with the notion of 'respect',
that go beyond these considerations. There are forms of exploiting

men or degrading them which would be thought to be excluded by these notions, but which cannot be excluded merely by considering how the exploited or degraded men see the situation. For it is precisely a mark of extreme exploitation or degradation that those who suffer it do not see themselves differently from the way they are seen by the exploiters; either they do not see themselves as anything at all, or they acquiesce passively in the role for which they have been cast. Here we evidently need something more than the precept that one should respect and try to understand another man's consciousness of his own activities; it is also that one may not suppress or destroy that consciousness.

All these I must confess to be vague and inconclusive considerations, but we are dealing with a vague notion: one, however, that we possess, and attach value to. To try to put these matters properly in order would be itself to try to reach conclusions about several fundamental questions of moral philosophy. What we must ask here is what these ideas have to do with equality. We started with the notion of men's equality as moral agents. This notion appeared unsatisfactory, for different reasons, in both an empirical and a transcendental interpretation. We then moved, via the idea of 'respect', to the different notion of regarding men not merely under professional, social, or technical titles, but with consideration of their own views and purposes. This notion has at least this much to do with equality: that the titles which it urges us to look behind are the conspicuous bearers of social, political, and technical inequality, whether they refer to achievement (as in the example of the inventor) or to social roles (as in the example of work titles). It enjoins us not to let our fundamental attitudes to men be dictated by the criteria of technical success or social position, and not to take them at the value carried by these titles and by the structures in which these titles place them. This does not mean, of course, that the more fundamental view that should be taken of men is in the case of every man the same: on the contrary. But it does mean that each man is owed the effort of understanding, and that in achieving it, each man is to be (as it were) abstracted from certain conspicuous structures of inequality in which we find him.

These injunctions are based on the proposition that men are beings who are necessarily to some extent conscious of themselves and of the world they live in. (I omit here, as throughout the discussion, the clinical cases of people who are mad or mentally defective, who always constitute special exceptions to what is in general true of men.) This proposition does not assert that men are equally conscious of themselves and of their situation. It was precisely one element in the notion of exploitation considered above that such consciousness can be decreased by social action and the environment; we may add that it can similarly be increased. But men are at least potentially conscious, to an indeterminate degree, of their situation and of what I have called their 'titles', are capable of reflectively standing back from the roles and positions in which they are cast; and this reflective consciousness may be enhanced or diminished by their social condition.

It is this last point that gives these considerations a particular relevance to the political aims of egalitarianism. The mere idea of regarding men from 'the human point of view', while it has a good deal to do with politics, and a certain amount to do with equality, has nothing specially to do with political equality. One could, I think, accept this as an ideal, and yet favour, for instance, some kind of hierarchical society, so long as the hierarchy maintained itself without compulsion, and there was human understanding between the orders. In such a society, each man would indeed have a very conspicuous title which related him to the social structure, but it might be that most people were aware of the human beings behind the titles, and found each other for the most part content, or even proud, to have the titles that they had. I do not know whether anything like this has been true of historical hierarchical societies; but I can see no inconsistency in someone's espousing it as an ideal, as some (influenced in many cases by a sentimental picture of the Middle Ages) have done. Such a person would be one who accepted the notion of 'the human view', the view of each man as something more than his title, as a valuable ideal, but rejected the ideals of political equality.

Once, however, one accepts the further notion that the degree of man's consciousness about such things as his role in society is itself in some part the product of social arrangements, and that it can be increased, this ideal of a stable hierarchy must, I think, disappear. For what keeps stable hierarchies together is the idea of necessity, that it is somehow fore-ordained or inevitable that there should be these orders; and this idea of necessity must be eventually undermined by the growth of people's reflective consciousness about their role, still more when it is combined with the thought that what they and the others have always thought about their roles in the social system was the product of the social system itself.

It might be suggested that a certain man who admitted that people's consciousness of their roles was conditioned in this way might nevertheless believe in the hierarchical ideal: but that in order to preserve the society of his ideal, he would have to make sure that the idea of the conditioning of consciousness did not get around to too many people, and that this consciousness about their roles did not increase too much. But such a view is really a very different thing from its naive predecessor. Such a man, no longer himself 'immersed' in the system, is beginning to think in terms of compulsion, the deliberate prevention of the growth of consciousness, which is a poisonous element absent from the original ideal. Moreover, his attitude (or that of rulers similar to himself) towards the other people in the ideal society must now contain an element of condescension or contempt, since he will be aware that their acceptance of what they suppose to be necessity is a delusion. This is alien to the spirit of human understanding on which the original ideal was based. The hierarchical idealist cannot escape the fact that certain things which can be done decently without self-consciousness can, with self-consciousness, be done only hypocritically. This is why even the rather hazy and very general notions that I have tried to bring together in this section contain some of the grounds of the ideal of political equality.

3   Equality in Unequal Circumstances

The notion of equality is invoked not only in connexions where men are claimed in some sense all to be equal, but in connexions where they are agreed to be unequal, and the question arises of the distribution of, or access to, certain goods to which their inequalities are relevant. It may be objected that the notion of equality is in fact misapplied in these connexions, and that the appropriate ideas are those of fairness or justice, in the sense of what Aristotle called 'distributive justice', where (as Aristotle argued) there is no question of regarding or treating everyone as equal, but solely a question of distributing certain goods in proportion to men's recognised inequalities.

I think it is reasonable to say against this objection that there is some foothold for the notion of equality even in these cases. It is useful here to make a rough distinction between two different types of inequality, inequality of *need* and inequality of *merit*, with a corresponding distinction between goods – on the one hand, goods demanded by the need, and on the other, goods that can be earned by the merit. In the case of needs, such as the need for medical treatment in case of illness, it can be presumed for practical purposes that the persons who have the need actually desire the goods in question, and so the question can indeed be regarded as one of distribution in a simple sense, the satisfaction of an existing desire. In the case of merit, such as for instance the possession of abilities to profit from a university education, there is not the same presumption that everyone who has the merit has the desire for the goods in question, though it may, of course, be the case. Moreover, the good of a university education may be legitimately, even if hopelessly, desired by those who do not possess the merit; while medical treatment or unemployment benefit are either not desired, or not legitimately desired, by those who are not ill or unemployed, i.e. do not have the appropriate need. Hence the distribution of goods in accordance with merit has a competitive aspect lacking in the case of distribution according to need. For these reasons, it is appropriate to speak, in the case of merit, not only of the distribution of the good, but of the distribution of the opportunity of achieving the good. But this, unlike the good itself, can be said to be distributed equally to everybody, and so one does encounter a notion of *general* equality, much vaunted in our society today, the notion of equality of opportunity.

Before considering this notion further, it is worth noticing certain resemblances and differences between the cases of need and of merit. In both cases, we encounter the matter (mentioned before in this paper) of the relevance of reasons. Leaving aside preventive medicine, the proper ground of distribution of medical care is ill health: this is a necessary truth. Now in very many societies, while ill health may work as a necessary condition of receiving treatment, it does not work as a sufficient condition, since such treatment costs money, and not all who are ill have the money; hence the possession of sufficient money becomes in fact an additional necessary condition of actually receiving treatment. Yet more extravagantly, money may work as a sufficient condition by itself, without any medical need, in which case the reasons that actually operate for the receipt of this good are just totally irrelevant to its nature; however, since only a few hypochrondriacs desire treatment when they do not need it, this is, in this case, a marginal phenomenon.

When we have the situation in which, for instance, wealth is a further necessary condition of the receipt of medical treatment, we can once more apply the notions of equality and inequality: not now in connexion with the inequality between the well and the ill, but in connexion with the inequality between the rich ill and the poor ill, since we have straightforwardly the situation of those whose needs are the same not receiving the same treatment, though the needs are the ground of the treatment. This is an irrational state of affairs.

It may be objected that I have neglected an important distinction here. For, it may be said, I have treated the ill health and the possession of money as though they were regarded on the same level, as 'reasons for receiving medical treatment', and this is a muddle. The ill health is, at most, a ground of the right to receive medical treatment; whereas the money is, in certain circumstances, the casually necessary condition of securing the right, which is a different thing. There is something in the distinction that this objection suggests: there is a distinction between a man's rights, the reasons why he should be treated in a certain way, and his power to secure those rights, the reasons why he can in fact get what he deserves. But this objection does not make it inappropriate to call the situation of inequality an 'irrational' situation: it just makes it clearer what is meant by so calling it. What is meant is that it is a situation in which reasons are insufficiently *operative*; it is a situation insufficiently controlled by reasons – and hence by reason itself. The same point arises with another form of equality and equal rights, equality before the law. It may be said that in a certain society, men have equal rights to a fair trial, to seek redress from the law for wrongs committed against them, etc. But if a fair trial or redress from the law can be secured in that society only by moneyed and educated persons, to insist that everyone has this right, though only these particular persons can secure it, rings hollow to the point of cynicism: we are concerned not with the abstract existence of rights, but with the extent to which those rights govern what actually happens.

Thus when we combine the notions of the relevance of reasons, and the operativeness of reasons, we have a genuine moral weapon, which can be applied in cases of what is appropriately called unequal treatment, even where one is not concerned with the equality of people as a whole. This represents a strengthening of the very weak principle mentioned at the beginning of this paper, that for every difference in the way men are treated, a reason should be given: when one requires further that the reasons should be relevant, and that they should be socially operative, this really says something.

Similar considerations will apply to cases of merit. There is, however, an important difference between the cases of need and merit, in respect of the relevance of reasons. It is a matter of logic that particular sorts of needs constitute a reason for receiving particular sorts of good. It is, however, in general a much more disputable question whether certain sorts of merit constitute a reason for receiving certain sorts of good. For instance, let it be supposed for the sake of argument, that private schools provide a superior type of education, which it is a good thing to receive. It is then objected that access to this type of education is unequally distributed, because of its cost: among children of equal promise or intelligence, only those from wealthy homes will receive it, and, indeed, children of little promise or intelligence will receive it, if from wealthy homes; and this, the objection continues, is irrational.

The defender of the private school system might give two quite different sorts of answer to this objection; besides, that is, the obvious type of answer which merely disputes the facts alleged by the objector. One is the sort of answer already discussed in the case of need: that we may agree, perhaps, that children of promise and intelligence have a right to a superior education, but in actual economic circumstances, this right cannot always be secured. The other is more radical: this would dispute the premiss of the objection that intelligence and promise are, at least by themselves, the grounds for receiving this superior type of education. While perhaps not asserting that wealth itself constitutes the ground, the defender of the system may claim that other characteristics significantly correlated with wealth are such grounds; or, again, that it is the purpose of this sort of school to maintain a tradition of leadership, and the best sort of people to maintain this will be people whose fathers were at such schools. We need not try to pursue such arguments here. The important point is that, while there can indeed be genuine disagreements about what constitutes the relevant sort of merit in such cases, such disagreements must also be disagreements about the nature of the good to be distributed. As such, the disagreements do not occur in a vacuum, nor are they logically free from restrictions. There is only a limited number of reasons for which education could be regarded as a good, and a limited number of purposes which education could rationally be said to serve; and to the limitations on this question, there correspond limitations on the sorts of merit or personal characteristic which could be rationally cited as grounds of access to this good. Here again we encounter a genuine strengthening of the very weak principle that, for differences in the way that people are treated, reasons should be given.

$\boxed{1}\rightarrow$ We may return now to the notion of equality of opportunity; understanding this in the normal political sense of equality of opportunity for *everyone in society* to secure certain goods. This notion is introduced into political discussion when there is question of the access to certain goods which, first, even if they are not desired by everyone in society, are desired by large numbers of people in all sections of society (either for themselves, or, as in the case of education, for their children), or would be desired by people in all sections of society if they knew about the goods in question and thought it possible for them to attain them; second, are goods which people may be said to earn or achieve; and third, are goods which not all the people who desire them can have. This third condition covers at least three different cases, however, which it is worth distinguishing. Some desired goods, like positions of prestige, management, etc., are by their very nature limited: whenever there are some people who are in command or prestigious positions, there are necessarily others who are not. Other goods are contingently limited, in the sense that there are certain conditions of access to them which in fact not everyone satisfies, but there is no intrinsic limit to the numbers who might gain access to them by satisfying the conditions; university education is usually regarded in this light nowadays, as something which requires certain conditions of admission to it which in fact not everyone satisfies, but which an indefinite proportion of people might satisfy. Third, there are goods which are fortuitously limited, in the sense that although everyone or large numbers of people satisfy the conditions of access to them, there is just not enough of them to go round; so some more stringent conditions or system of rationing have to be imposed, to govern access in an imperfect situation. A good can, of course, be both contingently and fortuitously limited at once: when, due to shortage of supply, not even the people who are qualified to have it, limited in numbers though they are, can in every case have it. It is particularly worth distinguishing those kinds of limitation, as there can be significant differences of view about the way in which a certain good is limited. While most would now agree that high education is contingently limited, a Platonic view would regard it as necessarily limited.

Now the notion of equality of opportunity might be said to be the notion that a limited good shall in fact be allocated on grounds which do not a priori exclude any section of those that desire it. But this formulation is not really very clear. For suppose grammar school education (a good perhaps contingently, and certainly fortuitously, limited) is allocated on grounds of ability as tested at the age of 11; this would normally be advanced as an example of equality of opportunity, as opposed to a system of allocation on grounds of parents' wealth. But does not the criterion of ability exclude a priori a certain section of people, viz. those that are not able – just as the other excludes a priori those who are not wealthy? Here it will obviously be said that this was not what was meant by a priori exclusion: the present argument just equates this with exclusion of anybody, i.e. with the mere existence of some condition that has to be satisfied. What then is a priori exclusion? It must mean exclusion on grounds other than those appropriate or rational for the good in question. But this still will not do as it stands. For it would follow from this that so long as those allocating grammar school education on grounds of wealth thought that such grounds were appropriate or rational (as they might in one of the ways discussed above in connexion with private schools), they could sincerely describe their system as one of equality of opportunity – which is absurd.

Hence it seems that the notion of equality of opportunity is more complex than it first appeared. It requires not merely that there should be no exclusion from access on grounds other than those appropriate or rational for the good in question, but that the grounds considered appropriate for the good should themselves be such that people from all sections of society have an equal chance of satisfying them. What now is a 'section of society'? Clearly we cannot include under this term sections of the populace identified just by the characteristics which figure in the grounds for allocating the good – since, once more, any grounds at all must exclude some section of the populace. But what about sections identified by characteristics which are correlated with the grounds of exclusion? There are important difficulties here: to illustrate this, it may help first to take an imaginary example.

Suppose that in a certain society great prestige is attached to membership of a warrior class, the duties of which require great physical strength. This class has in the past been recruited from certain wealthy families only; but egalitarian reformers achieve a change in the rules, by which warriors are recruited from all sections of the society, on the results of a suitable competition. The effect of this, however, is that the wealthy families still provide virtually all the warriors, because the rest of the populace is so under-nourished by reason of poverty that their physical strength is inferior to that of the wealthy and well nourished. The reformers protest that equality of opportunity has not really been achieved; the wealthy reply that in fact it has, and that the poor now have the opportunity of becoming warriors – it is just bad luck that their characteristics are such that they do not pass the test. 'We are not,' they might say, 'excluding anyone *for* being poor; we exclude people for being weak, and it is unfortunate that those who are poor are also weak.'

This answer would seem to most people feeble, and even cynical. This is for reasons similar to those discussed before in connexion with equality before the law; that the supposed equality of opportunity is quite empty – indeed, one may say that it does not really exist – unless it is made more effective than this. For one knows that it could be made more effective; one knows that there is a causal connexion between being poor and being under-nourished, and between being under-nourished and being physically weak. One supposes further that something could be done – subject to whatever economic conditions obtain in the imagined society – to alter the distribution of wealth. All this being so, the appeal by the wealthy to the 'bad luck' of the poor must appear as disingenuous.

It seems then that a system of allocation will fall short of equality of opportunity if the allocation of the good in question in fact works out unequally or disproportionately between different sections of society, if the unsuccessful sections are under a disadvantage which could be removed by further reform or social action. This was very clear in the imaginary example that was given, because the causal connexions involved are simple and well known. In actual fact, however, the situations of this type that arise are more complicated, and it is easier to overlook the causal connexions involved. This is particularly so in the case of educational selection, where such slippery concepts as 'intellectual ability' are involved. It is a known fact that the system of selection for grammar schools by the '11+' examination favours children in direct proportion to their social class, the children of professional homes having proportionately greater success than those from working-class homes. We have every reason to suppose that these results are the product, in good part, of environmental factors; and we further know that imaginative social reform, both of the primary educational system and of living conditions, would favourably affect those environmental factors. In these circumstances, this system of educational selection falls short of equality of opportunity.[2]

This line of thought points to a connexion between the idea of equality of opportunity, and the idea of equality of persons, which is stronger than might at first be suspected. We have seen that one is not really offering equality of opportunity to Smith and Jones if one contents oneself with applying the same criteria to Smith and Jones at, say, the age of 11; what one is doing there is to apply the same criteria to Smith as affected by favourable conditions and to Jones as affected by unfavourable but curable conditions. Here there is a necessary pressure to equal up the conditions: to give Smith and Jones equality of opportunity involves regarding their conditions, where curable, as themselves part of what is done to Smith and Jones, and not part of Smith and Jones themselves. Their identity, for these purposes, does not include their curable environment, which is itself unequal and a contributor of inequality. This abstraction of persons in themselves from unequal environments is a way, if not of regarding them as equal, at least of moving recognisably in that direction; and is itself involved in equality of opportunity.

One might speculate about how far this movement of thought might go. The most conservative user of the notion of equality of opportunity is, if sincere, prepared to abstract the individual from some effects of his environment. We have seen that there is good reason to press this further, and to allow that the individuals whose opportunities are to be equal should be abstracted from more features of social and family

---

[2] See on this C. A. R. Crosland, 'Public Schools and English Education', *Encounter* (July 1961).

background. Where should this stop? Should it even stop at the boundaries of heredity? Suppose it were discovered that when all curable environmental disadvantages had been dealt with, there was a residual genetic difference in brain constitution, for instance, which was correlated with differences in desired types of ability; but that the brain constitution could in fact be changed by an operation.[3] Suppose further that the wealthier classes could afford such an operation for their children, so that they always came out top of the educational system; would we then think that poorer children did not have equality of opportunity, because they had no opportunity to get rid of their genetic disadvantages?

Here we might think that our notion of personal identity itself was beginning to give way; we might well wonder who were the people whose advantages and disadvantages were being discussed in this way. But it would be wrong, I think, to try to solve this problem simply by saying that in the supposed circumstances our notion of personal identity would have collapsed in such a way that we could no longer speak of the individuals involved – in the end, we could still pick out the individuals by spatio-temporal criteria, if no more. Our objections to the system suggested in this fantasy must, I think, be moral rather than metaphysical. They need not concern us here. What is interesting about the fantasy, perhaps, is that if one reached this state of affairs, the individuals would be regarded as in all respects equal in themselves – for in themselves they would be, as it were, pure subjects or bearers of predicates, everything else about them, including their genetic inheritance, being regarded as a fortuitous and changeable characteristic. In these circumstances, where everything about a person is controllable, equality of opportunity and absolute equality seem to coincide; and this itself illustrates something about the notion of equality of opportunity.

I said that we need not discuss here the moral objections to the kind of world suggested in this fantasy. There is, however, one such point that is relevant to the different aspects of equality that have been discussed in this paper as a whole. One objection that we should feel to the fantasy world is that far too much emphasis was being placed on achieving high ability; that the children were just being regarded as locations of abilities. I think we should still feel this even if everybody (with results hard to imagine) were treated in this way; when not everybody was so treated, the able would also be more successful than others, and those very concerned with producing the ability

[3] A yet more radical situation – but one more likely to come about – would be that in which an individual's characteristics could be pre-arranged by interference with the genetic material. The dizzying consequences of this I shall not try to explore.

would probably also be over-concerned with success. The moral objections to the excessive concern with such aims are, interestingly, not unconnected with the ideal of equality itself; they are connected with equality in the sense discussed in the earlier sections of this paper, the equality of human beings despite their differences, and in particular with the complex of notions considered in the second section under the heading of 'respect'.

This conflict within the ideals of equality arises even without resort to the fantasy world. It exists today in the feeling that a thoroughgoing emphasis on equality of opportunity must destroy a certain sense of common humanity which is itself an ideal of equality.[4] The ideals that are felt to be in conflict with equality of opportunity are not necessarily other ideals of equality – there may be an independent appeal to the values of community life, or to the moral worth of a more integrated and less competitive society. Nevertheless, the idea of equality itself is often invoked in this connexion, and not, I think, inappropriately.

If the idea of equality ranges as widely as I have suggested, this type of conflict is bound to arise with it. It is an idea which, on the one hand, is invoked in connexion with the distribution of certain goods, some at least of which are bound to confer on their possessors some preferred status or prestige. On the other hand, the idea of equality of respect is one which urges us to give less consideration to those structures in which people enjoy status or prestige, and to consider people independently of those goods, on the distribution of which equality of opportunity precisely focuses our, and their, attention. There is perhaps nothing formally incompatible in these two applications of the idea of equality: one might hope for a society in which there existed both a fair, rational, and appropriate distribution of these goods, and no contempt, condescension, or lack of human communication between persons who were more and less successful recipients of the distribution. Yet in actual fact, there are deep psychological and social obstacles to the realisation of this hope; as things are, the competitiveness and considerations of prestige that surround the first application of equality certainly militate against the second. How far this situation is inevitable, and how far in an economically developed and dynamic society, in which certain skills and talents are necessarily at a premium, the obstacles to a wider realisation of equality might be overcome, I do not think that we know: these are in good part questions of psychology and sociology, to which we do not have the answers.

[4] See, for example, Michael Young, *The Rise of the Meritocracy* (London: Thames and Hudson, 1958).

When one is faced with the spectacle of the various elements of the idea of equality pulling in these different directions, there is a strong temptation, if one does not abandon the idea altogether, to abandon some of its elements: to claim, for instance, that equality of opportunity is the only ideal that is at all practicable, and equality of respect a vague and perhaps nostalgic illusion; or, alternatively, that equality of respect is genuine equality, and equality of opportunity an inegalitarian betrayal of the ideal – all the more so if it were thoroughly pursued, as now it is not. To succumb to either of these simplifying formulae would, I think, be a mistake. Certainly, a highly rational and efficient application of the ideas of equal opportunity, unmitigated by the other considerations, could lead to a quite inhuman society (if it worked – which, granted a well-known desire of parents to secure a position for their children at least as good as their own, is unlikely). On the other hand, an ideal of equality of respect that made no contact with such things as the economic needs of society for certain skills, and human desire for some sorts of prestige, would be condemned to a futile Utopianism, and to having no rational effect on the distribution of goods, position, and power that would inevitably proceed. If, moreover, as I have suggested, it is not really known how far, by new forms of social structure and of education, these conflicting claims might be reconciled, it is all the more obvious that we should not throw one set of claims out of the window; but should rather seek, in each situation, the best way of eating and having as much cake as possible. It is an uncomfortable situation, but the discomfort is just that of genuine political thought. It is no greater with equality than it is with liberty, or any other noble and substantial political ideal.

Commentary on Williams

The first four paragraphs describe the background and they determine the overall structure of the rest of the article. It is therefore very important that you appreciate what Williams is doing in them.

In his opening sentence, Williams says that equality figures in political discussion 'both in statements of fact' and 'in statements of political principles'.

What does he mean by each of these alternatives?

The factual claim is simply: human beings are equal; and the claim about political principle is: human beings ought to be treated equally. The idea that someone ought to be treated in a certain way is generally known as a *normative* claim – one that contrasts with the factual. It is normative because it requires us to think, not of how things are, but of what norm, rule or principle we have reason to institute. Williams notes that the factual and the normative can be combined so as to yield the claim: human beings ought to be treated as the equal beings that they in fact are, and this is a position typical of champions of equality. But Williams sees a problem with both the factual and the normative notions of equality.

What precisely is the problem that Williams finds in these two notions?

The worry expressed at $\boxed{a} \mapsto$ is that both factual and normative claims about equality seem to be either too strong or too weak, and, unless this worry is overcome, the notion of equality might turn out to be either trivial or absurd.

In the paragraph beginning at $\boxed{b} \mapsto$, Williams sets out to show how this difficulty infects the factual claim. On the one hand, the claim that human beings are equal in respect of those characteristics it makes sense to use in any comparison is simply false. Thus, people differ in intellectual and physical abilities, so the very strong claim that people are equal in these respects is patently false. On the other hand, if we try to weaken the claim so that it becomes: human beings are equal in being human beings, then, whilst the result is true, it 'does not do very much'. Williams concludes that as a result of this weakening: 'What looked like a paradox has turned into a platitude.'

Williams wonders (at $\boxed{c} \mapsto$) whether it even makes sense to say that human beings are equal in being human beings. Does it?

The normative claim about equality (described at $\boxed{d} \mapsto$ as the 'practical maxim of equality') is subject to the same kinds of problems. On the one hand, it seems just too strong to insist that human beings should be treated exactly alike in all circumstances; people are just too different to make this a plausible goal. On the other hand, it is too weak to say only that they should be treated alike in similar circumstances, since this would allow extremes of inequality if backed up by some reason or other suggesting that circumstances were not really similar.

Supposing that one was able to offer reasons for differences in treatment, why wouldn't this suffice to give us a workable norm of equality?

Williams's brief answer to this comes in the passage just before $\boxed{e} \mapsto$. The problem is not with the workability of the norm, but with the idea that it would be a norm of *equality*.

At this point, Williams has set the stage for the remainder of his article. His aim is clearly stated at $\boxed{e}\!\!\rightarrow$: he intends to advance considerations that will 'help to save the political notion of equality from these extremes of absurdity and of triviality'. You should read this paragraph carefully.

Section 1   Common humanity

Sections 1 and 2 explore ways of 'building up' the notion of equality. The first considers ways in which a notion of common humanity can non-trivially function to shape our treatment of each other in some more egalitarian way. In it there is an interesting argument which makes reference to the 'sharp distinction between fact and value' which is often encountered in moral philosophy and indeed in everyday moral argument. This is an important enough topic to warrant a close look, and the beginning of it can be set out as follows:

> Human beings are alike not only in their more general characteristics like their capacity to use language, live in societies, interbreed, etc., but also in their capacity to suffer pain, to feel affection and loss, and to experience frustration when thwarted in various ways. These are undoubted facts about us, but what follows from them about how we ought to treat each other? That is, what value judgements follow from the facts? One sort of position in moral philosophy suggests that you can never derive judgements about what we ought to do – what is of value – from judgements of a factual nature. If this position is adhered to in the present case, then one could imagine someone – perhaps a member of the 'ruling class' saying: 'I see that we are all alike in certain respects; it is after all obvious enough. But I do not see why this fact creates any moral claim. I can treat certain groups in my society as underlings: they are in fact like me, but this does not mean that I ought actually to treat them as like me.'

What do you find to be Williams's reply to this line of argument?

The point that Williams makes is a subtle one: at least when it comes to the issue of equality, the decision to ignore the fact of our common humanity in one's treatment of other human beings is already a moral commitment. And it is not one that can stand up to any scrutiny. As Williams says (in the passage in the paragraph marked $\boxed{f}\!\!\rightarrow$):

> [T]hose who neglect the moral claims of certain men that arise from their capacity to feel pain, etc., are *overlooking* or *disregarding* those capacities; and are not just operating with a special moral principle, conceding the capacities to these men, but denying the moral claim.

And he suggests that this is shown by the need felt by those who do neglect these moral claims to justify their behaviour, even by the most thinly veiled rationalizations and special pleading.

Looking back over the text around [f]→, summarize Williams's argument in more concrete terms using his example of colour discrimination.

Section 2   Moral capacities

In this section, Williams considers what he sees as some positive respects in which we might be said to be equal and, hence, deserving of equal treatment. (The capacities to suffer pain, and experience frustrations when our needs are not met, are negative in that they involve our reaction against certain kinds of treatment. A positive respect in which we are equal would be a respect in which our equality is shown by what we can do or achieve.)

The passage beginning with [g]→ and ending with [h]→ considers a candidate for some such positive characteristic. It is the idea that we are all equal in our capacity for virtue or moral achievement.

Read this passage and explain why, in the end, Williams does not find this capacity one which furthers his argument concerning equality.

In considering the idea that we are equal as moral agents – as persons capable of morally worthy action – and therefore equal worthy of respect, Williams makes special reference to the views of Immanuel Kant (1724–1804), an enormously influential German philosopher. Obviously enough, Williams expects that his philosophical readers will have some familiarity with Kant's moral philosophy, but of course the newcomer to philosophy will not share this familiarity. You can (and should at some point) have a look at Kant's *Foundations of the Metaphysics of Morals*, the work on which Williams's comments are based. This short, though complex, work is one of the most well known in the history of moral philosophy. However, even without reading this, you should be able to appreciate the main point that Williams makes against Kant. It comes roughly to this: in order to make plausible the idea that we are genuinely equal as moral agents – equal in respect of the things we can achieve morally – Kant has to abstract away from all the actual differences in motivation and ability that characterize human beings. This is because, as things are, we are not equally well placed in respect of intellectual capacity, sympathetic understanding and resoluteness. And these capacities, though they are not themselves purely moral, certainly make a difference to our capacities as moral agents. Therefore, if we took them into consideration, we would not be equal as moral agents, and this is why Kant needs to think of moral agency as not making any special reference to our actual or empirical natures. (This is what Williams means when he describes Kant's conception of moral agency as 'transcendental'.)

After the point in the text marked $\boxed{h}\!\mapsto$, Williams considers whether, independently of the now rejected idea that we can achieve equal things as moral agents, we can none the less be described as in some way equal in the respect owed to us.

> Before taking it further, Williams gives a good summary of his present position at the place marked $\boxed{i}\!\mapsto$. Most good philosophical writing contains this sort of guidance or sign-posting, and you must be alert to it. Using your own words, try to summarize Williams's own summary.

Having given some content to the idea that we are all equally deserving of respect – that we are all at least potentially capable of standing back and reflecting on ourselves and our roles in society – Williams goes on to consider what this has to do with the notion of political equality. At the point marked $\boxed{j}\!\mapsto$, Williams carefully distinguishes between this potentially equal reflective capacity and the ideal of political equality. He makes the interesting observation that our self-reflective potential does not as such stand in the way of someone's arguing for an unequal and hierarchical arrangement in society. But he goes on to find reason to reject the moral legitimacy of any such hierarchy.

> Can you say what this reason is?

What makes it impossible to maintain the ideal of a stable hierarchical – and therefore unequal – social arrangement is the fact that the degree to which we are each able to exercise our self-reflective capacities is itself a product of social arrangements. It is not simply inevitable that some persons occupy lesser roles in society and do so without any special consciousness of their being members of a 'lower' order. Rather, the ordering itself suppresses the consciousness of this lower status. If the arrangements had been different – if the capacity for reflecting on one's status had been fostered by some different social arrangement – then the hierarchy would be unstable. Put it this way: the perfectly reasonable recognition that there is nothing inevitable about the hierarchy is bound to undermine it.

Section 3　*Equality in unequal circumstances*

In this section, Williams presents the argument to which, as we will see, Nozick takes sharp exception. But before we turn to Nozick, it is very important that you appreciate Williams's argument in some detail.

Up to now, Williams has been discussing ways of building up the notion of equality so that it provides more bite in the debate about whether equality is a reasonable political goal. Having found that equality concerns certain universal features of human beings – our common humanity and our common potential for self-reflection – he thinks that we have some idea of why egalitarians are reasonable to believe in some political ideal of equality. In section 3, he considers how such an ideal might work in the familiar context of distribution of goods and opportunities in a society – a distribution which can be understood as taking place against a background of the inequalities that undoubtedly exist in abilities and capacities.

Is the issue of distribution one to which the issue of equality is relevant? Isn't it really an issue of justice or fairness, rather than one calling for egalitarian (or anti-egalitarian) argument? Williams considers this worry but rejects it, and in so doing makes an important distinction between need and merit (see $\boxed{k}$→).

> In your own words, explain the distinction between need and merit, and its relevance to Williams's argument.

Williams says that in the case of needs, such as the need for medical care, it can be presumed for practical purposes that virtually everyone who has the need for the good also has the desire to have it. But not everyone who merits some good, such as a university education, has the desire for it (and, of course, vice versa). And this difference is crucial. For in the case of merit, we can speak not only of the distribution of the good itself, but of the opportunities for obtaining the good. And it is plausibly – and commonly – argued that opportunity is something that should be distributed equally. This is at least one way in which the issue of fairness in distribution connects with the idea of equality.

At this point, and because of this distinction between need and merit, Williams's argument branches. He first goes into more detail about the basis for distribution of goods which depend upon need. His central point here is that a system that distributes goods such as medical services and rights before the law on the basis of actual inequalities in wealth or power is inherently irrational. (This is the topic of Nozick's challenge and we will consider it further below.) He then goes on to consider at some length the notion of equality of opportunity that comes with goods whose distribution requires some idea of merit – goods such as a university education which is of benefit to some, but not all, people. And his interesting conclusion is that, if we carry the reasoning through faithfully here, we will find that there is a deep conflict between the idea of equality of respect (described earlier) and equality of opportunity. These final pages of Williams's article (beginning at the place marked $\boxed{1}$→) are of fundamental importance to the debate about ideals of equality.

Carefully consider the argument that begins at $\boxed{1}$⊢> and goes to the end of the article, and do two things. First, summarize as clearly as you can the central strand of the argument. This will require you to set out Williams's premises and his conclusion. Second, offer reasons of your own for accepting or rejecting some or all of this argument. When you have done these two things, you will have written a philosophical essay on at least one aspect of the equality debate.

Introduction to Nozick

Robert Nozick (1940–2002) was professor of philosophy at Harvard University, and wrote the lively and challenging work on political philosophy, *Anarchy, State and Utopia* (1974), from which the extracts below are taken. He is also known for works in other areas of philosophy, including *Philosophical Explanations* (1981), which has made a substantial contribution to the theory of knowledge.

In *Anarchy, State and Utopia* Nozick defends what is essentially a form of individualism. Beginning from a moral position in which one is required to respect certain individual rights, Nozick argues that many forms of governmental activity are in fact without moral foundation. In particular, he argues against forms of redistribution of wealth and goods that many think are an essential feature of any acceptable political state. The fundamental rights that he considers are rather traditional, and can be found in political theorists of a broadly libertarian sort. Included in Nozick's list of inalienable rights are the right to one's life and the right to engage freely in any activity that one has chosen to pursue, subject only to not infringing the same rights in others.

Given the way Nozick develops his individualism, it is unsurprising that he is opposed to any sort of equality sponsored by the state or government. The first of the extracts takes aim at some of the things that Williams says, and the second provides a more detailed defence of the specific line of attack Nozick employed in the first.

Robert Nozick, *Anarchy, State and Utopia* (extracts)

1 Equality

The legitimacy of altering social institutions to achieve greater equality of material condition is, though often assumed, rarely *argued* for.

Writers note that in a given country the wealthiest n per cent of the population holds more than that percentage of the wealth, and the poorest n per cent holds less; that to get to the wealth of the top n per cent from the poorest, one must look at the bottom p per cent (where p is vastly greater than n), and so forth. They then proceed immediately to discuss how this might be altered. On the entitlement conception of justice in holdings, one cannot decide whether the state must do something to alter the situation merely by looking at a distributional profile or at facts such as these. It depends upon how the distribution came about. Some processes yielding these results would be legitimate, and the various parties would he entitled to their respective holdings. If these distributional facts *did* arise by a legitimate process, then they themselves are legitimate. This is, of course, *not* to say that they may not be changed, provided this can be done without violating people's entitlements. Any persons who favor a particular end-state pattern may choose to transfer some or all of their own holdings so as (at least temporarily) more nearly to realize their desired pattern.

[a] → The entitlement conception of justice in holdings makes no presumption in favor of equality, or any other overall end state or patterning. It cannot merely be *assumed* that equality must be built into any theory of justice. There is a surprising dearth of arguments for equality capable of coming to grips with the considerations that underlie a nonglobal and nonpatterned conception of justice in holdings. (However, there is no lack of unsupported statements of a presumption in favor of equality.) I shall consider the argument which has received the most attention from philosophers in recent years; that offered by Bernard Williams in his influential essay 'The Idea of Equality.' (No doubt many readers will feel that all hangs on some other argument; I would like to see that argument precisely set out, in detail.)

> Leaving aside preventive medicine, the proper ground of distribution of medical care is ill health: this is a necessary truth. Now in very many societies, while ill health may work as a necessary condition of receiving treatment, it does not work as a sufficient condition, since such treatment costs money, and not all who are ill have the money; hence the possession of sufficient money becomes in fact an additional necessary condition of actually receiving treatment. ... When we have the situation in which, for instance, wealth is a further necessary condition of the receipt of medical treatment, we can once more apply the notions of equality and inequality: not now in connexion with the inequality between the well and the ill, but in connexion with the inequality between the rich ill and the poor ill, since we have straightforwardly the situation of those whose

needs are the same not receiving the same treatment, though the needs are
the ground of the treatment. This is an irrational state of affairs. ... it is a
situation in which reasons are insufficiently *operative*; it is a situation
insufficiently controlled by reasons – and hence by reason itself.

Williams seems to be arguing that if among the different descriptions applying to an activity, there is one that contains an 'internal
goal' of the activity, then (it is a necessary truth that) the only proper
grounds for the performance of the activity, or its allocation if it is
scarce, are connected with the effective achievement of the internal
goal. If the activity is done upon others, the only proper criterion for
distributing the activity is their need for it, if any. Thus it is that
Williams says (it is a necessary truth that) the only proper criterion
for the distribution of medical care is medical need. Presumably, then,
the only proper criterion for the distribution of barbering services is
barbering need. But why must the internal goal of the activity take
precedence over, for example, the person's particular purpose in performing the activity? (We ignore the question of whether one activity
can fall under two different descriptions involving different internal
goals.) If someone becomes a barber because he likes talking to a
variety of different people, and so on, is it unjust of him to allocate
his services to those he most likes to talk to? Or if he works as a barber
in order to earn money to pay tuition at school, may he cut the hair of
only those who pay or tip well? Why may not a barber use exactly the
same criteria in allocating his services as someone else whose activities
have no internal goal involving others? Need a gardener allocate his
services to those lawns which need him most?

In what way does the situation of a doctor differ? Why must his
activities be allocated via the internal goal of medical care? (If there
was no 'shortage,' could some *then* be allocated using other criteria as
well?) It seems clear that *he* needn't do that; just because he has this
skill, why should *he* bear the costs of the desired allocation, why is he
less entitled to pursue his own goals, within the special circumstances
of practicing medicine, than everyone else? So it is *society* that, somehow, is to arrange things so that the doctor, in pursuing his own goals,
allocates according to need; for example, the society pays him to do
this. But why must the society do this? (Should they do it for barbering
as well?) Presumably, because medical care is important, people need it
very much. This is true of food as well, though farming does not have
an internal goal that refers to other people in the way doctoring does.
When the layers of Williams' argument are peeled away, what we
arrive at is the claim that society (that is, each of us acting together
in some organized fashion) should make provision for the important

needs of all of its members. This claim, of course, has been stated many times before. Despite appearances, Williams presents no argument for it. Like others, Williams looks only to questions of allocation. He ignores the question of where the things or actions to be allocated and distributed come from. Consequently, he does not consider whether they come already tied to people who have entitlements over them (surely the case for service activities, which are people's actions), people who therefore may decide for themselves to whom they will give the thing and on what grounds. [...]

2   How Liberty Upsets Patterns

It is not clear how those holding alternative conceptions of distributive justice can reject the entitlement conception of justice in holdings. For suppose a distribution favored by one of these non-entitlement conceptions is realized. Let us suppose it is your favorite one and let us call this distribution D1; perhaps everyone has an equal share, perhaps shares vary in accordance with some dimension you treasure. Now suppose that Wilt Chamberlain is greatly in demand by basketball teams, being a great gate attraction. (Also suppose contracts run only for a year, with players being free agents.) He signs the following sort of contract with a team: In each home game, twenty-five cents from the price of each ticket of admission goes to him. (We ignore the question of whether he is gouging the owners, letting them look out for themselves.) The season starts, and people cheerfully attend his team's games; they buy their tickets, each time dropping a separate twenty-five cents of their admission price into a special box with Chamberlain's name on it. They are excited about seeing him play; it is worth the total admission price to them. Let us suppose that in one season one million persons attend his home games, and Wilt Chamberlain winds up with $250,000, a much larger sum than the average income and larger even than anyone else has. Is he entitled to this income? Is this new distribution D2, unjust? If so, why? There is *no* question about whether each of the people was entitled to the control over the resources they held in D1; because that was the distribution (your favorite) that (for the purposes of argument) we assumed was acceptable. Each of these persons *chose* to give twenty-five cents of their money to Chamberlain. They could have spent it on going to the movies, or on candy bars, or on copies of *Dissent* magazine, or of *Monthly Review*. But they all, at least one million of them, converged on giving it to Wilt Chamberlain in exchange for watching him play basketball. If D1 was a just distribution, and people voluntarily moved from it to D2, transferring parts of their shares they were given under D1 (what was it for if not to do something with?), isn't D2 also just? If the people were entitled to dispose of the resources to which they were entitled (under D1), didn't this include their being entitled to give it to, or exchange it with, Wilt Chamberlain? Can anyone else complain on grounds of justice? Each other person already has his legitimate share under D1. Under D1, there is nothing that anyone has that anyone else has a claim of justice against. After someone transfers something to Wilt Chamberlain, third parties *still* have their legitimate shares; *their* shares are not changed. By what process could such a transfer among two persons give rise to a legitimate claim of distributive justice on a portion of what was transferred, by a third party who had no claim of justice on any holding of the others *before* the transfer? To cut off objections irrelevant here, we might imagine the exchanges occurring in a socialist society, after hours. After playing whatever basketball he does in his daily work, or doing whatever other daily work he does, Wilt Chamberlain decides to put in *overtime* to earn additional money. (First his work quota is set; he works time over that.) Or imagine it is a skilled juggler people like to see, who puts on shows after hours.

Why might someone work overtime in a society in which it is assumed their needs are satisfied? Perhaps because they care about things other than needs. I like to write in books that I read, and to have easy access to books for browsing at odd hours. It would be very pleasant and convenient to have the resources of Widener Library in my back yard. No society, I assume, will provide such resources close to each person who would like them as part of his regular allotment (under D1). Thus, persons either must do without some extra things that they want, or be allowed to do something extra to get some of these things. On what basis could the inequalities that would eventuate be forbidden? Notice also that small factories would spring up in a socialist society, unless forbidden. I melt down some of my personal possessions (under D1) and build a machine out of the material. I offer you, and others, a philosophy lecture once a week in exchange for your cranking the handle on my machine, whose products I exchange for yet other things, and so on. (The raw materials used by the machine are given to me by others who possess them under D1, in exchange for hearing lectures.) Each person might participate to gain things over and above their allotment under D1. Some persons even might want to leave their job in socialist industry and work full time in this private sector. I shall say something more about these issues in the next chapter. Here I wish merely to note how private property even in means of production would occur in a socialist society that did not forbid people to use as they wished some of the resources they are given under the socialist distribution D1. The socialist society would have to forbid capitalist acts between consenting adults.

The general point illustrated by the Wilt Chamberlain example and the example of the entrepreneur in a socialist society is that no end-state principle or distributional patterned principle of justice can be continuously realized without continuous interference with people's lives. Any favored pattern would be transformed into one unfavored by the principle, by people choosing to act in various ways; for example, by people exchanging goods and services with other people, or giving things to other people, things the transferrers are entitled to under the favored distributional pattern. To maintain a pattern one must either continually interfere to stop people from transferring resources as they wish to, or continually (or periodically) interfere to take from some persons resources that others for some reason chose to transfer to them. (But if some time limit is to be set on how long people may keep resources others voluntarily transfer to them, why let them keep these resources for *any* period of time? Why not have immediate confiscation?) It might be objected that all persons voluntarily will choose to refrain from actions which would upset the pattern. This presupposes unrealistically (1) that all will most want to maintain the pattern (are those who don't, to be 'reeducated' or forced to undergo 'self-criticism'?), (2) that each can gather enough information about his own actions and the ongoing activities of others to discover which of his actions will upset the pattern, and (3) that diverse and far-flung persons can coordinate their actions to dovetail into the pattern. Compare the manner in which the market is neutral among persons' desires, as it reflects and transmits widely scattered information via prices, and coordinates persons' activities.

It puts things perhaps a bit too strongly to say that every patterned (or end-state) principle is liable to be thwarted by the voluntary actions of the individual parties transferring some of their shares they receive under the principle. For perhaps some very weak patterns are not so thwarted. Any distributional pattern with any egalitarian component is overturnable by the voluntary actions of individual persons over time; as is every patterned condition with sufficient content so as actually to have been proposed as presenting the central core of distributive justice. Still, given the possibility that some weak conditions or patterns may not be unstable in this way, it would be better to formulate an explicit description of the kind of interesting and contentful patterns under discussion, and to prove a theorem about their instability. Since the weaker the patterning, the more likely it is that the entitlement system itself satisfies it, a plausible conjecture is that any patterning either is unstable or is satisfied by the entitlement system. [...]

Commentary on Nozick

The extracts from Nozick focus sharply on a particular argument of Williams. This commentary will begin with an explanation of some of the notions that Nozick introduces in the first paragraph (up to the place marked $\boxed{a}\rightarrow$). There is a lot condensed into this paragraph, and in order to understand it you will have to understand several notions that he uses but does not explain in the passage. They are discussed at length in the book from which the extracts are taken, but the following short summary will serve our purposes here.

In any society goods are distributed in some way or other, where by 'goods' is meant wealth, education, opportunity, healthcare and any other thing that can be reasonably said to be desired, needed or wanted. This is not to say that there is necessarily some social or political decision mechanism responsible for the distribution; merely that at a given time there will be some way in which things happen to be distributed. But of course there *may* be one or several distributional mechanisms. For example, there may be a tax system that takes wealth from one group and gives it to another; or there may be some centralized government that controls most of the wealth and distributes it according to some plan. In so far as there is some such mechanism, Nozick describes the distribution as *patterned*. In particular, he refers to an 'end-state pattern' and by this he means a distributional pattern, which for one reason or another sets the goal for the distributional mechanism. A pertinent example would be the end-state pattern of equality – an end state which would clearly involve some kind of mechanism that takes wealth from those who have more than an equal share and redistributes it to those who have less.

In his book, Nozick considers many kinds of end-state pattern and the arguments that might be offered in favour of them. A consistent theme is that none of them has more claim to legitimacy than his own favoured *entitlement* conception of distribution. The idea of entitlement is simple: if some distributional pattern happens to exist, and is judged to be fair or legitimate (by the best arguments that can be offered), then any later pattern of distribution that results from the initial one by legitimate exchanges is said to be just as fair or legitimate. Essentially, what Nozick insists is that once one has a legitimate ownership of some good, one is entitled to give it or spend it in any way one likes. Even if this spending results in a new form of distributional pattern – one which might not match the pattern of the original distribution – Nozick sees no problem. So long as the new pattern results from transactions involving those goods one is entitled to have, and by means one is entitled to engage in, the result is a fair or just distribution. It is, as Nozick insists, a distribution based on entitlement, as opposed to an end-state patterned one.

In the passage that Nozick cites from Williams, he finds what he recognizes as an argument for the kind of patterning distribution one would expect of an egalitarian. Williams says that the only rational ground for the distribution of medical care is ill health, and Nozick takes this as a general argument in favour of the distribution of goods and services equally to those in need of them, whether or not they have the money (or equivalent) to obtain them.

> Does Williams offer the general argument that Nozick takes him to be offering?

Before considering this issue, it will be useful to go on to consider the second of the Nozick extracts, the one called 'How Liberty Upsets Patterns'. The underlying theme of Nozick's alleged counter-examples to Williams – such as the barber who cuts hair because he likes conversation – is the entitlement conception of justice in distribution. Nozick believes that the only kind of distributional practice which could count as just is essentially that of the free market. Any attempt on the part of the state – or any quasi-governmental institution – to interfere with the operation of the market by either suppressing certain activities or redistributing funds by taxation is bound to result in injustice. His grounds for this can be found in the colourful example of Wilt Chamberlain that is described in the passage beginning at $\boxed{b}\!\!\mapsto$.

You are first to imagine that in some society the pattern of distribution of goods, tangible and otherwise, is completely in line with what is thought of as perfectly just. This distribution may be broadly egalitarian, or it may be based on some more complicated pattern, but that makes no difference to the argument. Next, Wilt Chamberlain enters the picture. Chamberlain was in fact a very famous basketball player in the USA, one so exciting as to make it reasonable to think that fans would have paid him directly to see him play. Nozick imagines that if in the society whose distributional pattern is described as perfectly just, Chamberlain is paid some small amount by each of the million or so fans who want to see him play, this will inevitably result in a vastly different distribution. Chamberlain will have a lot of money, will be able to buy many more of the goods of society, and the shape of the original patterned distribution will be disrupted. Yet, it is argued, there seems nothing illegitimate about this: Chamberlain gained the extra share of goods by the free exercise of his own efforts (and talent), and by others freely buying tickets. Nozick insists that only the entitlement conception of distribution is consistent both with justice and with the exercise of free choice that is evident in the Chamberlain example.

The overall conclusion of the argument is this: the exercise of liberty is bound to come into conflict with any sort of planned or patterned distribution, so the only way you can maintain an egalitarian society is by drastically restricting people's free choices. As Nozick puts it: 'The socialist society would have to forbid capitalist acts between consenting adults.'

> Nozick's argument relies for its effect on his use of a simple and immediately graspable example. Do you think that there are any special circumstances that, on reflection, make the Wilt Chamberlain example deceptively simple?

Nozick's underlying assumption seems to be that if we start with a just situation, then any new situation we arrive at is just, provided the steps we take to reach the new situation are also just.

> Does the assumption seem to you correct?

We raised a question above about Nozick's reading of Williams, which we can now look at in a little more detail. There are a number of considerations that make the situation more complicated than Nozick suggests. First of all, Williams's claim that it is irrational to let wealth be the basis for the distribution is intended to be less pervasive than Nozick imagines. Second, it can be thought of in a way that might make it less a target for Nozick's argument. As you may have realized in answering the question put earlier, Williams does not intend his claim about medical care to apply to all cases of distribution. Medical care is special in that it involves *need*, whereas other kinds of distribution depend on what Williams counts as *merit*.

> Go back to the Williams piece and re-read the passage on the distinction between need and merit. (This begins at the place marked ⟨k⟩→ in Williams's piece.) Also, consider carefully the kind of moral Williams draws from these cases.

Nozick's example shows someone benefiting from the free exercise of an ability or talent, but he says nothing about whether that benefit is to the detriment of anyone else, though the innocuousness of being paid to play basketball encourages us to doubt that it would be. However, consider another example. Suppose that someone has a particular talent for getting people to part with their life savings. (Assume here that the money is given freely and not because of any kind of lie or deception.) Would we regard this as a perfectly reasonable form of distribution by what Nozick calls 'entitlement'? Since it is likely that the loss of life savings would result in considerable harm, not just to an individual but to whole families, we are likely to be more cautious about thinking this acceptable. Certain exercises of freedom are perfectly fine, others are more problematic. Indeed, in his famous essay *On Liberty*, John Stuart Mill – a wholehearted defender of liberty – made the important distinction between liberty and licence. Liberty is the exercise of free choice when such choices do not cause harm to others, whereas licence is choice without such a restriction. Mill is not alone in insisting that only liberty is defensible, though care is needed, because licence often masquerades as liberty. Moreover, following Mill, it is generally reckoned that this condemnation of licence is in no way incompatible with the defence of liberty.

Of course, everything depends on whether you regard certain kinds of act as exercises of liberty or licence. And this is not something that can be settled by philosophical investigation alone; one would need to make a study of each sort of case. What Nozick seems to depend on in his argument is that the reader will all too easily generalize from the Chamberlain example without checking to see whether the choice exercised in other cases brings harms to others.

Can you think of realistic examples where what looks like an exercise of liberty could in fact be understood as mere licence?

Nozick also accuses Williams of making the assumption that where there are inequalities, there is reason for someone to interfere and put them right. He writes:

> When the layers of Williams' argument are peeled away, what we arrive at is the claim that society (that is, each of us acting together in some organized fashion) should make provision for the important needs of all of its members. This claim, of course, has been stated many times before. Despite appearances, Williams presents no argument for it.

Is it reasonable to require Williams to argue for the claim described in the passage?

The idea that a society should provide for the needs of its members is certainly not argued for in Williams's article, but this is not at all surprising, nor should it be counted a defect. As we have seen, Williams's overall aim is to deepen our understanding of equality, and thereby make its moral claim on us intelligible. Given this, it is certainly reasonable to make a background *assumption* about the relationship between individuals' needs and society in order to foreground the claims of equality in respect of that relationship. After all, to say that a society should make provision for its members' needs is not yet to say that this provision should be egalitarian.

5

Dilemma

Introduction to the Problem

Imagine the following: you have been invited to dinner with some friends on Saturday and you would very much like to accept. But when looking through a newspaper, you note that there is a concert on that very Saturday – a concert by a music group you very much like and which is playing only that one time in your locality. Together these facts put you in a dilemma.

Of course, the dilemma described is not all that serious. Your life wouldn't be dramatically affected one way or the other by whatever you decide, and it probably wouldn't matter all that much if you did neither of the things on offer. Still, before you make the choice, the situation you are in is certainly dilemmatic, and this simple example of what we can call a *practical dilemma* is a good place to start our investigation.

What we have in this example are two things which you would like to do – two things you desire – and circumstances that ended up making the fulfilment of both desires impossible. A little abbreviated notation will help to describe this case. We can say that you desire to do A and you also desire to do B, but it turns out that you cannot do both A and B. As a result you can: do A (and not B), or do B (and not A), or do neither A nor B. In effect, a practical dilemma is a forced choice.

Not all practical dilemmas are of precisely this form. In the above case, there was nothing problematic about your desires: if circumstances had been kinder – if the dinner and the concert were on different days – you could have satisfied both. However, it can happen that our desires conflict, apparently in and of themselves. For example, suppose you have been at home and haven't seen friends for some time. As a result you have a desire to get out of the house. But suppose also that you are comfortable at home and cannot be bothered to go out. In this case – and it is no doubt a familiar one – the problem lies with your conflicting desires and not with mere circumstance. In this case, you desire to do A and you also desire not to do A, and no change in outward circumstances could make the satisfaction of both of these possible.

Whichever form a practical dilemma takes, the key to resolving it is obvious enough. Since in one way or another, what gets you into a practical dilemma is your desires, the way out involves some kind of assessment or re-assessment of them. For example, you could resolve the dinner–concert dilemma by giving up on one or other desire, and you could resolve the problem of whether to go out by deciding which of your conflicting desires was the stronger. Of course, it is one thing to say what you need to do, and another thing to do it. The cases so far discussed might suggest that resolution of practical dilemmas is easy, but this is far from true. Sometimes the desires at the heart of a dilemma are so fundamental that giving them up or deciding between them is very difficult indeed. One way to put this is by saying that practical dilemmas can be very *real*, in the sense that their resolution involves genuine sacrifice.

Practical dilemma is an easily recognized feature of any life, and that is why it is a natural place to begin a discussion of moral dilemma. But, as we shall see, there are important differences between the practical and the moral. Using our original example, we can turn what was a practical dilemma into a moral one by changing the facts a bit. Imagine that you in fact had accepted the dinner-party invitation – you had promised you would be there on Saturday – and you knew that your hosts were relying on you. Imagine also that you had committed yourself to going to the concert on Saturday with another friend, one who would simply not go to the concert alone and who therefore counted on your using the ticket that he had bought for you. Let us assume you made these two engagements not realizing they conflicted, and that this only came to light when you updated your diary.

In this new situation, you not only *want* to do each of the things in the diary, you also are clearly *obligated* to do them. After all, each is the result of a promise you made. We can describe your dilemma this way: you ought to do A and you ought to do B, but circumstances have made it impossible for you actually to do both.

> What would happen if you decided either that you no longer wanted to go to the dinner party, or that you now wanted to go to the concert more than the dinner party?

Whilst these decisions would have resolved the practical dilemma described earlier, they would have no such effect on the moral dilemma. It can happen that what we desire to do coincides with what we ought to do, but we cannot depend on it. Nor of course can we avoid those things that we ought to do simply by finding we do not desire to do them. And this marks a fundamental difference between practical and moral dilemma. In the latter case, our obligations to do A and to do B hold, when they do, irrespective of what we want; in this sense their grip on us seems to lie outside of our immediate control.

It was noted that practical dilemmas sometimes come about because of inconvenient circumstances, but sometimes arise from desires that are inherently conflicting. Moral dilemmas seem to allow for these same two possibilities. Sometimes it is true that I ought to do A and ought to do B, but that circumstances just happen to make doing both impossible. But sometimes it can seem simply that I ought to do A and I ought not to do A. Indeed, it might be thought that real moral conflict is bound to take the latter form and, hence, that this difference in form is important. This is because the conflict would be inherent in the 'ought's and would owe nothing to external circumstances. If this is so, it would mark yet another difference between practical and moral dilemmas. For no such importance attaches to the two different forms of practical dilemma.

When we think about moral dilemma in the context of various philosophical theories about morality, the differences between the practical and the moral take on special significance. Philosophical theories of morality often have the form of proposals about goodness, rightness and virtue. In particular, these proposals are offered as guides to our moral decision-making. Appealing to them, it is suggested, will reveal to us what is good, or right or virtuous in any of the complex situations in which we find ourselves. Nor is this kind of advice found only in philosophical writings. The search for some universally applicable criterion of morality – whilst it is generally reckoned to be very difficult to discover – seems to many to be the defining feature of moral theory. Yet even the hypothetical possibility of such a criterion has a worrying, even paradoxical, consequence for our thinking about moral dilemma, and therefore for our thinking about morality itself.

The problem is this: if there were some criterion that would in every case (at least in principle) tell us what was good, or right or virtuous, then this would imply that moral dilemmas were simply not real. Yet, since they do in fact seem a central part of everyday moral experience – in this way, all too real – there is a tension between the attempt to establish a criterion of morality and our conception of moral experience. An appeal here to the differences between practical and moral dilemma will help to make the problem clearer.

What makes a *practical* dilemma real is that there are two things desired, but also there is a conflict in these desires, either through circumstances or in and of themselves. This means that acting in the face of a practical dilemma means giving up something desired – it means making a sacrifice. If you decided to go to the dinner party and not to the concert, then you would have resolved the dilemma, but your desire to go to the concert would not thereby disappear. You would be in effect sacrificing the concert for the dinner party. In contrast, if, on thinking things over, you were to find that you never really wanted to go to the concert, then it would seem more appropriate to say, not that you resolved the dilemma, but that you were never really in one in the first place.

Think now of the moral case, and suppose there to be some general rule or criterion that at least in principle tells us in every case what ought to be done. In the sharpest form of moral dilemma, you find yourself thinking that you ought to do A yet also ought *not* to do A. Because you believe that both of these 'oughts' make genuine demands, this dilemma seems real to you and calls for some kind of sacrifice as part of its resolution. However, if there were some general criterion of moral value that you accept, this reality is under threat. For example, suppose the criterion had the consequence that, in the circumstances, the thing you ought to do is not A. Then for all that you believed you ought to do it, you were simply mistaken. And this in turn suggests that you were not really in any sort of dilemma in the first place; you only thought you were. For, if the thought that you ought to do A is simply false, then like the desire you never had in the practical case, the dilemma just disappears. You can scarcely be said to sacrifice the satisfaction of a desire that you never really had, and, similarly, you can scarcely be said to sacrifice something you ought to do, when it is not true that you ought to do it.

In a nutshell the problem that will be investigated in the texts and commentary is this: the quest for fundamental moral principles – something often regarded as essential to moral thought – seems to rule out moral dilemma, even though most would regard dilemma as typical of, and fundamental to, genuine moral experience.

Introduction to Lemmon

E. J. Lemmon (1930–1966) was a British philosopher who taught in Oxford in the late 1950s and who died suddenly a few years after he had taken up a post in the University of California. He is perhaps best known for his textbook in logic entitled *Beginning Logic* which was widely used in American and British universities, as well as for articles on logic and moral philosophy. The article, 'Moral Dilemmas' appeared in the journal *Philosophical Review* in 1962. The extract below begins with section 3 and ends with section 5, the concluding section of the article, minus its last paragraph.

E. J. Lemmon, 'Moral Dilemmas' (extract)

3

It is well past time to reach the main topic of this paper. My third class of moral situation constitutes what I take to be the simplest variety of moral dilemma in the full sense. The characterization of this class is as follows: a man both ought to do something and ought not to do that thing. Here is a simple example, borrowed from Plato. A friend leaves me with his gun, saying that he will be back for it in the evening, and I promise to return it when he calls. He arrives in a distraught condition, demands his gun, and announces that he is going to shoot his wife because she has been unfaithful. I ought to return the gun, since I promised to do so – a case of obligation. And yet I ought not to do so, since to do so would be to be indirectly responsible for a murder, and my moral principles are such that I regard this as wrong. I am in an extremely straightforward moral dilemma, evidently resolved by not returning the gun.

The description of this class of cases may perhaps cause alarm; for it may well be thought to be contradictory that a man both ought and ought not to do something. To indicate why I do not think this is so, I will begin by considering the logic of the modal verb 'has to,' or 'must,' and then contrast this logic with that of the modal 'ought.' If a man has to do something, it does follow that he does that thing, in the sense that if he does not do it it cannot have been true that he must do it. This emerges quite clearly, I think, from the following fact of usage: a man announces that he must do something, but it later emerges that he has not done that thing. Then he will now repeat his earlier claim, not in the form that he *had* to do it, which would suggest falsely that he had done it, but in the form that he *ought* to have done it. Or, if at a party I say that I have to go, this will be taken as a sign heralding my departure. But if I merely say that I ought to go, this is entirely compatible, human weakness being what it is, with my staying for another hour.

It follows from this that 'must' and 'must not' are contraries in the logician's sense. That is, it cannot be both true that I must do something and that I must not do it: for if I must I will, and if I must not I will not, which is a contradiction. On the other hand, it may well be the case that I neither must do something nor must not do that thing. For example, it is neither true that I must light a cigarette nor that I must not light a cigarette. Hence 'must' and 'must not' may well both be false, though they may not be both true.

'Must not' should not be supposed to be the negation of 'must,' in the way that 'cannot' is the negation of 'can.' The proper negation of 'I must tell the truth' is, roughly, 'I do not have to tell the truth.' In an entirely similar way, 'ought not' is certainly not the negation of 'ought.' For example, it is true neither that I ought to be playing chess nor that I ought not to be playing chess; hence 'ought' and 'ought not' are not contradictory. But are they even contrary to one another? In the case of 'must' and 'must not' we showed them to be contrary by showing that 'must' implied 'will' and that consequently 'must not' implied 'will not.' Hence an explicit contradiction is derivable from the assumption that a man both must and must not do something. But no similar contradiction is derivable from the assumption that someone both ought and ought not to do something; for it certainly does not follow from the fact that a man ought to do something that he will do it, nor does it follow from the fact that a man ought not to do something that he will not do that thing. There seems no reason, therefore, why we should regard 'ought' and 'ought not' even as contraries, still less as contradictories. It seems to me that 'ought' and 'ought not' may well both be true, and that this description in fact characterizes a certain class of moral dilemma. Indeed, the Platonic example cited would not be a dilemma at all unless it was true that the man both ought to return the gun and ought not to return it. It is a nasty fact about human life that we sometimes both ought and ought not to do things; but it is not a logical contradiction.

My motive for carefully distinguishing some of the sources for 'ought's' earlier in this paper should now be apparent. For moral dilemmas of the sort we are at present considering will appear generally in the cases where these sources conflict. Our duty may conflict with our obligations, our duty may conflict with our moral principles, or our obligations may conflict with our moral principles. The Platonic case was an example of a conflict between principle and obligation. A simple variant illustrates a conflict between obligation and duty: the man with whom the gun is deposited may regard it as his duty as a friend not to return the gun, even though he is under an obligation to do so. And duty conflicts with principle every time that we are called on in our jobs to do things which we find morally repugnant.

A natural question to ask next is: how are moral dilemmas of this simple kind to be resolved? There are certain very simple resolutions, known from the philosophical literature, which we should discuss first; but I do not think they are in practice very common. First, we may hold to some very sweeping 'higher-order principle' such as 'Always prefer duty to obligation' or 'Always follow moral principles before duty or obligation.' This last precept, for example, at once resolves the Platonic dilemma mentioned earlier, which, as I described it, was a simple clash between principle and obligation. Secondly, and rather less simply, we may have in advance a complex ordering of our various duties, obligations, and the like – putting, for example, our duties as a citizen before our duties as a friend and our duties as a friend before any obligations we may have incurred – in virtue of which the moral dilemma is resolved. But dilemmas in which we are morally prepared, in which we, as it were, merely have to look up the solution in our private ethical code, are rare, I think, and in any case of little practical interest. Of greater importance are those dilemmas in this class where some decision of a moral character is required. And here it must be remembered that the failure to make a decision in one sense is itself to make a decision in another, broader, sense. For our predicament is here so described that, whatever we do, even if we do nothing at all (whatever that might mean), we are doing something which we ought not to do, and so can be called upon to justify either our activity or our inactivity. The only way we can avoid a decision is by ceasing to be any longer an agent (e.g., if we are arrested, or taken prisoner, or kidnapped, or die). This precise situation leads to another familiar pattern of bad faith, in which we pretend to ourselves either that no decision is called for or that in one way or another the decision has been taken out of our hands by others or that we are simply the victims of our own character in acting in this way or that, that we cannot help doing what we do and so cannot be reproached for resolving the dilemma in this way or that. If, however, we are to act here in good faith, we shall recognize that the dilemma is what it is and make the best decision we can.

Now what kind of considerations may or should affect the decision? The situation is such that no moral, or at least purely moral, considerations are relevant, in the sense that no appeal to our own given morality can decide the issue. We may of course consult a friend, take moral advice, find out what others have done in similar situations, appeal as it were to precedent. But again none of these appeals will be decisive – we still have to decide to act in accordance with advice or precedent. Or again we may approach our decisions by a consideration of ends – which course of action will, so far as we can see, lead to the best result. (I do not think it is an accident, by the way, that the word 'good,' or rather its superlative 'best,' makes its first appearance at this point in our discussion; for it is typically when we are torn between courses of conduct that the question of comparing different actions arises, and hence the word 'good,' a comparative

[j]→ adjective unlike 'right,' is at home here; the consequence, admittedly paradoxical, of this view of 'good' is that it is not properly a word of moral appraisal at all, despite the vast attention it receives from ethical philosophers; and I think I accept this conclusion.) Thus a consideration of ends determines a solution to the Platonic dilemma discussed earlier. Although I ought to return the gun and also ought not to return the gun, in fact it is evidently best, when we weigh up the expected outcome, not to return the gun, and so to sacrifice one's obligation to utilitarian considerations. Of course, when I say that this solution is evidently the best, I do not mean that it cannot be questioned. What I do mean is that it can only be seriously questioned by someone whose whole attitude toward human life is basically different from that of a civilized Western human being. Someone who thinks that it would really be better to return the gun must either hold the importance of a man's giving his word to be fantastically high or else hold human life to be extremely cheap, and I regard both these attitudes as morally primitive.

4

I shall pass on now to the next, more complex, class of moral situations which might be described as dilemmatic in the full sense. Roughly, the class I now have in mind may be described thus: there is some, but not conclusive, evidence that one ought to do something, and there is some, but not conclusive, evidence, that one ought not to do that thing. All the difficulties that arose in the way of making a decision in the last class of cases arise typically here too, but there are now difficulties of a new kind as well. Moreover, in this class of cases there can be no pre-assigned moral solution to the dilemma in virtue of higher-order principles or a given ordering of one's duties and obligations and the like, because part of the very dilemma is just one's uncertainty as to one's actual moral situation, one's situation with respect to duties, obligations, and principles. For example, it may be unclear whether it really is one's duty as a citizen to vote against the Communist candidate, and also unclear whether one is under an obligation to vote for the Communist candidate in view, let us say, of financial help received from the Communists in the Resistance during the war. Hence one is in a moral dilemma because there is some evidence that one should vote Communist and some that one should not, though in neither case is the evidence conclusive.

A good illustration of the kind of complexity this type of situation may embrace is from Sartre:

k→   I will refer to the case of a pupil of mine who sought me out in the
following circumstances. His father was quarrelling with his mother
and was also inclined to be a 'collaborator'; his elder brother had been
killed in the German offensive of 1940 and this young man, with a
sentiment somewhat primitive but generous, burned to avenge him. His
mother was living alone with him, deeply afflicted by the semi-treason
of his father and by the death of her oldest son, and her one consolation
was in this young man. But he, at this moment, had the choice between
going to England to join the Free French Forces or of staying near his
mother and helping her to live. He fully realized that this woman lived
only for him and that his disappearance – or perhaps his death – would
plunge her into despair. He also realized that, concretely and in fact,
every action he performed on his mother's behalf would be sure of effect
in the sense of aiding her to live, whereas anything he did in order to go
and fight would be an ambiguous action which might vanish like water
into sand and serve no purpose. For instance, to set out for England he
would have to wait indefinitely in a Spanish camp on the way through
Spain; or, on arriving in England or in Algiers he might be put into an
office to fill up forms. Consequently, he found himself confronted by
two very different modes of action; the one concrete, immediate, but
directed towards only one individual; the other an action addressed to
an end infinitely greater, a national collectivity, but for that reason
ambiguous – and it might be frustrated on the way. At the same time,
he was hesitating between two kinds of morality; on the one side, the
morality of sympathy, of personal devotion and, on the other side,
the morality of wider scope but of more debatable validity. He had to
choose between these two.

A crude oversimplification of this example might depict it thus: the
boy is under some obligation to stay with his mother; or, perhaps
better, his mother by her own position has put him under some
obligation to stay with her, since she is now dependent on him for
her own happiness. Consequently, he is conscious in some degree that
he ought to stay with her. On the other hand he feels some kind of duty
to join the Free French in England – a duty perhaps to his country as a
citizen. But this duty is far from being clearly given; as Sartre stresses,
it is felt only ambiguously. It may be his duty to fight, but can it really
be his duty, given his obligation to his mother, to sit in an office filling
l→   out forms? He is morally torn, but each limb of the moral dilemma is
not itself here clearly delineated.
An interesting feature of this case, and of the class of cases in general
which we are considering, is that, in attempting to reach a decision,
the arguments which try to establish exactly what one's moral situation is are not distinguishable from those which attempt to resolve
the dilemma itself. Thus the boy is unclear where his duty lies partly

because he is unclear what exactly would be the outcome of his decision to leave his mother, and this outcome is also relevant to the decision itself, as a utilitarian consideration affecting his choice.

Sartre's example has an important further feature, which marks out a particular subclass of the class of moral dilemmas in general: the dilemma is so grave a one, personally speaking, that either decision in effect marks the adoption on the part of the agent of a changed moral outlook. It does not seem to have been much observed by ethical philosophers that, speaking psychologically, the adoption of a new morality by an agent is frequently associated with the confrontation of a moral dilemma. Indeed, it is hard to see what else would be likely to bring about a change of moral outlook other than the having to make a difficult moral decision. On the nature of such a change there is time here only to say a few things. First, the change frequently and always in serious cases is associated with a change in fundamental attitudes, such as the change from liberalism to conservatism in politics or the change from Christianity to atheism in the field of religion. And the reasons given for the moral change may well be identical with the reasons given for the change in fundamental attitudes. This last kind of change is neither fully rational nor fully irrational. To persuade someone to change his fundamental attitudes is like getting someone to see an aesthetic point – to appreciate classical music or impressionist painting, for example. Arguments can be given, features of music or painting may be drawn to the person's attention, and so on and so forth, but none of these reasons is finally conclusive. Nonetheless, we should not rush to the opposite conclusion that matters of aesthetic taste are purely subjective. In a somewhat similar way we may persuade someone, or he may persuade himself, to change his fundamental attitudes, and so to change his moral outlook, at a time of moral crisis. Roughly speaking, Sartre's boy has to decide whether to be politically engaged or not, and this decision may well affect and be affected by his fundamental attitudes.

I am not at all saying that this kind of serious case is common; indeed, I think it is rare; but it is still of the greatest importance to ethics to investigate it, because it is of the greatest practical importance in a man's life. There may well be people who have never had to face a moral situation of these dimensions. But for Antigones and others who live faced with occasional major crises, the appropriate reasoning for this kind of moral dilemma is of vital importance. On the other hand, it is not at all clear what the role of the philosopher should be here. If we listen to much of contemporary ethical writing, his role is merely to analyze the discourse in which such reasoning is couched; the task of deciding what are good and what are bad ethical arguments belongs to someone else, though it is never quite made clear to whom. It is my own view that, even though it may be part and an important part of the philosopher's job to analyze the terminology of ethical arguments, his job does not stop there. Perhaps no one is properly equipped to give moral advice to anyone else, but if anyone is it is the philosopher, who at least may be supposed to be able to detect bad reasoning from good. It is a corollary of this view that a philosopher is not entitled to a private life – by which I mean that it is his duty to hold political and religious convictions in such a form as to be philosophically defensible or not to hold them at all. He is not entitled to hold such beliefs in the way in which many nonphilosophers hold them, as mere articles of faith.

5

After this brief digression, I must return to my classification of moral dilemmas: for there is one more kind that, with some hesitation, I should like to introduce. This is an even more extreme kind of dilemma than the last and probably of even rarer occurrence. I mean the kind of situation in which an agent has to make a decision of a recognizably moral character though he is completely unprepared for the situation by his present moral outlook. This case differs from the last in that there the question was rather of the applicability of his moral outlook to his present situation, while here the question is rather how to create a new moral outlook to meet unprecedented moral needs. This case is in some respects easier for the agent and in some respects harder to face than the last: easier, if he recognizes the situation for what it is, because he at least knows that for sure he has some basic moral rethinking to do, which is often not clear in the previous case; but harder, because basic moral rethinking is harder work in general than settling the applicability of given moral principles to a particular situation. A typical, but morally wrong, way of escape from this dilemma is again to act in bad faith, by pretending to oneself that the situation is one which one can handle with one's given moral apparatus.

A possible real instance of this kind of moral dilemma is that which faced Chamberlain in his negotiations with Hitler in 1938. He ought to have realized that he was dealing with a kind of person for which his own moral outlook had not prepared him, and that as prime minister he was called upon to rethink his moral and political approach in a more realistic way. This he failed to do, either because he was genuinely deceived as to Hitler's real character or, as I suspect, because he deceived himself on this point: if the latter, then he was guilty of the type of bad faith to which I am alluding.

q→   The main point of this variety of moral dilemma is that, at least if correctly resolved, it forces a man to develop a new morality; in the case of the last type of dilemma, this was a possible outcome but by no means a necessary one. So perhaps this is the place at which to say a little about what is involved in such a development. Here the analogy with aesthetics, which Sartre and others have cautiously drawn, may be useful. There may come a point in the development of a painter, say, or a composer, where he is no longer able to go on producing work that conforms to the canons of composition which he has hitherto accepted, where he is compelled by his authenticity as a creator to develop new procedures and new forms. It is difficult to describe what will guide him in the selection of new canons, but one consideration will often be the desire to be (whatever this means) *true to himself*. It may well be that an appropriate consideration in the development of a new moral outlook is the desire to be, in the relevant sense whatever that is, true to oneself and to one's own character. But I will not pursue this topic here, because I confess myself to be quite in the dark as to what the sense of these words is.

To conclude, I will not attempt to summarize, but rather I will say what I would like to see done and what I know I have here failed properly to do. I should like to see a detailed breakdown of the different kinds of difficult moral situations in which human beings, living as they do in societies, find themselves, because in my opinion too much attention has been paid in contemporary ethical writing to the easy, rule-guided, moral situation. The five types of ethical situation which I have here tried to distinguish might well be replaced by five hundred types, human life being what it is. Such an analysis will require sympathetic treatment of real moral problems considered in detail, and it will require a proper analysis of the concepts of choice and decision – active moral concepts, rather than the passive, spectatorlike, concepts of good and right. Secondly, I should like to see a proper discussion of the arguments that go to resolve moral dilemmas, because I do not believe that this is an area of total irrationality, though I do not believe that a traditional logical approach (the logic of imperatives, deontic logic, and whatnot) will do either. This will entail saying what constitutes a good and a bad moral reason for making a moral decision, and so will bring the moral philosopher out from his corner, where I think he has been too long, and back into the familiar but forgotten Socratic position of trying to answer the ever-present but ever-changing question: how should a man live?
[...]

Commentary on Lemmon

Lemmon (at ☐a⊢→) gives an example of a moral dilemma adapted from one that Plato described in his dialogue known as *Republic*.

> Is the dilemma at ☐a⊢→ one where two compatible obligations conflict *in the circumstances* or one where the conflict is *intrinsic* to the obligations themselves?

Answering this is not straightforward and a lot depends on how the obligations are described. On the one hand, we could say that Lemmon ought to return things lent to him, and that he ought to do what he can to prevent murder. So described, it is the circumstances of the case that make for the dilemma: it has turned out that returning the property cannot be done without encouraging murder. On the other hand, we could say that Lemmon ought to return the gun because he promised this, and also that he ought not to return the gun because it would encourage murder. So described, the conflict seems intrinsic to the obligations.

Lemmon chooses the latter sort of description of the obligations. As noted in the 'Introduction to the Problem', this choice has the effect of highlighting the conflict inherent in a dilemma. However, it also leads Lemmon straight into a consideration of features of what he calls 'the logic of modal verbs'. This discussion begins at ☐b⊢→, and continues to ☐e⊢→. (Note: In this context, modal verbs are words like 'ought' and 'must' which are reckoned to describe the mode with which, for example, certain requests or prescriptions are made. Imagine someone asking you to close the window. This request could be made in the 'must'-mode, as in 'You must close the window', or in the 'ought'-mode as in 'You ought to close the window.')

> At ☐b⊢→, Lemmon worries that his description of the dilemma 'may perhaps cause alarm'. Can you say why he thinks this?

If it were really contradictory to describe a moral dilemma as a case in which both 'S ought to do A' and 'S ought not to do A', then moral dilemmas would not only be distressing, they would be downright impossible. Yet surely most people think that they are possible and even common.

Lemmon suggests, however, that we can avoid such a result by paying attention to the differences between 'ought'-judgements and 'must'-judgements. There is indeed a contradiction between 'S must do A' and 'S must not do A', but this does not extend to 'ought'.

> What is the difference between 'S ought to do A' and 'S must do A'?

Lemmon points out (at $\boxed{c}\mapsto$) that when someone announces that he must leave the party at ten o'clock, this implies that he will leave at ten. If he is still there at eleven, then he will have to change his assessment. It would be misleading to say 'I had to leave at ten o'clock' since this implies that he did in fact leave, so he will likely say something like 'I ought to have left at ten.'

The plain fact is that 'must' and 'must not' are contraries: that is, they can both be false but they cannot both be true. So, this rules out the possibility that someone in a dilemma both 'must do A' and 'must not do A'; these two descriptions simply couldn't both be true. However, there is no logical bar to judgements of the form 'ought' and 'ought not' both being true (see $\boxed{d}\mapsto$). And this is precisely what is needed to allow Lemmon's description of the Platonic case as one in which 'I ought to return the gun' and 'I ought not to return the gun.' Such a description is at least logically in order, though it is thereby no less distressing for the agent who is in that situation.

At $\boxed{e}\mapsto$, Lemmon explains further why it was important to investigate the logic of 'ought'. By insisting that moral dilemmas can be put in the form 'ought' and 'ought not' – and demonstrating that this form is logically acceptable – he is able to show something about the sources of dilemmas. Each side of a moral dilemma – whether it is of the form 'ought' or 'ought not' – is supported by a different kind of moral consideration. Thus, you ought to return the gun because you put yourself under an *obligation* (You said: 'I promise'), but you ought not to return the gun because of a moral *principle* ('Do not encourage murder'). And other sorts of case can arise when duty enters the picture alongside obligation and principle.

> Think up some examples where the source of the dilemma is a conflict among duties, obligations or principles.

Lemmon next addresses a question (at $\boxed{f}\mapsto$) that might seem long overdue: how do we resolve moral dilemmas? For obvious enough reasons, his aim is to review certain very general considerations rather than offering specific moral advice. Two points that he makes are especially interesting. One is that moral dilemmas are such that even the failure to make a decision counts as a decision. This reflects something we noted earlier: you cannot 'solve' a moral dilemma simply by walking away from it. Moral dilemmas differ in just this way from practical dilemmas. Second, he says that, except in certain trivial cases, moral dilemmas cannot be solved by appeals to our own moral views (see here the passage at $\boxed{g}\mapsto$).

> Why does he say this?

Lemmon's claim here can seem surprising at first, but you must remember how he has described moral dilemmas. They are cases in which the agent's view of her obligations, duties and principles – in sum, the *whole* of her moral outlook – has led the agent to think that there is something she ought to do and also ought not to do. Given this, it is not surprising that a further consultation of that moral outlook will fail to resolve the dilemma.

What then can one do? Lemmon suggests (at $\boxed{h}$→) that someone in a moral dilemma might consult others, but he thinks this is unlikely to be decisive. In saying this, he is not casting doubt on the possibility of getting good moral advice from others; such a sweeping judgement would certainly be unreasonable. Instead, his point is that such moral advice would only work if the agent in the dilemma took it on board as part of her own moral outlook. And of course if this happened – and if the advice made one course of action the obviously right one – then the dilemma would have simply disappeared. Lemmon's point is that, whilst advice might sometimes have this effect, it does not generally do so, and this suggests that dilemmas are in general not real.

His wish to preserve the reality of a moral dilemma, whilst none the less allowing there to be considerations that might guide someone in its grip, leads Lemmon to write something that is rather surprising. What he says at $\boxed{i}$→ is that, in deciding whether or not to return the gun, we have to appeal to a consideration of ends or results in order to choose which thing to do. In the case at hand, this means taking into consideration a likely death, or a disappointment about a promise unfulfilled. This is not surprising in and of itself; what is surprising is his claim about 'good' and its superlative form 'best' as applied to ends. At $\boxed{j}$→, he says 'the consequence, admittedly paradoxical, of this view of "good" is that it is not properly a word of moral appraisal at all, despite the vast attention it receives from ethical philosophers; and I think I accept this conclusion.'

Lemmon's view is indeed paradoxical: how can it be that 'good' or 'better' as applied to such outcomes as death or the prevention of death are not used in a *moral* sense? We will have occasion to think this through more thoroughly in the context of the second reading. However, here it is sufficient to emphasize a reason why anyone might be tempted to hold such a view.

As noted above, Lemmon insists that moral dilemmas do occur, that they are real and that there is no logical bar to their being represented as a conflict between 'ought' and 'ought not' judgements, each of which is supported by an agent's moral outlook. He seems to think that if any such dilemma can be resolved by *moral* considerations – whether by elements of the agent's own moral outlook or by taking moral advice – then the dilemma would have turned out to be more apparent than real. However, he does want to allow that dilemmas do sometimes get resolved in this sense: there can be considerations that favour acting one way rather than another. Lemmon apparently takes the view that if these considerations are moral, then the dilemma was not real in the first place. So, he (paradoxically, perhaps) insists that we can speak of 'good' or 'better' outcomes in a *non-moral* sense, since he wants to make room for the obvious possibility of our making some kind of decision when faced with a dilemma.

In section 4, Lemmon considers an example of a moral dilemma that he finds to be more complex than the Platonic case, and he describes it as 'dilemmatic in the full sense'. The example (at ⬚k⬚↦) is due to Jean-Paul Sartre, the twentieth-century French philosopher, novelist and playwright who is one of the founders of the movement known as 'Existentialism'. (The passage that Lemmon cites is from *Existentialism and Humanism*, translated by P. Mairet, London, 1948, pp. 35–6.)

> Why does Lemmon think that the example at ⬚k⬚↦ is 'dilemmatic in the full sense'?

In the paragraphs before he presents the example, and in those that follow, Lemmon offers scattered remarks that suggest an answer to this question. But perhaps the key lies in the passage at and after ⬚l⬚↦. Here Lemmon suggests that the difference between the Platonic and Sartrean examples is this: in the Platonic case, we know what our obligations, duties and principles demand of us even though they conflict, whereas in the Sartrean case we do not even know that much. More specifically, whilst it is clear that the promise to return the gun places you under an obligation to do so, and that principle demands that you not assist in murder, Sartre's pupil is described as unsure even whether duty requires that he stay with his mother or whether principle requires him to fight for the Free French. This uncertainty adds an extra dimension to the Sartrean dilemma and this is perhaps why Lemmon describes it as 'dilemmatic in the full sense'. In such a dilemma, you do not know what morality requires of you, though you do recognize that whatever it is, it is bound to involve conflict. Lemmon says of the student: 'He is morally torn, but each limb of the moral dilemma is not itself here clearly delineated.'

At ⬚m⬚↦, Lemmon considers yet another consequence of the Sartrean kind of example: whatever the agent decides is bound to involve a change in moral outlook.

> Summarize in a paragraph Lemmon's reason for saying this.

Lemmon offers one further example of a kind of dilemma, but he does this after what he describes as a 'brief digression'. This digression begins at ⬚n⬚↦ and continues to ⬚o⬚↦. We do not need to discuss what he says there. But even though digressions generally do not serve the main line of argument, they can be important, and you should think about this one before moving on.

> Do you agree with what Lemmon says between ⬚n⬚↦ and ⬚o⬚↦?

The ground for the final example is prepared at $\boxed{o}\mapsto$ and the example given at $\boxed{p}\mapsto$. Lemmon insists that in this kind of case, not only is there lack of knowledge of what is morally required, but the agent is in fact completely unprepared for working it out. The example given is the 'moral dilemma ... which faced Chamberlain in his negotiations with Hitler'. Whilst one gets some sense of what Lemmon intends, it is not easy to pin down. Chamberlain's dealings with Hitler were enormously complicated – and historical investigation of this period continues – and it is not at all obvious which particular actions actually figure as dilemmatic. Lemmon also says that Chamberlain 'ought to have realized that he was dealing with a kind of person for which his own moral outlook had not prepared him'. Historical accuracy apart, it is difficult to know what to make of this. What if Chamberlain didn't realize this? What effect would such non-realization have on his dilemma? The claim is that he ought to have realized, but everything Lemmon says suggests that Chamberlain simply couldn't have understood what kind of person Hitler was.

Leaving aside the specifics of the Chamberlain example, Lemmon (at $\boxed{q}\mapsto$) amplifies his idea that this most extreme kind of dilemma can require us to develop a new morality, one in which the agent remains 'true to himself'. His remarks about this are, by his own admission, speculative and less than transparent, but they are certainly thought-provoking.

> Can you think of an example that illustrates, better than Lemmon's, this most extreme kind of moral dilemma?

Introduction to Mill

John Stuart Mill was born in London in 1806 and died in Avignon in 1873. His Scottish father, James Mill, was a distinguished writer and civil servant who, with Jeremy Bentham, was deeply involved in the political reform movement of the 1830s. James Mill and Bentham arranged for John Mill to be carefully educated, without what they saw as distracting contact with companions of his own age, so as to carry on the work of this movement. In his *Autobiography*, John Mill described his education – which most would regard as extraordinarily intensive – as one suitable for any normal child. That said, he also records a period of extreme depression that he suffered as a young man, and many now regard that depression as the direct result of his lack of anything one would count as a childhood.

A central philosophical view of the reformist movement of James Mill and Bentham was known as 'utilitarianism', and John Mill made a major contribution to this doctrine as well as to politics, economics, women's rights, philosophy and logic. He was by any standards a prolific writer and had an enormous influence on social and political life in nineteenth-century Britain and on the European continent.

Utilitarianism was originally published over three issues of the monthly *Fraser's Magazine* in 1861, and then collected together as a book in 1863. It should be noted that Mill's aim in *Utilitarianism* was expounding and defending the doctrine of utilitarianism for the more general public rather than constructing arguments for more narrowly philosophical purposes. The extracts that follow come from Book II.

John Stuart Mill, *Utilitarianism* (extracts)

a⊢→ The creed which accepts as the foundation of morals, Utility, or the Greatest Happiness Principle, holds that actions are right in proportion as they tend to promote happiness, wrong as they tend to produce the reverse of happiness. By happiness is intended pleasure, and the absence of pain; by unhappiness, pain, and the privation of pleasure. To give a clear view of the moral standard set up by the theory, much more requires to be said; in particular, what things it includes in the ideas of pain and pleasure; and to what extent this is left an open question. But these supplementary explanations do not affect the

b⊢→ theory of life on which this theory of morality is grounded – namely, that pleasure, and freedom from pain, are the only things desirable as ends; and that all desirable things (which are as numerous in the utilitarian as in any other scheme) are desirable either for the pleasure inherent in themselves, or as means to the promotion of pleasure and the prevention of pain.

Now, such a theory of life excites in many minds, and among them in some of the most estimable in feeling and purpose, inveterate

c⊢→ dislike. To suppose that life has (as they express it) no higher end than pleasure – no better and nobler object of desire and pursuit – they designate as utterly mean and grovelling; as a doctrine worthy only of swine, to whom the followers of Epicurus were, at a very early period, contemptuously likened; and modern holders of the doctrine are occasionally made the subject of equally polite comparisons by its German, French, and English assailants.

d⊢→ When thus attacked, the Epicureans have always answered, that it is not they, but their accusers, who represent human nature in a degrading light; since the accusation supposes human beings to be capable of no pleasures except those of which swine are capable. If this supposition

were true, the charge could not be gainsaid, but would then be no
longer an imputation; for if the sources of pleasure were precisely the
same to human beings and to swine, the rule of life which is good
enough for the one would be good enough for the other. The comparison of the Epicurean life to that of beasts is felt as degrading, precisely
because a beast's pleasures do not satisfy a human being's conceptions
of happiness. Human beings have faculties more elevated than the
animal appetites, and when once made conscious of them, do not
regard anything as happiness which does not include their gratifica-
tion. I do not, indeed, consider the Epicureans to have been by any
means faultless in drawing out their scheme of consequences from the
utilitarian principle. To do this in any sufficient manner, many Stoic, as
well as Christian elements require to be included. But there is no
known Epicurean theory of life which does not assign to the pleasures
of the intellect, of the feelings and imagination, and of the moral
sentiments, a much higher value as pleasures than to those of mere
sensation. It must be admitted, however, that utilitarian writers in
general have placed the superiority of mental over bodily pleasures
chiefly in the greater permanency, safety, uncostliness, &c., of the
former – that is, in their circumstantial advantages rather than in
their intrinsic nature. And on all these points utilitarians have fully
proved their case; but they might have taken the other, and, as it may
be called, higher ground, with entire consistency. It is quite compatible
with the principle of utility to recognise the fact, that some *kinds* of
pleasure are more desirable and more valuable than others. It would
be absurd that while, in estimating all other things, quality is considered as well as quantity, the estimation of pleasures should be
supposed to depend on quantity alone.

If I am asked, what I mean by difference of quality in pleasures, or
what makes one pleasure more valuable than another, merely as a
pleasure, except its being greater in amount, there is but one possible
answer. Of two pleasures, if there be one to which all or almost all who
have experience of both give a decided preference, irrespective of any
feeling of moral obligation to prefer it, that is the more desirable
pleasure. If one of the two is, by those who are competently ac-
quainted with both, placed so far above the other that they prefer it,
even though knowing it to be attended with a greater amount of
discontent, and would not resign it for any quantity of the other
pleasure which their nature is capable of, we are justified in ascribing
to the preferred enjoyment a superiority in quality, so far outweighing
quantity as to render it, in comparison, of small account.

Now it is an unquestionable fact that those who are equally ac-
quainted with, and equally capable of appreciating and enjoying, both,

h→ do give a most marked preference to the manner of existence which employs their higher faculties. Few human creatures would consent to be changed into any of the lower animals, for a promise of the fullest allowance of a beast's pleasures; no intelligent human being would consent to be a fool, no instructed person would be an ignoramus, no person of feeling and conscience would be selfish and base, even though they should be persuaded that the fool, the dunce, or the rascal is better satisfied with his lot than they are with theirs. They would not resign what they possess more than he, for the most complete satisfaction of all the desires which they have in common with him. If they ever fancy they would, it is only in cases of unhappiness so extreme, that to escape from it they would exchange their lot for almost any

i→ other, however undesirable in their own eyes. A being of higher faculties requires more to make him happy, is capable probably of more acute suffering, and is certainly accessible to it at more points, than one of an inferior type; but in spite of these liabilities, he can never really wish to sink into what he feels to be a lower grade of existence. We may give what explanation we please of this unwillingness; we may attribute it to pride, a name which is given indiscriminately to some of the most and to some of the least estimable feelings of which mankind are capable; we may refer it to the love of liberty and personal independence, an appeal to which was with the Stoics one of the most effective means for the inculcation of it; to the love of power, or to the love of excitement, both of which do really enter into and contribute to it: but its most appropriate appellation is a sense of dignity, which all human beings possess in one form or other, and in some, though by no means in exact, proportion to their higher faculties, and which is so essential a part of the happiness of those in whom it is strong, that nothing which conflicts with it could be, otherwise than momentarily, an object of desire to them. Whoever supposes that this preference takes place at a sacrifice of happiness – that the superior being, in anything like equal circumstances, is not happier than the inferior – confounds the two very different ideas, of happiness, and content. It is indisputable that the being whose capacities of enjoyment are low, has the greatest chance of having them fully satisfied; and a highly-endowed being will always feel that any happiness which he can look for, as the world is constituted, is imperfect. But he can learn to bear its imperfections, if they are at all bearable; and they will not make him envy the being who is indeed unconscious of the imperfections, but only because he feels not at all the good which those imperfections qualify. It is better to be a human being dissatisfied than

j→ a pig satisfied; better to be Socrates dissatisfied than a fool satisfied. And if the fool, or the pig, is of a different opinion, it is because they only know their own side of the question. The other party to the comparison knows both sides. [. . .]

$\boxed{k}\mapsto$ If utility is the ultimate source of moral obligations, utility may be invoked to decide between them when their demands are incompatible. Though the application of the standard may be difficult, it is better than none at all: while in other systems, the moral laws all claiming independent authority, there is no common umpire entitled to interfere between them; their claims to precedence one over another rest on little better than sophistry, and unless determined, as they generally are, by the unacknowledged influence of considerations of utility, afford a free scope for the action of personal desires and partialities. We must remember that only in these cases of conflict between secondary principles is it requisite that first principles should be appealed to. There is no case of moral obligation in which some secondary principle is not involved; and if only one, there can seldom be any real doubt which one it is, in the mind of any person by whom the principle itself is recognised.

Commentary on Mill

In his *System of Logic*, Mill writes: 'There are not only first principles of Knowledge, but first principles of Conduct' (Book 6, Chapter 12, Section 7). Understanding what he means by this, and gaining some general idea of how he thinks first principles of conduct actually work, is our initial task. But along the way we shall see what effect this idea has on our understanding of moral dilemma.

At $\boxed{a}\mapsto$ Mill gives a straightforward and unqualified statement of the principle which he describes as the foundation of morals.

> Before we consider this principle in any detail, write out a paragraph or two saying what you think Mill is claiming at $\boxed{a}\mapsto$ and what problems you can foresee in it.

The 'Greatest Happiness Principle' was one that Bentham, James Mill and others used to great effect in their critiques of existing social legislation. However, Mill goes further than they did: he sees it as 'the first principle of Conduct' alluded to above. That is, he uses it to *define* moral rightness. In concrete terms, what Mill claims is that whenever we find ourselves in a situation that requires us to decide what to do morally, we either explicitly or implicitly appeal to the principle of utility to tell us. Notice that he doesn't say that he thinks it would be good if people appealed to the principle of utility; he says that the action *is* right in proportion as it promotes happiness.

This is a very strong claim, one which puts an enormous burden on the principle of utility – a burden much stronger than it would have to bear if we regarded the promotion of happiness as one principle amongst others, and not as the sole one defining the standard of rightness. In the five chapters of *Utilitarianism*, Mill goes some way towards supporting the principle, and it is well beyond our task here to assess his arguments in full. However, as we will focus on the consequences of Mill's view for our understanding of moral dilemma, it is important to look a little more deeply into the kind of arguments Mill offers in favour of the greatest happiness principle.

As you may have anticipated when you did the earlier exercise, a major source of trouble for Mill comes from the widespread notion that concern with happiness is something wholly separate from the issue of what is morally right. At [b]→, Mill anticipates how he will deal with this worry. He claims that the only ends of human life are pleasure and the avoidance of pain, so that anything else is bound ultimately to turn in some way on these ends. His reasoning seems to be this: since the only thing desirable in and of itself is the pursuit of pleasure (and the avoidance of pain), only this can count as an *ultimate* end. If I happen to want to climb mountains, collect stamps, become a philosopher or, in some appropriate circumstances, if I make my life's work the fight for human rights and justice, all of these activities will in the final analysis be things that I undertake in order to increase pleasure and reduce pain.

It is important here to note that Mill's interest is in what is ultimately *desirable*. It may well be that some individuals do not pursue happiness, but that in itself would not undermine his claim that happiness is the sole thing that is desirable – the sole thing that is worth pursuing.

No less important is the need to be clear *whose* happiness is at issue in any application of the greatest happiness principle. Mill is less explicit in this first paragraph than in other places, but there can be no doubt that the principle is meant to apply to everyone, and to everyone equally. Thus, when we make a moral decision, or one about some social or legal arrangement, Mill insists that the sole criterion of rightness is the aggregated sum of human happiness or misery that will result from our decisions. As utilitarians generally put it: everyone counts for one.

The idea that the happiness of everyone affected by any moral or social decision counts – and counts equally – certainly makes it easier to see some plausibility in the connection between happiness and morality. But, as Mill himself notes, many continue to have doubts.

Mill articulates the first of these worries at [c]→. Explain what he says in your own words.

The Epicureans (followers of the fourth-century BC philosopher, Epicurus) maintained that pleasure and the avoidance of pain were the only things worth pursuing. Because of this they came to have a reputation for living lives of self-indulgence and excess – the very word 'Epicurean' conjures up images of over-indulgence – and it is in this context that Mill sets about giving his first rebuttal. Mill follows the Epicureans in answering those who think the pursuit of pleasure 'mean and grovelling' and 'worthy only of swine'. (Note, by the way, that the Epicureans in fact led almost ascetic lives, having decided that what was most important was the avoidance of pain attendant on disappointment in the pursuit of pleasure.)

At ⌈d⌉↦, Mill summarizes the Epicurean answer. Do you agree with what he says there?

The point that Mill derives from his discussion is that pleasures differ. There are many kinds of pleasures that human beings tend to seek in consequence of their possessing abilities they do not share with lower animals. Once recognized, these differences are all that a utilitarian needs to ward off the charge of demeaning human life. However, Mill goes further. In the passage marked ⌈e⌉↦, he introduces the idea of kinds of pleasure, some of which are of a higher quality than others.

  The distinction between quantity and quality of pleasures marked a radical departure from the views of Bentham. Bentham had insisted that everything came down in the end to a calculation of the quantity of pleasure. He thought that when due account was made of the fact that, for example, some pleasures were more likely to lead to others, or to be less ephemeral, we could fully account for the fact that mental pleasures outweighed those of the body. Mill, however, insists that quantity alone is not enough. It could happen that there were two equal quantities of pleasure, but that one of them would 'win' by being of a higher quality. But how exactly does Mill think we can come to decide this? Moreover, is it consistent to make increase in pleasure the sole criterion of moral value and then also to insist that pleasures differ in value? These are perennial questions raised by Mill's remarks in *Utilitarianism*, and we should devote a little time to considering them before returning to the issue of moral dilemma.

  Mill offers his method of distinguishing pleasures at ⌈f⌉↦ and he follows this up with an assertion of what he calls an 'unquestionable fact' at ⌈g⌉↦.

Do you find what he says at ⌈g⌉↦ unquestionably true?

There are two things to watch out for here. On the one hand, some have questioned just that thing which is described as 'unquestionable'. And, on the other hand, it is important to see whether Mill's way of arguing for his claim is wholly appropriate.

  Do those who have experienced the pleasures of the mind – the pleasures of learning, culture and the like – as well as the pleasures of the body, always prefer the former? So far from being an unquestionable fact, this is actually more a minefield of example and counter-example, if for no other reason than that many so-called 'pleasures of the body' are far from simply that. Would Mill count sport, gardening or wood-working as higher or lower pleasures?

It is not at all difficult to find those who, finding a certain emptiness in the pursuit of bodily pleasures, prefer those of the mind. But it is not difficult to find those who have become bored or disillusioned with what they see as the pretensions of culture and learning, and who therefore have a very different preference ranking. Mill might insist that those who come to prefer bodily pleasures have in some way not properly experienced learning and culture. But this would be a kind of sleight of hand. For if every possible example or counter-example is dismissed in this way, your claim is more a logical than a factual one. You would in essence be taking the idea of 'experiencing equally' to imply your favoured preference ranking rather than allowing the facts to speak for themselves.

At $\boxed{\text{h}}\!\!\rightarrow$, Mill offers a consideration which he takes to clinch his original claim. Does it?

It is one thing to insist that, if you have experienced each of two different kinds of pleasure, you will prefer one to the other. It is another to claim that that shows that the two kinds of pleasure differ qualitatively rather than merely quantitatively. But it is a third to support either of these contentions with the obvious fact that few human beings would consent to be changed into any of the lower animals. With respect to this third point, someone might, for example, insist that only human beings can truly appreciate even bodily pleasures, so that the option of being changed into a lower animal is just irrelevant to the issue of which pleasure is of a higher quality. And Mill himself seems to waver on the second point. The passage at $\boxed{\text{i}}\!\!\rightarrow$ speaks of a person of higher faculties requiring 'more to make him happy', and it sounds here as if Mill is claiming that the 'higher' pleasures are simply more pleasurable rather than of a greater value.

At the end of this complex paragraph, Mill makes what has become one of the most cited claims in *Utilitarianism*. At $\boxed{\text{j}}\!\!\rightarrow$, he says: 'It is better to be a human being dissatisfied than a pig satisfied; better to be Socrates dissatisfied than a fool satisfied.' Whilst it is difficult to disagree with him, it is unclear how this supports his method for distinguishing certain pleasures as of a higher value. Neither of the options described can be tested by Mill's method: the pig can scarcely possess human satisfactions, but then neither can the human being experience the pig's. And surely whilst the fool could not be Socrates, Socrates could not be the fool either.

In spite of all the justifiable qualms one has about Mill's claims and arguments, it is not difficult to see what he was getting at. The 'first principle of Conduct' – the greatest happiness principle – seemed to him to promise an unambiguous, secular and profoundly fair criterion of social and individual decision-making. To the charge that pleasure was in some way a demeaning basis for morality, Mill set out to show that seeking pleasure lay behind all of our judgements of desirability, so that morality was no special case. And he added considerations meant to show that the pursuit of individual human happiness was worthy of respect, and that seeking greater aggregate happiness in a society was morally compelling.

Nor is utilitarianism only of historical interest. In the first half of the nineteenth century, when James Mill and Bentham weighed into the field of social reform with the principle of utility on their banner, it was to many an unacceptably radical doctrine. However, over time, the idea that utilitarian considerations must figure in our determinations of social policy has come now to seem obvious. Indeed, in some ways, utilitarian notions, at least in many Western countries, have come to be viewed as part of an orthodoxy.

With this background, we can return to the issue of moral dilemma. In the last paragraph of Mill's Book II (the paragraph beginning at $\boxed{k}\mapsto$), Mill repeats his claim that the principle of utility is the ultimate source of moral obligations, and he also claims that by playing that role the principle can be used to decide between 'incompatible' moral demands. As he sees it, most moral systems give us little or no real moral guidance in difficult situations; they offer 'no common umpire'. But, however difficult it might be in practice to apply it, the greatest happiness principle is just such an umpire.

As applied to the Platonic dilemma, the idea would be this: you weigh up the effects of returning the gun and also of not returning the gun, on the happiness of all those directly involved and on all those who might in any way be touched by your decision. This is of course no easy thing to do, but, in this case, it would seem likely that the balance would lie heavily on the side of not returning the gun. According to Mill, this result would make it morally right for you not to return the gun, and wrong to return it. Thus, we can truly say that you ought not to return the gun, and we can also declare it false that you ought to return it.

> If you accept what Mill has said here, what happens to the moral dilemma?

The answer to this last question is clear: the dilemma has simply disappeared. It is similar to the case of a practical dilemma in which you no longer desire one of the options.

> Go back to the Lemmon extract to the place marked $\boxed{j}\mapsto$. What would Lemmon think of Mill's idea of a moral 'umpire'?

Lemmon considered the possibility that appeal to utility might well help us decide what to do. But he insisted that this help was practical and not moral. For, as just noted, if utility settles the moral issue, then the dilemma turns out not to have been real. And yet there is no doubt at all that the principle of utility in Mill's eyes is a first principle of *morality*. Indeed, Lemmon admitted that his own treatment of utility as a mere practical, decision-making device is 'paradoxical'.

It has been a goal of many moral theorists – including many who have disagreed with Mill about utility – to find a first principle of morality. But in so far as they are counted successful, we can use the reasoning above to show that moral dilemmas, at least in principle, are not real. And this is disturbing because it contradicts what seems obvious, namely that moral dilemmas are only too real.

6

Identity

Introduction to the Problem

Is the room in which I woke up this morning the same as the one in which I went to bed last night? Since nothing strange seems to have happened, I certainly believe that it is. But how can I be sure, and indeed what exactly does it mean to say that the room last night is one and the same as the room this morning? Those who are rash might think these are easy questions to deal with. The first they will dismiss as a typically exaggerated sceptical worry that philosophers can never seem to shake off, and they will say in answer to the second: the room at the two different times is the same, first, because it is in the same place and, second, because all of the objects in it are unchanged. But of course even a moment's thought shows both of these latter claims to be false. The room and the planet Earth on which it is located are in constant, extremely complicated, motion through space. Also, in myriad ways, the objects in the room will be affected, and therefore changed, by evaporation, ageing, the circulation of the molecules of air, etc., not to mention the more ordinary comings and going of a room's contents. Yet, through all these changes of place and content, it is not absurd to think that I did indeed wake up in the same room; it is just not easy to say what constitutes the relevant notion of 'the same' nor how to apply it to this case. And difficulties here suggest that the merely sceptical worries are not after all exaggerated.

The notion of being 'one and the same as' is important in philosophy (and especially in logic), but it is in no sense a merely technical notion. Often called *identity*, the idea of being 'one and the same as' is strictly speaking a relation, though, among relations, it is somewhat special. However, before I can say what this specialness comes to, some clarification of the notions of *same* and *different* is in order.

Think about the particular object that you are currently holding, viz. your copy of *Reading Philosophy*. Is this one and the same as the particular object that I am holding? It is certainly a work with the same title, it has the same authors, same number of pages, etc. Undoubtedly, your copy of *Reading Philosophy* is very similar to mine. Still, in that they are *different copies*, there is a perfectly good sense in which these books are not one and the same.

It is the notion of 'one and the same' in respect of our copies of *Reading Philosophy* that will figure in this chapter. However similar two books, or two rooms, happen to be, the very fact that there are *two* of them shows that, in the relevant sense, they are non-identical. When – and only when – particulars (be they books, rooms or other things) are one and the same in this sense, we shall say that they are strictly *identical*.

Let us now return to the fact that identity is a relation, and indeed a relation of a very special kind. In typical cases, relations hold between two or more things. As a first example, consider the relation 'is the sister of'. This relation is true of certain pairs of persons. In particular, it is true of those pairs in which the first member of the pair is a woman, the second is either a man or a woman, and the two are siblings. Thus, the pair containing first Emily Brontë and second Charlotte Brontë count as being in the 'is the sister of' relation, as do the pair containing Emily Brontë and Branwell Brontë. But the pair containing first Branwell and second Emily do not count, since Branwell, being male, cannot in fact be anyone's sister.

> Is it true to say that Emily Brontë is the sister of Emily Brontë?

The above question shouldn't have been difficult to answer: the relation 'is the sister of' is never true of the pair containing a person and herself. But not all relations are like this. Consider the relation: 'is as tall as'. One can certainly be as tall as oneself. Indeed, this relation seems bound to be true of those pairs whose first and second members are the same person. (Note that 'same' here is naturally understood as strict identity.) However, though 'is as tall as' is conveniently true of persons and themselves, it can also be true of different persons. If Bill is six-feet tall and Ben is six-feet tall then it is true that Bill is as tall as Ben.

An interestingly special feature of strict identity comes from the fact that it is like 'is as tall as' in that it can be true of pairs containing a person and herself, but it is unlike 'is the sister of' in that it can never be true of pairs like Emily and Charlotte or Bill and Ben. Identity turns out to be a relation true only of an object and itself.

Some find this puzzling. How can there be a relation between pairs of things that is only ever true of a thing and itself? And even if you do not find this odd – after all, you might say, what else would you expect of the identity relation than that it holds of pairs in which the first member is the *same* as the second – you might still wonder about its usefulness. Here are two examples which will give you some idea of just how common, and therefore useful, appeals to strict identity can be.

Imagine that Jones is accused of theft: a television was stolen during a burglary and the police have found a television of the same make and model in Jones's house. What would establish Jones's innocence is some evidence that the television in his house is not the television that was stolen. That is, Jones's innocence depends on the television in his house not being strictly identical to the one that was stolen. This can be made to sound puzzling. It seems that, if the police manage to make out their case, what they will have shown comes pretty much to this: a certain television is one and the same as itself. And this sounds trivially true. But of course it is less paradoxical to say that what the police have shown is that the two ways we have of singling out an object do in fact home in on the same object. The hard work for the prosecution came in establishing that the relevant identity is true.

Here is a second example. Some people – typically Italians – think of a certain city as 'Firenze'. Others – notably those in English-and French-speaking countries – think of that city as 'Florence'. Mostly, this difference causes no confusion, but it is all too easy to imagine someone who is not aware of these differing linguistic practices and for whom the claim that *Firenze is Florence* would be a useful piece of information. In this claim, the word 'is' marks strict identity. What is being said is (at least) that a certain city is one and the same as itself, but the use of the two different names in the identity claim somehow makes it informative. (It is no easy matter to explain how this claim, and the one that the police formulate in their case against Jones, can be informative, but that is another problem, one for philosophers of language.)

With this brief discussion of identity as background, let us now return to the question that opened the discussion, namely: how do I know – and what does it mean to say – that the room I slept in last night is the same as the one in which I woke up this morning? Our discussion of strict identity gives us a clue as to how we might construe the 'what it means to say' part of the question. When I wonder whether the room last night is the same as the one this morning, I am not simply wondering whether there is a similarity between the two. I am more likely wondering whether there is in fact more than one room. That is, I am wondering whether the room last night is really and strictly identical to the one in which I found myself this morning. Putting it slightly differently, the questions that exercise me are about the *re-identification* of the room over a stretch of time. If it turns out that there are *two* such rooms, then this will come as a surprise and will require further explanation; but if, as is more likely, there is only *one* such room, then all will be as I had thought. (This way of describing the possible outcomes show why strict identity is also known as *numerical* identity.)

Notice that the problem of re-identification is tied to, though often more difficult than, the problem of initial identification. Imagine that just before I went to sleep – and with the aim of eventual re-identification in mind – I considered the problem of saying what sort of thing a room is. A room seems to be a certain restricted area of space, one containing certain objects and reachable in certain ways from other locations. These considerations figure in what is called 'individuation', and it would seem that we need to have some idea about this before we can do any identifying or re-identifying. However, lying awake and thinking about the room, there is something that I could say truly and in advance of a definitive spelling out of individuation conditions. I could say that the room I was then in was one and the same as itself. This claim of numerical identity is bound to be true because, whatever it takes to individuate the room, in so far as I am truly thinking about the room, I am entitled to say that it is self-identical. After all, as we saw above, everything is strictly identical to itself.

Similarly, when I wake up the next morning in a room, I can say of the room I am in that it is one and the same as itself. The entitlement that I have to say this of the room in the morning is just as strong as it was for the room in the evening. However, what about the claim that the room in the evening is one and the same as the room in the morning? This, as was suggested above, is a surprisingly difficult question. Unlike the straightforward claim of self-identity, I cannot simply rely on the fact that things are identical to them-selves. Given that there was a time interval during which I was not keeping track – I was asleep – I cannot just assume that there is in fact only one room.

The case of the room is typical of our dealings with the world. We are constantly encountering and re-encountering things and taking for granted their continuing identity. But we do this even though, when challenged, we would have trouble justifying it, or even saying what it means for things such as rooms to have continuing identity. However, provided with a clear notion of strict identity, we can at least explain what we are doing when we re-identify something: to say that the room we wake up in is the same as the one we went to sleep in the night before is to say that there only ever was one room in question. But in saying this we make it more, rather than less, difficult to justify the re-identification. For, as noted, rooms change over time in all sorts of ways, and it is far from clear what grounds our assurance that there is really only one room in question.

The re-identification of rooms is an interesting example, and it raises certain general issues about re-identification which are more problematic than those in connection with ordinary, medium-sized, solid objects like tables. But, though genuinely puzzling, these cases of re-identification are all too easy to dismiss as mere philosopher's puzzles. However, such a dismissal is not so easy in the range of cases we are about to consider. For when it is a matter of recognizing whether, for example, a friend is one and the same *person* from one time to another, genuine puzzles become serious problems.

Our social and moral dealings with one another are built on often unexamined assumptions about personal identification and re-identification. Moreover, the problems of *personal identity* (as we will now call the issue of re-identification in respect of persons) infect not only our judgements about others; they threaten the ideas we have about our own continuing identity. The question of whether I am this morning one and the same person as the one who went to sleep last night is certainly of more concern to me than the question of whether the room is the same, or whether the colleague I am speaking to today is really one and the same person as the one I met last week.

Introduction to Locke

John Locke (1632–1704) was an English philosopher whose work had enormous influence on eighteenth-century Enlightenment thought, and which continues to form a central part of the philosophical curriculum. Moreover, while Locke's *An Essay Concerning Human Understanding* (1690) deals primarily with the nature of substance, knowledge and language, his work in political philosophy has also been of the first importance both theoretically and practically. Locke was by no means a spectator on the political events of his day; he was directly involved in the so-called Glorious Revolution of 1689 which saw William and Mary invited to be monarchs of England. In fact, dipping into a biography of Locke, you would come away surprised that any one person managed to fit so much into one lifetime.

The extracts below come from Locke's *Essay* Book II, Chapter XXVII, and present Locke's celebrated, and often criticized, discussion of personal identity. In it, he sketches a way of thinking about our continued identity as persons which was, for its time, bold in at least two ways: it was subtly critical of the religious tradition which, if it raised the question at all, treated our continuing identity as something deeply metaphysical; and it put in place a conception of persons which aimed to make our continued identity something accessible to each of us. (In the more recent literature, it is the second of these aspects which has been most prominent, and has given rise to no less bold 'neo-Lockean' views of personal identity.)

John Locke, *An Essay Concerning Human Understanding* (extracts)

a⟶   §1   Another occasion the mind often takes of comparing is the very being of things, when, considering anything as existing at any determined time and place, we compare it with itself existing at another time, and thereon form the *ideas* of *identity* and *diversity*. When we see any thing to be in any place in any instant of time, we are sure (be it what it will) that it is that very thing, and not another, which at that same time exists in another place, how like and undistinguishable soever it may be in all other respects; and in this consists *identity*, when the *ideas* it is attributed to vary not at all from what they were that moment wherein we consider their former existence, and to which we compare the present. For we never finding, nor conceiving it possible, that two things of the same kind should exist in the same place at the same time, we rightly conclude, that whatever exists any where at any time, excludes all of the same kind, and is there itself alone. When therefore we demand whether any thing be the same or no, it refers always to something that existed such a time in such a place, which it was certain at that instant, was the same with itself, and no other; from whence it follows, that one thing cannot have two beginnings of existence, nor two things one beginning: it being impossible for two things of the same kind to be or exist in the same instant in the very same place, or one and the same thing in different places. That therefore that had one beginning is the same thing; and that which had a different beginning in time and place from that, is not the same, but diverse. That which has made the difficulty about this relation has been the little care and attention used in having precise notions of the things to which it is attributed.

§2   We have the *ideas* but of three sorts of substances: (1) God. (2) Finite intelligences. (3) Bodies. First, God is without beginning, eternal, unalterable, and every where; and therefore concerning his identity, there can be no doubt. Secondly, Finite spirits having had each its determinate time and place of beginning to exist, the relation to that time and place will always determine to each of them its identity, as long as it exists.

Thirdly, the same will hold of every particle of matter to which, no addition or subtraction of matter being made, it is the same. For though these three sorts of substances, as we term them, do not exclude one another out of the same place, yet we cannot conceive but that they must necessarily each of them exclude any of the same kind out of the same place; or else the notions and names of identity and diversity would be in vain, and there could be no such distinctions of substances, or any thing else one from another. For example: could two bodies be in the same place at the same time, then those two parcels of matter must be one and the same, take them great or little; nay, all bodies must be one and the same. For by the same reason that two particles of matter may be in one place, all bodies may be in one place: which, when it can be supposed, takes away the distinction of identity and diversity of one and more, and renders it ridiculous. But it being a contradiction, that two or more should be one, identity and diversity are relations and ways of comparing well-founded, and of use to the understanding. All other things being but modes or relations ultimately terminated in substances, the identity and diversity of each particular existence of them too will be by the same way determined; only as to things whose existence is in succession, such as are the actions of finite beings, v.g. *motion* and *thought*, both which consist in a continued train of succession, concerning their diversity, there can be no question: because each perishing the moment it begins, they cannot exist in different times, or in different places, as permanent beings can at different times exist in distant places; and therefore no motion or thought, considered as at different times, can be the same, each part thereof having a different beginning of existence.

§3   From what has been said, it is easy to discover what is so much enquired after, the *principium individuationis*; and that, it is plain, is existence itself, which determines a being of any sort to a particular time and place, incommunicable to two beings of the same kind. This, though it seems easier to conceive in simple substances or modes, yet when reflected on, is not more difficult in compound ones, if care be taken to what it is applied: v.g. let us suppose an atom, i.e. a continued body under one immutable superficies, existing in a determined time and place; it is evident that, considered in any instant of its existence, it is in that instant the same with itself. For being at that instant what it is, and nothing else, it is the same, and so must continue as long as its existence is continued; for so long it will be the same, and no other. In like manner, if two or more atoms be joined together into the same mass, every one of those atoms will be the same, by the foregoing rule; and whilst they exist united together, the mass, consisting of the same atoms, must be the same mass, or the same body, let the parts be ever so differently jumbled; but if one of these atoms be taken away, or one new one added, it is no longer the same mass, or the same body. In the state of living creatures, their identity depends not on a mass of the same particles, but on something else. For in them the variation of great parcels of matter alters not the identity; an oak growing from a plant to a great tree, and then lopped, is still the same oak; and a colt grown up to a horse, sometimes fat, sometimes lean, is all the while the same horse, though in both these cases, there may be a manifest change of the parts, so that truly they are not either of them the same masses of matter, though they be truly one of them the same oak, and the other the same horse. The reason whereof is, that in these two cases of a mass of matter and a living body, *identity* is not applied to the same thing.

§4   We must therefore consider wherein an oak differs from a mass of matter; and that seems to me to be in this: that the one is only the cohesion of particles of matter any how united; the other such a disposition of them as constitutes the parts of an oak, and such an organization of those parts as is fit to receive and distribute nourishment, so as to continue and frame the wood, bark, and leaves, etc., of an oak, in which consists the vegetable life. That being then one plant which has such an organization of parts in one coherent body, partaking of one common life, it continues to be the same plant as long as it partakes of the same life, though that life be communicated to new particles of matter vitally united to the living plant, in a like continued organization conformable to that sort of plants. For this organization, being at any one instant in any one collection of *matter*, is in that particular concrete distinguished from all other and is that individual life; which existing constantly from that moment both forwards and backwards, in the same continuity of insensibly succeeding parts united to the living body of the plant, it has that identity, which makes the same plant and all the parts of it parts of the same plant during all the time that they exist united in that continued organization, which is fit to convey that common life to all the parts so united.

§5   The case is not so much different in *brutes* but that any one may hence see what makes an animal and continues it the same. Something we have like this in machines, and may serve to illustrate it. For example, what is a watch? It is plain it is nothing but a fit organization or construction of parts to a certain end, which, when a sufficient force is added to it, it is capable to attain. If we would suppose this machine one continued body, all whose organized parts were repaired, increased, or diminished by a constant addition or separation of insensible parts, with one common life, we should have some thing very much like the body of an animal, with this difference: that in an animal the fitness of the organization and the motion wherein life consists begin together, the motion coming from within; but in machines, the force coming sensibly from without, is often away when the organ is in order and well fitted to receive it.

§6   This also shows wherein the identity of the same *man* consists: viz. in nothing but a participation of the same continued life, by constantly fleeting particles of matter, in succession vitally united to the same organized body. He that shall place the identity of man in any thing else but, like that of other animals, in one fitly organized body, taken in any one instant and from thence continued under one organ-ization of life in several successively fleeting particles of matter united to it, will find it hard to make an *embryo*, one of years, mad and sober, the same man, by any supposition that will not make it possible for *Seth, Ismael, Socrates, Pilate, St. Austin,* and *Caesar Borgia,* to be the same man. For if the *identity* of soul alone makes the same man, and there be nothing in the nature of matter why the same individual spirit may not be united to different bodies, it will be possible that those men living in distant ages, and of different tempers, may have been the same man: which way of speaking must be, from a very strange use of the word *man,* applied to an *idea* out of which body and shape are excluded. And that way of speaking would agree yet worse with the notions of those philosophers who allow of transmigration, and are of opinion that the souls of men may, for their miscarriages, be detruded into the bodies of beasts, as fit habitations, with organs suited to the satisfaction of their brutal inclinations. But yet I think, nobody, could he be sure that the soul of *Heliogabalus* were in one of his hogs, would yet say that hog were a *man* or *Heliogabalus.*

§7   It is not therefore unity of substance that comprehends all sorts of *identity* or will determine it in every case; but to conceive and judge of it aright, we must consider what *idea* the word it is applied to stands for: it being one thing to be the same *substance,* another the same *man,* and a third the same *person,* if *person, man,* and *substance* are three names standing for three different *ideas*; for such as is the *idea* belonging to that name, such must be the *identity*; which, if it had been a little more carefully attended to, would possibly have prevented a great deal of that confusion which often occurs about this matter, with no small seeming difficulties, especially concerning *personal identity,* which therefore we shall, in the next place, a little consider. [...]

§9   This being premised, to find wherein *personal identity* consists, we must consider what *person* stands for; which, I think, is a thinking intelligent being, that has reason and reflection, and can consider itself as itself, the same thinking thing in different times and places; which it does only by that consciousness which is inseparable from thinking, and, as it seems to me, essential to it: it being impossible for any one to perceive, without perceiving that he does perceive. When we see, hear, smell, taste, feel, meditate, or will any thing, we know that we do so. Thus it is always as to our present sensations and perceptions, and by this every one is to himself that which he calls *self*: it not being considered in this case whether the same *self* be continued in the same or divers substances. For since consciousness always accompanies thinking, and it is that which makes every one to be what he calls *self*, and thereby distinguishes himself from all other thinking things: in this alone consists *personal identity*, i.e. the sameness of a rational being. And as far as this consciousness can be extended backwards to any past action or thought, so far reaches the identity of that *person:* it is the same *self* now it was then, and it is by the same *self* with this present one that now reflects on it, that that action was done. [...]

§15   And thus we may be able, without any difficulty, to conceive the same person at the resurrection, though in a body not exactly in make or parts the same which he had here, the same consciousness going along with the soul that inhabits it. But yet the soul alone, in the change of bodies, would scarce to any one, but to him that makes the soul the *man*, be enough to make the same *man*. For should the soul of a prince, carrying with it the consciousness of the prince's past life, enter and inform the body of a cobbler as soon as deserted by his own soul, every one sees he would be the same person with the prince, accountable only for the prince's actions; but who would say it was the same man? The body too goes to the making the man, and would, I guess, to everybody determine the man in this case, wherein the soul, with all its princely thoughts about it, would not make another man: but he would be the same cobbler to every one besides himself. I know that in the ordinary way of speaking, the same person and the same man stand for one and the same thing. And indeed, every one will always have a liberty to speak as he pleases, and to apply what articulate sounds to what *ideas* he thinks fit, and change them as often as he pleases. But yet when we will enquire what makes the same *spirit, man,* or *person*, we must fix the *ideas* of *spirit, man,* or *person* in our minds; and having resolved with ourselves what we mean by them, it will not be hard to determine in either of them, or the like, when it is the *same*, and when not.

§16   But though the same immaterial substance or soul does not alone, wherever it be, and in whatsoever state, make the same man: yet it is plain, consciousness, as far as ever it can be extended, should it be to ages past, unites existences and actions, very remote in time, into the same person, as well as it does the existences and actions of the immediately preceding moment, so that whatever has the consciousness of present and past actions is the same person to whom they both belong. Had I the same consciousness that I saw the ark and *Noah's* flood as that I saw an overflowing of the *Thames* last winter, or as that I write now, I could no more doubt that I who write this now, that saw the Thames overflowed last winter, and that viewed the flood at the general deluge, was the same *self*, place that *self* in what substance you please, than that I who write this am the same *myself* now, whilst I write (whether I consist of all the same substance, material or immaterial, or no) that I was yesterday. For as to this point of being the same *self*, it matters not whether this present *self* be made up of the same or other substances, I being as much concerned and as justly accountable for any action that was done a thousand years since, appropriated to me now by this self-consciousness, as I am for what I did the last moment.

§17   Self is that conscious thinking thing, whatever substance made up of (whether spiritual or material, simple or compounded, it matters not), which is sensible, or conscious of pleasure and pain, capable of happiness or misery, and so is concerned for itself, as far as that consciousness extends. Thus every one finds that, whilst comprehended under that consciousness, the little finger is as much a part of himself as what is most so. Upon separation of this little finger, should this consciousness go along with the little finger, and leave the rest of the body, it is evident the little finger would be the person, the same person; and self then would have nothing to do with the rest of the body. As in this case it is the consciousness that goes along with the substance, when one part is separate from another, which makes the same person, and constitutes this inseparable self; so it is in reference to substances remote in time. That with which the consciousness of this present thinking thing can join itself, makes the same person, and is one self with it, and with nothing else; and so attributes to itself, and owns all the actions of that thing as its own, as far as that consciousness reaches, and no farther; as every one who reflects will perceive.

§18   In this *personal identity*, is founded all the right and justice of reward and punishment: happiness and misery being that for which every one is concerned for *himself*, not mattering what becomes of any substance not joined to or affected with that consciousness. For, as it is evident in the instance I gave but now, if the consciousness went along with the little finger when it was cut off, that would be the same *self* which was concerned for the whole body yesterday, as making part of itself, whose actions then it cannot but admit as its own now. Though, if the same body should still live, and immediately from the separation of the little finger, have its own peculiar consciousness, whereof the little finger knew nothing, it would not at all be concerned for it as a part of *itself*, or could own any of its actions, or have any of them imputed to him.

§19   This may show us wherein personal identity consists: not in the identity of substance but, as I have said, in the identity of *consciousness*, wherein, if *Socrates* and the present mayor of *Queenborough* agree, they are the same person; if the same *Socrates* waking and sleeping do not partake of the same *consciousness*, *Socrates* waking and sleeping is not the same person. And to punish *Socrates* waking for what sleeping *Socrates* thought, and waking *Socrates* was never conscious of, would be no more of right than to punish one twin for what his brother-twin did, whereof he knew nothing, because their outsides were so like that they could not be distinguished; for such twins have been seen.

§20   But yet possibly it will still be objected, suppose I wholly lose the memory of some parts of my life beyond a possibility of retrieving them, so that perhaps I shall never be conscious of them again: yet am I not the same person that did those actions, had those thoughts that I once was conscious of, though I have now forgot them? To which I answer, that we must here take notice what the word *I* is applied to, which, in this case, is the man only. And the same man being presumed to be the same person, *I* is easily here supposed to stand also for the same person. But if it be possible for the same man to have distinct incommunicable consciousness at different times, it is past doubt the same man would at different times make different persons; which, we see, is the sense of mankind in the solemnest declaration of their opinions, human laws not punishing the *mad man* for the *sober man's* actions, nor the *sober man* for what the *mad man* did, thereby making them two persons: which is somewhat explained by our way of speaking in *English* when we say such an one *is not himself*, or is *beside himself*; in which phrases it is insinuated, as if those who now, or at least first used them, thought that *self* was changed, the *self*-same person was no longer in that man.

§21   But yet it is hard to conceive that *Socrates*, the same individual *man*, should be two persons. To help us a little in this, we must consider what is meant by *Socrates*, or the same individual *man*.

First, it must be either the same individual, immaterial, thinking substance; in short, the same numerical soul, and nothing else.

Secondly, or the same animal, without any regard to an immaterial soul.

Thirdly, or the same immaterial spirit united to the same animal.

Now take which of these suppositions you please, it is impossible to make personal identity to consist in any thing but consciousness, or reach any farther than that does.

For by the first of them, it must be allowed possible that a man born of different women, and in distant times, may be the same man. A way of speaking, which, whoever admits, must allow it possible for the same man to be two distinct persons, as any two that have lived in different ages, without the knowledge of one another's thoughts.

By the second and third, *Socrates*, in this life and after it, cannot be the same man any way, but by the same consciousness; and so making *human identity* to consist in the same thing wherein we place *personal identity*, there will be no difficulty to allow the same man to be the same person. But then they who place *human identity* in consciousness only, and not in something else, must consider how they will make the infant *Socrates* the same man with *Socrates* after the resurrection. But whatsoever to some men makes a *man*, and consequently the same individual man, wherein perhaps few are agreed, personal identity can by us be placed in nothing but consciousness (which is that alone which makes what we call *self*) without involving us in great absurdities.

§22   But is not a man drunk and sober the same person? Why else is he punished for the fact he commits when drunk, though he be never afterwards conscious of it? Just as much the same person as a man that walks and does other things in his sleep is the same person and is answerable for any mischief he shall do in it. Human laws punish both, with a justice suitable to their way of knowledge; because, in these cases, they cannot distinguish certainly what is real, what counterfeit; and so the ignorance in drunkenness or sleep is not admitted as a plea. For, though punishment be annexed to personality, and personality to consciousness, and the drunkard perhaps be not conscious of what he did, yet human judicatures justly punish him, because the fact is proved against him, but want of consciousness cannot be proved for him. But in the Great Day, wherein the secrets of all hearts shall be laid open, it may be reasonable to think no one shall be made to answer for what he knows nothing of, but shall receive his doom, his conscience accusing or excusing him.

§23   Nothing but consciousness can unite remote existences into the same person: the identity of substance will not do it; for whatever substance there is, however framed, without consciousness there is no person; and a carcass may be a person, as well as any sort of substance be so, without consciousness.

Could we suppose two distinct incommunicable consciousnesses acting the same body, the one constantly by day, the other by night; and, on the other side, the same consciousness, acting by intervals, two distinct bodies: I ask in the first case, whether the *day-* and the *night-man* would not be two as distinct persons as *Socrates* and *Plato*? And whether, in the second case, there would not be one person in two distinct bodies, as much as one man is the same in two distinct clothings? Nor is it at all material to say, that this same, and this distinct *consciousness*, in the cases above mentioned, is owing to the same and distinct immaterial substances, bringing it with them to those bodies; which, whether true or no, alters not the case, since it is evident the *personal identity* would equally be determined by the consciousness, whether that consciousness were annexed to some individual immaterial substance or no. For, granting that the thinking substance in man must be necessarily supposed immaterial, it is evident that immaterial thinking thing may sometimes part with its past consciousness and be restored to it again, as appears in the forgetfulness men often have of their past actions; and the mind many times recovers the memory of a past consciousness, which it had lost for twenty years together. Make these intervals of memory and forgetfulness to take their turns regularly by day and night, and you have two persons with the same immaterial spirit, as much as in the former instance two persons with the same body. So that *self* is not determined by identity or diversity of substance, which it cannot be sure of, but only by identity of consciousness.

Commentary on Locke

The extracts from Locke's *Essay* require close attention, not least because the prose, as well as the punctuation, of seventeenth-century writers is quite different from contemporary styles. What you should aim for in the first instance is some sense of how Locke sees the problem developing, and what he offers as a solution, so you should take the time necessary to complete the task in the box below.

> The Locke extract contains sixteen of the twenty-six sections in Book II, Chapter XXVII of Locke's *Essay*. (Each section is indicated by '§', followed by a number.) Write one or two sentences summarizing the main point of each of these sections. If you do this carefully, you will end up with a compact summary in your own words of Locke's arguments and assumptions.

If you have done this exercise diligently, you will probably have realized that, whilst Locke's central theme is pretty clear, the details of his discussion can often seem confusing and even incoherent. (This latter feature of Locke's *Essay* is not all that surprising: it was written over a period of twenty years during which Locke was engaged in delicate, and even dangerous, political dealings, and during which he spent a number of years in exile in The Netherlands.)

In §1, Locke introduces the topic that will occupy him in succeeding sections. He describes it this way (at $\boxed{a}\!\!\rightarrow$): 'the very being of things, when, considering anything as existing at any determined time and place, we compare it with itself existing at another time, and thereon form the *ideas* of *identity* and *diversity*.' Clearly, what is announced here is the notion of identity (and non-identity or, in Locke's term, 'diversity') through time – the very notion that figured in the introduction to this chapter as re-identification. Locke goes on to make a point about the role that origin plays in helping us to understand whether we have identity or diversity.

His view of this is given at $\boxed{b}\!\!\rightarrow$. Do you think that it would have helped to solve the earlier problem of re-identification in respect of rooms? To what does Locke apply the notions of identity and diversity?

In §1, Locke speaks of the identity and diversity of 'things of the same kind', but, in §2, he is more specific. He insists that we have ideas of three different kinds of substance to which the notion of identity can apply. The first substance is God, and, aside from the observation that identity cannot be in doubt in respect of God, no more is said of this. The second kind Locke calls 'finite intelligences', by which he means immaterial souls, a notion which we encountered in Descartes in chapter 2. Of these, Locke says that they have their identity and diversity determined no differently from the 'things of the same kind' that he spoke of in §1. That is, the identity of a finite intelligence comes from its origin in 'time and place'. (Nothing more is said of souls or immaterial substance until later on.) It is about the third kind of substance – bodies – that Locke has the most to say, and we will come to this shortly.

First, consider Locke's claim that the above kinds of substance 'do not exclude one another out of the same place.' What this means is that there is nothing to prevent, say, a finite intelligence occupying the same time and place as a material body. However, he also says that no two substances of the same kind can occupy the same time and place: 'could two bodies be in the same place at the same time, then those two parcels of matter must be one and the same . . .' This last brings to the foreground an idea that was already present in §1, namely that, when it comes to deciding the identity (or diversity) of things, the *kind* that those things belong to is crucial. A finite intelligence and a body – being two different kinds of thing – could occupy the same time and place without being identical, whilst this could not happen with two finite intelligences or two bodies. (We will come back to this idea.)

Returning to the idea of identity and diversity of bodies (or material substances), Locke notes that this is something easier to think about in the simplest case, e.g. the continued existence and identity of a single atom or particle of matter. His discussion of this is at $\boxed{d}\!\!\rightarrow$. (Remember that Locke and his contemporaries would have had no idea of atoms as themselves complex.)

Before considering the more complex cases that are introduced at the end of §3, have a look at the passage marked $\boxed{c}\!\!\rightarrow$. Here Locke claims that there is a kind of existence where there is no persisting thing to re-identify.

Say what kind of example he has in mind at $\boxed{c}\!\!\rightarrow$ and also whether you think he is right about this.

When Locke says that identity depends only upon the coming into, and continuing, existence of a thing he is not saying all that much. Whilst no doubt true, it falls short of helping us tell whether an object is or was not identical to one encountered earlier; it would, for example, be of very little help in answering the earlier question about the room, since we would need first to be sure about there being only a single room in order to decide the issue of its origin. But Locke's insistence on the uniqueness of origin as a necessary feature of identity allows him to take a further important step. For he argues from the fact that a single continuing thing cannot have two separate origins, and that two different things cannot have the same origin, that we must attend very carefully to the *kind* of thing that is in question.

A single atom that comes into being at a time is the easiest case: so long as it continues, its identity consists in precisely its being just this one item (see $\boxed{d}\!\!\rightarrow$ again). If a material body consists of twenty atoms, then its identity depends on these twenty staying together; if one of them strays, the original body, according to Locke, no longer counts as persisting. However, with living things, whilst the origin counts in just the same way, the principle of continued identity is not like that of simple material bodies. An oak tree can lose a branch and still remain that very tree. As he spells it out in §4 and §5, what matters for the continued existence of an oak tree or a horse is having a continued organization and life, and not merely being composed of the same atoms.

In §6, Locke carries this thought over to the case of man or human being. The biological kind to which we belong has, like the oak tree and the horse, identity conditions which depend on the organization and participation in a common life. Locke's argument for this consists in trying to show that the opposite view would lead to absurdity (see here the passage at the place marked $\boxed{e}\!\!\rightarrow$).

Spell out Locke's argument and say why you find it convincing or unconvincing.

What he shows is that if you try to leave out material substance and ground the idea of human identity on the identity of immaterial substances, i.e. souls, then you will have no defence against someone who insists that Socrates and Pilate are one and the same man. In effect, what Locke shows here is that the notion of soul, a notion he does not otherwise challenge, is simply of no real use when we think about what grounds strict identity over time in respect of human beings.

In §7, Locke summarizes his position and introduces a distinction between *man* and *person*. Man is the biological kind – think here of *human being* or *homo sapiens* – which therefore has the same general identity conditions as *oak* and *horse*; whereas the *person* is distinguished from *man* as a 'different idea'. This constitutes the beginning of Locke's contribution to the debate on personal identity. Whereas it might seem natural to think of the *man* Socrates and the *person* Socrates as requiring the same conditions of identity, Locke claims that these two notions come apart. And it is at this point that Locke develops his account of persons and their identity.

In what is the most famous passage on this subject in the *Essay*, Locke says (you will find this at [f]→) that a person 'is a thinking intelligent being, that has reason and reflection, and can consider itself as itself, the same thinking thing in different times and places'. Following on from this, Locke suggests that his account shows us how to distinguish the identity of persons from the identity of biological body and from the idea of a special kind of substance called 'soul'.

In §15, he considers a case intended to make his point, the case of the prince and the cobbler. You are to imagine that the consciousness of the prince has entered the body of the cobbler (whose own consciousness has departed). Is the resultant the same *man* as the prince or the cobbler? Is the resultant the same *person* as the prince or the cobbler?

> What are Locke's answers to these questions? Are they the same as those you would give? Can you defend your own answers if they differ from Locke's?

The moral of his resolution of these questions is drawn out in §16 and §17. In §16, he notes that it is not the transfer of soul alone that determines our answers, but rather the consciousness that one might think accompanies this transfer. And this leads him to imagine the possibility that a single person could have both witnessed the floods in Noah's time and the flooding of the Thames in Locke's own. In §17, he develops the idea that it is not the material parts of human beings that determine their identity as persons, but only their conscious states. Your finger is part of you, but if you lose it, this will normally make no difference at all to your identity as a person. However, if your consciousness were in some way to be contained in your little finger, then Locke says: 'it is evident the little finger would be the person.'

> This last conclusion is, for all Locke says, far from evident. What do you think? In answering this question, go back over the paragraphs from the *Essay* and pick out those parts which say what Locke means by

'consciousness'. Having done that, ask yourself what you think Locke would mean by 'same consciousness'? Everything in Locke's account hinges on this notion.

It is clear enough what Locke was aiming at in his account of personal identity: he thought that there is some kind of mental occurrence which each of us can recognize and which brings with it the idea of our continued existence as persons. It is as if he thought each of us could just tell when it is me by somehow introspecting. And I suspect that many people have some such idea, even if they don't articulate it. However, the notion of consciousness which Locke uses to characterize these inner goings on is very problematic. Locke's discussion suggests that both memory and what we might now call 'self-consciousness' are crucial to self-identification, but neither, taken in isolation, is as helpful as Locke seems to have thought. In order for my memories to help in self-identification, they must be *my* memories. But then doesn't this mean that memory presupposes personal identity rather than being a ground for it? Similarly, it seems right to say that, if I can introspect and catch myself thinking, then this presupposes that I have some idea of what myself – my personhood – is even before I introspect. Finally, what about cases in which I suffer memory lapses, or loss of self-consciousness? Do I thereby lose myself? Locke raises these difficult questions, later in §§ 20 and 22 where he responds to an imaginary objector.

In §§18 and 19, one finds Locke, not so much addressing these questions about the criteria of identity, but rather filling in his reasons for giving the notion of person such a prominent place. Locke suggests that we use the notion of person when we are thinking of two things: the kind of concern that we each have for ourselves, and the kind of concern that we have for the actions of others. The first shows that the notion of personal identity is a necessary part of the concern we have for our own welfare, at a given time and in the future. The second is about the accountability that we attribute to other people's actions and characters. With this as background, Locke's discussion returns to certain issues of identity. He asks whether genuine and complete loss of memory constitutes grounds for denying a continuity of personal identity (§20). And he follows this up with a question about real, even if temporary, loss of self-consciousness, as in the case of someone who does something when very drunk (§22).

Do you think that the answers he provides in these two cases are sensible? In what way, if any, do they illuminate his account of personal identity?

In §§21 and 23, Locke further defends the idea that consciousness (in some sense) is what lies behind our judgements of personal identity, but many feel that his discussion here takes him beyond the limit of what is plausible.

Do you think that our ordinary notion of a person would genuinely allow us to think that one and the same human being could be two different persons, one existing by day and the other by night?

Introduction to Williams

Background information about Bernard Williams was given in chapter 4. In the article below, he presents an argument which could be used to cast doubt on certain of the things that Locke says about the role of consciousness in personal identity. The centrepiece of the article is a sustained discussion of a fascinating example, one which bears a close initial resemblance to an example that Locke mentions.

In order to get the most out of your reading of Williams, you might begin with a little experiment on yourself.

Do you think it possible that you could exchange bodies with someone else? (Here you are to understand 'possible' not as 'practical' or as 'physically possible', but only as something that is coherent or possible in thought.)

If you think it is possible, describe the circumstances that would have to be fulfilled for this to happen. And if you think it impossible, say why.

As you will recall, Locke seems to find no difficulty in imagining such an exchange, as witness his example of the prince and the cobbler. Go back to the Locke reading and see how he would answer the above questions. In contrast to Locke, Williams does not regard the possibility of body exchange as straightforward, though he nowhere suggests that it is simply incoherent. What he does is to make us think harder about the kinds of thing that Locke and others tend to say about personal identity – things that may in the end have been said in too much haste.

Bernard Williams, 'The Self and the Future'

Suppose that there were some process to which two persons, A and B, could be subjected as a result of which they might be said – question-beggingly – to have *exchanged bodies*. That is to say – less question-beggingly – there is a certain human body which is such that when previously we were confronted with it, we were confronted with person A, certain utterances coming from it were expressive of memories of the past experiences of A, certain movements of it partly constituted the actions of A and were taken as expressive of the character of A, and so forth; but now, after the process is completed, utterances coming from this body are expressive of what seem to be just those memories which previously we identified as memories of the past experiences of B, its movements partly constitute actions expressive of the character of B, and so forth; and conversely with the other body.

There are certain important philosophical limitations on how such imaginary cases are to be constructed, and how they are to be taken when constructed in various ways. I shall mention two principal limitations, not in order to pursue them further here, but precisely in order to get them out of the way.

There are certain limitations, particularly with regard to character and mannerisms, to our ability to imagine such cases even in the most restricted sense of our being disposed to take the later performances of that body which was previously A's as expressive of B's character; if the previous A and B were extremely unlike one another both physically and psychologically, and if, say, in addition, they were of different sex, there might be grave difficulties in reading B's dispositions in any possible performances of A's body. Let us forget this, and for the present purpose just take A and B as being sufficiently alike (however alike that has to be) for the difficulty not to arise; after the experiment, persons familiar with A and B are just *overwhelmingly struck* by the B-ish character of the doings associated with what was previously A's body, and conversely. Thus the feat of imagining an exchange of bodies is supposed possible in the most restricted sense. But now there is a further limitation which has to be overcome if the feat is to be not merely possible in the most restricted sense but also is to have an outcome which, on serious reflection, we are prepared to describe as A and B having changed bodies – that is, an outcome where, confronted with what was previously A's body, we are prepared seriously to say that we are now confronted with B.

It would seem a necessary condition of so doing that the utterances coming from that body be taken as genuinely expressive of memories of B's past. But memory is a causal notion; and as we actually use it, it seems a necessary condition of x's present knowledge of x's earlier experiences constituting memory of those experiences that the causal chain linking the experiences and the knowledge should not run outside x's body. Hence if utterances coming from a given body are to be taken as expressive of memories of the experiences of B, there should be some suitable causal link between the appropriate state of that body and the original happening of those experiences to B. One radical way of securing that condition in the imagined exchange case is to suppose, with Shoemaker,[1] that the brains of A and of B are transposed. We may not need so radical a condition. Thus suppose it were possible to extract information from a man's brain and store it in a device while his brain was repaired, or even renewed, the information then being replaced: it would seem exaggerated to insist that the resultant man could not possibly have the memories he had before the operation. With regard to our knowledge of our own past, we draw distinctions between merely recalling, being reminded, and learning again, and those distinctions correspond (roughly) to distinctions between no new input, partial new input, and total new input with regard to the information in question; and it seems clear that the information-parking case just imagined would not count as new input in the sense necessary and sufficient for 'learning again'. Hence we can imagine the case we are concerned with in terms of information extracted into such devices from A's and B's brains and replaced in the other brain; this is the sort of model which, I think not unfairly for the present argument, I shall have in mind.

We imagine the following. The process considered above exists; two persons can enter some machine, let us say, and emerge changed in the appropriate ways. If A and B are the persons who enter, let us call the persons who emerge the *A-body-person* and *the B-body-person*: the A-body-person is that person (whoever it is) with whom I am confronted when, after the experiment, I am confronted with that body which previously was A's body – that is to say, that person who would naturally be taken for A by someone who just saw this person, was familiar with A's appearance before the experiment, and did not know about the happening of the experiment. A non-question-begging description of the experiment will leave it open which (if either) of the persons A and B the A-body-person is; the description of the experiment as 'persons changing bodies' of course implies that the A-body-person is actually B.

We take two persons A and B who are going to have the process carried out on them. (We can suppose, rather hazily, that they are willing for this to happen; to investigate at all closely at this stage why they might be willing or unwilling, what they would fear, and so forth, would anticipate some later issues.) We further announce that one of the two resultant persons, the A-body-person and the B-body-person, is going after the experiment to be given $100,000, while the other is going to be tortured. We then ask each of A and B to choose which

[1]   *Self-knowledge and Self-identity* (Ithaca, NY, 1963), pp. 23 et seq.

treatment should be dealt out to which of the persons who will emerge from the experiment, the choice to be made (if it can be) on selfish grounds.

Suppose that A chooses that the B-body-person should get the pleasant treatment and the A-body-person the unpleasant treatment; and B chooses conversely (this might indicate that they thought that 'changing bodies' was indeed a good description of the outcome). The experimenter cannot act in accordance with both these sets of preferences, those expressed by A and those expressed by B. Hence there is one clear sense in which A and B cannot both get what they want: namely, that if the experimenter, before the experiment, announces to A and B that he intends to carry out the alternative (for example), of treating the B-body-person unpleasantly and the A-body-person pleasantly, then A can say rightly, 'That's not the outcome I chose to happen', and B can say rightly, 'That's just the outcome I chose to happen'. So, evidently, A and B before the experiment can each come to know either that the outcome he chose will be that which will happen, or that the one he chose will not happen, and in that sense they can get or fail to get what they wanted. But is it also true that when the experimenter proceeds after the experiment to act in accordance with one of the preferences and not the other, then one of A and B will have got what he wanted, and the other not?

[a]→ There seems very good ground for saying so. For suppose the experimenter, having elicited A's and B's preference, says nothing to A and B about what he will do; conducts the experiment; and then, for example, gives the unpleasant treatment to the B-body-person and the pleasant treatment to the A-body-person. Then the B-body-person will not only complain of the unpleasant treatment as such, but will complain (since he has A's memories) that that was not the outcome he chose, since he chose that the B-body-person should be well treated; and since A made his choice in selfish spirit, he may add that he precisely chose in that way because he did not want the unpleasant things to happen to him. The A-body-person meanwhile will express satisfaction both at the receipt of the $100,000 and also at the fact that the experimenter has chosen to act in the way that he, B, so wisely chose. These facts make a strong case for saying that the experimenter has brought it about that B did in the outcome get what he wanted and A did not. It is therefore a strong case for saying that the B-body-person really is A, and the A-body-person really is B; and therefore for saying that the process of the experiment really is that of changing bodies. For the same reasons it would seem that A and B in our example really did choose wisely, and that it was A's bad luck that the choice he correctly made was not carried out, B's good luck that

the choice he correctly made was carried out. This seems to show that to care about what happens to me in the future is not necessarily to care about what happens to *this* body (the one I now have); and this in turn might be taken to show that in some sense of Descartes's obscure phrase, I and my body are 'really distinct' (though, of course, nothing in these considerations could support the idea that I could exist without a body at all).

These suggestions seem to be reinforced if we consider the cases where A and B make other choices with regard to the experiment. Suppose that A chooses that the A-body-person should get the money, and the B-body-person get the pain, and B chooses conversely. Here again there can be no outcome which matches the expressed preferences of both of them: they cannot both get what they want. The experimenter announces, before the experiment, that the A-body-person will in fact get the money, and the B-body-person will get the pain. So A at this stage gets what he wants (the announced outcome matches his expressed preference). After the experiment, the distribution is carried out as announced. Both the A-body-person and the B-body-person will have to agree that what is happening is in accordance with the preference that A originally expressed. The B-body-person will naturally express this acknowledgement (since he has A's memories) by saying that this is the distribution he chose; he will recall, among other things, the experimenter announcing this outcome, his approving it as what he chose, and so forth. However, he (the B-body-person) certainly does not like what is now happening to him, and would much prefer to be receiving what the A-body-person is receiving – namely, $100,000. The A-body-person will on the other hand recall choosing an outcome other than this one, but will reckon it good luck that the experimenter did not do what he recalls choosing. It looks, then, as though the A-body-person has got what he wanted, but not what he chose, while the B-body-person has got what he chose, but not what he wanted. So once more it looks as though they are, respectively, B and A; and that in this case the original choices of both A and B were unwise.

Suppose, lastly, that in the original choice A takes the line of the first case and B of the second: that is, A chooses that the B-body-person should get the money and the A-body-person the pain, and B chooses exactly the same thing. In this case, the experimenter would seem to be in the happy situation of giving both persons what they want – or at least, like God, what they have chosen. In this case, the B-body-person likes what he is receiving, recalls choosing it, and congratulates himself on the wisdom of (as he puts it) his choice; while the A-body-person does not like what he is receiving, recalls choosing it, and is forced to acknowledge that (as he puts it) his choice was unwise. So once more we seem to get results to support the suggestions drawn from the first case.

Let us now consider the question, not of A and B choosing certain outcomes to take place after the experiment, but of their willingness to engage in the experiment at all. If they were initially inclined to accept the description of the experiment as 'changing bodies' then one thing that would interest them would be the character of the other person's body. In this respect also what would happen after the experiment would seem to suggest that 'changing bodies' was a good description of the experiment. If A and B agreed to the experiment, being each not displeased with the appearance, physique, and so forth of the other person's body; after the experiment the B-body-person might well be found saying such things as: 'When I agreed to this experiment, I thought that B's face was quite attractive, but now I look at it in the mirror, I am not so sure'; or the A-body-person might say 'When I agreed to this experiment I did not know that A had a wooden leg; but now, after it is over, I find that I have this wooden leg, and I want the experiment reversed.' It is possible that he might say further that he finds the leg very uncomfortable, and that the B-body-person should say, for instance, that he recalls that he found it very uncomfortable at first, but one gets used to it: but perhaps one would need to know more than at least I do about the physiology of habituation to artificial limbs to know whether the A-body-person would find the leg uncomfortable: that body, after all, has had the leg on it for some time. But apart from this sort of detail, the general line of the outcome regarded from this point of view seems to confirm our previous conclusions about the experiment.

Now let us suppose that when the experiment is proposed (in non-question-begging terms) A and B think rather of their psychological advantages and disadvantages. A's thoughts turn primarily to certain sorts of anxiety to which he is very prone, while B is concerned with the frightful memories he has of past experiences which still distress him. They each hope that the experiment will in some way result in their being able to get away from these things. They may even have been impressed by philosophical arguments to the effect that bodily continuity is at least a necessary condition of personal identity: A, for example, reasons that, granted the experiment comes off, then the person who is bodily continuous with him will not have this anxiety, and while the other person will no doubt have some anxiety – perhaps in some sense his anxiety – at least that person will not be he. The experiment is performed and the experimenter (to whom A and B previously revealed privately their several difficulties and hopes) asks the A-body-person whether he has got rid of his anxiety. This person presumably replies that he does not know what the man is talking about; he never had such anxiety, but he did have some very disagreeable memories, and recalls engaging in the experiment to get rid of them, and is disappointed to discover that he still has them. The B-body-person will react in a similar way to questions about his painful memories, pointing out that he still has his anxiety. These results seem to confirm still further the description of the experiment as 'changing bodies'. And all the results suggest that the only rational thing to do, confronted with such an experiment, would be to identify oneself with one's memories, and so forth, and not with one's body. The philosophical arguments designed to show that bodily continuity was at least a necessary condition of personal identity would seem to be just mistaken.

b⟶   Let us now consider something apparently different. Someone in whose power I am tells me that I am going to be tortured tomorrow. I am frightened, and look forward to tomorrow in great apprehension. He adds that when the time comes, I shall not remember being told that this was going to happen to me, since shortly before the torture something else will be done to me which will make me forget the announcement. This certainly will not cheer me up, since I know perfectly well that I can forget things, and that there is such a thing as indeed being tortured unexpectedly because I had forgotten or been made to forget a prediction of the torture: that will still be a torture which, so long as I do know about the prediction, I look forward to in fear. He then adds that my forgetting the announcement will be only part of a larger process: when the moment of torture comes, I shall not remember any of the things I am now in a position to remember. This does not cheer me up, either, since I can readily conceive of being involved in an accident, for instance, as a result of which I wake up in a completely amnesiac state and also in great pain; that could certainly happen to me, I should not like it to happen to me, nor to know that it was going to happen to me. He now further adds that at the moment of torture I shall not only not remember the things I am now in a position to remember, but will have a different set of impressions of my past, quite different from the memories I now have. I do not think that this would cheer me up, either. For I can at least conceive the possibility, if not the concrete reality, of going completely mad, and thinking perhaps that I am George IV or somebody; and being told that something like that was going to happen to me would have no tendency to reduce the terror of being told authoritatively that I was going to be tortured, but would merely compound the horror. Nor do I see why I should be put into any better frame of mind by the person in charge adding lastly that the impressions of my past with which I shall be equipped on the eve of torture will exactly fit the past of another person now living, and that indeed I shall acquire these impressions by (for instance) information now in his brain being copied into mine. Fear, surely, would still be the proper reaction: and not because one did not know what was going to happen, but because in one vital respect at least one did know what was going to happen – torture, which one can indeed expect to happen to oneself, and to be preceded by certain mental derangements as well.

 If this is right, the whole question seems now to be totally mysterious. For what we have just been through is of course merely one side, differently represented, of the transaction which we considered before, and it represents it as a perfectly hateful prospect, while the previous considerations represented it as something one should rationally, perhaps even cheerfully, choose out of the options there presented. It is differently presented, of course, and in two notable respects; but when we look at these two differences of presentation, can we really convince ourselves that the second presentation is wrong or misleading, thus leaving the road open to the first version which at the time seemed so convincing? Surely not.

The first difference is that in the second version the torture is throughout represented as going to happen to me: 'you', the man in charge persistently says. Thus he is not very neutral. But should he have been neutral? Or, to put it another way, does his use of the second person have a merely emotional and rhetorical effect on me, making me afraid when further reflection would have shown that I had no reason to be? It is certainly not obviously so. The problem just is that through every step of his predictions I seem to be able to follow him successfully. And if I reflect on whether what he has said gives me grounds for fearing that I shall be tortured, I could consider that behind my fears lies some principle such as this: that my undergoing physical pain in the future is not excluded by any psychological state I may be in at the time, with the platitudinous exception of those psychological states which in themselves exclude experiencing pain, notably (if it is a psychological state) unconsciousness. In particular, what impressions I have about the past will not have any effect on whether I undergo the pain or not. This principle seems sound enough.

It is an important fact that not everything I would, as things are, regard as an evil would be something that I should rationally fear as an evil if it were predicted that it would happen to me in the future and also predicted that I should undergo significant psychological changes in the meantime. For the fact that I regard that happening, things being as they are, as an evil can be dependent on factors of belief or character which might themselves be modified by the psychological changes in question. Thus if I am appallingly subject to acrophobia, and am told that I shall find myself on top of a steep mountain in the near future, I shall to that extent be afraid; but if I am told that I shall be psychologically changed in the meantime in such a way as to rid me of my acrophobia (and as with the other prediction, I believe it), then I have no reason to be afraid of the predicted happening, or at least not the same reason. Again, I might look forward to meeting a certain person again with either alarm or excitement because of my memories of our past relations. In some part, these memories operate in connexion with my emotion, not only on the present time, but projectively forward: for it is to a meeting itself affected by the presence of those memories that I look forward. If I am convinced that when the time comes I shall not have those memories, then I shall not have just the same reasons as before for looking forward to that meeting with the one emotion or the other. (Spiritualism, incidentally, appears to involve the belief that I have just the same reasons for a given attitude toward encountering people again after I am dead, as I did before: with the one modification that I can be sure it will all be very nice.)

Physical pain, however, the example which for simplicity (and not for any obsessional reason) I have taken, is absolutely minimally dependent on character or belief. No amount of change in my character or my beliefs would seem to affect substantially the nastiness of tortures applied to me; correspondingly, no degree of predicted change in my character and beliefs can unseat the fear of torture which, together with those changes, is predicted for me.

I am not at all suggesting that the *only* basis, or indeed the only rational basis, for fear in the face of these various predictions is how things will be relative to my psychological state in the eventual outcome. I am merely pointing out that this is one component; it is not the only one. For certainly one will fear and otherwise reject the changes themselves, or in very many cases one would. Thus one of the old paradoxes of hedonistic utilitarianism; if one had assurances that undergoing certain operations and being attached to a machine would provide one for the rest of one's existence with an unending sequence of delicious and varied experiences, one might very well reject the option, and react with fear if someone proposed to apply it compulsorily; and that fear and horror would seem appropriate reactions in the second case may help to discredit the interpretation (if anyone has the nerve to propose it) that one's reason for rejecting the option voluntarily would be a consciousness of duties to others which one in one's hedonic state would leave undone. The prospect of contented madness or vegetableness is found by many (not perhaps by all) appalling in ways which are obviously not a function of how things would then be for them, for things would then be for them not appalling. In the case we are at present discussing, these sorts of considerations seem merely to make it clearer that the predictions of the man in charge provide a double ground of horror: at the prospect of torture, and at the prospect of the change in character and in impressions of the past that will precede it. And certainly, to repeat what has already been said, the prospect of the second certainly seems to provide no ground for rejecting or not fearing the prospect of the first.

I said that there were two notable differences between the second presentation of our situation and the first. The first difference, which we have just said something about, was that the man predicted the torture for *me*, a psychologically very changed 'me'. We have yet to find a reason for saying that he should not have done this, or that I really should be unable to follow him if he does; I seem to be able to follow him only too well. The second difference is that in this presentation he does not mention the other man, except in the somewhat incidental role of being the provenance of the impressions of the past I end up with. He does not mention him at all as someone who will end up with impressions of the past derived from me (and, incidentally, with $100,000 as well – a consideration which, in the frame of mind appropriate to this version, will merely make me jealous).

But why *should* he mention this man and what is going to happen to him? My selfish concern is to be told what is going to happen to me, and now I know: torture, preceded by changes of character, brain operations, changes in impressions of the past. The knowledge that one other person, or none, or many will be similarly mistreated may affect me in other ways, of sympathy, greater horror at the power of this tyrant, and so forth; but surely it cannot affect my expectations of torture? But – someone will say – this is to leave out exactly the feature which, as the first presentation of the case showed, makes all the difference: for it is to leave out the person who, as the first presentation showed, will be you. It is to leave out not merely a feature which should fundamentally affect your fears, it is to leave out the very person for whom you are fearful. So of course, the objector will say, this makes all the difference.

But can it? Consider the following series of cases. In each case we are to suppose that after what is described, A is, as before, to be tortured; we are also to suppose the person A is informed beforehand that just these things followed by the torture will happen to him:

(i)   A is subjected to an operation which produces total amnesia;
(ii) amnesia is produced in A, and other interference leads to certain changes in his character;

(iii)   changes in his character are produced, and at the same time
        certain illusory 'memory' beliefs are induced in him: these are
        of a quite fictitious kind and do not fit the life of any actual
        person;

(iv)   the same as (iii), except that both the character traits and the
        'memory' impressions are designed to be appropriate to another
        actual person, B;

 (v)   the same as (iv), except that both the result is produced by
        putting the information into A from the brain of B, by a method
        which leaves B the same as he was before;

(vi)   the same happens to A as in (v), but B is not left the same, since a
        similar operation is conducted in the reverse direction.

I take it that no-one is going to dispute that A has reasons, and fairly
straightforward reasons, for fear of pain when the prospect is that of
situation (i); there seems no conceivable reason why this should not
extend to situation (ii), and the situation (iii) can surely introduce no
difference of principle – it just seems a situation which for more than
one reason we should have grounds for fearing, as suggested above.
Situation (iv) at least introduces the person B, who was the focus of the
objection we are now discussing. But it does not seem to introduce him
in any way which makes a material difference; if I can expect pain
through a transformation which involves new 'memory'-impressions,
it would seem a purely external fact, relative to that, that the
'memory'-impressions had a model. Nor, in (iv), do we satisfy a causal
condition which I mentioned at the beginning for the 'memories'
actually being memories; though notice that if the job were done
thoroughly, I might well be able to elicit from the A-body-person the
kinds of remarks about his previous expectations of the experiment –
remarks appropriate to the original B – which so impressed us in the
first version of the story. I shall have a similar assurance of this being
so in situation (v), where, moreover, a plausible application of the
causal condition is available.

But two things are to be noticed about this situation. First, if we
concentrate on A and the A-body-person, we do not seem to have
added anything which from the point of view of his fears makes any
material difference; just as, in the move from (iii) to (iv), it made no
relevant difference that the new 'memory'-impressions which precede
the pain had, as it happened, a model, so in the move from (iv) to (v)
all we have added is that they have a model which is also their cause:
and it is still difficult to see why that, to him looking forward, could
possibly make the difference between expecting pain and not
expecting pain. To illustrate that point from the case of character: if A

is capable of expecting pain, he is capable of expecting pain preceded by a change in his dispositions – and to that expectation it can make no difference, whether that change in his dispositions is modelled on, or indeed indirectly caused by, the dispositions of some other person. If his fears can, as it were, reach through the change, it seems a mere trimming how the change is in fact induced. The second point about situation (v) is that if the crucial question for A's fears with regard to what befalls the A-body-person is whether the A-body-person is or is not the person B,[2] then that condition has not yet been satisfied in situation (v): for there we have an undisputed B in addition to the A-body-person, and certainly those two are not the same person.

But in situation (vi), we seemed to think, that is finally what he is. But if A's original fears could reach through the expected changes in (v), as they did in (iv) and (iii), then certainly they can reach through in (vi). Indeed, from the point of view of A's expectations and fears, there is less difference between (vi) and (v) than there is between (v) and (iv) or between (iv) and (iii). In those transitions, there were at least differences – though we could not see that they were really relevant differences – in the content or cause of what happened to him; in the present case there is absolutely no difference at all in what happens to him, the only difference being in what happens to someone else. If he can fear pain when (v) is predicted, why should he cease to when (vi) is?

I can see only one way of relevantly laying great weight on the transition from (v) to (vi); and this involves a considerable difficulty. This is to deny that, as I put it, the transition from (v) to (vi) involves merely the addition of something happening to somebody else; what rather it does, it will be said, is to involve the reintroduction of A himself, as the B-body-person; since he has reappeared in this form, it is for this person, and not for the unfortunate A-body-person, that A will have his expectations. This is to reassert, in effect, the viewpoint emphasised in our first presentation of the experiment. But this surely has the consequence that A should not have fears for the A-body-person who appeared in situation (v). For by the present argument, the A-body-person in (vi) is not A; the B-body-person is. But the A-body-person in (v) is, in character history, everything, exactly the same as the A-body-person in (vi); so if the latter is not A, then neither is the former. (It is this point, no doubt, that encourages one to speak of the difference that goes with (vi) as being, on the present view, the reintroduction of A.) But no one else in (v) has any better claim to be A. So in

---

[2]   This of course does not have to be the crucial question, but it seems one fair way of taking up the present objection.

(v), it seems, A just does not exist. This would certainly explain why A should have no fears for the state of things in (v) though he might well have fears for the path to it. But it rather looked earlier as though he could well have fears for the state of things in (v). Let us grant, however, that that was an illusion, and that A really does not exist in (v); then does he exist in (iv), (iii), (ii), or (i)? It seems very difficult to deny it for (i) and (ii); are we perhaps to draw the line between (iii) and (iv)?

$f\rightarrow$ Here someone will say: you must not insist on drawing a line – borderline cases are borderline cases, and you must not push our concepts beyond their limits. But this well-known piece of advice, sensible as it is in many cases, seems in the present case to involve an extraordinary difficulty. It may intellectually comfort observers of A's situation; but what is A supposed to make of it? To be told that a future situation is a borderline one for its being myself that is hurt, that it is conceptually undecidable whether it will be me or not, is something which, it seems, I can do nothing with; because, in particular, it seems to have no comprehensible representation in my expectations and the emotions that go with them.

If I expect that a certain situation, S, will come about in the future, there is of course a wide range of emotions and concerns, directed on S, which I may experience now in relation to my expectation. Unless I am exceptionally egoistic, it is not a condition on my being concerned in relation to this expectation, that I myself will be involved in S – where my being 'involved' in S means that I figure in S as someone doing something at that time or having something done to me, or, again, that S will have consequences affecting me at that or some subsequent time. There are some emotions, however, which I will feel only if I will be involved in S, and fear is an obvious example.

Now the description of S under which it figures in my expectations will necessarily be, in various ways, indeterminate; and one way in which it may be indeterminate is that it leaves open whether I shall be involved in S or not. Thus I may have good reason to expect that one of us five is going to get hurt, but no reason to expect it to be me rather than one of the others. My present emotions will be correspondingly affected by this indeterminacy. Thus, sticking to the egoistic concern involved in fear, I shall presumably be somewhat more cheerful than if I knew it was going to be me, somewhat less cheerful than if I had been left out altogether. Fear will be mixed with, and qualified by, apprehension; and so forth. These emotions revolve around the thought of the eventual determination of the indeterminacy; moments of straight fear focus on its really turning out to be me, of hope on its turning out not to be me. All the emotions are related to the coming about of what

I expect: and what I expect in such a case just cannot come about save by coming about in one of the ways or another.

There are other ways in which indeterminate expectations can be related to fear. Thus I may expect (perhaps neurotically) that something nasty is going to happen to me, indeed expect that when it happens it will take some determinate form, but have no range, or no closed range, of candidates for the determinate form to rehearse in my present thought. Different from this would be the fear of something radically indeterminate – the fear (one might say) of a nameless horror. If somebody had such a fear, one could even say that he had, in a sense, a perfectly determinate expectation: if what he expects indeed comes about, there will be nothing more determinate to be said about it after the event than was said in the expectation. Both these cases of course are cases of *fear* because one thing that is fixed amid the indeterminacy is the belief that it is me to whom the things will happen.

Central to the expectation of S is the thought of what it will be like when it happens – thought which may be indeterminate, range over alternatives, and so forth. When S involves me, there can be the possibility of a special form of such thought: the thought of how it will be for me, the imaginative projection of myself as participant in S.[3] I do not have to think about S in this way, when it involves me; but I may be able to. (It might be suggested that this possibility was even mirrored in the language, in the distinction between 'expecting to be hurt' and 'expecting that I shall be hurt'; but I am very doubtful about this point, which is in any case of no importance.)

Suppose now that there is an S with regard to which it is for conceptual reasons undecidable whether it involves me or not, as is proposed for the experimental situation by the line we are discussing. It is important that the expectation of S is not *indeterminate* in any of the ways we have just been considering. It is not like the nameless horror, since the fixed point of that case was that it was going to happen to the subject, and that made his state unequivocally fear. Nor is it like the expectation of the man who expects one of the five to be hurt; his fear was indeed equivocal, but its focus, and that of the expectation, was that when S came about, it would certainly come about in one way or the other. In the present case, fear (of the torture, that is to say, not of the initial experiment) seems neither appropriate, nor inappropriate, nor appropriately equivocal. Relatedly, the subject has an incurable difficulty about how he may think about S. If he

[3] For a more detailed treatment of issues related to this, see 'Imagination and the Self', pp. 38 et seq. [Note that this latter essay is found in Williams's *Problems of the Self* (Cambridge University Press, 1973), the collection from which 'The Self and the Future' was taken.]

engages in projective imaginative thinking (about how it will be for him), he implicitly answers the necessarily unanswerable question; if he thinks that he cannot engage in such thinking, it looks very much as if he also answers it, though in the opposite direction. Perhaps he must just refrain from such thinking; but is he just refraining from it, if it is incurably undecidable whether he can or cannot engage in it?

It may be said that all that these considerations can show is that fear, at any rate, does not get its proper footing in this case; but that there could be some other, more ambivalent, form of concern which would indeed be appropriate to this particular expectation, the expectation of the conceptually undecidable situation. There are, perhaps, analogous feelings that actually occur in actual situations. Thus material objects do occasionally undergo puzzling transformations which leave a conceptual shadow over their identity. Suppose I were sentimentally attached to an object to which this sort of thing then happened; it might be that I could neither feel about it quite as I did originally, nor be totally indifferent to it, but would have some other and rather ambivalent feeling towards it. Similarly, it may be said, toward the prospective sufferer of pain, my identity relations with whom are conceptually shadowed, I can feel neither as I would if he were certainly me, nor as I would if he were certainly not, but rather some such ambivalent concern.

But this analogy does little to remove the most baffling aspect of the present case – an aspect which has already turned up in what was said about the subject's difficulty in thinking either projectively or non-projectively about the situation. For to regard the prospective pain-sufferer *just* like the transmogrified object of sentiment, and to conceive of my ambivalent distress about his future pain as just like ambivalent distress about some future damage to such an object, is of course to leave him and me clearly distinct from one another, and thus to displace the conceptual shadow from its proper place. I have to get nearer to him than that. But is there any nearer that I can get to him without expecting his pain? If there is, the analogy has not shown us it. We can certainly not get nearer by expecting, as it were, ambivalent pain; there is no place at all for that. There seems to be an obstinate bafflement to mirroring in my expectations a situation in which it is conceptually undecidable whether I occur.

The bafflement seems, moreover, to turn to plain absurdity if we move from conceptual undecidability to its close friend and neighbour, conventionalist decision. This comes out if we consider another description, overtly conventionalist, of the series of cases which occasioned the present discussion. This description would reject a point I relied on in an earlier argument – namely, that if we deny that the A-body-person in (vi) is A (because the B-body-person is), then we must deny that the A-body-person in (v) is A, since they are exactly similar. 'No', it may be said, 'this is just to assume that we say the same in different sorts of situation. No doubt when we have the very good candidate for being A – namely, the B-body-person – we call him A; but this does not mean that we should not call the A-body-person A in that other situation when we have no better candidate around. Different situations call for different descriptions.' This line of talk is the sort of thing indeed appropriate to lawyers deciding the ownership of some property which has undergone some bewildering set of transformations; they just have to decide, and in each situation, let us suppose, it has got to go to somebody, on as reasonable grounds as the facts and the law admit. But as a line to deal with a person's fears or expectations about his own future, it seems to have no sense at all. If A's fears can extend to what will happen to the A-body-person in (v), I do not see how they can be rationally diverted from the fate of the exactly similar person in (vi) by his being told that someone would have a reason in the latter situation which he would not have in the former for deciding to call another person A.

[j] →   Thus, to sum up, it looks as though there are two presentations of the imagined experiment and the choice associated with it, each of which carries conviction, and which lead to contrary conclusions. The idea, moreover, that the situation after the experiment is conceptually undecidable in the relevant respect seems not to assist, but rather to increase, the puzzlement; while the idea (so often appealed to in these matters) that it is conventionally decidable is even worse. Following from all that, I am not in the least clear which option it would be wise to take if one were presented with them before the experiment. I find that rather disturbing.

[k] →   Whatever the puzzlement, there is one feature of the arguments which have led to it which is worth picking out, since it runs counter to something which is, I think, often rather vaguely supposed. It is often recognised that there are 'first-personal' and 'third-personal' aspects of questions about persons, and that there are difficulties about the relations between them. It is also recognised that 'mentalistic' considerations (as we may vaguely call them) and considerations of bodily continuity are involved in questions of personal identity (which is not to say that there are mentalistic and bodily criteria of personal identity). It is tempting to think that the two distinctions run in parallel: roughly, that a first-person approach concentrates attention on mentalistic considerations, while a third-personal approach emphasises considerations of bodily continuity. The present discussion is an illustration of exactly the opposite. The first argument, which led to the 'mentalistic' conclusion that A and B would change bodies and that each person should

identify himself with the destination of his memories and character, was an argument entirely conducted in third-personal terms. The second argument, which suggested the bodily continuity identification, concerned itself with the first-personal issue of what A could expect. That this is so seems to me (though I will not discuss it further here) of some significance.

1→ I will end by suggesting one rather shaky way in which one might approach a resolution of the problem, using only the limited materials already available.

The apparently decisive arguments of the first presentation, which suggested that A should identify himself with the B-body-person, turned on the extreme neatness of the situation in satisfying, if any could, the description of 'changing bodies'. But this neatness is basically artificial; it is the product of the will of the experimenter to produce a situation which would naturally elicit, with minimum hesitation, that description. By the sorts of methods he employed, he could easily have left off earlier or gone on further. He could have stopped at situation (v), leaving B as he was; or he could have gone on and produced two persons each with A-like character and memories, as well as one or two with B-like characteristics. If he had done either of those, we should have been in yet greater difficulty about what to say; he just chose to make it as easy as possible for us to find something to say. Now if we had some model of ghostly persons in bodies, which were in some sense actually moved around by certain procedures, we could regard the neat experiment just as the *effective* experiment: the one method that really did result in the ghostly persons' changing places without being destroyed, dispersed, or whatever. But we cannot seriously use such a model. The experimenter has not in the sense of that model *induced* a change of bodies; he has rather produced the one situation out of a range of equally possible situations which we should be most disposed to call a change of bodies. As against this, the principle that one's fears can extend to future pain whatever psychological changes precede it seems positively straightforward. Perhaps, indeed, it is not; but we need to be shown what is wrong with it. Until we are shown what is wrong with it, we should perhaps decide that if we were the person A then, if we were to decide selfishly, we should pass the pain to the B-body-person. It would be risky: that there is room for the notion of a risk here is itself a major feature of the problem.

Commentary on Williams

The first paragraphs present an example which is largely science-fictional. In this example, we are told about an operation done to two human beings, A and B, and we are invited to think about how we would describe the changes that result from this. In brief, what happens is that the two individuals either undergo an operation that interchanges their brains, or they have a kind of read/write recording of their brains' contents which has the same effect as the operation. It is further assumed that two perfectly healthy individuals emerge from the operation.

What is important about this is not the issue of whether it is now practical, or ever will be, but how we can best describe what is imagined as having taken place in respect of A and B, especially as it bears on the issue of the identity of both.

Taking into account only the material up to [a]→, say which of the following seems the best account of what will have happened:
(a) A ando B have swapped personalities.
(b) A has come to inhabit B's body, and B has come to inhabit A's body.
(c) A and B have both died and two other people, say A* and B*, have emerged.
Can you think of any other descriptions that fit what happens more closely?

Williams's example is very much like one that Locke had imagined: the case of the prince and the cobbler. Locke wrote:

> For should the soul of a prince, carrying with it the consciousness of the prince's past life, enter and inform the body of a cobbler as soon as deserted by his own soul, every one sees he would be the same person with the prince, accountable only for the prince's actions ...

Of course, as we saw earlier in the chapter, Locke thought that this judgement was one about *personal* identity only, and not about human identity. He went on to say:

> but who would say it was the same man? The body too goes to the making the man, and would, I guess, to everybody determine the man in this case, wherein the soul, with all its princely thoughts about it, would not make another man: but he would be the same cobbler to every one besides himself.

It is this last sentence which is difficult to understand. On the one hand, it seems to say that we (from outside) would judge that the cobbler – whatever his princely protestations – would remain the cobbler, and similarly in respect of the prince. But on the other hand, it suggests that this judgement might not be wholly right because the man we judge to be the cobbler would count himself the prince. The burning question here, which Locke does not adequately address, is whether our perspective – the one that sees the same cobbler after the switch – is the right one, or whether it is the 'cobbler's' own perspective that is right. From the latter perspective, he regards himself as in fact the prince.

> Locke's suggestion that the first answer is merely about 'same *man*' and the second about 'same *person*' does not seem satisfying here. Can you say why?

There is a lot that could be said here, but perhaps the most obvious is this: the *man* we judge to be the cobbler will insist that he is in fact a prince; but then again, the *person* we judge to be the cobbler would be no less insistent on being a prince. The problem seems therefore not to be about whether 'man' or 'person' is at issue, but about a tension between the two answers that Locke envisages. Williams's article goes on to probe these answers by modifying the example in certain crucial respects.

One of the ways in which Williams's treatment differs sharply from Locke's is that Williams gets us to imagine the kinds of thing that A and B might say about their own identity *before* the operation, as well as what we might say then about the outcome. These are elicited by sharply differentiating between the fates of the various persons after the operation. In particular, A and B are told that one of the resultant persons will be given $100,000, and that the other will be tortured. For ease of reference, though without any commitment on the issue of personal identity, we can think of these resulting persons as the A- and B-body-persons.

> Williams considers different things that A and B might say if they were asked to choose the fate of the A- and B-body-persons, and also what they would say about their willingness to undergo the experimental operation. These are described in the text between $\boxed{a}\!\mapsto$ and $\boxed{b}\!\mapsto$. Summarize these various options in your own words.

Everything about Williams's discussion tends to make it natural, even inevitable, that we come to think of the experiment as that of A and B *changing bodies*.

> If, when you answered an earlier exercise, you thought 'changing bodies' was not the best description of the case, has the series of choices and estimates of outcome changed your mind? If not, what do you think might be wrong with the way these choices are described?

Next read the paragraph beginning at $\boxed{b}\!\mapsto$. If you find this account coherent, then you will agree with Williams (apparently the 'I' in the story) that the transitions described are frightening and unpleasant. But, as Williams reveals at $\boxed{c}\!\mapsto$, the operation and its effects as recounted by the experimenter are in reality the same as are described at the beginning of the article. In the first run through of the story, the operation is described from the 'outside', or *third-person* point of view. It is we who consider the matter and who are told what will happen to A and B, and what they think of it. In this second run through, however, the experimenter addresses his remarks to *me*. I am told that I will be tortured, but that I will not remember being told this, that I will have other memories, that these other memories exactly match those of someone else … etc. In sum, the second way of recounting the operation and its effects is in the *first-person*; it is directed to me.

It is not really surprising that the third- and first-person ways of describing the operation are different, nor that this makes it difficult, on first hearing, to recognize them as two sides of the same coin. However, what is surprising and important is that the two accounts lead to incompatible conclusions.

As we saw, if you begin with the third-person account, it is easy to think of the operation as resulting in the switching of bodies. But think carefully about the first-person account. (Here refer to the series of cases that begin at d↦.) It seems clear that the changes described as you move from (i) to (vi) are changes that affect *oneself*. At no stage does it seem as if your own self drops out in favour of the other self whose memories you end up with. In short, at no stage does it seem as if you and the other change places. This is shown by the fact that it seems perfectly reasonable for you (whom we can think of as A) to fear what is going to happen to you and your body throughout the sequence of changes.

In the first presentation of the case, this is not how we expected A to act. There, we were led to believe, A would think of his future as tied up with the B-body-person, and so would be pretty detached from the fact that the A-body-person was going to be tortured.

> The paragraphs between e↦ and f↦ consider ways in which one might resist this conclusion about the second of the perspectives on the example. The arguments here are careful and sometimes dense, but you should read them over several times, and try to summarize them in your own words.

Reaching two such different conclusions, each of which seems so plausible, suggests that our concept of a person is not fully coherent. But perhaps the way forward here is to relax the requirement that we must know, in every case, precisely how our concept of personhood functions. After all, the Williams case (and Locke's before him) are unlikely actually to arise. And if they do, we can then see what we shall say about the possibility of there being two perspectives on these sorts of case.

This strategy is anticipated by Williams and he in fact discusses two variants of it. The first variant is that of undecidability (see f↦). The idea here is that we possess the concept of a person, and with it a concept of *same* person, but, like many of our other concepts, there can be borderline cases.

We all know what it is to be bald, and we can usually sort people into those that are bald and those that aren't. But of course there are undecidable or borderline cases of baldness. And why shouldn't we be perfectly at ease with this same kind of borderline status in the case of the identity of persons?

Williams presents several arguments against this undecidability strategy (see especially the passages marked $g \mapsto$ and $h \mapsto$). Summarize his points in your own words.

The second strategy that Williams considers he calls 'conventionalist'. The idea here is that, recognizing these examples to be difficult, we simply wait to see how we and the relevant experimental subjects would actually come to decide the matter. An analogy here would be the settling of some kind of property dispute. When it is unclear who owns, say, a certain parcel of land, we leave it to courts and lawyers to make some decision about ownership. Treating A and B, and A's and B's friends and neighbours, as like the courts and lawyers, perhaps we should say that we will leave it up to them to determine the facts of what is so far in our experience merely a fictional case.

Williams dismisses this second, conventionalist, way of evading the problem at the very end of the paragraph marked $i \mapsto$. What is his reason for dismissing it?

At $j \mapsto$, Williams summarizes his arguments and finds it disturbing that he himself is unsure which of the options is the better one. He suggests that the clash of perspectives on his example is more than a mere philosophical puzzle, though it certainly is philosophically puzzling. Moreover, he suggests that the perspectives on the example do not conform to the usual expectations that one might have about the roles of our mental lives and bodies in decisions about personal identity (here see $k \mapsto$).

One might think from an outside or third-person perspective that our personhood is tied up with bodies and that our mental states or consciousness figures only when we adopt the first-person perspective. But if you think carefully about Williams's description of the two perspectives you will see that they run counter to this. When, in the first instance, A and B and we contemplate their future, they do so by estimating what they will think and feel. In short, in the first run through of the example – the one which we came to think of as exchanging bodies – conscious states were central even though the perspective was third person. However, in the second and clearly first-person case, continuity, rather than exchange, of body seemed more cogent.

In the final paragraph (marked by ☐→), Williams tentatively suggests a resolution to the conflict between the two cases. Say what his conclusion is, and what argument he uses to reach it. Finally, give some reasons for either agreeing or disagreeing with him.

7

Freedom

Introduction to the Problem

The problem of free will is one of the deepest and most troubling in philosophy. Each of us has a point of view from which we regard our own actions. From your own point of view it is natural to think that many of your actions – much of what you do – is 'up to you', rather than depending on factors outside your control. You have wants (or desires), you make choices, you take decisions, and when you act to carry out these desires, choices and decisions, you commonly regard yourself as acting freely. Examples great and small permeate life, from choosing to drink tea rather than coffee, to voting for a political party or deciding to go and settle in another country.

But there is another point of view on your actions. They are events which occur at a certain place and time. And no less than any other event in the world, what you do issues from causes. *Determinism* is the name given to various doctrines which appear to conflict with free will: the doctrine that every event has a cause, or that, given an event's causes, the happening of the event is determined or necessary, or that anything that happens could in principle be predicted if we knew enough about its causes. The debate about free will is driven by the initial thought that we cannot be genuinely free if determinism is true. If our actions have causes which determine them, and from which they could in principle be predicted, in what sense is what we do 'up to us'?

One question in this debate is whether there is some doctrine of determinism which is actually true. But philosophers have often concentrated on another question: *if* determinism were true, *would* that mean we had to deny that human beings have free will? People who answer Yes to this question are known as Incompatibilists – they think free will is incompatible with determinism. People who answer No are known as Compatibilists – they think that the truth of determinism is compatible with the truth of the claim 'human beings have free will'.

This debate is a central one in philosophy because it raises both metaphysical and ethical problems. That is to say, it makes us ask both how human beings are placed within the world at large (what kind of things are human beings and their actions?) and how we regard actions from the point of view of their ethical value (for example, what is the basis of our assigning praise, blame and responsibility to ourselves and others?).

Introduction to Schopenhauer

Arthur Schopenhauer was a German philosopher who lived from 1788 to 1860. He was an independent thinker who rebelled against the academic establishment of his day. Although *will* was one of the central concepts in his philosophy, he did not believe that individual human beings have free will in the sense usually accepted. His *Prize Essay on the Freedom of the Will*, from which we have taken some extracts here, dates from 1839. The Royal Norwegian Society of Sciences had announced a competition to answer the question 'Can the freedom of the will be demonstrated from self-consciousness?' Schopenhauer submitted his essay and won the prize. Because his previous work was at that time unknown, he could not assume that the judges of the competition would be familiar with it. Hence the reader does not need to know anything more about Schopenhauer's philosophy in order to read these extracts, in which he presents a clear, self-contained argument, and answers *No* to the question set.

Arthur Schopenhauer, *Prize Essay on the Freedom of the Will* (extracts)

The question set by the Royal Society is as follows:

> *Num liberum hominum arbitrium e sui ipsius conscientia demonstrari potest?*
> 'Can the freedom of the human will be demonstrated from self-consciousness?'

I Definitions

With so important, serious, and difficult a question that is essentially identical with one of the main problems of all medieval and modern philosophy, great accuracy and hence an analysis of the principal concepts coming within its purview are certainly not out of place.

(1) What is meant by freedom?

Carefully considered, this concept is *negative*. By it we understand simply the absence of everything that impedes and obstructs; however, the latter as something manifesting force must be something positive. In keeping with the possible nature of this impeding something, the concept has three very different subspecies, namely physical, intellectual, and moral freedom.

(a) *Physical freedom* is the absence of *material* obstacles of every kind. Thus we speak of free sky, free view, free air, free field, a free place, free heat (that is not chemically bound), free electricality, free course of a stream where it is no longer checked by mountains or sluices, and so on.[1] Even free room, free board, free press, postage-free indicate the absence of onerous conditions that, as hindrances to pleasure, usually attach to such things. But in our thinking, the concept of freedom is most frequently predicated of animals. The characteristic of animals is that their movements proceed from *their will*, are voluntary, and consequently are called *free* when no material obstacle makes this impossible. Now since these obstacles may be of very different kinds, but that which they obstruct is always *the will*, it is preferable, for the sake of simplicity, to take the concept from the positive side, and with it to think of everything that moves only by its will or acts only from its will. This transformation of the concept essentially alters nothing. Accordingly, in this *physical* meaning of the concept of freedom, animals and human beings are called *free* when neither chains, dungeon, nor paralysis, and thus generally no *physical, material* obstacle impedes their actions, but these occur in accordance with their *will*.

This *physical meaning* of the concept of freedom, and especially as the predicate of animals, is the original, immediate, and therefore most frequent one. For this reason, the concept given this meaning is not subject to any doubt or controversy, but its reality can always be verified by experience. For as soon as an animal acts only from its *will*, it is in this sense *free*; and no account is taken here of what may have influenced its will itself. For in this, its original, immediate, and therefore popular meaning, the concept of freedom refers only to an *ability*, that is, precisely to the absence of *physical* obstacles to the

---

[1]   The extensive use of 'free' to designate the lack of physical obstacle is more idiomatic in German than in English. [Footnotes are by the translator and editor of the Cambridge University Press translation.]

actions of the animal. Thus we say that the birds of the air, the animals of the forest are free; human beings are free by nature; only the free are happy. A people is also called free, and by this we understand that it is governed only by laws and that it itself has issued them; for then in every case it obeys only its own will. Accordingly, political freedom is to be classed under physical freedom.

But as soon as we leave this *physical* freedom and consider the other two kinds, we are concerned no longer with the popular, but with the *philosophical* sense of the concept, which, as is well known, opens the way to many difficulties. It is divisible into two entirely different kinds, namely intellectual and moral freedom.

(b) *Intellectual freedom, to hekousion kai akousion kata dianoian*[2] in Aristotle,[3] is taken into consideration here merely for the purpose of making the classification complete. I therefore propose to defer its discussion until the very end of this essay, for by then the concepts to be used therein will have found their explanation already in what has gone before, so that it can be dealt with briefly then. But in the classification it had to come next to physical freedom, since it is most closely related to the latter.

(c) I therefore turn at once to the third kind, to *moral freedom*, which is really the *liberum arbitrium*[4] mentioned in the question of the Royal Society.

This concept is connected with that of physical freedom in a manner that also enables us to see its necessarily much later origin. As I have said, physical freedom refers only to material obstacles, and exists at once with the absence of the latter. But in a good many cases it was observed that, without being impeded by material obstacles, a human being was restrained from acting as otherwise would certainly have been in accordance with his will, by mere motives, such as threats, promises, dangers, and the like. The question was therefore raised whether such a human being had still been *free*, or whether, like a physical obstacle, a strong countermotive could actually prevent and render impossible an action according to the will proper. The answer to this could not be difficult for sound common sense, namely that a motive could never act like a physical obstacle, since the latter might easily exceed absolutely the physical forces of a human being, whereas a motive can never be irresistible in itself or have absolute power but may still always be overcome by a *stronger countermotive*, if only it were present and the human being in the given individual case could be

---

[2] 'The voluntary and involuntary with respect to thought.'
[3] Aristotle (384–322 BC): Greek philosopher; the phrase cited by Schopenhauer can be found in *Eudemian Ethics*, 11, 7, 1223a 23–25 and elsewhere.
[4] 'Free choice of the will.'

determined by it. For we frequently see that even what is usually the strongest of all motives, the preservation of life, is nevertheless overcome by others, e.g., in suicide and the sacrifice of life for others, for opinions and for interests of many kinds; and conversely, that occasionally all degrees of the most extreme tortures on the rack have been surmounted by the mere thought that life would otherwise be lost. But although it was evident from this that motives have no purely objective and absolute compulsion, a subjective and relative one could nevertheless belong to them, namely for the person concerned; and in the end this was the same thing. Hence there remains the question: Is the will itself free? – Here then the concept of freedom, which one had hitherto thought of only in reference to the *ability to act*, was now brought in relation to *willing*, and the problem arose whether willing itself was *free*. But on further consideration, the original, purely empirical, and hence popular concept of freedom proved incapable of entering into this connection with *willing*. For according to this concept, *'free'* means *'in conformity with one's own will.'* Now if we ask whether the will itself is free, we are asking whether it is in conformity with itself; and this of course is self-evident, but it also tells us nothing. As a result of the empirical concept of freedom we have: 'I am free, if I can *do what I will*,' and the freedom is already decided by this 'what I will.' But now since we are asking about the freedom of *willing* itself, this question should accordingly be expressed as follows: 'Can you also *will* what you will?' This appears as if the willing depended on yet another willing lying behind it. And supposing that this question were answered in the affirmative, there would soon arise the second question:

b→ 'Can you also will what you will to will?' and thus it would be pushed back to infinity, since we would always think of *one* willing as being dependent on a previous or deeper willing, and thus in vain endeavor to arrive ultimately at a willing that we were bound to conceive and accept as being dependent on absolutely nothing. However, if we wanted to assume such a willing, we could just as well assume the first as any final willing that had been arbitrarily chosen. Yet in this way the question would be reduced to the quite simple one of 'can you will?' But whether the mere answering of it in the affirmative decides the freedom of willing is what we wanted to know, and is left unsettled. The original, empirical concept of freedom, a concept drawn from doing, thus refuses to enter into a direct connection with that of willing. Therefore to be able to apply to the will the concept of freedom, one had to modify it by grasping it in a more abstract way. This was

c→ done by conceiving through the concept of *freedom* only the absence of all *necessity* in general. Here the concept retains the *negative* character which I had assigned to it at the very beginning. Accordingly, the concept of *necessity*, as the positive concept establishing the former's negative meaning, would have to be discussed first.

We therefore ask what is meant by *necessary*. The usual explanation, that 'necessary is that the opposite of which is impossible, or which cannot be otherwise' is merely verbal, a paraphrase of the concept which does not increase our insight. But as the real definition I give the following: *necessary is that which follows from a given sufficient ground*. Like every correct definition, this proposition is capable also of inversion. Now depending on whether this sufficient ground is logical, mathematical, or physical (i.e., causal), the *necessity* will be logical (like that of the conclusion when the premises are given), mathematical (e.g., the equality of the sides of the triangle if the angles are equal), or physical and real (like the occurrence of the effect as soon as the cause exists). In each case, the necessity adheres to the consequent with equal strictness if the ground is given. Only insofar as we understand something as the consequent of a given ground do we recognize it as necessary; and conversely, as soon as we recognize something as a consequent of a sufficient ground, we see that it is necessary; for all grounds are compelling. This real definition is so adequate and exhaustive that necessity and being the consequence of a given sufficient ground are outright convertible terms, in other words, the one can always be put in the place of the other. – Accordingly, absence of necessity would be

d⟶ identical with absence of a determining sufficient ground. Now the contingent is conceived as the opposite of the *necessary*; but the one does not contradict the other. For everything contingent is only *relatively* so. For in the real world, where only the contingent is to be found, every event is *necessary* in regard to its cause; but in regard to everything else with which it coincides in time and space, it is *contingent*. Now as absence of necessity is characteristic of what is free, the latter would have to be dependent on absolutely no cause at all, and consequently would have to be defined as the *absolutely contingent*. This is an extremely problematical concept, one whose conceivability I cannot vouch for, and one which nevertheless coincides in a curious way with the concept of *freedom*. In any case, the *free* remains that which is in no relation necessary; and this means that which is dependent on no ground. Now this concept, applied to the will of a human being, would state that in its manifestations (acts of will) an individual will would not be determined by causes or sufficient reasons in general, for otherwise its acts would not be free but necessary, since the consequent of a given ground (whatever the nature of that ground) is always *necessary*. On this rests *Kant's* definition according to which freedom is the power to initiate *of itself* a series of changes.[5] For this

---

[5]   See Immanuel Kant, *Critique of Pure Reason*, A 445/B 473.

'of itself,' when reduced to its true meaning, signifies 'without antecedent cause'; this, however, is identical with 'without necessity.' Thus, although that definition gives the concept of freedom the appearance of being positive, on closer examination its negative nature is again apparent. – A free will would therefore be one that was not determined by grounds; and since everything determining something else must be a ground – a real ground, i.e., a cause, in the case of real things – a free will would be one that was determined by nothing at all. The particular manifestations of such a will (acts of will) would therefore proceed absolutely and quite originally from itself, without being brought about necessarily by antecedent conditions, and thus without being determined by anything according to a rule. In the case of such a concept clear thinking is at an end because the principle of sufficient reason in all its meanings is the essential form of our whole faculty of cognition, yet here it is supposed to be given up. However, we are not left without even a *terminus technicus* for this concept; it is *liberum arbitrium indifferentiae*.[6] Moreover, this is the only clearly determined, firm, and settled concept of that which is called freedom of the will. Therefore one cannot depart from it without falling into vague and hazy explanations behind which lurks a hesitant insufficiency, as when one speaks of grounds that do not necessarily bring about their consequents. Every consequence of a ground is necessary, and every necessity is a consequence of a ground. From the assumption of such a *liberum arbitrium indifferentiae*, the immediate consequence that characterizes this concept itself and is therefore to be stated as its mark is that for a human individual endowed with it, under given external circumstances that are determined quite individually and thoroughly, two diametrically opposed actions are equally possible. [...]

II   The Will before Self-consciousness

[...] The feeling residing in self-consciousness that 'I can do what I will' does constantly accompany us, but states merely that, although the decisions or decided acts of will spring from the dim depths of our inner being, they will always pass over at once into the world of intuition, for our body, like everything else, belongs to that world. This consciousness forms the bridge between the inner and outer worlds that would otherwise remain separated by an insurmountable gap [...]. If we were to ask someone who is wholly impartial, he would express somewhat as follows that immediate consciousness which is so frequently taken to be that of a supposed freedom of the

6   'Free choice of indifference.'

will: 'I can do what I will; if I want to go to the left, I go to the left; if I want to go to the right, I go to the right. This depends entirely on my will alone; I am therefore free.' Certainly this statement is perfectly true and correct, yet with it the will is already presupposed; for it assumes that the will has already made its decision, and hence nothing can be settled thereby concerning the will itself being free. For the statement in no way speaks of the dependence or independence of the *occurrence* of the act of will itself, but only of the *consequences* of this act as soon as it occurs, or, to speak more accurately, of the act's inevitable appearance as bodily action. But it is simply and solely the consciousness underlying that statement which causes the naive, i.e., the philosophically untutored human being, who in spite of this may yet be a great scholar in other disciplines, to regard the freedom of the will as something so absolutely and immediately certain that he expresses it as an unquestionable truth, and really cannot believe that philosophers seriously doubt it, but thinks in his heart that all the talk about it is mere dialectical school-fencing and at bottom play. Now the undoubtedly important certainty given by that consciousness is always quite close at hand; moreover the human being, as primarily and essentially a practical and not a theoretical being, is much more clearly conscious of the active side of his acts of will, i.e., of their effectiveness, than of the *passive*, i.e., of their dependence. For this reason, it is so difficult to make the human being who is philosophically untrained understand the real meaning of our problem, and to get him to see that the question is now not one of the *consequences* but of the *grounds* of his willing in each case. It is true that his *action* depends simply and solely on his *willing*, but we now want to know on what *his willing itself* depends, if on nothing at all or on something. He can certainly *do* one thing if he wants to, and can just as well *do* the other thing if he wants to; but he should now ask himself whether he is also capable of *willing* one thing as well as the other. Now with this object in view, let us put the question to the human being in some such terms as the following: 'Of two opposite wishes that have arisen in you, can you really satisfy the one as well as the other? For example, when choosing between two mutually exclusive objects, can you prefer the possession of the one just as well as that of the other?' He will then say: 'Perhaps the choice may be difficult for me, yet it will always depend entirely on me whether I *will* to choose the one or the other, and will not depend on any other authority; for I have complete freedom to choose what I will, and here I shall always follow only my *will*.' – Now if we say to him: 'But on what does your willing itself depend?' he will reply out of his self-consciousness: 'On absolutely nothing but me! I can will what I will; what I will, that I will.' – The latter he says without meaning to be tautological, or without relying in his inmost consciousness on the principle of identity by virtue of which alone this is true. On the contrary, when pressed to the very limit here, he speaks of a willing of his willing, which is as if he were to speak of an I of his I. He has been driven back to the very core of his self-consciousness, where he finds his I and his will to be indistinguishable, but nothing is left for assessing the two. Whether in that choice his *willing itself* of one thing and not of the other, for his person and the objects of choice are here assumed as given, could possibly turn out differently from what it ultimately does; or whether, by the data just mentioned, it is determined just as necessarily as that in a triangle the greatest angle is subtended by the greatest side – this is a question so remote from natural *self-consciousness* that it cannot even understand it, much less have a ready answer for it, or even only the undeveloped germ of one, which it could give out only naively. – Therefore in the way just indicated, the impartial but philosophically untutored human being will still always try to run away from the perplexity that the question, when really understood, is bound to cause, and will take refuge behind that immediate certainty 'what I will I can do, and I will what I will,' as was said above. He will attempt to do this over and over again innumerable times, so that it will be difficult to pin him down to the real question from which he is always trying to slip away. And for this he is not to be blamed, for the question is really extremely ticklish. It thrusts a searching hand into the inmost recesses of the human being; it wants to know whether he too, like everything else in the world, is a being once and for all determined by its own constitution; a being, like every other in nature, having its definite constant qualities from which there necessarily spring its reactions to the external occasion that arises and which accordingly, from this point of view, bear their unalterable character, and consequently are wholly abandoned, in whatever may be modifiable in them, to determination by occasion from without; or whether he alone is an exception to the whole of nature. If, however, we finally succeed in pinning him down to this so ticklish question, and in making it clear to him that we are here inquiring about the origin of his acts of will themselves, and are asking whether they arise in accordance with some rule or entirely without any, we shall discover that immediate self-consciousness contains no information about this. For the untutored human being himself here departs from self-consciousness and reveals his perplexity through speculation and all kinds of attempted explanations. He tries to draw the arguments for them at first from the experience he has acquired of himself and others, and then from universal rules of the understanding. But through the uncertainty and hesitancy of his explanation he here shows plainly enough that his immediate self-consciousness furnishes no information about the question when correctly understood, although previously it was ready with an answer when the question was incorrectly understood.

III   The Will before the Consciousness of Other Things

All *changes* that occur in given objects in the real external world are [...] subject to the law of *causality*, and thus always occur as *necessary* and inevitable, whenever and wherever they occur. – To this law there can be no exception, for the rule holds *a priori* for all possibility of experience. But as regards its *application* to a given case, we have merely to ask whether we are dealing with a *change* of a real object that is given in external experience. When this is so, its changes are subject to the application of the law of causality; in other words, they must be brought about by a cause, and for that very reason must *necessarily* be brought about.

If we now approach this experience itself with our universal, *a priori* certain rule, which is therefore valid without exception for all possible experience, and consider the real objects given in experience to whose possible changes our rule refers, we soon notice in those objects some fundamentally striking main differences in accordance with which they also have long been classified. Thus some objects are inorganic, i.e., inanimate; others are organic, i.e., animate, and the latter again are either plants or animals. Animals again, although essentially similar and conforming to their concept, are still found in an extremely varied and finely shaded hierarchy of perfection, from those still closely akin to a plant, and hardly distinguishable from it, up to those that are most perfect and conform most perfectly to the concept of an animal. At the summit of this hierarchy we see the human being – ourselves.

Now if, without allowing ourselves to be confused by that multiplicity and variety, we consider all those beings together merely as external, real objects of experience, and accordingly proceed to apply to the changes occurring in such beings our law of causality that stands *a priori* firm for the possibility of all experience, we shall find that experience certainly does turn out everywhere in accordance with the *a priori* certain law, yet to the mentioned great *diversity* in the essential nature of all those objects of experience there also corresponds a modification, appropriate to that diversity, of the way in which causality asserts its right in them. Thus, in keeping with the threefold distinction of inorganic bodies, plants, and animals, causality that guides and directs all their changes likewise shows itself in three forms, as *cause* in the narrowest sense of the word, or as *stimulus*, or as *motivation*; and yet this modification does not in the least detract from the *a priori* validity of causality and consequently from the necessity, thereby established, with which the effect follows the cause.

Cause in the narrowest sense of the word is that by virtue of which all mechanical, physical, and chemical changes occur in the objects of experience. It is everywhere characterized by two distinctive features; first by the fact that Newton's third law that 'action and reaction are equal' finds its application here; in other words, the antecedent state, called cause, undergoes a change equal to that undergone by the ensuing state, called the effect. – Secondly, cause in the narrowest sense is characterized by the fact that, according to Newton's second law, the degree of the effect is always exactly proportionate to that of the cause; consequently an intensification of the cause likewise brings about an equal intensification of the effect. Thus once the mode of operation is known, the degree of the effect can also be known, measured, and calculated at once from the degree of the intensity of the cause, and vice versa. [...] Now it is such *causes in the narrowest sense* that produce the changes in all *inanimate, i.e., inorganic* bodies. The cognition and presupposition of causes of this kind guide our consideration of all the changes that form the subject of mechanics, hydrodynamics, physics, and chemistry. To be determined exclusively by causes of this kind is, therefore, the proper and essential characteristic of an inorganic or inanimate body.

The second kind of causes is *stimulus*, i.e., that cause which in the first place does *not* itself undergo a reaction proportionate to its action; and, in the second place, that in which there is absolutely no uniformity between the intensity of the cause and that of the effect. Consequently, the degree of the effect here cannot be measured and previously determined in accordance with that of the cause. On the contrary, a small increase in the stimulus may cause a very great increase in the effect; or conversely it may eliminate the previous effect entirely, or even bring about an opposite one. For example, it is well known that plants can be forced to an extraordinarily rapid growth by heat or the addition of lime to the soil, because those causes act as stimuli to the plants' vital force. If, however, the appropriate degree of stimulus is very minutely exceeded, then, instead of an enhanced and quickened life, the result will be the death of the plant. Thus we can also exert and considerably heighten our mental powers by wine or opium, but if the right amount of stimulus is exceeded, the result will be the very opposite. – It is causes of this kind, namely *stimuli*, that determine all the changes of organisms *as such*. All the changes and developments of plants and all the merely organic and vegetative changes or functions of animal bodies occur through *stimuli*. Light, heat, air, nutrition, every drug, touch, fructification, and so on act on them in this way. But the life of animals still has quite a different sphere, about which I shall speak in a moment; the entire life of *plants* takes place exclusively in accordance with *stimuli*. All their assimilation, growth, the striving of their crowns to reach the light and of their roots toward the better soil, their fructification, germination, and so on are changes brought about by *stimuli*. In a few isolated species there is also a characteristic swift movement that is likewise solely the result of stimuli, and for this reason they are called sensitive plants. The best-known of these are *Mimosa pudica, Hedysarum gyrans*, and *Dionaea muscipula*.[7] To be determined by stimuli exclusively and without exception is the character of the plant. Consequently, a plant is any body whose movements and changes peculiar and appropriate to its nature always and exclusively follow on *stimuli*.

The third kind of moving cause, which characterizes *animals*, is *motivation*, i.e., causality that passes through *cognition*. It enters in the gradual scale of natural beings, at that point where a being which is more complex, and thus has more manifold needs, was no longer able to satisfy them merely on the occasion of a stimulus that must be awaited, but had to be in a position to choose, seize, and even seek out the means of satisfaction. And so with beings of this kind, mere susceptibility to *stimuli* and movement therefrom are replaced by susceptibility to *motives*, i.e., by a faculty of representation, an intellect in innumerable degrees of perfection. This manifests itself materially as a nervous system and brain and thus entails consciousness. It is well known that the basis of animal life is a plant life that as such takes place only on *stimuli*. But all movements performed by an animal *as an animal*, and hence depending on what physiology calls *animal functions*, occur in consequence of a known object, and hence *on motives*. Accordingly, an *animal* is any body whose external movements and changes, peculiar and appropriate to its nature, always ensue *on motives*, i.e., on certain *representations* that are present to its here already presupposed consciousness. However infinite graduations there may be of the capacity for representations and thus for consciousness in the series of animals, there is nevertheless in every animal enough of it for the motive to present itself to it and cause it to move.

---

[7] *Mimosa pudica* or 'sensitive plant' is a tropical American plant whose leaves are sensitive to tactile stimulation. *Hedysarum gyrans*, a tropical Asian plant whose leaves rotate slowly but visibly in daylight at temperatures above 72°F, has been reclassified at least twice since the nineteenth century, most recently as *Codariocalyx motorius*. The English name of the plant is 'telegraph plant' or 'semaphore plant'. *Dionaea muscipula* is the familiar Venus's-flytrap.

Here the inner moving force whose particular manifestation is called forth by the motive proclaims itself to the now existing self-consciousness as that which we denote by the word *will*.

[I]→   […] I cannot omit discussing the difference brought about in motivation by that which distinguishes human consciousness from all animal consciousness. This trait, which is properly expressed by the word *reason*, consists in a human being not merely capable, like an animal, of an *intuitive* apprehension of the external world, but also of abstracting universal concepts (*notiones universales*) from it. To be able to fix and retain these in his sensuous consciousness, he denotes them by words, and then makes innumerable combinations with them. These, like the concepts of which they consist, are of course related always to the world that is known through intuition, yet they properly constitute what we call *thinking*. The great advantages of the human species over all the rest thus become possible, such as speech, reflectiveness, looking back at the past, care about the future, purpose, deliberation, the planned and systematic action of many in common, the state, the sciences, the arts, and so on. All this rests solely on the unique ability to have nonintuitive, abstract, universal representations, called *concepts* (i.e., conceptual complexes of things),[8] because each of them contains or comprehends under itself many particular things. Animals, even the cleverest, lack this ability, and therefore have no other representations than *intuitive representations*. Accordingly, they know only what is actually present, and live solely in the present moment. The motive by which their will is moved must therefore always be intuitive and present. But the result of this is that an exceedingly limited *choice* is granted to them, namely only among those things which are present in intuition for their limited range of view and power of apprehension and thus are present in time and space. The stronger of these then at once determines their will as motive, whereby the causality of the motive here becomes very obvious. An *apparent* exception is made by *training*, which is fear operating through the medium of habit. But instinct is to a certain extent a *real* exception insofar as, by reason of it, the animal is set into motion in the *whole* of its mode of action not by motives proper, but by an inner urge and drive. But in the details of the *particular* actions and at every moment the latter receives again its closer determination through motives, and thus returns to the rule. […] On the other hand, owing to his capacity for nonintuitive representations, by means of which he *thinks and reflects*, a human being has an infinitely wider range of view, which encompasses the absent, the past, and the future.

---

[8]   The German words are 'Begriffe' and 'Inbegriffe der Dinge,' respectively.

He thus has a far greater sphere of influence of motives and consequently also of choice than an animal has, restricted as it is to the
narrowness of the present moment. As a rule, it is not the thing lying
before his sensible intuition and present in time and space which
determines his action, but rather mere *thoughts*, which he carries
about in his head wherever he goes, and which make him independent
of the impression of the present moment. Whenever the latter fail to do
this, however, we call his conduct irrational; on the other hand, his
conduct is commended as *rational* when it takes place exclusively
according to well-considered thoughts, and thus quite independently
of the impression of what is present in intuition. A human being is
actuated by a special class of representations (abstract concepts,
thoughts), which an animal does not have, and this is evident even
externally; for this circumstance impresses the character of the *deliberate and intentional* on all his actions, even the most insignificant, in
fact on all his steps and movements. Thus his whole line of conduct is
so obviously different from that of animals that one almost sees how,
as it were, fine, invisible threads (motives consisting of mere thoughts)
guide his movements, whereas those of animals are drawn by the
coarse, visible ropes of what is present in intuition. But the difference
does not go beyond this. A thought becomes *motive*, as does an
intuition, as soon as it is able to act on the will that lies before it.
But all motives are causes, and all causality entails necessity. Now by
means of his ability to think, a human being can represent to himself
the motives whose influence he feels on his will in any order he likes,
alternately and repeatedly, in order to hold them before the will; and
this is called *reflecting*. He has a capacity for deliberation and, by
virtue of it, a far greater *choice* than is possible for the animal. In this
way, he certainly is *relatively free*, namely from the immediate compulsion of objects that are *present through intuition* and act as motives
on his will, a compulsion to which the animal is absolutely subject. A
human being, on the other hand, determines himself independently of
present objects, in accordance with thoughts, which are *his* motives.
At bottom it is this *relative* freedom that educated but not deep-
thinking people understand by freedom of the will, which, they say,
obviously gives the human being the advantage over the animal. But
such freedom is merely *relative*, namely in reference to what is present
through intuition, and merely *comparative*, namely in comparison
with the *animal*. Only *the mode* of motivation is changed by it; on
the other hand, the *necessity* of the effect of the motives is not in the
least suspended or even only diminished. The *abstract* motive that
consists in a mere *thought* is an external cause determining the will
just as is the intuitive motive, which consists in a real object that is

present. Consequently, it is a cause like every other and is even, like other causes, at all times something real and material insofar as it always rests ultimately on an impression received *from without* at some time and place. Its advantage lies merely in the length of the guiding wire. By this I mean that it is not, like the merely intuitive motives, bound to a certain *proximity* in space and time, but can operate through the greatest distance and longest time by means of concepts and thoughts in a long concatenation. This is a consequence of the constitution and eminent susceptibility of the organ which first experiences and receives its impression, namely the human brain or *reason*. But this does not in the least suspend its causality and the *necessity* associated with it. Therefore only a very superficial view can regard that relative and comparative freedom as absolute, as a *liberum arbitrium indifferentiae*. Indeed, the capacity for deliberation, arising from that comparative freedom, gives us nothing but a *conflict of motives*, one that is very often painful, over which irresolution presides, and whose scene of conflict is the whole mind and consciousness of the human being. For he allows the motives repeatedly to try their strength on his will, one against the other. His will is thus put in the same position as that of a body that is acted on by different forces in opposite directions – until at last the decidedly strongest motive drives the others from the field and determines the will. This outcome is called decision and as the result of the struggle, appears with complete *necessity*.

n ⊳   [...] To render as clearly as possible the origin of that error which is so important to our theme, and thus to supplement the investigation of self-consciousness that was given in the preceding section, let us think of a man in the street who says to himself: 'It is six o'clock; the day's work is over. I can now go for a walk, or go to the club; I can also climb the tower to see the sun set; I can also go to the theater; I can also visit this or that friend; in fact I can also run out by the city gate into the wide world and never come back. All that is entirely up to me; I have complete freedom; however, I do none of them, but just as voluntarily go home to my wife.' This is just as if water were to say: 'I can form high waves (as in a storm at sea); I can rush down a hill (as in the bed of a torrent); I can dash down foaming and splashing (as in the waterfall); I can rise freely as a jet into the air (as in a fountain); finally, I can even boil away and disappear (as at 212 degrees Fahrenheit); however, I do none of these things now, but voluntarily remain calm and clear in the mirroring pond.' Just as water can do all those things only when the determining causes enter for one or the other, so is the condition just the same for that man with respect to what he imagines he can do. Until the causes enter, it is impossible for him to do anything; but then he *must* do it, just as water must act as soon as it is placed in the respective circumstances. When the matter is closely considered, his error and the deception in general which arises from the wrongly interpreted self-consciousness that he is now equally capable of doing all those things are due to the fact that only *one* image at a time can be present in his imagination and that for the moment this image excludes all others. Now if he pictures to himself the motive for one of those actions that are suggested as possible, he at once feels its effect on his will that is thus solicited. In technical language this is called a *velleitas*;[9] but now he thinks he can raise the latter to a *voluntas*,[10] i.e., carry out the proposed action; but this is a deception. For reflection would at once step in and remind him of the motives that pull in other or opposite directions, whereupon he would see to it that no such action ensue. With such a successive presentation of different and mutually exclusive motives, to the constant accompaniment of the inner refrain: 'I can do what I will,' the will turns at once, like a weathervane on a well-oiled pivot in a changeable wind, to every motive that is presented to it by the imagination. It turns successively to all the motives that lie before it as possible, and with each the human being thinks he can *will* it, and thus fix the weathervane at this point; but this is a mere deception. For his 'I can will this' is in truth hypothetical and carries with it the clause, 'if I did not rather will that other thing'; but this abolishes that ability to will. – Let us turn to the man whom we left deliberating at six o'clock, and imagine that he now notices that I am standing behind him, philosophizing about him, and disputing his freedom to do all those actions that to him are possible. It might easily happen that he carries out one of them in order to refute me; but then my denial of his freedom and its effect on his spirit of contradiction would have been the motive that compelled him to do it. Yet this could induce him to carry out only one or other of the *easier* of the above-listed actions, e.g., to go to the theater, but certainly not the last-mentioned one, namely to run out into the wide world; for such an action, that motive would be much too weak. – In just the same way, many a human being erroneously imagines that, by holding a loaded pistol in his hand, he can shoot himself. The least thing for doing this is the mechanical means of carrying it out, but the main thing is an exceedingly powerful and therefore very rare motive that has the immense strength necessary to overcome the desire for life or rather the fear of death. Only after such a motive has entered can he actually shoot himself, and then he must, unless the deed is prevented by an even stronger countermotive, if such is at all possible.

9 'Wish' or 'act of wishing.'
10 'Will' or 'act of willing.'

I can do what I will; I can, *if I will*, give all I have to the poor, and thus become poor myself – if I *will*! – But I am not able to *will* this because the opposing motives have far too much power over me. If, on the other hand, I had another character, indeed to the extent of being a saint, then I could will it; but then I could not help willing it and would therefore have to do it. – All this is perfectly consistent with the 'I can *do* what I *will*' of self-consciousness, in which even today some thoughtless philosophasters imagine they see the freedom of the will, and accordingly advance this as a given fact of consciousness.

Commentary on Schopenhauer

Schopenhauer's strategy in the passages selected is first to define the concept of freedom, then to examine it in the light of the distinction between 'self-consciousness' and 'consciousness of other things'. Self-consciousness means a person's awareness of their own states of mind, in this case their desires and aims – their will, or what they want to do. Schopenhauer sometimes calls this a consciousness of the 'inner' world and contrasts it with consciousness of ordinary things that belong to the 'outer' world in space and time.

Schopenhauer addresses a precise question, namely 'Can the freedom of the human will be demonstrated from self-consciousness?'

> Read the selections from Schopenhauer and decide the following for yourself: Where does Schopenhauer answer this precise question?

Schopenhauer's answer comes most explicitly in the section entitled 'The will before self-consciousness', in the sentence marked $\boxed{j} \mapsto$: 'immediate self-consciousness contains no information about this'. What is the 'this'? If you read back a little in the text, you find that it is 'whether human acts of will arise in accordance with some rule that determines them'. So Schopenhauer's answer to the question is No: self-consciousness does not tell us whether or not our will is free or determined.

To see how Schopenhauer arrives here, you will need to examine two points especially. First, what is Schopenhauer's definition of freedom of the will? Second, what are his grounds for saying that self-consciousness does not tell us whether we have free will?

Section I   Definitions

In the section 'What is meant by freedom?' Schopenhauer states a first definition of freedom, but then moves on to another definition.

Read from [a]→ to [c]→ in the text, and formulate your answer to these questions: (1) What is the definition of freedom Schopenhauer starts with? (2) What is the revised definition he reaches? (3) Why does he need the revised definition?

On (1): Schopenhauer starts by discussing animals, which at this stage include human beings. The initial definition in the passage starting at [a]→ is that an animal is free when it acts 'only from its will'. The opposite of free action, in this sense, is action impeded by some obstacle.

On (2): The revised definition is reached at [c]→ in the text, and states that freedom is the absence of all necessity. The notion of what can impede action has been broadened from that of a physical obstacle, and now includes necessity in general. We might suggest a simple example: if it was necessary that I chose to drink tea and not coffee this morning, then I was not free to choose coffee at that very time.

On (3): The revised definition is needed because Schopenhauer makes a transition from 'freedom to do' to 'freedom to will'. And this makes the first definition problematic, because according to it my will would be free if it arose 'only from my will'. Schopenhauer's objection to this (at [b]→) is that it leads to an infinite regress: if we ask whether the will from which my will arises is free, that means it springs only from my will, and so on. (Pointing to an infinite regress is a common device in philosophy. Most often philosophers use it as a form of objection: if we start with an initial proposition and it leads to an infinite regress, there is probably something wrong with the initial proposition.)

The remainder of the discussion in the section 'What is meant by freedom?' is taken up with the concept of necessity. The term 'contingent' as used by philosophers does indeed mean the opposite of necessary (as Schopenhauer says at [d]→). If something happens contingently, that means it happens but did not have to happen. Schopenhauer's point here is that, although an event may not be absolutely necessary (in which case its not happening would just be impossible), it is necessary relative to its cause. In other words, Schopenhauer is claiming that if the cause of an event happens, then the event must happen.

At [e]→ and [f]→ in the text Schopenhauer makes two final claims about the notion of free will. First, that a free will would be one 'determined by nothing at all'; second, that this is the only clear conception of free will.

You might pause here to consider some philosophical questions: (1) How does the conception of free will at [e]→ relate to Schopenhauer's preceding discussion? (2) Has Schopenhauer done anything to persuade us that the conception stated at [e]→ is the only clear conception of free will we can

have? (3) Has Schopenhauer made things too easy for himself by constructing a definition of free will so extreme that nobody would be likely to
support it?

Pay some attention to this last point. Sometimes when a philosopher has
produced an argument against a proposition, the reader may think that it
was not the best proposition to be attacking in the first place, and it can be
good philosophy to point this out. Here you might think: 'If that's what free
will means, then there is probably no free will, but are there not other senses
of free will that are more plausible?'

Section II   *The will before self-consciousness*

We have seen at $\boxed{j}\vdash$ Schopenhauer's overall answer to the question he was
set. Self-consciousness cannot inform us that we have free will. But there is
something which, according to Schopenhauer, self-consciousness can inform
us about.

In the section 'The will before self-consciousness', what is it that self-
consciousness can tell us about the will? What is it that self-consciousness
cannot tell us about the will? It should help to write down answers to these
two questions before continuing.

A simple diagram might clarify Schopenhauer's argument here. He thinks of
an act of will being preceded by a cause and followed by a bodily action (see
especially the passage around $\boxed{g}\vdash$). Thus:

Cause   →   My act of will   →   My bodily action
(the ground   (the consequence
of my act of will)   of my act of will)

With this diagram in mind, invent for yourself a concrete example based
around, e.g. your willing to eat a chocolate bar, or your willing to jump into
a swimming pool.

According to Schopenhauer, what self-consciousness can tell me is that if I
have willed to jump into the pool (or whatever example you like), I can jump
into the pool. But he argues that self-consciousness cannot tell me whether the
occurrence of my act of will itself was or was not determined (see $\boxed{h}\vdash$). Self-
consciousness can tell me what is going to happen when I have willed something, but can tell me nothing about whether my act of will had a cause or
ground, or what that cause or ground might have been.

Hence, as Schopenhauer says at ☐j↦, self-consciousness cannot pronounce on the question: Could I have willed something different? Could I have willed at that moment not to eat the chocolate, or not to jump into the pool?

Section III   *The will before the consciousness of other things*

Having answered his central question already, Schopenhauer asks what we can know about what grounds or causes our acts of will. Self-consciousness is unhelpful here, but what he calls 'consciousness of other things' does give us information. 'Consciousness of other things' means effectively our ordinary experience of the world. The chief point here is that changes we can experience in the world follow a rule: they are all brought about by causes (see ☐k↦).

Schopenhauer refers to this rule as an *a priori* one. This means that it is a universal rule which we can establish prior to any particular experiences. He thinks that all events without exception have causes, but that is not something we have to discover from the evidence of our experience; rather, it is so basic that all experience presupposes it.

Instead of changes, we might equally say events (or occurrences or happenings). The basic argument of section III is then very simple:

1   All events in nature are determined by causes.
2   My acts of will are events in nature.
3   My acts of will are determined by causes.

The alternative, for Schopenhauer, is to turn my acts of will into a strange kind of event that is 'an exception to the whole of nature' (see ☐i↦ in the previous section). This idea of continuity with nature leads, in the culmination of Schopenhauer's argument, to his vivid comparison between the behaviour of a man and the behaviour of a body of water.

> Read the passage from ☐n↦ to the end of the extract. What is Schopenhauer's aim in comparing the man to water? Is the comparison justified?

Schopenhauer's idea is that given my character, and those experiences I have which bring about my acts of will, I could never have willed to act otherwise than I did in fact will.

The big question for Schopenhauer is this: Is the fact that *something* causes our actions enough to render them unfree? What *differentiates* human action from other occurrences in nature is that it is caused by rational thinking and decision-taking. Schopenhauer agrees with this in the long passage beginning at ☐l↦. He even acknowledges (at ☐m↦) that rationality gives us a kind of freedom no other creatures have. (Note: other animals lack rationality, but have perception of objects in the here and now, which Schopenhauer refers to as *intuition* or *intuitive representation*.)

At this point, we might remember the worry raised about Schopenhauer's definition of freedom. Is he too extreme in equating freedom with the absence of every kind of cause or necessity? A Compatibilist reply to Schopenhauer might start by pointing to his own idea of relative freedom at $\boxed{m}\!\!\rightarrow$, and suggesting that if we are free in *this* sense, it is perhaps enough. Perhaps we should not worry about not being free in the extreme metaphysical sense Schopenhauer uses in his definition of freedom.

Towards the end of his essay (in a passage not included in the above extracts) Schopenhauer acknowledges that what he has said cannot really be the end of the matter. For, as he says, we have a:

> perfectly clear and certain feeling of *responsibility* for what we do, of *account-ability* for our actions – a feeling that rests on an unshakable certainty that we ourselves are *the doers of our deeds*. On the strength of that consciousness, it never occurs to anyone, not even to someone who is convinced of the necessity (previously discussed) with which our actions occur, to make use of this necessity as an excuse for a transgression, and to throw the blame on the motives because their appearance rendered the deed inevitable.

This passage eloquently states one reason why philosophers have found the issue of free will and determinism so problematic. It also leads us on to our second reading on free will.

Introduction to Strawson

'Freedom and Resentment' is another piece by P. F. Strawson, who featured in chapter 2 above. 'Freedom and Resentment' was originally delivered as a lecture to the British Academy and published in *Proceedings of the British Academy* (1962), then reprinted in the collection of Strawson's essays also entitled *Freedom and Resentment* (Methuen, 1974). What follows is an extract, consisting of approximately two-thirds of the piece.

Strawson's approach is to look away from the question of determinism, and to describe various ways in which we take attitudes towards other human beings in the light of their actions: resenting them, feeling grateful to them, blaming them, or being morally approving towards them. This is supposed to be a reflection on quite ordinary aspects of human life. Strawson explains how there can be reasons to withhold such attitudes towards people in certain situations. We do not resent, or blame, or morally approve someone's actions if we believe that he or she lacked various kinds of control over his or her actions. Sections IV and V of the piece are full of diverse examples of this. Strawson's overall aim is to show that determinism's being true would never be a reason to stop adopting the moral and other interpersonal attitudes he identifies. So there is not the clash between morality and determinism that many have imagined. Indeed, we do not have to know very much about determinism to see that our moral concepts and practices are not genuinely called into question by it.

This is an intricately written piece, whose structure may not be fully apparent on first reading. You should be prepared to re-read it, and re-read at least parts of it more than once, with the aid of the commentary that follows. It is a piece which repays careful attention.

P. F. Strawson, 'Freedom and Resentment' (extract)

I

Some philosophers say they do not know what the thesis of determinism is. Others say, or imply, that they do know what it is. Of these, some – the pessimists perhaps – hold that if the thesis is true, then the concepts of moral obligation and responsibility really have no application, and the practices of punishing and blaming, of expressing moral condemnation and approval, are really unjustified. Others – the optimists perhaps – hold that these concepts and practices in no way lose their *raison d'être* if the thesis of determinism is true. Some hold even that the justification of these concepts and practices requires the truth of the thesis. There is another opinion which is less frequently voiced: the opinion, it might be said, of the genuine moral sceptic. This is that the notions of moral guilt, of blame, of moral responsibility are inherently confused and that we can see this to be so if we consider the consequences either of the truth of determinism or of its falsity. The holders of this opinion agree with the pessimists that these notions lack application if determinism is true, and add simply that they also [a]→ lack it if determinism is false. If I am asked which of these parties I belong to, I must say it is the first of all, the party of those who do not know what the thesis of determinism is. But this does not stop me from having some sympathy with the others, and a wish to reconcile them. Should not ignorance, rationally, inhibit such sympathies? Well, of course, though darkling, one has some inkling – some notion of [b]→ what sort of thing is being talked about. This lecture is intended as a move towards reconciliation; so is likely to seem wrongheaded to everyone.

But can there be any possibility of reconciliation between such clearly opposed positions as those of pessimists and optimists about determinism? Well, there might be a formal withdrawal on one side in return for a substantial concession on the other. Thus, suppose the optimist's position were put like this: (1) the facts as we know them do not show determinism to be false; (2) the facts as we know them supply an adequate basis for the concepts and practices which the pessimist feels to be imperilled by the possibility of determinism's truth. Now it might be that the optimist is right in this, but is apt to give an inadequate account of the facts as we know them, and of how they constitute an adequate basis for the problematic concepts and practices; that the reasons he gives for the adequacy of the basis are themselves inadequate and leave out something vital. It might be that the pessimist is rightly anxious to get this vital thing back and, in the grip of his anxiety, feels he has to go beyond the facts as we know them; feels that the vital thing can be secure only if, beyond the facts as we know them, there is the further fact that determinism is false. Might he not be brought to make a formal withdrawal in return for a vital concession?

II

Let me enlarge very briefly on this, by way of preliminary only. Some optimists about determinism point to the efficacy of the practices of punishment, and of moral condemnation and approval, in regulating behaviour in socially desirable ways.[1] In the fact of their efficacy, they suggest, is an adequate basis for these practices; and this fact certainly does not show determinism to be false. To this the pessimists reply, all in a rush, that *just* punishment and moral condemnation imply moral guilt and guilt implies moral responsibility and moral responsibility implies freedom and freedom implies the falsity of determinism. And to this the optimists are wont to reply in turn that it is true that these practices require freedom in a sense, and the existence of freedom in this sense is one of the facts as we know them. But what 'freedom' means here is nothing but the absence of certain conditions the presence of which would make moral condemnation or punishment inappropriate. They have in mind conditions like compulsion by another, or innate incapacity, or insanity, or other less extreme forms of psychological disorder, or the existence of circumstances in which the making of any other choice would be morally inadmissible or would be too much to expect of any man. To this list they are

[1] Cf. P. H. Nowell-Smith, 'Freewill and moral responsibility', *Mind*, vol. LVII, 1948.

constrained to add other factors which, without exactly being limitations of freedom, may also make moral condemnation or punishment inappropriate or mitigate their force: as some forms of ignorance, mistake, or accident. And the general reason why moral condemnation or punishment are inappropriate when these factors or conditions are present is held to be that the practices in question will be generally efficacious means of regulating behaviour in desirable ways only in cases where these factors are not present. Now the pessimist admits that the facts as we know them include the existence of freedom, the occurrence of cases of free action, in the negative sense which the optimist concedes; and admits, or rather insists, that the existence of freedom in this sense is compatible with the truth of determinism. Then what does the pessimist find missing? When he tries to answer this question, his language is apt to alternate between the very familiar and the very unfamiliar.[2] Thus he may say, familiarly enough, that the man who is the subject of justified punishment, blame or moral condemnation must really deserve it; and then add, perhaps, that, in the case at least where he is blamed for a positive act rather than an omission, the condition of his really deserving blame is something that goes beyond the negative freedoms that the optimist concedes. It is, say, a genuinely free identification of the will with the act. And this is the condition that is incompatible with the truth of determinism.

The conventional, but conciliatory, optimist need not give up yet. He may say: Well, people often decide to do things, really intend to do what they do, know just what they're doing in doing it; the reasons they think they have for doing what they do, often really are their reasons and not their rationalizations. These facts, too, are included in the facts as we know them. If this is what you mean by freedom – by the identification of the will with the act – then freedom may again be conceded. But again the concession is compatible with the truth of the determinist thesis. For it would not follow from that thesis that nobody decides to do anything; that nobody ever does anything intentionally; that it is false that people sometimes know perfectly well what they are doing. I tried to define freedom negatively. You want to give it a more positive look. But it comes to the same thing. Nobody denies freedom in this sense, or these senses, and nobody claims that the existence of freedom in these senses shows determinism to be false.

But it is here that the lacuna in the optimistic story can be made to show. For the pessimist may be supposed to ask: But why does freedom in this sense justify blame, etc.? You turn towards me first the negative, and then the positive, faces of a freedom which nobody

[2] As Nowell-Smith pointed out in a later article: 'Determinists and libertarians', *Mind*, vol. LXIII, 1954.

challenges. But the only reason you have given for the practices of moral condemnation and punishment in cases where this freedom is present is the efficacy of these practices in regulating behaviour in socially desirable ways. But this is not a sufficient basis, it is not even the right sort of basis, for these practices as we understand them.

Now my optimist, being the sort of man he is, is not likely to invoke an intuition of fittingness at this point. So he really has no more to say. And my pessimist, being the sort of man he is, has only one more thing to say; and that is that the admissibility of these practices, as we understand them, demands another kind of freedom, the kind that in turn demands the falsity of the thesis of determinism. But might we not induce the pessimist to give up saying this by giving the optimist something more to say?

III

I have mentioned punishing and moral condemnation and approval; and it is in connection with these practices or attitudes that the issue between optimists and pessimists – or, if one is a pessimist, the issue between determinists and libertarians – is felt to be particularly important. But it is not of these practices and attitudes that I propose, at first, to speak. These practices or attitudes permit, where they do not imply, a certain detachment from the actions or agents which are their objects. I want to speak, at least at first, of something else: of the non-detached attitudes and reactions of people directly involved in trans-actions with each other; of the attitudes and reactions of offended parties and beneficiaries; of such things as gratitude, resentment, forgiveness, love, and hurt feelings. Perhaps something like the issue between optimists and pessimists arises in this neighbouring field too; and since this field is less crowded with disputants, the issue might here be easier to settle; and if it is settled here, then it might become easier to settle it in the disputant-crowded field.

What I have to say consists largely of commonplaces. So my language, like that of commonplaces generally, will be quite unscientific and imprecise. The central commonplace that I want to insist on is the very great importance that we attach to the attitudes and intentions towards us of other human beings, and the great extent to which our personal feelings and reactions depend upon, or involve, our beliefs about these attitudes and intentions. I can give no simple description of the field of phenomena at the centre of which stands this common-place truth; for the field is too complex. Much imaginative literature is devoted to exploring its complexities; and we have a large vocabulary for the purpose. There are simplifying styles of handling it in a general way. Thus we may, like La Rochefoucauld, put self-love or self-esteem or vanity at the centre of the picture and point out how it may be caressed by the esteem, or wounded by the indifference or contempt, of others. We might speak, in another jargon, of the need for love, and the loss of security which results from its withdrawal; or, in another, of human self-respect and its connection with the recognition of the individual's dignity. These simplifications are of use to me only if they help to emphasize how much we actually mind, how much it matters to us, whether the actions of other people – and particularly of *some* other people – reflect attitudes towards us of goodwill, affection, or esteem on the one hand or contempt, indifference, or malevolence on the other. If someone treads on my hand accidentally, while trying to help me, the pain may be no less acute than if he treads on it in contemptuous disregard of my existence or with a malevolent wish to injure me. But I shall generally feel in the second case a kind and degree of resentment that I shall not feel in the first. If someone's actions help me to some benefit I desire, then I am benefited in any case; but if he intended them so to benefit me because of his general goodwill towards me, I shall reasonably feel a gratitude which I should not feel at all if the benefit was an incidental consequence, unintended or even regretted by him, of some plan of action with a different aim.

These examples are of actions which confer benefits or inflict injuries over and above any conferred or inflicted by the mere manifestation of attitude and intention themselves. We should consider also in how much of our behaviour the benefit or injury resides mainly, or entirely, in the manifestation of attitude itself. So it is with good manners, and much of what we call kindness, on the one hand; with deliberate rudeness, studied indifference, or insult on the other.

Besides resentment and gratitude, I mentioned just now forgiveness. This is a rather unfashionable subject in moral philosophy at present; but to be forgiven is something we sometimes ask, and forgiving is something we sometimes say we do. To ask to be forgiven is in part to acknowledge that the attitude displayed in our actions was such as might properly be resented and in part to repudiate that attitude for the future (or at least for the immediate future); and to forgive is to accept the repudiation and to forswear the resentment.

We should think of the many different kinds of relationship which we can have with other people – as sharers of a common interest; as members of the same family; as colleagues; as friends; as lovers; as chance parties to an enormous range of transactions and encounters. Then we should think, in each of these connections in turn, and in others, of the kind of importance we attach to the attitudes and intentions towards us of those who stand in these relationships to us, and of the kinds of *reactive* attitudes and feelings to which we ourselves are prone. In general, we demand some degree of goodwill or regard on the part of those who stand in these relationships to us, though the forms we require it to take vary widely in different connections. The range and intensity of our reactive attitudes towards goodwill, its absence or its opposite vary no less widely. I have mentioned, specifically, resentment and gratitude; and they are a usefully opposed pair. But, of course, there is a whole continuum of reactive attitude and feeling stretching on both sides of these and – the most comfortable area – in between them.

The object of these commonplaces is to try to keep before our minds something it is easy to forget when we are engaged in philosophy, especially in our cool, contemporary style, viz. what it is actually like to be involved in ordinary interpersonal relationships, ranging from the most intimate to the most casual.

IV

It is one thing to ask about the general causes of these reactive attitudes I have alluded to; it is another to ask about the variations to which they are subject, the particular conditions in which they do or do not seem natural or reasonable or appropriate; and it is a third thing to ask what it would be like, what it is like, not to suffer them. I am not much concerned with the first question; but I am with the second; and perhaps even more with the third.

Let us consider, then, occasions for resentment: situations in which one person is offended or injured by the action of another and in which – in the absence of special considerations – the offended person might naturally or normally be expected to feel resentment. Then let us consider what sorts of special considerations might be expected to modify or mollify this feeling or remove it altogether. It needs no saying now how multifarious these considerations are. But, for my purpose, I think they can be roughly divided into two kinds. To the first group belong all those which might give occasion for the employment of such expressions as 'He didn't mean to', 'He hadn't realized', 'He didn't know'; and also all those which might give occasion for the use of the phrase 'He couldn't help it', when this is supported by such phrases as 'He was pushed', 'He had to do it', 'It was the only way', 'They left him no alternative', etc. Obviously these various pleas, and the kinds of situations in which they would be appropriate, differ from each other in striking and important ways. But for my present purpose they have something still more important in common. None of them invites us to suspend towards the agent, either at the time of his action or in general, our ordinary reactive attitudes. They do not invite us to view the agent as one in respect of whom these attitudes are in any way inappropriate. They invite us to view the *injury* as one in respect of which a particular one of these attitudes is inappropriate. They do not invite us to see the agent as other than a fully responsible agent. They invite us to see the injury as one for which he was not fully, or at all, responsible. They do not suggest that the agent is in any way an inappropriate object of that kind of demand for goodwill or regard which is reflected in our ordinary reactive attitudes. They suggest instead that the fact of injury was not in this case incompatible with that demand's being fulfilled, that the fact of injury was quite consistent with the agent's attitude and intentions being just what we demand they should be.[3] The agent was just ignorant of the injury he was causing, or had lost his balance through being pushed or had reluctantly to cause the injury for reasons which acceptably override his reluctance. The offering of such pleas by the agent and their acceptance by the sufferer is something in no way opposed to, or outside the context of, ordinary interpersonal relationships and the manifestation of ordinary reactive attitudes. Since things go wrong and situations are complicated, it is an essential and integral element in the transactions which are the life of these relationships.

The second group of considerations is very different. I shall take them in two subgroups of which the first is far less important than the second. In connection with the first subgroup we may think of such statements as 'He wasn't himself', 'He has been under very great strain recently', 'He was acting under post-hypnotic suggestion'; in connection with the second, we may think of 'He's only a child', 'He's a hopeless schizophrenic', 'His mind has been systematically perverted', 'That's purely compulsive behaviour on his part'. Such pleas as these do, as pleas of my first general group do not, invite us to suspend our ordinary reactive attitudes towards the agent, either at the time of his action or all the time. They do not invite us to see the agent's action in a way consistent with the full retention of ordinary interpersonal attitudes and merely inconsistent with one particular attitude. They invite us to view the agent himself in a different light from the light in which we should normally view one who has acted as he has acted. I shall not linger over the first subgroup of cases. Though they perhaps raise, in the short term, questions akin to those raised, in the long term, by the second subgroup, we may dismiss them without considering

---

[3] Perhaps not in every case just what we demand they should be, but in any case not just what we demand they should not be. For my present purpose these differences do not matter.

those questions by taking that admirably suggestive phrase, 'He wasn't himself', with the seriousness that – for all its being logically comic – it deserves. We shall not feel resentment against the man he is for the action done by the man he is not; or at least we shall feel less. We normally have to deal with him under normal stresses; so we shall not feel towards him, when he acts as he does under abnormal stresses, as we should have felt towards him had he acted as he did under normal stresses.

g⊦→   The second and more important subgroup of cases allows that the circumstances were normal, but presents the agent as psychologically abnormal – or as morally undeveloped. The agent was himself; but he is warped or deranged, neurotic or just a child. When we see someone in such a light as this, all our reactive attitudes tend to be profoundly modified. I must deal here in crude dichotomies and ignore the ever-interesting and ever-illuminating varieties of case. What I want to contrast is the attitude (or range of attitudes) of involvement or partici-pation in a human relationship, on the one hand, and what might be called the objective attitude (or range of attitudes) to another human being, on the other. Even in the same situation, I must add, they are not altogether exclusive of each other; but they are, profoundly, *opposed* to each other. To adopt the objective attitude to another human being is to see him, perhaps, as an object of social policy; as a subject for what, in a wide range of sense, might be called treatment; as something certainly to be taken account, perhaps precautionary account, of; to be managed or handled or cured or trained; perhaps simply to be avoided, though *this* gerundive is not peculiar to cases of objectivity of attitude. The objective attitude may be emotionally toned in many ways, but not in all ways: it may include repulsion or fear, it may include pity or even love, though not all kinds of love. But it cannot include the range of reactive feelings and attitudes which belong to involvement or participation with others in interpersonal human relationships; it cannot include resentment, gratitude, forgiveness, anger, or the sort of love which two adults can sometimes be said to feel reciprocally, for each other. If your attitude towards someone is wholly objective, then though you may fight him, you cannot quarrel with him, and though you may talk to him, even negotiate with him, you cannot reason with him. You can at most pretend to quarrel, or to reason, with him.

    Seeing someone, then, as warped or deranged or compulsive in behaviour or peculiarly unfortunate in his formative circumstances – seeing someone so tends, at least to some extent, to set him apart from normal participant reactive attitudes on the part of one who so sees him, tends to promote, at least in the civilized, objective attitudes. But there is something curious to add to this. The objective attitude is not only something we naturally tend to fall into in cases like these, where participant attitudes are partially or wholly inhibited by abnormalities or by immaturity. It is also something which is available as a resource in other cases too. We look with an objective eye on the compulsive behaviour of the neurotic or the tiresome behaviour of a very young child, thinking in terms of treatment or training. But we *can* sometimes look with something like the same eye on the behaviour of the normal and the mature. We *have* this resource and can sometimes use it: as a refuge, say, from the strains of involvement; or as an aid to policy; or simply out of intellectual curiosity. Being human, we cannot, in the normal case, do this for long, or altogether. If the strains of involvement, say, continue to be too great, then we have to do something else – like severing a relationship. But what is above all interesting is the tension there is, in us, between the participant attitude and the object-ive attitude. One is tempted to say: between our humanity and our intelligence. But to say this would be to distort both notions.

h→ What I have called the participant reactive attitudes are essentially natural human reactions to the good or ill will or indifference of others towards us, as displayed in *their* attitudes and actions. The question we have to ask is: What effect would, or should, the acceptance of the truth of a general thesis of determinism have upon these reactive attitudes? More specifically, would, or should, the acceptance of the truth of the thesis lead to the decay or the repudiation of all such attitudes? Would, or should, it mean the end of gratitude, resentment, and forgiveness; of all reciprocated adult loves; of all the essentially *personal* antagonisms?

But how can I answer, or even pose, this question without knowing *exactly* what the thesis of determinism is? Well, there is one thing we do know: that if there is a coherent thesis of determinism, then there must be a sense of 'determined' such that, if that thesis is true, then all behaviour whatever is determined in that sense. Remembering this, we can consider at least what possibilities lie formally open; and then perhaps we shall see that the question can be answered *without* knowing exactly what the thesis of determinism is. We can consider what possibilities lie open because we have already before us an account of the ways in which particular reactive attitudes, or reactive attitudes in general, may be, and, sometimes, we judge, should be, inhibited. Thus I considered earlier a group of considerations which tend to inhibit, and, we judge, should inhibit, resentment, in particular cases of an agent causing an injury, without inhibiting reactive atti-tudes in general towards that agent. Obviously this group of consider-ations cannot strictly bear upon our question; for that question concerns reactive attitudes in general. But resentment has a particular interest; so it is worth adding that it has never been claimed as a

consequence of the truth of determinism that one or another of these
considerations was operative in every case of an injury being caused by
an agent; that it would follow from the truth of determinism that
anyone who caused an injury *either* was quite simply ignorant of
causing it *or...*, etc. The prevalence of this happy state of affairs
would not be a consequence of the reign of universal determinism,
but of the reign of universal goodwill. We cannot, then, find here the
possibility of an affirmative answer to our question, even for the
particular case of resentment.

Next, I remarked that the participant attitude, and the personal
reactive attitudes in general, tend to give place, and it is judged by
the civilized should give place, to objective attitudes, just in so far as
the agent is seen as excluded from ordinary adult human relationships
by deep-rooted psychological abnormality – or simply by being a
child. But it cannot be a consequence of any thesis which is not itself
self-contradictory that abnormality is the universal condition.

Now this dismissal might seem altogether too facile; and so, in a
sense, it is. But whatever is too quickly dismissed in this dismissal is
allowed for in the only possible form of affirmative answer that
remains. We can sometimes, and in part, I have remarked, look on
the normal (those we rate as 'normal') in the objective way in which we
have learned to look on certain classified cases of abnormality. And
our question reduces to this: could, or should, the acceptance of the
determinist thesis lead us always to look on everyone exclusively in
this way? For this is the only condition worth considering under which
the acceptance of determinism could lead to the decay or repudiation
of participant reactive attitudes.

It does not seem to be self-contradictory to suppose that this might
happen. So I suppose we must say that it is not absolutely inconceivable that it should happen. But I am strongly inclined to think that it is,
for us as we are, practically inconceivable. The human commitment to
participation in ordinary interpersonal relationships is, I think, too
thoroughgoing and deeply rooted for us to take seriously the thought
that a general theoretical conviction might so change our world that,
in it, there were no longer any such things as interpersonal relationships as we normally understand them; and being involved in interpersonal relationships as we normally understand them precisely is being
exposed to the range of reactive attitudes and feelings that is in
question.

This, then, is a part of the reply to our question. A sustained
objectivity of interpersonal attitude, and the human isolation which
that would entail, does not seem to be something of which human
beings would be capable, even if some general truth were a theoretical

ground for it. But this is not all. There is a further point, implicit in the foregoing, which must be made explicit. Exceptionally, I have said, we can have direct dealings with human beings without any degree of personal involvement, treating them simply as creatures to be handled in our own interests, or our side's, or society's – or even theirs. In the extreme case of the mentally deranged, it is easy to see the connection between the possibility of a wholly objective attitude and the impossibility of what we understand by ordinary interpersonal relationships. Given this latter impossibility, no other civilized attitude is available than that of viewing the deranged person simply as something to be understood and controlled in the most desirable fashion. To view him as outside the reach of personal relationships is already, for the civilized, to view him in this way. For reasons of policy or self-protection we may have occasion, perhaps temporary, to adopt a fundamentally similar attitude to a 'normal' human being; to concentrate, that is, on understanding 'how he works', with a view to determining our policy accordingly or to finding in that very understanding a relief from the strains of involvement. Now it is certainly true that in the case of the abnormal, though not in the case of the normal, our adoption of the objective attitude is a consequence of our viewing the agent as *incapacitated* in some or all respects for ordinary interpersonal relationships. He is thus incapacitated, perhaps, by the fact that his picture of reality is pure fantasy, that he does not, in a sense, live in the real world at all; or by the fact that his behaviour is, in part, an unrealistic acting out of unconscious purposes; or by the fact that he is an idiot, or a moral idiot. But there is something else which, *because* this is true, is equally certainly *not* true. And that is that there is a sense of 'determined' such that (1) if determinism is true, all behaviour is determined in this sense, and (2) determinism might be true, i.e. it is not inconsistent with the facts as we know them to suppose that all behaviour might be determined in this sense, and (3) our adoption of the objective attitude towards the abnormal is the result of a prior embracing of the belief that the behaviour, or the relevant stretch of behaviour, of the human being in question is determined in this sense. Neither in the case of the normal, then, nor in the case of the abnormal is it true that, when we adopt an objective attitude, we do so *because* we hold such a belief. So my answer has two parts. The first is that we cannot, as we are, seriously envisage ourselves adopting a thoroughgoing objectivity of attitude to others as a result of theoretical conviction of the truth of determinism; and the second is that when we do in fact adopt such an attitude in a particular case, our doing so is not the consequence of a theoretical conviction which might be expressed as 'Determinism in this case', but is a consequence of our abandoning, for different reasons in different cases, the ordinary interpersonal attitudes.

$\boxed{k} \mapsto$ It might be said that all this leaves the real question unanswered, and that we cannot hope to answer it without knowing exactly what the thesis of determinism is. For the real question is not a question about what we actually do, or why we do it. It is not even a question about what we would *in fact* do if a certain theoretical conviction gained general acceptance. It is a question about what it would be rational to do if determinism were true, a question about the rational justification of ordinary interpersonal attitudes in general. To this I shall reply, first, that such a question could seem real only to one who had utterly failed to grasp the purport of the preceding answer, the fact of our natural human commitment to ordinary interpersonal attitudes. This commitment is part of the general framework of human life, not something that can come up for review as particular cases can come up for review within this general framework. And I shall reply, second, that if we could imagine what we cannot have, viz. a choice in this matter, then we could choose rationally only in the light of an assessment of the gains and losses to human life, its enrichment or impoverishment; and the truth or falsity of a general thesis of determinism would not bear on the rationality of *this* choice.[4]

V

The point of this discussion of the reactive attitudes in their relation – or lack of it – to the thesis of determinism was to bring us, if possible, nearer to a position of compromise in a more usual area of debate. We are not now to discuss reactive attitudes which are essentially those of offended parties or beneficiaries. We are to discuss reactive attitudes which are essentially not those, or only incidentally are those, of offended parties or beneficiaries, but are nevertheless, I shall claim, kindred attitudes to those I have discussed. I put resentment in the centre of the previous discussion. I shall put moral indignation – or, more weakly, moral disapprobation – in the centre of this one.

---

[4] The question, then, of the connection between rationality and the adoption of the objective attitude to others is misposed when it is made to seem dependent on the issue of determinism. But there is another question which should be raised, if only to distinguish it from the misposed question. Quite apart from the issue of determinism might it not be said that we should be nearer to being purely rational creatures in proportion as our relation to others was in fact dominated by the objective attitude? I think this might be said; only it would have to be added, once more, that if such a choice were possible, it would not necessarily be rational to choose to be more purely rational than we are.

The reactive attitudes I have so far discussed are essentially reactions to the quality of others' wills towards us, as manifested in their behaviour: to their good or ill will or indifference or lack of concern. Thus resentment, or what I have called resentment, is a reaction to injury or indifference. The reactive attitudes I have now to discuss might be described as the sympathetic or vicarious or impersonal or disinterested or generalized analogues of the reactive attitudes I have already discussed. They are reactions to the qualities of others' wills, not towards ourselves, but towards others. Because of this impersonal or vicarious character, we give them different names. Thus one who experiences the vicarious analogue of resentment is said to be indignant or disapproving, or morally indignant or disapproving. What we have here is, as it were, resentment on behalf of another, where one's own interest and dignity are not involved; and it is this impersonal or vicarious character of the attitude, added to its others, which entitle it to the qualification 'moral'. Both my description of, and my name for, these attitudes are, in one important respect, a little misleading. It is not that these attitudes are essentially vicarious – one can feel indignation on one's own account – but that they are essentially capable of being vicarious. But I shall retain the name for the sake of its suggestiveness; and I hope that what is misleading about it will be corrected in what follows.

The personal reactive attitudes rest on, and reflect, an expectation of, and demand for, the manifestation of a certain degree of goodwill or regard on the part of other human beings towards ourselves; or at least on the expectation of, and demand for, an absence of the manifestation of active ill will or indifferent disregard. (What will, in particular cases, *count* as manifestations of good or ill will or disregard will vary in accordance with the particular relationship in which we stand to another human being.) The generalized or vicarious analogues of the personal reactive attitudes rest on, and reflect, exactly the same expectation or demand in a generalized form; they rest on, or reflect, that is, the demand for the manifestation of a reasonable degree of goodwill or regard, on the part of others, not simply towards oneself, but towards all those on whose behalf moral indignation may be felt, i.e., as we now think, towards all men. The generalized and non-generalized forms of demand, and the vicarious and personal reactive attitudes which rest upon, and reflect, them are connected not merely logically. They are connected humanly; and not merely with each other. They are connected also with yet another set of attitudes which I must mention now in order to complete the picture. I have considered from two points of view the demands we make on others and our reactions to their possibly injurious actions. These were the points of view of one whose interest was directly involved (who suffers, say, the injury) and of others whose interest was not directly involved (who do not themselves suffer the injury). Thus I have spoken of personal reactive attitudes in the first connection and of their vicarious analogues in the second. But the picture is not complete unless we consider also the correlates of these attitudes on the part of those on whom the demands are made, on the part of the agents. Just as there are personal and vicarious reactive attitudes associated with demands on others for oneself and demands on others for others, so there are self-reactive attitudes associated with demands on oneself for others. And here we have to mention such phenomena as feeling bound or obliged (the 'sense of obligation'); feeling compunction; feeling guilty or remorseful or at least responsible; and the more complicated phenomenon of shame.

[m]→   All these three types of attitude are humanly connected. One who manifested the personal reactive attitudes in a high degree but showed no inclination at all to their vicarious analogues would appear as an abnormal case of moral egocentricity, as a kind of moral solipsist. Let him be supposed fully to acknowledge the claims to regard that others had on him, to be susceptible of the whole range of self-reactive attitudes. He would then see himself as unique both as one (*the* one) who had a general claim on human regard and as one (*the* one) on whom human beings in general had such a claim. This would be a kind of moral solipsism. But it is barely more than a conceptual possibility; if it is that. In general, though within varying limits, we demand of others for others, as well as of ourselves for others, something of the regard which we demand of others for ourselves. Can we imagine, besides that of the moral solipsist, any other case of one or two of these three types of attitude being fully developed, but quite unaccompanied by any trace, however slight, of the remaining two or one? If we can, then we imagine something far below or far above the level of our common humanity – a moral idiot or a saint. For all these types of attitude alike have common roots in our human nature and our membership of human communities.

Now, as of the personal reactive attitudes, so of their vicarious analogues, we must ask in what ways, and by what considerations, they tend to be inhibited. Both types of attitude involve, or express, a certain sort of demand for interpersonal regard. The fact of injury constitutes a prima facie appearance of this demand's being flouted or unfulfilled. We saw, in the case of resentment, how one class of considerations may show this appearance to be mere appearance, and hence inhibit resentment, *without* inhibiting, or displacing, the sort of demand of which resentment can be an expression, without in any way tending to make us suspend our ordinary interpersonal attitudes to the agent. Considerations of this class operate in just the same way, for just the same reasons, in connection with moral disapprobation or indignation; they inhibit indignation without in any way inhibiting the sort of demand on the agent of which indignation can be an expression, the range of attitudes towards him to which it belongs. But in this connection we may express the facts with a new emphasis. We may say, stressing the moral, the generalized aspect of the demand, considerations of this group have no tendency to make us see the agent as other than a morally responsible agent; they simply make us see the injury as one for which he was not morally responsible. The offering and acceptance of such exculpatory pleas as are here in question in no way detracts in our eyes from the agent's status as a term of moral relationships. On the contrary, since things go wrong and situations are complicated, it is an essential part of the life of such relationships.

But suppose we see the agent in a different light: as one whose picture of the world is an insane delusion; or as one whose behaviour, or a part of whose behaviour, is unintelligible to us, perhaps even to him, in terms of conscious purposes, and intelligible only in terms of unconscious purposes; or even, perhaps, as one wholly impervious to the self-reactive attitudes I spoke of, wholly lacking, as we say, in moral sense. Seeing an agent in such a light as this tends, I said, to inhibit resentment in a wholly different way. It tends to inhibit resentment because it tends to inhibit ordinary interpersonal attitudes in general, and the kind of demand and expectation which those attitudes involve; and tends to promote instead the purely objective view of the agent as one posing problems simply of intellectual understanding, management, treatment, and control. Again the parallel holds for those generalized or moral attitudes towards the agent which we are now concerned with. The same abnormal light which shows the agent to us as one in respect of whom the personal attitudes, the personal demand, are to be suspended, shows him to us also as one in respect of whom the impersonal attitudes, the generalized demand, are to be suspended. Only, abstracting now from direct personal interest, we may express the facts with a new emphasis. We may say: to the extent to which the agent is seen in this light, he is not seen as one on whom demands and expectations lie in that particular way in which we think of them as lying when we speak of moral obligation; he is not, to that extent, seen as a morally responsible agent, as a term of moral relationships, as a member of the moral community.

I remarked also that the suspension of ordinary interpersonal attitudes and the cultivation of a purely objective view is sometimes possible even when we have no such reasons for it as I have just

mentioned. Is this possible also in the case of the moral reactive attitudes? I think so; and perhaps it is easier. But the motives for a total
suspension of moral reactive attitudes are fewer, and perhaps weaker:
fewer, because only where there is antecedent personal involvement can
there be the motive of seeking refuge from the strains of such involvement; perhaps weaker, because the tension between objectivity of view
and the moral reactive attitudes is perhaps less than the tension between
objectivity of view and the personal reactive attitudes, so that we can in
the case of the moral reactive attitudes more easily secure the speculative or political gains of objectivity of view by a kind of setting on one
side, rather than a total suspension, of those attitudes.

n→   These last remarks are uncertain; but also, for the present purpose,
unimportant. What concerns us now is to inquire, as previously in
connection with the personal reactive attitudes, what relevance any
general thesis of determinism might have to their vicarious analogues.
The answers once more are parallel; though I shall take them in a
slightly different order. First, we must note, as before, that when the
suspension of such an attitude or such attitudes occurs in a particular
case, it is *never* the consequence of the belief that the piece of behaviour in question was determined in a sense such that all behaviour
might be, and, if determinism is true, all behaviour is, determined in
that sense. For it is not a consequence of any general thesis of determinism which might be true that nobody knows what he's doing or
that everybody's behaviour is unintelligible in terms of conscious
purposes or that everybody lives in a world of delusion or that nobody
has a moral sense, i.e. is susceptible of self-reactive attitudes, etc. In
fact no such sense of 'determined' as would be required for a general
thesis of determinism is ever relevant to our actual suspensions of
o→   moral reactive attitudes. Second, suppose it granted, as I have already
argued, that we cannot take seriously the thought that theoretical
conviction of such a general thesis would lead to the total decay of
the personal reactive attitudes. Can we then take seriously the thought
that such a conviction – a conviction, after all, that many have held or
said they held – would nevertheless lead to the total decay or repudiation of the vicarious analogues of these attitudes? I think that the
change in our social world which would leave us exposed to the
personal reactive attitudes but not at all to their vicarious analogues,
the generalization of abnormal egocentricity which this would entail,
is perhaps even harder for us to envisage as a real possibility than the
decay of both kinds of attitude together. Though there are some necessary and some contingent differences between the ways and cases in
which these two kinds of attitudes operate or are inhibited in their
operation, yet, as general human capacities or pronenesses, they

p→ stand or lapse together. Finally, to the further question whether it would not be *rational*, given a general theoretical conviction of the truth of determinism, so to change our world that in it all these attitudes were wholly suspended, I must answer, as before, that one who presses this question has wholly failed to grasp the import of the preceding answer, the nature of the human commitment that is here involved: it is useless to ask whether it would not be rational for us to do what it is not in our nature to (be able to) do. To this I must add, as before, that if there were, say, for a moment open to us the possibility of such a godlike choice, the rationality of making or refusing it would be determined by quite other considerations than the truth or falsity of the general theoretical doctrine in question. The latter would be simply irrelevant; and this becomes ironically clear when we remember that for those convinced that the truth of determinism nevertheless really would make the one choice rational, there has always been the insuperable difficulty of explaining in intelligible terms how its falsity would make the opposite choice rational.

Commentary on Strawson

It can be hard initially to see where the argument of this piece by Strawson is going. He makes many distinctions at the beginning, and is being extremely careful throughout, so there are passages of orientation and qualification that can strike the reader as quite complicated. However, there is a clear architecture to the piece, which this commentary is designed to help you find.

The overall point of the piece is to raise doubts about the significance of *determinism* for morality, especially the ways in which human beings regard one another as responsible or blameworthy for what they do. Strawson says he himself does not know what the thesis of determinism is (see a→). Is this not disconcerting? How can we say what the significance of determinism is, if we do not know what determinism is?

It will be worth recalling the rough statements of determinism made at the beginning of this chapter: that every event has a cause, or that, given an event's causes, the happening of the event is determined or necessary, or that anything that happens could in principle be predicted if we knew enough about its causes. Strawson, of course, understands this much about what determinism might say, and assumes that the reader does too. His approach could be put in this way: even knowing very roughly the sort of doctrine that determinism is supposed to be, what difference would it make to morality if determinism were true? The answer will tell us something about where to invest more philosophical labour. Perhaps if we can tell from even a vague notion of determinism that its truth would make no difference to morality, then we won't have to worry too much about making determinism a more precise doctrine, or about whether it is true?

Sections I and II may make for difficult reading at first. What the author is doing here is, as it were, drawing a map of the philosophical terrain, which later (in section III) he refers to as a 'field [...] crowded with disputants'. And at ⬚b⬚→ he states that his intention is to make a reconciliation. It should be a prime task to discover what this reconciliation is – who is to be reconciled with whom?

Strawson uses the common technique of personifying philosophical positions. He starts by describing a debate in which there are different voices putting forward different arguments. But his stance is to place himself outside the debate looking on, as it were. So the question is always what the participants in the debate would or might say to each other. Strawson wants to suggest that the participants need not disagree as much as they might think.

> Read just the first paragraph of 'Freedom and Resentment'. Write down a precise answer to the following question: which *two* philosophical positions does the author say he intends to reconcile here?

There are four basic positions in the first paragraph, which Strawson represents as held by four schematic kinds of person: (1) philosophers who 'say they do not know what the thesis of determinism is', (2) 'pessimists', (3) 'optimists', (4) a 'genuine moral sceptic'. Each holds a distinct view about determinism. But which views need we concern ourselves with in what follows? Strawson's intention is quite clearly to reconcile the positions held by (2) and (3). So we must concentrate on making clear what the so-called 'pessimists' and the so-called 'optimists' would believe.

Note that Strawson uses 'pessimist' and 'optimist' as terms of convenience, and that he means no more than 'pessimist about the compatibility of determinism and morality' and 'optimist about the compatibility of determinism and morality'. (He is not talking about people who are generally pessimistic or optimistic in the ordinary sense.)

I said the issue is the relationship between determinism and morality. Do we at least know what we mean by the term 'morality'? It is a large question, but for present purposes it will be sufficient to concentrate on what Strawson himself says.

> In the first paragraph Strawson refers to 'concepts and practices' that belong to morality. Make a note of what concepts he means, and of what practices he means.

The concepts in question are those of moral obligation and responsibility, which are fairly familiar notions in ordinary life. Obligation concerns what we ought to do, or perhaps what we have a duty to do. Responsibility relates (as

Schopenhauer said) to the notion of being 'the doers of our deeds' and to the notion of 'accountability' (or perhaps 'answerability'). Often in philosophy the doer is referred to as an *agent*, a word which comes from the Latin for 'doer'. An agent is a person who *acts*, in the sense of a person who *does something*.

Take an example. If we want to know who is responsible for, say, a window's being broken, then one thing we want to know is simply whose action it was that brought about the window's breaking. We might say that a falling tree was 'responsible' for breaking the window – if all we meant by 'responsible for X happening' is 'causing X to happen'. But 'responsibility' when applied to human beings usually means something more than that. A tree is not an agent. A tree could never be accountable or answerable for breaking the window, but we assume that most human beings, most of the time, could. We have a sense that the action of breaking the window is in some way under the control of the person who is responsible.

Answerability or accountability is closely related to the 'practices' characteristic of morality that Strawson lists, namely: punishing, blaming, expressing moral condemnation or approval. Again, we could not enter into any of these practices with the tree that broke our window. We might destroy the tree, we might even curse it for causing the damage, but the specific moral behaviour Strawson lists would not happen in this case. Only if we believe someone to have been somehow in control of what they did, and then to have done what they *ought not* to have done, do we *morally* condemn, blame or properly punish them. So it seems that only someone who uses the *concepts* of moral obligation and responsibility, and applies them to people, can take part in the moral *practices* Strawson mentions.

All of this – believing people to have responsibility and obligations, and treating them in specifically moral ways if they do or do not fulfil their obligations – is what Strawson's 'pessimist' thinks is unfounded if determinism is true. The 'optimist' thinks just the opposite: namely, that, if determinism is true, it makes no difference to all of these moral beliefs and ways of treating people.

The architecture of Strawson's argument

After a first read through, you will face the task of reading again more analytically to find the structure of the argument. The architecture of this piece requires some comment.

Section I sketches the philosophical terrain, and states the intention to reconcile optimists about determinism and morality with pessimists about determinism and morality.

Section II characterizes the kind of debate likely to occur between such 'optimists' and 'pessimists'.

Section III begins Strawson's own argument proper. He distinguishes 'personal reactive attitudes' from moral ones, and gives some examples of the place of personal reactive attitudes (such as resentment and gratitude) in our lives.

Section IV makes two chief points: (1) that there are reasons we can give for seeing resentment or gratitude as inappropriate attitudes towards someone; (2) that the truth of determinism would *not* be one of these reasons.

Section V returns to moral attitudes (which Strawson now calls 'vicarious analogues' of the personal reactive attitudes), and argues that determinism would likewise *not* be a reason to suspend moral attitudes.

The rest of this commentary will concentrate on sections III–V only, where Strawson presents his own argument.

Reactive attitudes

Read section III of 'Freedom and Resentment'. Give examples of what Strawson calls 'reactive attitudes'. Explain why they are 'reactive'.

At ⌐c⌐→ Strawson lists the kinds of attitude between people that he is generally concerned with in section III. But it is in the paragraph labelled ⌐d⌐→ that he explains why certain attitudes are reactive: they are attitudes we take to someone because of the attitude they display towards us. If someone's attitude to you is generous, your attitude to them in return may well be grateful. If their attitude to you is neglectful or aggressive, your attitude to them may well be resentful. Resentment and gratitude are the chief examples of reactive attitudes, and they are reactive because you adopt them in reaction to another attitude shown towards you by someone else.

Now we can move on to section IV, where Strawson argues for his central points about these reactive attitudes. The first five paragraphs, finishing just before ⌐h⌐→, raise the question about occasions when, despite some injury, it would not be appropriate to feel resentment towards the agent who brought about the injury.

Make a list of the different reasons Strawson gives for not feeling resentment over an injury. State how each relates to the responsibility of the agent who causes the injury.

The major distinction Strawson makes is between reasons for not feeling resentment about the particular action of an agent, and reasons for not feeling resentment towards the agent at all. The former 'do not invite us to see the agent as other than a fully responsible agent' (see ⌐e⌐→). The second group 'do . . . invite us to suspend our ordinary reactive attitudes towards the agent' (see ⌐f⌐→). That presumably means seeing the agent as less than fully responsible.

The most important group of cases for Strawson's argument is those where we take the 'objective attitude' to another human being. In the paragraph marked $\boxed{g}\!\mapsto$ Strawson explains this attitude as one in which we suspend our ordinary reactive attitudes.

But by now the reader may be wondering: how does all this relate to free will and determinism?

> What question does Strawson pose about reactive attitudes and determinism in section IV? What answer does he give? Pay especial attention to the passages marked $\boxed{h}\!\mapsto$, $\boxed{i}\!\mapsto$ and $\boxed{j}\!\mapsto$.

In the short paragraph marked $\boxed{h}\!\mapsto$ Strawson poses really the key question of his whole essay. Since it is cases of the 'objective attitude' that involve some removal of responsibility from agents, it is these cases where determinism might be thought to impact upon our taking of reactive attitudes towards agents. Hence the posing of a more restricted question at $\boxed{i}\!\mapsto$: if we believed determinism to be true, would it mean that we would begin to regard everybody with the 'objective attitude'?

> Pause to consider the question just raised. In other words, do you think we would stop feeling resentment and gratitude towards anyone if we thought that all of everyone's behaviour was determined?

Turning to $\boxed{j}\!\mapsto$, we discover that Strawson's answer is a confident No. Determinism is never a reason for suspending our reactive attitudes; and we cannot imagine having no reactive attitudes at all. Having them is just part of the way we are as human beings. Strawson's whole case depends upon this answer. (Some may feel that a Yes answer is also conceivable: a large debate could develop at this point.)

Moral attitudes

In section V Strawson moves back to moral attitudes, and concentrates on moral indignation or moral disapprobation. He is going to argue that the same answer to the question about determinism applies in this case too: believing determinism true would not lead us to abandon moral disapprobation of agents. The paragraph marked $\boxed{n}\!\mapsto$ makes this parallel clear.

> What do the moral attitudes Strawson discusses have in common with the previously discussed personal reactive attitudes (such as resentment)? How do the moral attitudes differ from the personal reactive attitudes?

Strawson calls the moral attitudes 'vicarious analogues' of the personal reactive attitudes he discussed earlier. They are analogues because both kinds of attitude are reactive attitudes. And 'vicarious' means 'on behalf of someone else'. So a moral reactive attitude is here construed as (1) an attitude we can take towards an agent on behalf of a third person who has been injured by the agent, (2) an attitude we take to the agent in reaction to the attitude the agent takes to the third person. Instead of 'vicarious' Strawson also uses the terms 'sympathetic', 'impersonal', 'disinterested' or 'generalized'. The idea is that to disapprove *morally* of what you do, I don't have to have been injured directly by you, or feel personally resentful myself.

At $\boxed{\text{l}} \mapsto$ Strawson mentions another morally important set of attitudes, which he calls 'self-reactive' and associates with 'demands on oneself for others'. This includes feeling oneself obliged to do something, feeling guilty, feeling ashamed. He states at $\boxed{\text{m}} \mapsto$ that all three types of attitude are 'humanly connected', and that we cannot imagine the different types existing without one another.

So to Strawson's grand conclusion, which he sets out in the paragraph marked $\boxed{\text{n}} \mapsto$. There are in fact three conclusions here: first, the reasons for suspending moral reactive attitudes towards some agent never include the truth of determinism; second, we cannot imagine a world in which we gave up our moral attitudes to one another.

> This second conclusion, running from $\boxed{\text{o}} \mapsto$ to $\boxed{\text{p}} \mapsto$ in the text, is stated in more complicated form, making a connection between moral attitudes and personal reactive attitudes: what is that connection?

Strawson here gives a miniature argument of the form:

(1) we cannot imagine giving up our personal reactive attitudes because of a belief in determinism,
(2) we cannot imagine a world in which we kept our personal reactive attitudes but lost our moral reactive attitudes; therefore
(3) we cannot imagine losing our moral reactive attitudes because of a belief in determinism.

Much depends here on the plausibility of Strawson's claim about 'what we can imagine' under step (2). Why could there not be a human world in which we became resentful or grateful to other agents in reaction to the attitudes they showed to us personally, but felt no moral disapproval on behalf of anyone else? That might be a strange and repellent world, but if it can be imagined, then this part of Strawson's argument is weakened.

The third conclusion Strawson reaches in our extract (see $\boxed{\text{p}} \mapsto$) is about what it would be rational to do if we believed determinism was true.

> Read from $\boxed{\text{p}} \mapsto$ to the end of the extract. Also read the paragraph marked $\boxed{\text{k}} \mapsto$ in section IV, which makes the parallel point in the case of personal reactive attitudes. How does Strawson respond to the question about the rationality of abandoning our reactive attitudes?

The point here could be put as follows. You might think it was one thing to say we *are unable to abandon* our practices of resentment and moral indignation, but quite another to say we *have good reason to retain* them. And if determinism is true, surely we ought to stop treating agents as responsible and ought to stop feeling resentment and moral indignation? The 'ought' here is that of rationality: we ought only to believe what we have good reason to believe, and if there is good reason not to believe it, we should stop believing it. The fact that we could not give up feeling resentment and moral indignation might show only the limits of our abilities. Some people, irrationally, simply cannot stop being afraid of spiders, even when they are convinced spiders are harmless. Would we not be like those people, if we simply could not stop having reactive attitudes, even when we were convinced that every agent's behaviour was determined?

Strawson's response is subtle. He suggests that the question of whether it is rational to retain our reactive attitudes should not even be askable if we have grasped what he has said already. If it is part of our very nature – part of being what we are – that we have reactive attitudes towards one another, then the rationality of doing so is not an issue at all. And even supposing we could imagine ourselves, in an entirely hypothetical situation, making a rational choice here, it might indeed not be rational to choose to abandon our reactive attitudes, once we considered overall 'the gains and losses to human life'.

In conclusion, notice how far we have travelled from our original question 'Do we have free will?' In effect, Strawson has invited us to forget that question, and to ask first 'How do we actually react to one another's behaviour?' and then 'Can we imagine remaining human and ceasing to react to one another's behaviour in this way?' From this we learn, if we are convinced by Strawson, that determinism is not really a threat to the concepts and practices of morality.

The debate need not end here. There is room for someone to come back with a better defined version of determinism, and try to show that this determinism is true, so that there is at least a sense in which we do not have free will. One might agree with Strawson that we could never abandon our attitudes, moral and personal, to one another, but argue that this shows nothing about free will as such – perhaps all it means is that we have to remain under an illusion of freedom, come what may? (Strawson would presumably reply that this view missed the point and that 'free will as such' was a red herring.) There is also the position of the moral sceptic Strawson mentioned at the outset: the position which says that morality is ill founded anyway, whether or nor determinism is true.

Another idea sometimes voiced about the problem of free will is that it shows we do not have a single consistent outlook on ourselves and our place in the world. On the one hand, we cannot cease to view ourselves 'humanly' as agents, subjects of thought, decision and action, and recipients of blame and other reactive attitudes. On the other hand, we want to understand the world objectively, in terms of what can be explained causally from a non-subjective or scientific point of view. But then we human beings have to be part of the scientific picture of the world of events with causes. And perhaps there is a fundamental, even insuperable difficulty for us in understanding ourselves both in that way and in ordinary human, interpersonal terms. Some other problems, including the mind–body problem and the problem of personal identity, might have a similar origin. That would suggest that the continuing difficulty over the question of free will is a symptom of an even deeper difficulty we have in comprehending ourselves.

8

Causality

Introduction to the Problem

What conditions obtain when true causal statements are made – when it is said, for instance, that John's seeing the papers mounting up *caused* his feeling of despair, or that the ringing of Jane's alarm bell *caused* her to wake up this morning? When something is a cause, it doesn't simply happen before the effect it has: in some sense or other it *produces* its effect. In some sense or other his seeing the papers mounting up *produced* despair in John. But what does this mean? What is it for one thing to cause, or to produce, another, or to make it happen?

In these examples – John's feeling despair, Jane's waking up – we find the word 'cause' in statements which could be used to give ordinary, everyday causal explanations. Our everyday use of causal notions extends far beyond statements containing the word 'cause' itself. One might have said 'John's despair resulted from his seeing the papers mounting up.' And one might have said 'Jane woke up *because* her alarm bell rang', or simply 'Jane's alarm bell woke her up.' There are many words which invoke a causal connection between things. When you appreciate how widespread is the use of causal language (of words such as 'cause', 'because', 'produce', 'make happen', 'result from', 'wake up' etc.), you see how pervasive and fundamental is an idea of causal connection. It seems that we need to recognize causality in order to find the world at all intelligible. It is no wonder that the nature of casuality is something that philosophers through the centuries have wanted to understand.

Causality is not only appealed to everyday but also both in science and in philosophy. In many people's view, science provides us with knowledge of causes; and much of the debate about causality has been conducted on the assumption that the projects of science, and their authority, can be better understood if we know better what causality is. Causality's importance within philosophy can be illustrated with some examples. Remember Descartes (whose First and Second Meditations came in chapters 1 and 2): he believed in *causal interaction* between mind and body; in the Third Meditation, he concludes that he is not the only thing that exists by arguing that only God could *cause* him to have the idea of a perfect being. The Schopenhauer reading in chapter 7 shows how a question about free will may be thought to turn on a question about causality. Philosophers of the past and present have wanted to use causal notions to understand a range of concepts, including freedom, agency, perception, memory and reference.

There are many more philosophical questions concerned with the phenomenon of causality than the one asked in the opening paragraph. But this is the leading question addressed in the two readings that follow. Both of the authors here are concerned with a particular aspect of the question – *What sort of necessity, if any, attaches to the relation between cause and effect*? If Jane wakes up *because* her alarm bell rings, then we take there to be a connection between Jane's alarm bell's ringing and Jane's waking up – a connection that would be missing in another case in which Jane's waking up came after the ringing of her alarm bell but was not caused by it. If one thinks that there is something about a cause which *makes* it be followed by its effect, then one seems to suppose that in the case in which Jane's waking up is caused by the ringing, it *necessarily* follows it. What exactly does it mean to say that two events (such as the ringing and the waking) are *necessarily* connected? Is it true that two events are necessarily connected when one causes the other? What sort of necessity would this be?

Introduction to Hume

David Hume's essay 'Of Tragedy' is a text in chapter 3. We are concerned now with Hume's writings in metaphysics, which take up Book One of *A Treatise of Human Nature* (1739–40), and *Enquiry Concerning Human Understanding* (1748).

Hume was the last of the three philosophers known as the British empiricists. (Locke and Berkeley are the other two; there are texts of both in chapter 9.) The doctrine of empiricism claims that experience is the ultimate source of all our knowledge, and observation of the world is the way to gain knowledge. As an empiricist, Hume sought to apply the method of observation to a study of human nature itself. He thought that abstract metaphysical speculation cannot yield progress in philosophy. Human beings live and function in the world, and philosophers should try to observe how they do so – in particular how they come by their ideas and their beliefs. We shall see that in his discussion of causality, Hume's principal concern is the question of how people come to have the idea that one thing is the cause of another.

Hume's account of causality has immense historical importance. On the one hand, it is central to a debate which occupied philosophers for the last forty years of the twentieth century and which still carries on. On the other hand, many historians of philosophy see Hume's contribution to the topic as the final chapter in a particular debate that began with Descartes. There are passages in Hume in which he engages in this particular debate by arguing against accounts of causation given by his predecessors and contemporaries. Most of these passages have been omitted from the extracts from the *Treatise* printed here. Here the focus is on Hume's positive arguments for his own view. When he expounds these arguments, Hume helps himself to pieces of terminology he has set up and assumptions for which he has argued earlier in the book. The rest of this introduction will explain some of Hume's terminology and assumptions.

Humean background

Hume's *Treatise* starts with a distinction among the contents of our minds. This is the distinction between impressions and ideas. It corresponds, Hume tells us, to the distinction between 'feeling and thinking': when we feel, we have impressions in our minds; when we think, ideas. Among 'feeling' Hume includes not only the experiencing of emotions, but also what we should now call perception (which Hume calls 'sensing') – seeing, hearing, touching etc. Among 'thinking', Hume includes not only pondering or wondering about things, but also remembering and imagining. Hume says that impressions are 'direct', 'vivid' and 'forceful', and that ideas are 'feeble', 'faint images'. (To observe Hume's distinction in operation, you might look at the book you are reading, and then close your eyes and think about the book, perhaps imagining that it might be a different colour. In Hume's view, you move from having an impression of the book to having an idea of the book.)

Hume claims that ideas are *copies* of impressions. This claim puts his empiricism in place: in saying that an idea can only be in one's mind if it is a copy of an impression previously there, Hume ensures that all our ideas can be traced back to sense experience. Hume calls some ideas *compound*: such ideas are made up out of simple ones. A compound idea need not be directly copied as such from a corresponding impression; but each of its components (each of the simple ideas of which it is made up) must be copied from a simple impression, according to Hume. Thus Hume thinks that we can always ask the question, about any idea we have, which impression or impressions it is derived from.

Hume's 'feeling'/'thinking' division corresponds to another distinction he works with – a distinction now between two different kinds of knowledge. Some propositions can only be known through observation – through 'feeling' in Hume's very broad sense of that term. These propositions say how things are in the world. On the other side of the distinction are propositions which can be known 'by the mere operation of thought'. These latter propositions are the 'certain' ones. Propositions that are certain in Hume's sense 'do not depend on what is anywhere existent in the universe', as he puts it. They may be 'intuitively certain' or 'demonstrably certain'. By an 'intuitively' certain proposition, Hume means one that can be known simply by understanding what it says. By a 'demonstrably' certain proposition, Hume means one that follows logically from, and thus can be proved from, intuitively certain propositions.

Hume holds that intuitively certain propositions owe their certainty to relationships between terms (as we shall see at $\boxed{h}$→). For example, one can know the proposition that 'Orange is more like red than blue' just by understanding what it says, because if one understands it, one sees that the relations of *resemblance* that it states are exactly what it states them to be; and one can know the proposition that 'It is never day and night' just by understanding what it says, because if one understands it, one sees that 'day' and 'night' stand in a relation of *contrariety* (i.e. they are contrary terms – terms which cannot both apply to something). Notice that Hume would not classify 'I am thinking', whose certainty Descartes underlined, as a certain proposition. To know that one is thinking, it is not enough, at least in Hume's view, to understand what the proposition says.

Hume believes that the only propositions that are necessary are the ones he calls certain. This belief helps explain why he opposes accounts of casuality in terms of *necessary connection*. We shall see that, although such accounts are Hume's main target, Hume does not deny that *necessary connection* is a crucial part of our thinking about *cause*. In Hume's account, it can be correct to say that '*c* is necessarily connected with *e*', but it is wrong to suppose that this states a simple fact about a relation holding between *c* and *e*.

Note: These extracts are from *A Treatise of Human Nature, Book I: Of the Understanding*. They come from Part III, entitled 'Of Knowledge and Probability'. Hume's spelling has been modernized, and to a small extent the punctuation has been too.

David Hume, *A Treatise of Human Nature, Book I* (extracts from Part III)

Section 2 Of Probability; and of the Idea of Cause and Effect

$\boxed{a}$→ [. . .] We must consider the idea of *causation*, and see from what origin it is derived. It is impossible to reason justly, without understanding perfectly the idea concerning which we reason; and it is impossible perfectly to understand any idea, without tracing it up to its origin, and examining that primary impression, from which it arises. The examination of the impression bestows a clearness on the idea; and the examination of the idea bestows a like clearness on all our reasoning.

b→ Let us therefore cast our eye on any two objects, which we call cause and effect, and turn them on all sides, in order to find that impression, which produces an idea, of such prodigious consequence. At first sight I perceive, that I must not search for it in any of the particular *qualities* of the objects; since, whichever of these qualities I pitch on, I find some object, that is not possessed of it, and yet falls under the denomination of cause or effect. And indeed there is nothing existent, either externally or internally, which is not to be considered either as a cause or an effect; though it is plain there is no one quality, which universally belongs to all beings, and gives them a title to that denomination.

The idea, then, of causation must be derived from some *relation* among objects; and that relation we must now endeavour to discover. I find in the first place, that whatever objects are considered as causes or effects, are *contiguous*; and that nothing can operate in a time or place,
c→ which is ever so little removed from those of its existence. Though distant objects may sometimes seem productive of each other, they are commonly found upon examination to be linked by a chain of causes, which are contiguous among themselves, and to the distant objects; and when in any particular instance we cannot discover this connection, we still presume it to exist. We may therefore consider the relation of contiguity as essential to that of causation; at least may suppose it such, according to the general opinion, till we can find a more proper occasion to clear up this matter, by examining what objects are or are not susceptible of juxtaposition and conjunction.

d→ The second relation I shall observe as essential to causes and effects, is not so universally acknowledged, but is liable to some controversy. It is that of PRIORITY of time in the cause before the effect. Some pretend that it is not absolutely necessary a cause should precede its effect; but that any object or action, in the very first moment of its existence, may exert its productive quality, and give rise to another object or action, perfectly co-temporary with itself. But beside that experience in most instances seems to contradict this opinion, we may establish the relation of priority by a kind of inference or reasoning. It is an established maxim both in natural and moral philosophy, that an object, which exists for any time in its full perfection without producing another, is not its sole cause; but is assisted by some other principle, which pushes it from its state of inactivity, and makes it exert that energy, of which it was secretly possessed. Now if any cause may be perfectly co-temporary with its effect, it is certain, according to this maxim, that they must all of them be so; since any one of them, which retards its operation for a single moment, exerts not itself at that very individual time, in which it might have operated; and therefore is no proper cause. The consequence of this would be no less than the destruction of that succession of causes, which we observe in the world; and indeed, the utter annihilation of time. For if one cause were co-temporary with its effect, and this effect with its effect, and so on, it is plain there would be no such thing as succession, and all objects must be co-existent.

If this argument appear satisfactory, it is well. If not, I beg the reader to allow me the same liberty, which I have used in the preceding case, of supposing it such. For he shall find, that the affair is of no great importance. [...]

e ⊢→ Shall we then rest contented with these two relations of contiguity and succession, as affording a complete idea of causation? By no means. An object may be contiguous and prior to another, without being considered as its cause. There is a NECESSARY CONNEC-TION to be taken into consideration; and that relation is of much greater importance, than any of the other two above-mentioned. [...]

It is necessary for us to leave the direct survey of this question concerning the nature of that *necessary connection* which enters into our idea of cause and effect; and endeavour to find some other questions, the examination of which will perhaps afford a hint that may serve to clear up the present difficulty. Of these questions there occur two, which I shall proceed to examine, *viz.*

f ⊢→ First, for what reason we pronounce it *necessary*, that every thing whose existence has a beginning, should also have a cause.

Secondly, why we conclude, that such particular causes must *necessarily* have such particular effects; and what is the nature of that inference we draw from the one to the other, and of the *belief* we repose in it? [...]

Section 3 Why a Cause is always Necessary

To begin with the first question concerning the necessity of a cause. It is a general maxim in philosophy, that *whatever begins to exist, must*
g ⊢→ *have a cause of existence.* This is commonly taken for granted in all reasonings, without any proof given or demanded. It is supposed to be

founded on intuition, and to be one of those maxims, which though they may be denied with the lips, it is impossible for men in their hearts really to doubt of. But if we examine this maxim by the idea of knowledge above explained, we shall discover in it no mark of any such intuitive certainty; but on the contrary shall find, that it is of a nature quite foreign to that species of conviction.

[h]→ All certainty arises from the comparison of ideas, and from the discovery of such relations as are unalterable, so long as the ideas continue the same. These relations are *resemblance, proportions in quantity and number, degrees of any quality*, and *contrariety*; none of which are implied in this proposition, *Whatever has a beginning has also a cause of existence*. That proposition therefore is not intuitively certain. At least any one, who would assert it to be intuitively certain, must deny these to be the only infallible relations, and must find some other relation of that kind to be implied in it; which it will then be time enough to examine.

[i]→ But here is an argument, which proves at once, that the foregoing proposition is neither intuitively nor demonstrably certain. We can never demonstrate the necessity of a cause to every new existence, or new modification of existence, without showing at the same time the impossibility there is, that any thing can ever begin to exist without some productive principle; and where the latter proposition cannot be proved, we must despair of ever being able to prove the former. Now that the latter proposition is utterly incapable of a demonstrative

[j]→ proof, we may satisfy ourselves by considering that as all distinct ideas are separable from each other, and as the ideas of cause and effect are evidently distinct, it will be easy for us to conceive any object to be non-existent this moment, and existent the next, without conjoining to it the distinct idea of a cause or productive principle. The separation, therefore, of the idea of a cause from that of a beginning of existence, is plainly possible for the imagination; and consequently the actual separation of these objects is so far possible, that it implies no contradiction nor absurdity; and is therefore incapable of being refuted by any reasoning from mere ideas; without which it is impossible to demonstrate the necessity of a cause. [...]

Section 6   Of the Inference from the Impression to the Idea

[k]→ It is easy to observe, that in tracing th[e] relation [of cause and effect], the inference we draw from cause to effect, is not derived merely from a

survey of these particular objects, and from such a penetration into their essences as may discover the dependence of the one upon the other. There is no object, which implies the existence of any other if we consider these objects in themselves, and never look beyond the ideas which we form of them. Such an inference would amount to knowledge, and would imply the absolute contradiction and impossibility of conceiving any thing different. But as all distinct ideas are separable, it is evident there can be no impossibility of that kind. When we pass from a present impression to the idea of any object, we might possibly have separated the idea from the impression, and have substituted any other idea in its room.

l⟩ It is therefore by EXPERIENCE only, that we can infer the existence of one object from that of another. The nature of experience is this. We remember to have had frequent instances of the existence of one species of objects; and also remember, that the individuals of another species of objects have always attended them, and have existed in a regular order of contiguity and succession with regard to them. Thus we remember, to have seen that species of object we call flame, and to have felt that species of sensation we call heat. We likewise call to mind their constant conjunction in all past instances. Without any farther ceremony, we call the one cause and the other effect, and infer the existence of the one from that of the other. In all those instances, from which we learn the conjunction of particular causes and effects, both the causes and effects have been perceived by the senses, and are remembered. But in all cases, wherein we reason concerning them, there is only one perceived or remembered, and the other is supplied in conformity to our past experience.

Thus in advancing we have insensibly discovered a new relation betwixt cause and effect, when we least expected it, and were entirely employed upon another subject. This relation is their CONSTANT CONJUNCTION. Contiguity and succession are not sufficient to make us pronounce any two objects to be causes and effect, unless we perceive, that these two relations are preserved in several instances.

m⟩ [...] We shall continue the thread of our discourse; and having found, that after the discovery of the constant conjunction of any objects, we always draw an inference from one object to another, we shall now examine the nature of that inference, and of the transition from the impression to the idea. Perhaps it will appear in the end, that the necessary connection depends on the inference, instead of the inference's depending on the necessary connection. [...]

Section 14 Of the Idea of Necessary
Connection

n → [...] We must now return upon our footsteps to examine that question, which[1] first occurred to us, and which we dropped in our way, viz. *What is our idea of necessity, when we say that two objects are necessarily connected together?* Upon this head I repeat what I have often had occasion to observe, that as we have no idea, that is not derived from an impression, we must find some impression, that gives rise to this idea of necessity, if we assert we have really such an idea. In order to this I consider, in what objects necessity is commonly supposed to lie; and finding that it is always ascribed to causes and effects, I turn my eye to two objects supposed to be placed in that relation; and examine them in all the situations, of which they are susceptible. I immediately perceive, that they are *contiguous* in time and place, and that the object we call cause *precedes* the other we call effect. In no one instance can I go any farther, nor is it possible for me to discover any third relation betwixt these objects. I therefore enlarge my view to comprehend several instances; where I find like objects always existing in like relations of contiguity and succession. At first sight this seems to serve but little to my purpose. The reflection on several instances only repeats the same objects; and therefore can never give rise to a new idea. But upon farther enquiry I find, that the repetition is not in every particular the same, but produces a new impression, and by that means the idea, which I at present examine. For after a frequent repetition, I find, that upon the appearance of one of the objects, the mind is *determined* by custom to consider its usual attendant, and to consider it in a stronger light upon account of its relation to the first object. It is this impression, then, or determination, which affords me the idea of necessity. [...]

There is no question, which on account of its importance, as well as difficulty, has caused more disputes both among ancient and modern philosophers, than this concerning the efficacy of causes, or that quality which makes them be followed by their effects. But before they entered upon these disputes, methinks it would not have been improper to have examined what idea we have of that efficacy, which is the subject of the controversy. This is what I find principally wanting in their reasonings, and what I shall here endeavour to supply.

o → I begin with observing that the terms of *efficacy, agency, power, force, energy, necessity, connection,* and *productive quality,* are all nearly synonymous; and therefore it is an absurdity to employ any of

---

[1] Section 2.

them in defining the rest. By this observation we reject at once all the vulgar definitions, which philosophers have given of power and efficacy; and instead of searching for the idea in these definitions, must look for it in the impressions, from which it is originally derived. If it be a compound idea, it must arise from compound impressions. If simple, from simple impressions.

I believe the most general and most popular explication of this matter, is to say,[2] that finding from experience, that there are several new productions in matter, such as the motions and variations of body, and concluding that there must somewhere be a power capable of producing them, we arrive at last by this reasoning at the idea of power and efficacy. But to be convinced that this explication is more popular than philosophical, we need but reflect on two very obvious principles. First, that reason alone can never give rise to any original idea, and secondly, that reason, as distinguished from experience, can never make us conclude, that a cause or productive quality is absolutely requisite to every beginning of existence. Both these considerations have been sufficiently explained: and therefore shall not at present be any farther insisted on.

I shall only infer from them, that since reason can never give rise to the idea of efficacy, that idea must be derived from experience, and from some particular instances of this efficacy, which make their passage into the mind by the common channels of sensation or reflection. [...]

p⊢→   Suppose two objects to be presented to us, of which the one is the cause and the other the effect; it is plain, that from the simple consideration of one, or both these objects we never shall perceive the tie by which they are united, or be able certainly to pronounce, that there is a connection betwixt them. It is not, therefore, from any one instance, that we arrive at the idea of cause and effect, of a necessary connection of power, of force, of energy, and of efficacy. Did we never see any but particular conjunctions of objects, entirely different from each other, we should never be able to form any such ideas.

q⊢→   But again, suppose we observe several instances, in which the same objects are always conjoined together, we immediately conceive a connection betwixt them, and begin to draw an inference from one to another. This multiplicity of resembling instances, therefore, constitutes the very essence of power or connection, and is the source from which the idea of it arises. In order, then, to understand the idea of power, we must consider that multiplicity; nor do I ask more to give a solution of that difficulty, which has so long perplexed us. For thus I reason. The repetition of perfectly similar instances can never *alone*

---

[2]   See Mr *Locke*; chapter of power.

give rise to an original idea, different from what is to be found in any particular instance, as has been observed, and as evidently follows from our fundamental principle, that *all ideas are copied from impressions*. Since therefore the idea of power is a new original idea, not to be found in any one instance, and which yet arises from the repetition of several instances, it follows, that the repetition *alone* has not that effect, but must either *discover* or *produce* something new, which is the source of that idea. Did the repetition neither discover nor produce anything new, our ideas might be multiplied by it, but would not be enlarged above what they are upon the observation of one single instance. Every enlargement, therefore, (such as the idea of power or connection) which arises from the multiplicity of similar instances, is copied from some effects of the multiplicity, and will be perfectly understood by understanding these effects. Wherever we find anything new to be discovered or produced by the repetition, there we must place the power, and must never look for it in any other object.

But it is evident, in the first place, that the repetition of like objects in like relations of succession and contiguity *discovers* nothing new in any one of them.

Secondly, it is certain that this repetition of similar objects in similar situations *produces* nothing new either in these objects, or in any external body. For it will readily be allowed, that the several instances we have of the conjunction of resembling causes and effects are in themselves entirely independent, and that the communication of motion, which I see result at present from the shock of two billiard balls, is totally distinct from that which I saw result from such an impulse a twelve-month ago. These impulses have no influence on each other. They are entirely divided by time and place; and the one might have existed and communicated motion, though the other never had been in being.

There is, then, nothing new either discovered or produced in any objects by their constant conjunction, and by the uninterrupted resemblance of their relations of succession and contiguity. But it is from this resemblance, that the ideas of necessity, of power, and of efficacy, are derived. These ideas, therefore, represent not anything, that does or can belong to the objects, which are constantly conjoined. This is an argument, which, in every view we can examine it, will be found perfectly unanswerable. Similar instances are still the first source of our idea of power or necessity; at the same time that they have no influence by their similarity either on each other, or on any external object. We must, therefore, turn ourselves to some other quarter to seek the origin of that idea.

Though the several resembling instances, which give rise to the idea of power, have no influence on each other, and can never produce any new quality *in the object*, which can be the model of that idea, yet the *observation* of this resemblance produces a new impression *in the mind*, which is its real model. For after we have observed the resemblance in a sufficient number of instances, we immediately feel a determination of the mind to pass from one object to its usual attendant, and to conceive it in a stronger light upon account of that relation. This determination is the only effect of the resemblance; and therefore must be the same with power or efficacy, whose idea is derived from the resemblance. The several instances of resembling conjunctions lead us into the notion of power and necessity. These instances are in themselves totally distinct from each other, and have no union but in the mind, which observes them, and collects their ideas. Necessity, then, is the effect of this observation, and is nothing but an internal impression of the mind, or a determination to carry our thoughts from one object to another. Without considering it in this view, we can never arrive at the most distant notion of it, or be able to attribute it either to external or internal objects, to spirit or body, to causes or effects.

The necessary connection betwixt causes and effects is the foundation of our inference from one to the other. The foundation of our inference is the transition arising from the accustomed union. These are, therefore, the same.

The idea of necessity arises from some impression. There is no impression conveyed by our senses, which can give rise to that idea. It must, therefore, be derived from some internal impression, or impression of reflection. There is no internal impression, which has any relation to the present business, but that propensity, which custom produces, to pass from an object to the idea of its usual attendant. This therefore is the essence of necessity. Upon the whole, necessity is something, that exists in the mind, not in objects; nor is it possible for us ever to form the most distant idea of it, considered as a quality in bodies. Either we have no idea of necessity, or necessity is nothing but that determination of the thought to pass from causes to effects, and from effects to causes, according to their experienced union.
[...]

It is now time to collect all the different parts of this reasoning, and by joining them together form an exact definition of the relation of cause and effect, which makes the subject of the present enquiry. This order would not have been excusable, of first examining our inference from the relation before we had explained the relation itself, had it been possible to proceed in a different method. But as the nature of the relation depends so much on that of the inference, we have been obliged to advance in this seemingly preposterous manner, and make use of terms before we were able exactly to define them, or fix their meaning. We shall now correct this fault by giving a precise definition of cause and effect.

There may two definitions be given of this relation, which are only different, by their presenting a different view of the same object, and making us consider it either as a *philosophical* or as a *natural* relation; either as a comparison of two ideas, or as an association betwixt them. We may define a CAUSE to be 'An object precedent and contiguous to another, and where all the objects resembling the former are placed in like relations of precedence and contiguity to those objects that resemble the latter.' If this definition be esteemed defective, because drawn from objects foreign to the cause, we may substitute this other definition in its place, viz. 'A CAUSE is an object precedent and contiguous to another, and so united with it, that the idea of the one determines the mind to form the idea of the other, and the impression of the one to form a more lively idea of the other.' Should this definition also be rejected for the same reason, I know no other remedy, than that the persons, who express this delicacy, should substitute a juster definition in its place. But for my part I must own my incapacity for such an undertaking. When I examine with the utmost accuracy those objects, which are commonly denominated causes and effects, I find, in considering a single instance, that the one object is precedent and contiguous to the other; and in enlarging my view to consider several instances, I find only, that like objects are constantly placed in like relations of succession and contiguity. Again, when I consider the influence of this constant conjunction, I perceive, that such a relation can never be an object of reasoning, and can never operate upon the mind, but by means of custom, which determines the imagination to make a transition from the idea of one object to that of its usual attendant, and from the impression of one to a more lively idea of the other. However extraordinary these sentiments may appear, I think it fruitless to trouble myself with any farther enquiry or reasoning upon the subject, but shall repose myself on them as on established maxims.

Section 15   Rules by which to Judge of Causes and Effects

According to the precedent doctrine, there are no objects which by the mere survey, without consulting experience, we can determine to be the causes of any other; and no objects, which we can certainly determine in the same manner not to be the causes. Any thing may produce any thing. Creation, annihilation, motion, reason, volition; all these may arise from one another, or from any other object we can imagine. Nor will this appear strange, if we compare two principles explained above, *that the constant conjunction of objects determines their causation*, and *that properly speaking, no objects are contrary to each other but existence and non-existence.* Where objects are not contrary, nothing hinders them from having that constant conjunction, on which the relation of cause and effect totally depends.

Since therefore it is possible for all objects to become causes or effects to each other, it may be proper to fix some general rules, by which we may know when they really are so.

1   The cause and effect must be contiguous in space and time.
2   The cause must be prior to the effect.
3   There must be a constant union betwixt the cause and effect. It is chiefly this quality, that constitutes the relation.
4   The same cause always produces the same effect, and the same effect never arises but from the same cause. This principle we derive from experience, and is the source of most of our philosophical reasonings. For when by any clear experiment we have discovered the causes or effects of any phenomenon, we immediately extend our observation to every phenomenon of the same kind, without waiting for that constant repetition, from which the first idea of this relation is derived.
5   There is another principle, which hangs upon this, viz. that where several different objects produce the same effect, it must be by means of some quality, which we discover to be common amongst them. For as like effects imply like causes, we must always ascribe the causation to the circumstance, wherein we discover the resemblance.
6   The following principle is founded on the same reason. The difference in the effects of two resembling objects must proceed from that particular, in which they differ. For as like causes always produce like effects, when in any instance we find our expectation to be disappointed, we must conclude that this irregularity proceeds from some difference in the causes.
7   When any object increases or diminishes with the increase or diminution of its cause, it is to be regarded as a compounded effect, derived from the union of the several different effects, which arise from the several different parts of the cause. The absence or presence of one part of the cause is here supposed to be always attended with the absence or presence of a proportionable part of the effect. This constant conjunction sufficiently proves, that the

one part is the cause of the other. We must, however, beware not to draw such a conclusion from a few experiments. A certain degree of heat gives pleasure; if you diminish that heat, the pleasure diminishes; but it does not follow, that if you augment it beyond a certain degree, the pleasure will likewise augment; for we find that it degenerates into pain.

8   The eighth and last rule I shall take notice of is, that an object, which exists for any time in its full perfection without any effect, is not the sole cause of that effect, but requires to be assisted by some other principle, which may forward its influence and operation. For as like effects necessarily follow from like causes, and in a contiguous time and place, their separation for a moment shows, that these causes are not complete ones.

Commentary on Hume

Section 2

We saw in the 'Humean Background' (in 'Introduction to Hume' above) why he thinks that we can always ask the question, about any idea we have, which impression or impressions it is derived from. At $\boxed{a}\!\rightarrow$ we see that an instance of this question sets in motion Hume's treatment of causality.

At $\boxed{b}\!\rightarrow$ Hume invites us to look for an impression of causation in the objects that are causes and effects. In claiming that we cannot find such an impression, he denies that causality can be observed in the individual case.

Hume appears to mean *events* when he uses the word 'objects' in this context. We saw some examples of events at the beginning of the chapter – John's seeing the papers mounting up, the ringing of Jane's alarm bell. An example that Hume gives himself is the collision of two billiard balls. (You probably use 'object' so that a billiard ball counts as an object. But a billiard ball – as opposed to the movement of one, or a collision of two balls – seems not to belong in the category of things that Hume intends by 'objects' here.) Hume tells us that however hard we look at the individual objects that are causes and effects, we will not be able to come up with any impression from which we could get our idea of 'cause' or 'effect'.

To see what is meant by the conclusion of the argument Hume gives here (a conclusion he states in the first sentence of the next paragraph) that our idea of causation must come from some *relation*, you might consider the idea of *being a mother*. Someone is a mother not because she is herself some way but because something else (in this case another human being who is her son or daughter) is *related* to her in a certain way. (There is a discussion of relations – of which *identity* is a special case – in the 'Introduction to the Problem' in chapter 6.)

How does the argument that Hume gives in the second and third sentences of the paragraph marked [b]→ work? Think of examples to help you consider this question.

Hume's argument is that 'being a cause' and 'being an effect' cannot be qualities (i.e. properties) of events, because (a) whatever quality we might latch on to as the candidate for being the quality in question, we can find another event which has that quality but which isn't a cause or effect, and (b) that whatever event we latch on to, we can bring it under the head either of 'cause' or 'effect', yet a candidate for the quality in question can hardly be something that belongs to *all* events.

Hume's word 'contiguous' means neighbouring, or adjacent, in space and time. At [c]→ Hume allows that 'distant' (i.e. non-contiguous) objects some-times seem to stand to one another as cause to effect. He explains why it should seem so, even though it isn't really so: really there is no action at a distance.

State Hume's explanation at [c]→ in your own words, giving examples of causal chains.
Do you agree with Hume that there is no action at a distance?

Some people find it natural to think that when iron filings are attracted towards a magnet, the magnet acts on filings that are not touching it. This seems to be an example of action at a distance.

In the paragraph that starts at [d]→ Hume makes, and then argues for, the claim that causes must be temporally prior to their effects, i.e. come before them in time.

Ask yourself the following questions about the argument in [d]→:
  (i) What is Hume's attitude to his argument?
 (ii) Where does the argument start?
(iii) What are its premises?
(iv) Do you accept its conclusion or do you think that a cause might be simultaneous with its effect?

Hume seems not to be very bothered about whether his argument will be persuasive. He appears to rely on two premises: (a) that time or duration cannot itself produce any change (this is one way of understanding Hume's 'established maxim'), and (b) that if we thought that there was a time when cause and effect were both in existence, then we should have to allow that time or duration had produced some change. Those who do not accept the argument will want to produce a counter-example to its conclusion that causes precede their effects. (A counter-example is a case that shows a generalization to be false.) One such counter-example might be this: a piece of iron's reaching 1,535 °C causes the iron to start to melt, and is simultaneous with – not temporally prior to – its starting to melt.

At e⟩→ Hume suggests that he will be looking for something like a definition of 'cause'. In Hume's scheme of things, our idea of cause is a compound idea, so that it ought in principle to be possible to break it down into the simple ideas that it is made up from. Hume thinks it is obvious that, besides an event's being contiguous with another and temporally prior to that other, the further ingredient we need, to understand what it is for the event to be the cause of the other, has to do with necessary connection. But Hume sees a difficulty about supposing that we have an idea of necessary connection. This difficulty will be explained in his discussion in section 14.

At f⟩→ Hume introduces two questions. We shall see that he is to devote section 3 to the first question, and much of section 14 to the second.

Section 3

Hume's first question might be put like this: 'Does every event necessarily have a cause?' Hume himself, when he asks the question, moves away from speaking of 'objects' as what are caused: he speaks now of 'every thing whose existence has a beginning'. He sums up his question as one about 'the necessity of the cause', and he uses various different formulations in his discussion.

At g⟩→ we learn that Hume thinks that everyone assumes the answer to his question to be *Yes*. (Perhaps Hume thinks that everyone assumes that everything which comes to be in the world – whether it is an 'object' in Hume's special sense [i.e. an event] or an 'object' in a more ordinary sense – must be caused to be there. That would explain why he uses such formulations as 'every thing whose existence has a beginning' and 'whatever begins to exist'.) Hume says that 'we shall discover' that the correct answer is *No*: it is not the case that every event necessarily has a cause. Notice that in answering *No*, Hume does not deny that every event *does* have a cause; he is concerned with whether this is '*certain*' in his sense. If it is certain, then every event *must* have a cause. Hume devotes the paragraph marked h⟩→ to showing that it is not intuitively certain that every event has a cause, and the paragraph that starts at i⟩→ to showing that it is not certain, either intuitively or demonstrably.

Hume's argument at h⟩→ turns on claims about relations which he has made earlier (see the 'Humean Background' for his notion of intuitive certainty).

Do you think there are examples of intuitively certain propositions whose certainty is not owed to any of the four relations among ideas that Hume mentions at h⟩→ ? Do you find it plausible that the proposition whose intuitive certainty is at issue here – that every event has a cause – is intuitively certain?

Many would argue against Hume that a statement such as 'If I am thinking, then I exist' is intuitively certain but does not owe its intuitive certainty to any of Hume's four relations. But not many people would disagree with Hume about the proposition whose intuitive certainty is at issue here: they don't find it plausible that understanding the proposition that every event has a cause is enough to know its truth.

Hume's argument in the paragraph that starts at ⌐i⌐⟶ is rather complex. In the second sentence, Hume asserts that there are two propositions whose proofs go hand in hand. This enables him to direct his argument against what he calls the latter proposition, in order to demolish the former.

At ⌐j⌐⟶ Hume has 'we may satisfy ourselves by considering that'. This signals the beginning of an argument – one that starts with the words 'as all distinct ideas are separable'. The argument is given in two convoluted sentences, and it may be useful, before unpicking it, to try to say what Hume's basic contention is.

> Try to say in your own words what Hume's basic contention is following
> ⌐j⌐⟶ .

Hume seems to be telling us that where two events are actually related causally, it is possible that only one of them should have occurred, i.e. that the two are separable. He apparently relies on two principles: (1) that distinct ideas are separable, and (2) that what we can imagine (i.e. what is 'possible for the imagination') is really possible.

> Ask yourself how the principles (1) and (2) work in Hume's argument at
> ⌐j⌐⟶. What does Hume mean by the distinctness of two ideas? How is the
> separability of two *events* which are cause and effect supposed to be
> shown?
> Do you accept principle (2): can you find an example of something which
> you can imagine and which you think isn't really possible?

Some philosophers have wondered how the distinctness of *ideas* is supposed to be used to establish the separability of *events*. And many philosophers have doubted whether our ability to imagine something is enough to show that it is really possible. For example we can, perhaps, imagine a cow jumping over the moon, but it would seem not to be really possible that a cow should jump over the moon.

Section 6

In this section Hume enquires into the basis of the 'inference we draw from cause to effect'. He wants to know what makes us expect an event of a certain sort when we observe an event that we take to be its cause. For example: we hear Jane's alarm bell ringing (we have an impression of this), and we infer that Jane will wake up (we have the idea that she will). Why do we make this inference and have the expectation that we do?

At $\boxed{k}\mapsto$ Hume argues that the inferences we make cannot be based on our knowing something which renders it impossible that an event's effect should not occur. Thus Hume would say that there can be nothing about the impression we have of the ringing of Jane's alarm bell which makes it impossible that there not be an event of Jane's waking up. Even if the idea that we get when we have an impression of the bell ringing is actually an idea of Jane's waking up, we could perfectly well get a different idea.

In the two paragraphs following $\boxed{l}\mapsto$ Hume says that our inferences depend on our memory of past connections. For instance, we have in the past observed that Jane has regularly woken up after her alarm bell rings, and we infer that Jane will wake up this time. Events of the two sorts have regularly been observed together: we have experienced their 'constant conjunction'. Experience of constant conjunction is what our causal inferences are based upon, according to Hume.

At $\boxed{m}\mapsto$ Hume gives an indication of what the drift of his argument is going to be. In considering $\boxed{e}\mapsto$ above, we saw that Hume thinks that one ingredient we need, if we are to understand c's being the cause of e, has to do with necessary connection. What we see now is that Hume thinks that (perhaps!) our idea of necessary connection needs to be explained in terms of the inferences from cause to effect that we actually make.

Section 14

At $\boxed{n}\mapsto$ Hume goes back to his question about our idea of necessary connection, and again applies his claim that all ideas are copies of impressions (see 'Humean Background'). This paragraph summarizes arguments that Hume is soon to spell out in more detail.

At $\boxed{o}\mapsto$ Hume again (cp. at $\boxed{e}\mapsto$) suggests that what he is after is a definition of 'cause'. He thinks that we would make no advance with definition if we brought in terms such as 'efficacy', 'agency' etc. because these all mean the same as one another near enough ('are all nearly synonymous'). Well, one might think that we *want* to use words which mean the same as the term in a definition of that term. Still, in any helpful definition, we shall also want to use words which are easier to understand than the term being defined. Hume's remarks here about the compound and the simple reveal that his own conception of a definition is of something which serves to break down an idea into simpler ones. If a definition achieved such breaking down, then presumably it would be a helpful one.

Consider in turn the following pairs that come on Hume's list of 'nearly synonymous' terms in the paragraph marked $\boxed{o}\mapsto$: (a) *agency, energy*; (b) agency, necessity; (c) power, necessity; (d) power, connection; (e) connection, productive quality. Do you think that the terms in these pairs mean nearly the same as one another?

It doesn't actually seem at all plausible that we have pairs of near synonyms here. Of course this may not affect Hume's main point – that in defining 'cause', one does not want to find oneself explaining something obscure in terms of something just as obscure. But if one thinks that 'agency', 'energy', 'power', 'productive quality' all mean rather different things, then it can seem as though there is more variety in our causal language than Hume thinks there is. And one might start to question whether the kind of definition that Hume seeks – by which a compound idea is broken down into simple ones – can always be given.

At $\boxed{p}\mapsto$ Hume argues that the idea of necessary connection cannot be derived from perceiving any individual pair of events. An example of such a pair might be the ringing of Jane's alarm bell yesterday morning and Jane's waking up yesterday morning. Hume is soon to use the example of one billiard ball's moving and another ball's moving after the two balls collide.

Between $\boxed{q}\mapsto$ and $\boxed{r}\mapsto$ Hume makes his vital move in explaining how it is that we have an idea of necessary connection. He argues that (1) the idea of necessary connection cannot be arrived at simply from repeated observations of individual pairs of events: if we don't observe a necessary connection in experiencing one case, then we are not going to observe such a connection merely by having the experience repeated. But he thinks that (2) something about the repetition of causally related pairs of events must account for our getting the idea of necessary connection. And (3) repetition has no effect on the events we observe. It must then be that (4) observation of repeated instances of pairs of events creates a new impression in our minds. Thus (5) our habit (or 'custom') of making causal inferences when we have observed repeated instances – a habit which was described in section 6 – is the basis of our conception of necessary connection. The necessity in question is a habit of the mind – a 'determination of the thought to pass from causes to effects'.

To ensure that you have understood the passage from $\boxed{q}\mapsto$ to $\boxed{r}\mapsto$, identify the places at which Hume is making the claims labelled above as (1), (2), (3), (4), (5). (Hume makes some of these claims more than once.) Find places where any of these claims are supported, and places where Hume moves from one to another of them.

At $\boxed{s}\mapsto$ Hume explains why his discussion of causality has taken the route that it has. One might have thought that an account of the inferences that we make from cause to effect should be based on a definition of 'cause'. But since, according to Hume, we can't understand what we mean by 'cause' unless we know how our causal inferences work, he has had to examine causal inference before giving a definition. He thinks that the fact that he is now in a position to give a definition justifies his procedure.

Hume gives *two* definitions of 'cause', telling us that they differ only in 'presenting a different view'. Both definitions respond to the fact (as Hume sees it) that an idea of necessary connection cannot be a simple ingredient in the idea of cause. The first definition comes at $\boxed{t} \mapsto$, and it is given in terms of spatial contiguity, temporal priority and regularity. No mention is made of necessary connection. The second comes at $\boxed{u} \mapsto$, where the definition is given in terms of an idea's being produced in the mind (the mind is 'determined' to 'form' an idea). This definition introduces necessary connection of the sort that Hume admits we can have an idea of. ('Necessary connection' is not explicitly brought in, Hume having argued that necessary connection is really nothing other than the mind's determination to form an idea.)

Hume thinks that we might not like the first definition because it draws on terms 'foreign to the cause'. Presumably he means that if we accept this first definition, then we have to allow that when we make the claim that two particular events are causally connected, we are committing ourselves to a claim about many other events which resemble them and which occurred long ago. Thus our claim about the particular case is implicitly a general one. Hume acknowledges that we might find this objectionable.

Does it seem to you an objection to Hume's definition of 'cause' at $\boxed{t} \mapsto$ that if it is correct, then all our particular causal claims are implicitly general ones?

Hume thinks that we also might not like his second definition 'for the same reason'. This time the 'foreign element' on which the definition draws is not other events but the states of the mind of someone who makes a causal claim.

Does it seem to you to be an objection to Hume's definition of 'cause' at $\boxed{u} \mapsto$ that if it is correct, then when we make causal claims we are implicitly saying something about our own minds?

Hume's first definition requires regularities in the world – 'resembling' events standing in 'like relations'. The second requires associations in our minds. Hume speaks as if we could take our pick, and use whichever of his definitions we prefer.

Do you think that Hume is right to say that his definitions differ only in presenting a different view?
Do you think that there can be real regularities without any associations in our minds?
Do you think that there can be associations in our minds without any real regularities?

Hume's two definitions cannot be simple alternatives between which we can take our pick, if they differ in respect of what they admit as cases of causal relations. And they do seem to differ so. Presumably we have not observed all the phenomena of causality that there are in the world, so that there are real regularities without any associations in our minds. Again, presumably we can have wrong expectations about what will happen, so that there need be no actual regularity corresponding to an association in our mind upon which an expectation is based.

The definitions appear not to be equivalent, then. It might be suggested that Hume's first definition is designed to say *when* we judge c to have caused e, and the second to say *why* we judge c to have caused e.

Section 15

Hume begins this section by reminding us that we rely on experience to have knowledge of causal connections. He repeats his claim that any event could cause any old other event. Given that any particular event does not actually cause any old other one, we ought to be able to say when we actually have cases of causal connection. Thus Hume moves away from his question of what it is for one event to cause another, and turns to a new question – of what our basis is for judging that one event is cause of another. He sets out eight rules to be followed by someone who seeks knowledge of causal connections. Theories of causality which understand 'cause' along the lines of Hume's first definition (at $\boxed{t} \mapsto$) are known as regularity theories. The remaining commentary on Hume will be devoted to becoming clear about what Hume means by 'resembling' events standing in 'like relations', and thus to becoming clearer about what a regularity theory says.

Hume doesn't always speak of 'resembling' events standing in 'like relations'. At $\boxed{v} \mapsto$ he speaks of the *same* cause as always producing the *same* effect, and of the *same* effect as always arising from the *same* cause. In similar vein, he spoke of a 'constant conjunction' between cause and effect (see paragraph marked $\boxed{1} \mapsto$). When Hume speaks this way, we evidently have to understand 'cause' and 'effect' as standing for things that may be repeated: you can find the same one twice. Like Hume, we sometimes speak this way. Consider that we might say: 'Jane bought an alarm clock in January; she used to wake up spontaneously, but nowadays her alarm bell's ringing causes her to wake up'. Here 'her alarm bell's ringing' seems to stand for something repeatable, which has happened every day for several months. If Jane's alarm bell has rung every day, then the *same* thing has happened frequently.

We know what Hume means by 'cause' and 'effect' at $\boxed{v} \mapsto$, then. Still Hume usually speaks of his 'objects' as if they were *un*repeatable things. And when events were introduced above, we thought of them as unrepeatable. When we used the example 'The ringing of Jane's alarm bell caused Jane's waking up', we could have described the two events so as to show that they are not repeatable: we could have said 'The ringing of Jane's alarm bell's at 7.00.00a.m., 1st May 2002 caused Jane's waking up at 7.00.01a.m., 1st May 2002.' These more elaborate descriptions of the events, which give them dates, make it plain that the events couldn't happen more than once. These events are not the right sort of thing to be 'constantly conjoined'. But they are the right sort of thing to stand to one another in a relation such as 'was earlier in time than'. (The fact that Hume thinks of causally related things as standing in relations of temporal priority and contiguity makes it plain that he usually intends 'objects' or 'causes' in the sense of one-off things rather than of repeatable things. The ambiguity we have noted in 'event' and in phrases such as 'Jane's waking up' – sometimes standing for repeatable, sometimes for unrepeatable, one-off things – is one that philosophers nowadays sometimes try to avoid by speaking of 'type events' [repeatable] and 'token events' [unrepeatable].)

It is when Hume thinks of causes as unrepeatable, one-off things, as he usually does, that he speaks of *like* effects as implying *like* causes. See $\boxed{w}\mapsto$. The question that arises is: how alike do two events have to be to count as 'like', or (to use Hume's other word) to count as 'resembling' one another'? The question is sure to arise because any unrepeatable, one-off event has a range of different properties, so that it can be like another event in some ways and unlike it in other ways.

We can raise this question in connection with Hume's first definition of 'cause' at $\boxed{t}\mapsto$. Simplifying a bit so as to focus on Hume's 'resembles', this tells us that where *c* caused *e*, we have the following generalization:

All events which resemble *c* are followed by events which resemble *e*.

Consider then our case in which examples of *c* and *e* were the ringing of Jane's alarm bell on a certain day and Jane's waking up that day. What is it for an event to *resemble c*? If we say that it must be *exactly* like *c* – exactly like that very ringing of Jane's alarm bell – then *c* itself will be the only event that fills the bill. We seem then not to have any real *generalization*. But if we say that for an event to resemble the ringing of Jane's alarm bell, it is enough that it should be a ringing of Jane's alarm bell, then Hume's definition will not seem plausible. Suppose that Jane one day leaves her house very early and forgets to switch her alarm off before she goes. That day, with Jane away from her house, we have an event which is her alarm bell's ringing, but it is not followed by an event which resembles Jane's waking up.

In order to have a definite idea of the sorts of generalization which come into Hume's first definition of 'cause', we need to be able to say something definite about the respects in which events must resemble one another when the definition applies. Some philosophers think that the generalizations that are relevant here are causal *laws*. They think that the respects in which we have to think of events resembling one another in order to think of causality as in operation are *law-like* respects – i.e. features of events that would be recognized in statements of causal laws.

At ⟨x⟩↦ Hume himself appreciates that two one-off events might resemble one another in some respects and not in others.

Consider Hume's rule 6 at ⟨x⟩↦ , and try to say exactly what claim Hume is making here. Think of examples.

Hume is concerned with cases in which 'two resembling objects' have different effects. So there are two events which resemble one another in some respect, although there is a respect in which their effects don't resemble one another. To provide an example, we might take the two resembling objects both to be events of Jane's alarm bell's ringing, and suppose that whereas the effect of one is Jane's waking up, the effect of the other is Jane's neighbour's becoming annoyed (Jane is away from the house, and the neighbour can hear the bell going on and on). It would be false to make a generalization saying that all events which are Jane's alarm bell's ringing are followed by events which are Jane's waking up. We have 'an irregularity', in Hume's sense.

Hume tells us that such an irregularity has its source in 'some difference in the causes': in our example, the two events of Jane's alarm bell's ringing (one of which did, the other of which didn't, have Jane's waking up as effect) must be different in some way. Well, in the example we have described, it is all too obvious why an event of Jane's alarm bell's ringing should have caused an event of her waking up in one instance and not the other. Jane's alarm bell's ringing happened close to Jane's ear in one instance, and in the other it did not, and that is surely a relevant difference.

Although we know a 'difference in the causes' in our example, Hume seems to think that we do not always know what the relevant differences are. He says that 'we must *conclude*' that the irregularity has its source in some difference in the causes. Thus at ⟨x⟩↦ Hume suggests that although we must assume that there is a corresponding generalization wherever two particular events are causally connected, we might not know what the generalization is. People who think that some causal *law* is at work in each particular instance of causality would probably agree with Hume on this point: they will say that one can know that a law is at work without knowing what the law is. They might think that the obvious difference we have noted between the two cases of Jane's alarm bell's ringing (that her alarm clock was near her ear in the one case and not the other) is not enough to substantiate a real causal connection in the first case. We need to point towards an *underlying* regularity to substantiate a real causal connection. (These theorists may also justify their appeal to causal *laws* by saying that an account of causality should not concern itself with regularities that are merely accidental, i.e. that just happen to obtain.)

We shall see that Anscombe puts into question the assumption that Hume thinks we must make. This is the assumption which is common to regularity theorists – that there are generalizations corresponding to every particular instance of causality, i.e. that wherever it is true that *c* caused *e*, it is also true that all events which resemble *c* are followed by events which resemble *e*. Anscombe takes those who accept such a regularity theory to believe that the generalizations in question (saying that *all* events which resemble *c* are followed by events which resemble *e*) are deterministic laws of nature.

Introduction to Anscombe

G. E. M. Anscombe (1919–2001) was a pupil of the great philosopher Wittgenstein and one of his literary executors. She taught philosophy in Oxford, and later as a professor in Cambridge, England. The essay, of whose two parts the first is reproduced here, was delivered as her inaugural lecture at Cambridge in 1971. Her book *Intention* (1957) initiated extensive discussion of human action and its explanation. The three volumes of her *Collected Philosophical Papers* (1981) put together her numerous writing in metaphysics, philosophy of mind and ethics.

Much of Elizabeth Anscombe's writing challenges received philosophical views. Her writing on causality is no exception. In the text below, having indicated what view she will attack, she makes it plain how widely she takes the view to be held, and describes it as 'a bit of *Weltanschauung*'. (*Weltanschauung*, literally translated from the German, means 'world-outlook'.) She gives historical examples of philosophers who have held the view, and then proceeds to say what she takes to be wrong with it, contrasting it with an alternative view of her own.

G. E. M. Anscombe, 'Causality and Determination' (extract)

I

a→ It is often declared or evidently assumed that causality is some kind of necessary connection, or alternatively, that being caused is – non-trivially – instancing some exceptionless generalization saying that such an event always follows such antecedents. Or the two conceptions are combined.

Obviously there can be, and are, a lot of divergent views covered by this account. Any view that it covers nevertheless manifests one particular doctrine or assumption. Namely:

b→   If an effect occurs in one case and a similar effect does not occur in an
      apparently similar case, there must be a relevant further difference.

Any radically different account of causation, then, by contrast with
which all those diverse views will be as one, will deny this assumption.
Such a radically opposing view can grant that often – though it is
difficult to say generally when – the assumption of relevant difference
is a sound principle of investigation. It may grant that there are
necessitating causes, but will refuse to identify causation as such
with necessitation. It can grant that there are situations in which,
given the initial conditions and no interference, only one result will
accord with the laws of nature; but it will not see general reason, in
advance of discovery, to suppose that any given course of things has
been so determined. So it may grant that in many cases difference of
issue can rightly convince us of a relevant difference of circumstances;
but it will deny that, quite generally, this *must* be so.

The first view is common to many philosophers of the past. It is also,
usually but not always in a neo-Humeian form, the prevailing received
opinion throughout the currently busy and productive philosophical
schools of the English-speaking world, and also in some of the European and Latin American schools where philosophy is pursued in at all
the same sort of way; nor is it confined to these schools. So firmly rooted
is it that for many even outside pure philosophy, it routinely determines
the meaning of 'cause', when consciously used as a theoretical term:
witness the terminology of the contrast between 'causal' and 'statistical'
laws, which is drawn by writers on physics – writers, note, who would
not conceive themselves to be addicts of any philosophic school when
they use this language to express that contrast.

The truth of this conception is hardly debated. It is, indeed, a bit of
Weltanschauung: it helps to form a cast of mind which is characteristic
of our whole culture.

The association between causation and necessity is old; it occurs for
c→   example in Aristotle's *Metaphysics*: 'When the agent and patient meet
suitably to their powers, the one acts and the other is acted on OF
NECESSITY.' Only with 'rational powers' an extra feature is needed
to determine the result: 'What has a rational power [e.g. medical
knowledge, which can kill *or* cure] OF NECESSITY does what it has
the power to do and as it has the power, when it has the desire.'[1]

d→   Overleaping the centuries, we find it an axiom in Spinoza, 'Given a
determinate cause, the effect follows OF NECESSITY, and without its

---

[1] *Metaphysics*, book IX, chapter V.

e ⊢→ cause, no effect follows.'[2] And in the English philosopher Hobbes: 'A cause simply, or an entire cause, is the aggregate of all the accidents both of the agents how many soever they be, and of the patients, put together; which when they are supposed to be present, IT CANNOT BE UNDERSTOOD BUT THAT THE EFFECT IS PRODUCED at the same instant; and if any of them be wanting, IT CANNOT BE UNDERSTOOD BUT THAT THE EFFECT IS NOT PRODUCED.'[3]

f ⊢→ It was this last view, where the connection between cause and effect is evidently seen as *logical* connection of some sort, that was overthrown by Hume, the most influential of all philosophers on this subject in the English-speaking and allied schools. For he made us see that, given any particular cause – or 'total causal situation' for that matter – and its effect, there is not in general any contradiction in supposing the one to occur and the other not to occur. That is to say, we'd know what was being described – what it would be like for it to be true – if it were reported for example that a kettle of water was put, and kept, directly on a hot fire, but the water did not heat up.

Were it not for the preceding philosophers who had made causality out as some species of logical connection, one would wonder at this being called a discovery on Hume's part: for vulgar humanity has always been over-willing to believe in miracles and marvels and *lusus naturae*. Mankind at large saw no contradiction, where Hume worked so hard to show the philosophic world – the Republic of Letters – that there was none.

The discovery was thought to be great. But as touching the equation
g ⊢→ of causality with necessitation, Hume's thinking did nothing against this but curiously reinforced it. For he himself assumed that NECESSARY CONNECTION is an essential part of the idea of the relation of cause and effect,[4] and he sought for its nature. He thought this could not be found in the situations, objects, or events called 'causes' and 'effects', but was to be found in the human mind's being determined, by experience of CONSTANT CONJUNCTION, to pass from the sensible impression or memory of one term of the relation to the convinced idea of the other. Thus to say that an event was caused was to say that its occurrence was an instance of some exceptionless generalization connecting such an event with such antecedents as it occurred in. The twist that Hume gave to the topic thus suggested a connection of the notion of causality with that of deterministic laws – i.e. laws such that always, given initial conditions and the laws, a unique result is determined.

[2] *Ethics*, book I, axiom III.
[3] *Elements of Philosophy Concerning Body*, chapter IX.
[4] *Treatise of Human Nature*, book I, part III, sections II and VI.

The well-known philosophers who have lived after Hume may have aimed at following him and developing at least some of his ideas, or they may have put up a resistance; but in no case, so far as I know,[5] has the resistance called in question the equation of causality with necessitation.

⟦h⟧→ Kant, roused by learning of Hume's discovery, laboured to establish causality as an *a priori* conception and argued that the objective time order consists 'in that order of the manifold of appearance according to which, IN CONFORMITY WITH A RULE, the apprehension of that which happens follows upon the apprehension of that which precedes ... In conformity with such a rule there must be in that which precedes an event the condition of a rule according to which this event INVARI-ABLY and NECESSARILY follows.'[6] Thus Kant tried to give back to causality the character of a *justified* concept which Hume's consider-ations had taken away from it. Once again the connection between causation and necessity was reinforced. And this has been the general characteristic of those who have sought to oppose Hume's conception of causality. They have always tried to establish the necessitation that they saw in causality: either *a priori*, or somehow out of experience.

⟦i⟧→ Since Mill it has been fairly common to explain causation one way or another in terms of 'necessary' and 'sufficient' conditions. Now 'sufficient condition' is a term of art whose users may therefore lay down its meaning as they please. So they are in their rights to rule out the query: 'May not the sufficient conditions of an event be present, and the event yet not take place?' For 'sufficient condition' is so used that if the sufficient conditions for X are there, X occurs. But at the same time, the phrase cozens the understanding into not noticing an assumption. For 'sufficient condition' sounds like: 'enough'. And one certainly *can* ask: 'May there not be *enough* to have made something happen – and yet it not have happened?'

⟦j⟧→ Russell wrote of the notion of cause, or at any rate of the 'law of causation' (and he seemed to feel the same way about 'cause' itself), that, like the British monarchy, it had been allowed to survive because it had been erroneously thought to do no harm. In a destructive essay of great brilliance he cast doubt on the notion of necessity involved, unless it is explained in terms of universality, and he argued that upon examination the concepts of determination and of invariable succes-sion of like objects upon like turn out to be empty: they do not differentiate between any conceivable course of things and any other. Thus Russell too assumes that necessity or universality is what is in

[5] My colleague Ian Hacking has pointed out C. S. Peirce to me as an exception to this generalization.
[6] *Critique of Pure Reason*, book II, chapter II, section III, Second Analogy.

question, and it never occurs to him that there may be any other conception of causality.[7]

k⊢→ Now it's not difficult to shew it prima facie wrong to associate the notion of cause with necessity or universality in this way. For, it being much easier to trace effects back to causes with certainty than to predict effects from causes, we often know a cause without knowing whether there is an exceptionless generalization of the kind envisaged, or whether there is a necessity.

l⊢→ For example, we have found certain diseases to be contagious. If, then, I have had one and only one contact with someone suffering from such a disease, and I get it myself, we suppose I got it from him. But what if, having had the contact, I ask a doctor whether I will get the disease? He will usually only be able to say, 'I don't know – maybe you will, maybe not.'

But, it is said, knowledge of causes here is partial; doctors seldom even know any of the conditions under which one invariably gets a m⊢→ disease, let alone all the sets of conditions. This comment betrays the assumption that there is such a thing to know. Suppose there is: still, the question whether there is does not have to be settled before we can know what we mean by speaking of the contact as cause of my getting the disease.

n⊢→ All the same, might it not be like this: knowledge of causes is possible without any satisfactory grasp of what is involved in causation? Compare the possibility of wanting clarification of 'valency' or 'long-run frequency', which yet have been handled by chemists and statisticians without such clarification; and valencies and long-run frequencies, whatever the right way of explaining them, have been known. Thus one of the familiar philosophic analyses of causality, or a new one in the same line, may be correct, though knowledge of it is not necessary for knowledge of causes.

There is something to observe here, that lies under our noses. It is o⊢→ little attended to, and yet still so obvious as to seem trite. It is this: causality consists in the derivativeness of an effect from its causes. This is the core, the common feature, of causality in its various kinds. Effects derive from, arise out of, come of, their causes. For example, everyone will grant that physical parenthood is a causal relation. Here the derivation is material, by fission. Now analysis in terms of necessity or universality does not tell us of this derivedness of the effect; rather it forgets about that. For the necessity will be that of laws of nature; through it *we* shall be able to derive knowledge of the effect from knowledge of the cause, or vice versa, but that does not shew us

---

[7] 'The Notion of Cause', in *Mysticism and Logic*.

the cause as source of the effect. Causation, then, is not to be identified with necessitation.

p→ If *A* comes from *B*, this does not imply that every *A*-like thing comes from some *B*-like thing or set-up or that every *B*-like thing or set-up has an *A*-like thing coming from it; or that given *B*, *A* had to come from it, or that given *A*, there had to be *B* for it to come from. Any of these may be true, but if any is, that will be an additional fact, not comprised in *A*'s coming from *B*. If we take 'coming from' in the sense of travel, this is perfectly evident.

q→ 'But that's because we can observe travel!' The influential Humeian argument at this point is that we can't similarly observe causality in the individual case.[8] So the reason why we connect what we call the cause and what we call the effect as we do must lie elsewhere. It must lie in the fact that the succession of the latter upon the former is of a kind regularly observed.

r→ There are two things for me to say about this. *First*, as to the statement that we can never observe causality in the individual case. Someone who says this is just not going to count anything as 'observation of causality'. This often happens in philosophy; it is argued that 'all we find' is such-and-such, and it turns out that the arguer has excluded from his idea of 'finding' the sort of thing he says we don't 'find'. And when we consider what we are allowed to say we do 'find', we have the right to turn the tables on Hume, and say that neither do we perceive bodies, such as billiard balls, approaching one another. When we 'consider the matter with the utmost attention', we find only an impression of travel made by the successive positions of a round white patch in our visual fields ..etc. Now a 'Humeian' account of causality has to be given in terms of constant conjunction of physical things, events etc., not of experiences of them. If, then, it must be allowed that we 'find' bodies in motion, for example, then what theory

s→ of perception can justly disallow the perception of a lot of causality? The truthful – though unhelpful – answer to the question: How did we come by our primary knowledge of causality? is that in learning to speak we learned the linguistic representation and application of a host of causal concepts. Very many of them were represented by transitive and other verbs of action used in reporting what is observed. Others – a good example is 'infect' – form, not observation statements, but rather expressions of causal hypotheses. The word 'cause' itself is highly general. How does someone show that he has the concept *cause*? We may wish to say: only by having such a word in his vocabulary. If so, then the manifest possession of the concept presupposes the mastery of much else in language. I mean: the word

8 *Treatise of Human Nature*, book I, part III, section II.

'cause' can be *added* to a language in which are already represented many causal concepts. A small selection: *scrape, push, wet, carry, eat, burn, knock over, keep off, squash, make* (e.g. noises, paper boats), *hurt*. But if we care to imagine languages in which no special causal concepts are represented, then no description of the use of a word in such languages will be able to present it as meaning *cause*. Nor will it even contain words for natural kinds of stuff, nor yet words equivalent to 'body', 'wind', or 'fire'. For learning to use special causal verbs is part and parcel of learning to apply the concepts answering to these, and many other, substantives. As surely as we learned to call people by name or to report from seeing it that the cat was on the table, we also learned to report from having observed it that someone drank up the milk or that the dog made a funny noise or that things were cut or broken by whatever we saw cut or break them.

(I will mention, only to set on one side, one of the roots of Hume's argument, the implicit appeal to Cartesian scepticism. He confidently challenges us to 'produce some instance, wherein the efficacy is plainly discoverable to the mind, and its operations obvious to our conscious-ness or sensation'.[9] Nothing easier: is cutting, is drinking, is purring not 'efficacy'? But it is true that the apparent perception of such things may be only apparent: we may be deceived by false appearances. Hume presumably wants us to 'produce an instance' in which *efficacy* is related to sensation as *red* is. It is true that we can't do that; it is not *so* related to sensation. He is also helped, in making his argument that we don't perceive 'efficacy', by his curious belief that 'efficacy' means much the same thing as 'necessary connection'! But as to the Carte-sian-sceptical root of the argument, I will not delay upon it, as my present topic is not the philosophy of perception.)

Second, as to that instancing of a universal generalization, which was supposed to supply what could not be observed in the individual case, the causal relation, the needed examples are none too common. 'Motion in one body in all past instances that have fallen under our observation, is follow'd upon impulse by motion in another':[10] so Hume. But, as is always a danger in making large generalizations, he was thinking only of the cases where we do observe this – billiard balls against free-standing billiard balls in an ordinary situation; not billiard balls against stone walls. Neo-Humeians are more cautious. They realize that if you take a case of cause and effect, and relevantly describe the cause *A* and the effect *B*, and then construct a universal proposition, 'Always, given an *A*, a *B* follows' you usually won't get anything true. You have got to describe the absence of circumstances

9 Ibid., book I, part III, section XIV.
10 Ibid., book II, part III, section I.

in which an *A* would not cause a *B*. But the task of excluding all such circumstances can't be carried out. There is, I suppose, a vague association in people's minds between the universal propositions which would be examples of the required type of generalizations, and scientific laws. But there is no similarity.

x ⊢→   Suppose we were to call propositions giving the properties of substances 'laws of nature'. Then there will be a law of nature running 'The flash-point of such a substance is . . .', and this will be important in explaining why striking matches usually causes them to light. This law of nature has not the form of a generalization running 'Always, if a sample of such a substance is raised to such a temperature, it ignites'; nor is it equivalent to such a generalization, but rather to: 'If a sample of such a substance is raised to such a temperature and doesn't ignite, there must be a cause of its not doing so.' Leaving aside questions connected with the idea of a pure sample, the point here is that 'normal conditions' is quite properly a vague notion. That fact makes generalizations running 'Always . . .' merely fraudulent in such cases; it will always be necessary for them to be hedged about with clauses referring to normal conditions; and we may not know in advance whether conditions are normal or not, or what to count as an abnormal condition. In exemplar analytical practice, I suspect, it will simply be a relevant condition in which the generalization, 'Always, if such-and-such, such-and-such happens . . .', supplemented with a few obvious conditions that have occurred to the author, turns out to be untrue. Thus the conditional 'If it doesn't ignite then there must be some cause' is the better gloss upon the original proposition, for it does not pretend to say specifically, or even disjunctively specifically, what *always* happens. It is probably these facts which make one hesitate to call propositions about the action of substances 'laws of nature'. The law of inertia, for example, would hardly be glossed: 'If a body accelerates without any force acting on it, there must be some cause of its doing so.' (Though I wonder what the author of *Principia* himself would have thought of that.) On the other hand just such 'laws' as that about a substance's flash-point are connected with the match's igniting because struck.

y ⊢→   Returning to the medical example, medicine is of course not interested in the hopeless task of constructing lists of all the sets of conditions under each of which people always get a certain disease. It is interested in finding what that is special, if anything, is always the case when people get a particular disease; and, given such a cause or condition (or in any case), in finding circumstances in which people don't get the disease, or tend not to. This is connected with medicine's concern first, and last, with things as they happen in the messy and mixed up conditions of life: only between its first and its last concern can it look for what happens unaffected by uncontrolled and inconstant conditions. [. . .]

Commentary on Anscombe

Anscombe starts by laying out the account of causality she is to challenge. The 'two conceptions' of which she speaks at $\boxed{a}\!\!\mapsto$ are both present in Hume.

> Look again at $\boxed{t}\!\!\mapsto$ and $\boxed{u}\!\!\mapsto$ in the Hume extracts, and consider how Hume's two definitions relate to the 'two conceptions' that Anscombe speaks of at $\boxed{a}\!\!\mapsto$.

The idea that causality is 'some kind of necessary connection' is present in Hume's second definition of 'cause' (although, as we saw, Hume deliberately avoids the words 'necessary connection', thinking as he does that 'necessary connection' means something very different from what we might suppose). The idea that causality is 'instancing some exceptionless generalization' is present in Hume's first definition.

At $\boxed{b}\!\!\mapsto$, Anscombe states the particular assumption made by all her opponents.

> Do you think Hume makes the assumption which Anscombe displays at $\boxed{b}\!\!\mapsto$?

Look again at $\boxed{x}\!\!\mapsto$ in the Hume extract, where Hume says that if there appears to be some irregularity, 'we must conclude that' it has it source in 'some difference in the causes'. It seems that Hume here makes the assumption that is Anscombe's target.

Between $\boxed{c}\!\!\mapsto$ and $\boxed{k}\!\!\mapsto$ Anscombe shows how deeply embedded in past philosophical thinking are the conceptions that she wishes to attack. Hume is pivotal in Anscombe's historical sketch: she moves from ancient and early modern philosophy, through Hume, to philosophers from the eighteenth, nineteenth and twentieth centuries. These are the nationalities and dates of the six philosophers Anscombe mentions: Aristotle, classical Greek, 384–322 BC; Benedict de Spinoza, Dutch, 1632–1677; Thomas Hobbes, British, 1588–1679; Immanuel Kant, German, 1724–1804; John Stuart Mill, British, 1806–1873; Bertrand Russell, British, 1872–1970. (In a footnote she mentions Charles S. Peirce, American, 1839–1914.)

Anscombe gives her first example of a philosopher holding that causation and necessity are connected at $\boxed{c}\!\!\mapsto$.

Think about the claims of Aristotle, Spinoza and Hobbes at $\boxed{c}\mapsto$, $\boxed{d}\mapsto$ and $\boxed{e}\mapsto$. Consider how each of them relates to one or other (or both) of the two conceptions Anscombe introduced at $\boxed{a}\mapsto$.

At $\boxed{f}\mapsto$ we find something that Hume and Anscombe agree about: cause and effect are not logically connected. Anscombe suggests that no one would have thought otherwise if earlier philosophers such as Hobbes had not given the accounts they did. Thus she says that Hume's claim that any event could cause any old other event is fine if it means that false causal claims never state logical impossibilities, or contradictions. (You were asked above, in connection with the argument at $\boxed{j}\mapsto$ in the Hume text, whether you could find an example of something you can imagine but you think is really impossible. The notion of possibility at issue there was not *logical* possibility. It is logically possible – it is not a contradiction to say – that a cow jumps over the moon. Hume did not distinguish between different kinds of possibility: he believed that there was only one kind.)

At $\boxed{g}\mapsto$ Anscombe tells us how she understands Hume's distinctive contribution to thinking about causality.

Find sentences in the extracts from Hume's *Treatise* which show that Hume's thinking about causality matches Anscombe's account of it.

Hume first claims that necessary connection is an essential part of the idea of the relation of cause and effect at $\boxed{e}\mapsto$ in his section 2. That he gives no argument for the claim justifies Anscombe's saying that he *assumed* this. Anscombe's description of Hume fits with the argument between $\boxed{q}\mapsto$ and $\boxed{r}\mapsto$ in his section 14.

Anscombe also says that a link between the notions of causality and of deterministic laws is suggested by Humean thinking. The commentary on section 15 explains how Hume's way of thinking about causality can lead to the idea of laws as underlying causal connections. (Hume himself does not allude to the notion of a deterministic law in any of the passages we have looked at. When deterministic laws are introduced, it seems that a new source of *necessity* enters into the account. For when laws are distinguished from accidental generalizations, laws are considered to be statements which do not just happen to be true but which, in some sense, *must* be true.)

At $\boxed{h}\mapsto$, Anscombe speaks of Kant's claims about causality, saying that although these were made in opposition to Hume, they cling to an assumption of a link between causation and necessity. Kant's claim that causality is an *a priori* conception is the claim that no particular experiences are needed to have a conception of causality. (Kant means by '*a priori*' something like what Hume means by 'certain' as explained in the 'Humean Background'. But the two philosophers disagree significantly on how the *a priori* and the *necessary* are related.)

At ⌐i⌐→ Anscombe suggests that talk of causes as 'sufficient conditions' can surreptitiously lead us into supposing that causes make their effects necessary. She acknowledges that someone might stipulate that they will use 'sufficient condition' in such a way that a sufficient condition for an event makes it impossible that the event should not occur. But she suggests that talk of 'sufficient conditions' can bamboozle us into thinking that an effect has to have happened if its cause did. Consider, for example, the statement that striking a match caused it to ignite. If we say that a cause is a sufficient condition, then (according to Anscombe) this may mean only that the match's being struck was enough to ignite it, and it need not mean that it was impossible that the match should have been struck and not ignited. (Notice that when Hume speaks of a 'complete' cause at the very end of the printed extracts, he seems to be thinking that a 'complete cause' would be a sufficient condition.)

At ⌐j⌐→ Anscombe applauds an essay in which Russell attacked the whole notion of cause. She suggests that Russell didn't realize that what he really put under attack was only a particular notion of cause – a notion bound up with ideas of universal regularities and necessity.

If there were exceptionless generalizations covering all cases of causality (of the sort that Anscombe's opponent believes in), then, if we knew these generalizations, we should always be able to make accurate predictions. At ⌐k⌐→ Anscombe points out that this is not our situation: we often know the causes of things even when we are not in a position to have made predictions of them.

In the paragraphs following ⌐l⌐→ Anscombe takes an example in which she knows the cause of something although even an expert would not have been able to predict it. She knows that her contact with a certain person was what resulted in her having a disease, but a doctor would not have been able to say whether her contact with that person who had the disease would transmit the disease to her.

> What is Anscombe's response at ⌐m⌐→ to an opponent who says that when we aren't able to predict, that is because we don't know enough?

Anscombe points out that such an opponent simply assumes that there is something to know which would enable predictions. Even if that assumption is allowed, the opponent must grant that we can understand perfectly well what it is for a disease to result from contact with someone without thinking that there is something that might be known which would enable predictions.

With 'All the same' at ⌐n⌐→ Anscombe imagines her opponent coming back.

> Try to express in your own words the possibility that Anscombe illustrates using the analogy of 'valency' or 'long-run frequency'.

It is possible that an account of causality is a correct account, even though we can understand causality perfectly well without accepting the account. This is the possibility that Anscombe's opponent relies on: the opponent thinks that an account of causality which requires underlying unknown regularities is correct, even though those who have the idea of causality may not accept that there are such regularities.

At o⊢→ Anscombe turns from arguing against opponents to draw attention to what she thinks is an obvious but overlooked way of understanding causality. And here we find her own positive claim – that causality consists in *derivativeness*. It is noteworthy that Anscombe speaks of 'causality in its various kinds', and uses parenthood as an example of a causal relation. There is an implicit criticism of Hume here: he wrote as if there was only one kind of causality – the kind in which cause and effect are events ('objects').

At p⊢→ Anscombe shows how, if we follow her in thinking of effects as coming (or deriving) from causes, we shall not be committed to the various claims about regularity and necessitation made by her opponents. She says that this will be obvious if we think about 'coming from' in a certain way – 'in the sense of travel'.

> There are four things which at p⊢→ Anscombe says are not implied by 'A comes from B'. Take as example: 'A farmer came from (i.e. travelled from) Idaho.' In order to see the overall point that Anscombe is making, go through each of the four things. In each case find the statement that Anscombe will say is not implied by 'A farmer came from Idaho.'

It is, as Anscombe says, 'perfectly evident' that 'A farmer came from Idaho' does not imply that every farmer-like thing comes from somewhere like Idaho. And the other three seem equally evident.

At q⊢→ Anscombe imagines that her opponent will challenge the parallel she suggests between 'comes from' in the sense of travel and 'comes from' as a way of understanding 'causes'. Her opponent thinks that travel is observable, and causality is not. (Anscombe here refers to Hume: his argument was at b⊢→ in the extracts above.) The opponent argues that since causality is not observable, we must look outside the things that are cause and effect to find the connection between them (the connection is 'drawn from objects foreign to the cause' was how Hume put this).

Anscombe spends the rest of the extract responding to this argument. Her remarks are directed first (from r⊢→) against its premise that causality is not observable, and second (from v⊢→) against its conclusion that every individual case of causality is an instance of some generalization.

Between r⊢→ and s⊢→ Anscombe wonders what idea of observation/perception is used by someone (whom she calls a 'Humeian') who says that we don't observe/perceive causality.

What are Anscombe's two main points against the Humean between [r]→ and [s]→?

(1) Anscombe says that a Humean may employ a conception of what we 'find' in perception which is inconsistent with our 'finding' causality when we perceive things. But if so, the Humean gives no argument for the unobservability of causality. (2) Anscombe says that a Humean about causality must allow that we perceive bodies in motion for instance. But if it is admitted that we can perceive such things as this, then why should it not be admitted that we perceive causality?

Between [s]→ and [u]→ Anscombe offers an alternative way to Hume's of thinking about how we get our idea of causality. We acquire causal concepts when we learn a language. We don't have to acquire a word for Hume's idea of 'cause': such a word might be something we came to understand as a result of understanding the various other causal concepts which we use to report ordinary things that we see.

At [t]→ Anscombe offers 'a small selection' of causal concepts to illustrate how widespread ordinary causal language is, and thus how very various are the ways in which we might gain a conception of causality in coming to speak a language.

Find a few other concepts that Anscombe might have introduced at [t]→ as examples to make her point.

Many examples might be given which show how pervasively verbs introduce causality, including *raise, kill, drop, alter, change, turn, melt something, sink something, wake someone up.*

(In a parenthetic paragraph starting at [u]→, Anscombe mentions 'Cartesian scepticism' as a possible source of Hume's view. In chapter 2, at the end of the 'Commentary on Descartes', we saw how Descartes separates what he calls 'sensory perception in a restricted sense' from seeing; he bases a distinction between these two in his division between what we could, and what we could not, be deceived about. Anscombe's point is that if we were asked to show that our experiences of causality were things that we could not be deceived about, then the challenge would be impossible to meet. But she thinks the challenge is inappropriate.)

At [v]→ Anscombe reminds us of how rarely we can find universal generalizations which back up causal claims in particular instances. And she says that it isn't possible to patch up such generalizations as we might arrive at – not possible to make the generalizations exceptionless by talking of the absence of circumstances. She doubts that scientific laws are really at all like the sort of universal generalizations that people think about when they imagine universal generalizations as backing up causal claims.

As a particular case of 'Always, given an *A*, a *B* follows' (see Anscombe at
$\boxed{\text{w}}$→) consider 'Always given the ringing of an alarm bell, an event of
someone's waking up follows.' Taking this example, illustrate Anscombe's
claims about the difficulty of finding any truly universal generalizations.

At $\boxed{\text{x}}$→ Anscombe introduces a conception of a 'law of nature'. She thinks
that laws of nature according to this conception have a genuine connection
with our ideas of causality, and that they can be used for making predictions
in normal conditions. She shows how very different such laws of nature are
from the sort of generalizations that followers of Hume make appeal to. She
acknowledges that the fact that laws of nature matching her conception don't
tell us what *always* happens means that people probably won't call these 'laws
of nature'. (The author of *Principia*, whom she mentions in brackets, is Isaac
Newton, 1642–1727, whose work Hume knew.)

Consider these two ways of spelling out what is meant by 'The flashpoint
of a certain substance is 500 °C (i.e. is a temperature of 500 degrees
Celsius)'.
(i)   'Always if a sample of the substance is raised to 500 °C, it ignites.'
(ii)   'If a sample of the substance doesn't ignite at 500 °C, then there must
be some cause.'
What are Anscombe's reasons for saying we should accept (ii) rather than
(i)?

At $\boxed{\text{y}}$→ Anscombe returns to the example she introduced at $\boxed{\text{l}}$→, pointing
out that medicine is not interested in discovering the kind of exceptionless
generalizations which Humeans suppose underlie causal claims.

A useful final exercise would be to consider what, if anything, Anscombe
has persuaded you of. Try to isolate two or three things that Hume and
Anscombe clearly disagree about. Ask yourself where you stand.

Examples of things which Hume assents to, and about which Anscombe
disagrees with Hume, might be the following:

1   Causal relations cannot be perceived directly in a single case; they can only
    be inferred from many similar cases.
2   Causal relations are instances of universal generalizations that admit no
    exceptions.
3   It is possible to give the kind of definition of 'cause' that Hume sought – in
    which a compound idea is broken down into simple ones.

9

Qualities

Introduction to Some Problems

If you say that the tomato is round and red, then you attribute two qualities (sometimes called properties or attributes) to the tomato – roundness and redness. According to the philosopher John Locke, these two qualities are of very different sorts. For roundness belongs among what Locke called primary qualities – 'solidity, extension, figure, motion or rest'; and redness belongs among what Locke called secondary qualities – 'colours, sounds, tastes'. Locke attached great significance to a distinction between primary and secondary qualities.

George Berkeley denied that the distinction had the significance that Locke believed it did. Hence there is a debate about the primary/secondary quality distinction. The debate is an important one because of its connection with a range of philosophical problems. In this 'Introduction', three interrelated problems are set out. Two more problems will be presented after the texts and commentaries, in 'Further Questions' below. All five problems are ones on which the question of whether the primary/secondary quality distinction is a genuine and important one has a bearing.

The following problems are all rather abstract. It won't be obvious how they relate to the debate about the primary/secondary quality distinction until you have read some of the texts. But you are advised to read through the rest of this 'Introduction' before reading the texts of the three authors, and to re-read it along with the 'Further Questions' section when you have read the texts and commentaries. Some of the tasks that accompany the commentaries are not at all easy. If you find some of them difficult, don't let that discourage you from continuing with the texts.

Are things as they seem?

If a tomato *looks* red to us, is it *really* red? This question is an example of a more general question that philosophers raise when they ask whether things are as they seem. Is the world that we encounter in perceptual experience, when we keep our eyes and ears open, the world as it really is?

Locke's answer to the question 'Are things really as they seem?' is '*Yes* in so far as things seem to have primary qualities; but *No* in so far as they seem to have secondary qualities.' According to Locke, when someone perceives something to possess one of the primary qualities, they perceive it as it really is; whereas when they perceive something to possess one of the secondary qualities, they don't perceive it as it really is, since then the idea they have is not an idea of any quality actually present in the thing. So, for example, on this view, if you have ideas of roundness and redness when you look at the tomato, roundness, being a primary quality, is a quality that the tomato indeed has; redness, being a secondary quality, is a feature of your experience of the tomato.

Are all truths scientific truths?

It is sometimes said that the picture of the world around us given to us by science clashes with the picture of the world got by perceiving it in everyday circumstances. We perceive the world as made up of coloured, macroscopic, stable things. (Macroscopic things are those that it doesn't need a microscope to see.) Today's physics tells us that the world is made up of clouds of colourless, microscopic, mobile particles. What is the relationship between these two pictures? Can we endorse both?

If one accepts that the everyday qualities of things are just as real as the ones that the scientists deal with, then one thinks that a scientific account of the world gives only a partial description of reality. But some people think that the only true view of the world is a scientific one. Since qualities like redness cannot be attributed to the clouds of colourless microscopic particles of which physicists speak, these people say that the quality of redness simply doesn't belong in a correct account of how things are. They say that tomatoes aren't really red (however ripe they may be!).

On one understanding of the distinction between primary and secondary qualities, it corresponds to a distinction between qualities attributed by science and qualities that do not come into a scientific account of things. Thus your answer to a question about the relationship between the two pictures of the world around us – the picture given by science and the picture got by perceiving it in everyday circumstances – may affect your view about the status of the secondary qualities.

Subjective and objective

Something is objective in so far as it is independent of either a particular mind or minds in general. The idea that we want to know how things *objectively* are is an idea upon which those who appeal to science as telling us the true nature of things often rely. When they tell us that an account of things' secondary qualities does not belong in an account of the true nature of things, they point out that there is something subjective about the secondary qualities. Secondary qualities, they say, are dependent on a particular mind or on minds in general.

One can understand why the secondary qualities should be thought to be subjective, or mind dependent. For Locke defined the secondary qualities in terms of sensations produced in us, in human subjects – 'in our minds'. At the end of the 'Commentary on Boyle' below, we shall see that more than one thing might be meant by the claim that secondary qualities are subjective.

Introduction to Boyle and Locke

Robert Boyle (1627–1691) is often treated nowadays as a scientist rather than a philosopher (although a distinction between scientists and philosophers is much easier to draw among people today than it is in the case of seventeenth- or eighteenth-century figures). You have encountered Boyle if you have come across Boyle's Law in studying physics: he did important work on temperature and on gases. Boyle defended a mechanistic picture of nature. He was convinced that experimental data provided the best means of undermining the non-mechanistic worldview that was prevalent in his day.

Boyle was a contemporary of Locke's, and a friend. By reading his work alongside Locke's, one is able to see the extent to which Locke's philosophy was bound up with the science of his day. The Boyle extracts reprinted here are from *The Origin of Forms and Qualities According to the Corpuscularian Philosophy* – a work first published in 1666, consisting of a number of papers that Boyle wrote in the 1650s. The Locke extracts are from the work introduced in chapter 6: *An Essay Concerning Human Understanding*. (There is an introduction to Locke in that chapter.)

These reprinted extracts from Boyle, Locke and Berkeley do not cover everything that these authors had to say on primary and secondary qualities. They have been selected so that you will encounter most of the main arguments while having a manageable amount to read. If you take the texts in this chapter in two parts, then it is recommended that you take the Boyle and Locke together, and treat the Berkeley texts as the second part.

Robert Boyle, *The Origin of Forms and Qualities* (extracts)

I   I agree with the generality of philosophers, so far as to allow that there is one catholic or universal matter common to all bodies, by which I mean a substance extended, divisible, and impenetrable.

II   But because, this matter being in its own nature but one, the diversity we see in bodies must necessarily arise from somewhat else than the matter they consist of, and since we see not how there could be any change in matter if all its (actual or designable) parts were perpetually at rest among themselves, it will follow that, to discriminate the catholic matter into variety of natural bodies, it must have motion in some or all its designable parts; and that motion must have various tendencies, that which is in this part of the matter tending one way, and that which is in that part tending another: as we plainly see in the universe or general mass of matter there is really a great quantity of motion, and that variously determined, and that yet divers portions of matter are at rest.

III   These two grand and most catholic principles of bodies, matter and motion, being thus established, it will follow both that matter must be actually divided into parts, that being the genuine effect of variously determined motion; and that each of the primitive fragments, or other distinct and entire masses of matter, must have two attributes – its own magnitude, or rather *size*, and its own *figure* or *shape*. And since experience shows us (especially that which is afforded us by chemical operations, in many of which matter is divided into parts too small to be singly sensible) that this division of matter is frequently made into insensible corpuscles or particles, may conclude that the minutest fragments, as well as the biggest masses, of the universal matter are likewise endowed each with peculiar bulk and shape. For, being a finite body, its dimensions must be terminated and measurable; and though it may change its figure, yet for the same reason it must necessarily have *some figure* or other. [...]

V   [...] But now we are to consider that there are *de facto* in the world certain sensible and rational beings that we call men, and the body of man having several of its external parts, as the eye, the ear, &c., each of a distinct and peculiar texture, whereby it is capable to receive impressions from the bodies about it, and upon that account it is called an organ of sense – we must consider, I say, that these sensories may be wrought upon by the figure, shape, motion and texture of bodies without them after several ways, some of those external bodies being fitted to affect the eye, others the ear, others the nostrils, &c. And to these operations of the objects on the sensories, the mind of man, which upon the account of its union with the body perceives them, giveth distinct names, calling the one *light* or *colour*, the other *sound*, the other *odour*, &c. And because also each organ of sense, as the eye or the palate, may be itself differingly affected by external objects, the mind likewise gives the objects of the same sense distinct appellations, calling one colour *green*, the other *blue*, and one taste *sweet* and another *bitter*, &c.: whence men have been induced to frame a long catalogue of such things as, for their relating to our senses, we call *sensible* qualities. And because we have been conversant with them before we had the use of reason, and the mind of man is prone to conceive almost everything (nay, even privations, as blindness, death, &c.) under the notion of a true entity or sub-

[b] ⇥ stance, as itself is, we have been from our infancy apt to imagine that these sensible qualities are real beings in the objects they denominate, and have the faculty or power to work such and such things, as gravity hath a power to stop the motion of a bullet shot upwards and carry that solid globe of matter toward the centre of the earth: whereas

[c] ⇥ indeed (according to what we have largely shown above) there is in the body to which these sensible qualities are attributed nothing of real and physical but the size, shape, and motion or rest, of its component particles, together with that texture of the whole which results from their being so contrived as they are. Nor is it necessary they should have in them anything more, like to the ideas they occasion in us – those ideas being either the effects of our prejudices or inconsiderate-ness, or else to be fetched from the relation that happens to be betwixt those primary accidents of the sensible object and the peculiar texture

[d] ⇥ of the organ it affects: as, when a pin being run into my finger causeth pain, there is no distinct quality in the pin answerable to what I am apt to fancy pain to be; but the pin in itself is only slender, stiff, and sharp, and by those qualities happens to make a solution of continuity in my organ of touching, upon which, by reason of the fabric of the body and the intimate union of the soul with it, there ariseth that troublesome kind of perception which we call *pain*. [...]

VI   But here I foresee a difficulty, which being perhaps the chiefest that we shall meet with against the Corpuscular hypothesis, it will deserve to be, before we proceed any farther, taken notice of. And it is this, that whereas we explicate colours, odours, and the like sensible qualities, by a *relation to our senses*, it seems evident that they have an *absolute* being irrelative to *us*; for snow (for instance) would be white, and a glowing coal would be hot, though there were no man or any other animal in the world. And it is plain that bodies do not only by their qualities work upon *our senses*, but upon *other*, and those inanimate, *bodies*: as the coal will not only heat or burn a *man's hand* if he touch it, but would likewise heat wax (even so much as to melt it and make it flow), and thaw ice into water, though all the men and sensitive beings in the world were annihilated. To clear this difficulty, I have several things to represent: and

1   I say not that there are no other accidents in bodies than colours, odours and the like: for I have already taught that there are simpler and more primitive affections of matter, from which these secondary qualities, if I may so call them, do depend; and that the operations of bodies upon one another spring from the same, we shall see by and by.

2   Nor do I say that all qualities of bodies are *directly sensible*: but I observe that, when one body works upon another, the knowledge we have of their operation proceeds either from some sensible quality, or some more catholic affection of matter, as motion, rest, or texture, generated or destroyed in one of them; for else it is hard to conceive how we should come to discover what passes betwixt them.

3   We must not look upon every distinct body that works upon our senses as a bare lump of matter of that bigness and outward shape that it appears of: many of them having their parts curiously contrived, and most of them perhaps in motion too. Nor must we look upon the universe that surrounds us as upon a moveless and undistinguished heap of matter, but as upon a great engine, [. . .]

4   I do not deny but that bodies may be said in a very favourable sense to have those qualities we call *sensible*, though there were no animals in the world. For a body in that case may differ from those bodies which now are quite devoid of quality, in its having such a disposition of its constituent corpuscles that, in case it were duly applied to the sensory of an animal, it would produce such a sensible quality which a body of another texture would not: as, though if there were no animals there would be no such thing as pain, yet a pin may, upon the account of its figure, be fitted to cause pain, in case it were moved against a man's finger; whereas a bullet or other blunt body, moved against it with no greater force, will not cause any such perception of pain. And thus snow, though, if there were no lucid body nor organ of sight in the world, it

would exhibit no colour at all (for I could not find it had any in places exactly darkened), yet it hath a greater disposition than a coal or soot to reflect a store of light outwards, when the sun shines upon them all three. And so we say that a lute is in tune, whether it be actually played upon or no, if the strings be all so duly stretched as that it would appear to be in tune if it were played upon. But as, if you should thrust a pin into a man's finger, both a while before and after his death, though the pin be as sharp at one time as at another and maketh in both cases alike a solution of continuity, yet in the former case the action of the pin will produce pain, and not in the latter, because in this the pricked body wants the soul and consequently the perceptive faculty: so, if there were no sensitive beings, those bodies that are now the objects of our senses would be but *dispositively*, if I may so speak, endowed with colours, tastes, and the like, and *actually* but only with those more catholic affections of bodies – figure, motion, texture, &c.

Commentary on Boyle

Try not to be put off by Boyle's seventeenth-century English. Where Boyle writes 'giveth', for instance, we should nowadays say 'gives'. If you find Boyle's long sentences difficult, see whether you can express what Boyle is saying in shorter sentences of your own.

Boyle speaks as an advocate of the corpuscularian hypothesis, according to which material things are made of indivisible particles. You might think of the corpuscularian hypothesis as a precursor to atomic theory. But the atoms which scientists now tell us make up everything are themselves made up of even smaller particles, whereas the corpuscles of the hypothesis are the very smallest (Boyle says 'minutest') things.

The extract starts with Boyle's enunciation of his two basic principles. Like other philosophers of his day, he thinks that what all material things share is matter. But unlike other philosophers of his day, he thinks that what accounts for the differences between different material things must ultimately be differences of motion.

Boyle says that it follows from his general principles that matter must be divisible into different parts, but that it cannot be divided into parts indefinitely (cannot be infinitely divisible, one might say). 'Corpuscles' is the name for the parts – 'too small to be singly sensed' – into which Boyle argues that material things (or 'bodies') must be ultimately divisible.

The mechanistic world – of matter and motion – portrayed by Boyle in sections I, II, and III is conceived in the absence of human beings. In section V Boyle turns his attention to human beings' experience of the world. We experience material things as having what Boyle calls 'sensible qualities': these are qualities that things are perceived as having – qualities that things look to us to have, or sound or feel or taste or smell to us to have. Boyle wants to explain how our varied sense experiences can fit into the mechanistic world of matter and motion. At ⊡→ he speaks of sense organs (Boyle says 'sensories') as affected by (Boyle says 'wrought upon by') certain qualities of objects outside them (Boyle says 'without them'). Notice that the qualities in terms of which Boyle explains sense experience – figure, shape, motion and texture – are the qualities that belong to matter according to Boyle's basic principles. Boyle is soon to call these the *primary* qualities (though he uses the word 'accidents' for qualities when he introduces the term 'primary').

Boyle tells us what we are 'apt to imagine' at ⓑ→, and he contrasts this with what is 'indeed' the case at ⓒ→.

> In order to be clear about the difference between what Boyle thinks we are inclined falsely to believe at ⓑ→, and what Boyle thinks the truth is, at ⓒ→, try to put these things in your own words.

Boyle thinks that we are inclined to believe that qualities such as greenness or sweetness can make a real impact in the world, as gravity does. His own view is that a thing's having a certain colour or taste is a matter of its affecting our minds, *via* our sense organs, in a particular way.

At ⓓ→ Boyle uses the example of pain to make clear his point about such qualities as greenness or sweetness. When a pin affects us by causing us pain, we don't suppose that there is anything like painfulness in the pin. No more, thinks Boyle, should we suppose that there are qualities in objects which are like (Boyle says 'like to') our experiences of greenness or sweetness. To understand human beings' experience, we have to take account not only of the fact that the figure, shape, motion and texture of things (i.e. their primary qualities) have effects on sense organs, but also of the fact that the soul is affected by the bodily goings on that result from such effects on sense organs. Boyle is soon to call those experienced qualities, the likes of which are not in material objects and which need to be understood by reference to the effects that they have on the mind (Boyle says 'soul'), secondary qualities.

Here we should notice that for Boyle the distinction between qualities of two sorts relies upon a distinction between the world of material things – wherein there are only primary qualities – and a world containing souls as well as material things – wherein there is experience of secondary qualities. Evidently a dualism like Descartes's is at work in Boyle. We saw that Descartes treats seeing as made up of distinguishable mental and physical components (end of 'Commentary on Descartes' in chapter 2 above). It seems that Boyle holds an account of perception similar to Descartes's: in order to account for things' sensible qualities we need to allude to a specifically mental component in perception.

At the start of section VI, Boyle makes it clear that he is going to confront an objection to what he has been saying. Bringing in the notion of *subjectivity* (which Boyle doesn't use himself), one might put the objection in this way: 'You're saying, Boyle, that sensible qualities such as the colours we see things as having and the sounds we hear things as making, are subjective: you understand these qualities in relation to us. But surely things really have these qualities, and have them objectively, independently of us. Even if there weren't any human beings or other animals in the world, snow would still be white; and things that feel hot to us would still have effects on other things – coal would make wax hot and melt it, for example.'

Boyle enumerates the various points he makes in answer to the objection he envisages, the first four of which are reproduced in the extract. In his 1–3, Boyle points up features of his view which are meant to help to lessen the force of the objection.

1   Boyle reminds us that he hasn't said that *all* of things' qualities are sensible qualities; indeed he has relied upon the idea that the sensible qualities depend upon other qualities.
2   He points out that one can know about things' qualities other than by sensing them directly.
3   He suggests that when we think of the world in primary quality terms, we shouldn't think only of things we perceive as having size and shape, but should remember that much goes on in the 'great engine' that is 'the universe' which we are not aware of. The 'parts', most of which Boyle says are 'perhaps in motion', are the tiny corpuscles which Boyle thinks all material things are made up of.

Try to see how Boyle's points 1, 2 and 3 in his section VI bear on the objection he is responding to.

At the start of 4, Boyle tells us that there is a sense – 'a very favourable sense' he says – in which things may be said still to have sensible qualities even in the absence of animals. And he spends this paragraph getting clear about what this sense is. His initial idea is that what makes the difference to whether something has a certain sensible quality is whether its constituent corpuscles have a disposition to produce such a quality when they affect an animal via its sense organs (or 'sensory').

At $\boxed{e} \!\!\rightarrow$ Boyle tell us what it is for a lute (a stringed musical instrument) to be in tune. He compares what it is for a lute to be in tune with what it is for snow to be white.

What is the relevant point of comparison between 'being in tune', in the example of the lute at $\boxed{e} \!\!\rightarrow$, and 'being white'?

A lute's being in tune is not a matter of its being played upon, but of its strings being such that it would seem to be in tune if it were played upon. Similarly, Boyle seems to be suggesting, snow's being white is not a matter of anyone's seeing it, but of its being such that it would look white if it did affect a sense organ suitably connected to a soul.

Some of today's philosophers claim that, as Boyle suggests, any secondary quality is a disposition of a certain sort – a disposition to produce a particular kind of experience, they say. These people think, for instance, that something's being white is a matter of its being so disposed as normally to cause experiences of whiteness in human beings and other animals. They may feel entitled to claim that snow would actually be white in a world without animals. (This is something that Boyle appears to deny at the very end of the passage when he says that in the absence of animals, things would be 'dispositively ... endowed' with sensible qualities.) Of course snow wouldn't actually *look* white in such a world, but perhaps it would still have the disposition that these people say whiteness is – perhaps it would still be such that it *would* cause certain experiences in human beings *if* human beings were present.

> Do you think that snow would (actually) be white if there were no humans or other animals? Even if you think the answer to this question is obvious, you should ask yourself what considerations might lead someone to answer *Yes*, and what considerations might lead someone to answer *No*.

When Boyle responds to the objection which starts section VI, he appears to be trying to steer a path between saying that secondary qualities are quite simply subjective (and thus absent from a world without human or other animals' minds) and saying that secondary qualities are quite simply objective (and thus independent of humans and other animals). In thinking about the subjectivity of secondary qualities, it can be helpful to distinguish between two different questions:

1   Are secondary qualities best understood by thinking about how things appear to human subjects?
2   Is the fact that something has a secondary quality a fact which is dependent upon human subjects?

Thus, to take a particular case, one can ask:

1   Is what whiteness is (what it is for something to be white) best understood by thinking about how white things look to human subjects?
2   Is the fact of snow's being white dependent on human subjects?

In answer to question (1) Boyle says *Yes*. But in answer to (2) he seems *not* to want to say *Yes* straightforwardly.

Consider whether a middle course, such as Boyle wants to steer, is made available by distinguishing between questions (1) and (2).

John Locke, *An Essay Concerning Human Understanding* (extract from Book II, Chapter VIII)

§8 Whatsoever the mind perceives in itself, or is the immediate object of perception, thought, or understanding, that I call idea; and the power to produce any idea in our mind, I call quality of the subject wherein that power is. Thus a snowball having the power to produce in us the ideas of white, cold, and round, the power to produce those ideas in us, as they are in the snowball, I call qualities; and as they are sensations or perceptions in our understandings, I call them ideas; which ideas, if I speak of sometimes as in the things themselves, I would be understood to mean those qualities in the objects which produce them in us.

§9 Qualities thus considered in bodies are: First, such as are utterly inseparable from the body, in what state soever it be; and such as in all the alterations and changes it suffers, all the force can be used upon it, it constantly keeps; and such as sense constantly finds in every particle of matter which has bulk enough to be perceived; and the mind finds inseparable from every particle of matter, though less than to make itself singly be perceived by our senses: v.g. Take a grain of wheat, divide it into two parts; each part has still solidity, extension, figure, and mobility: divide it again, and it retains still the same qualities; and so divide it on, till the parts become insensible; they must retain still each of them all those qualities. For division (which is all that a mill, or pestle, or any other body, does upon another, in reducing it to insensible parts) can never take away either solidity, extension, figure, or mobility from any body, but only makes two or more distinct separate masses of matter, of that which was but one before; all which distinct masses, reckoned as so many distinct bodies, after division, make a certain number. These I call original or primary qualities of body, which I think we may observe to produce simple ideas in us, viz. solidity, extension, figure, motion or rest, and number.

§10   Secondly, such qualities which in truth are nothing in the objects themselves but powers to produce various sensations in us by their primary qualities, i.e. by the bulk, figure, texture, and motion of their insensible parts, as colours, sounds, tastes, &c. These I call secondary qualities. To these might be added a third sort, which are allowed to be barely powers; though they are as much real qualities in the subject as those which I, to comply with the common way of speaking, call qualities, but for distinction, secondary qualities. For the power in fire to produce a new colour, or consistency, in wax or clay, by its primary qualities, is as much a quality in fire, as the power it has to produce in me a new idea or sensation of warmth or burning, which I felt not before, by the same primary qualities, viz. the bulk, texture, and motion of its insensible parts.

§11   The next thing to be considered is, how bodies produce ideas in us; and that is manifestly by impulse, the only way which we can conceive bodies to operate in.

§12   If then external objects be not united to our minds when they produce ideas therein; and yet we perceive these original qualities in such of them as singly fall under our senses, it is evident that some motion must be thence continued by our nerves, or animal spirits, by some parts of our bodies, to the brains or the seat of sensation, there to produce in our minds the particular ideas we have of them. And since the extension, figure, number, and motion of bodies of an observable bigness, may be perceived at a distance by the sight, it is evident some singly imperceptible bodies must come from them to the eyes, and thereby convey to the brain some motion; which produces these ideas which we have of them in us.

§13   After the same manner, that the ideas of these original qualities are produced in us, we may conceive that the ideas of secondary qualities are also produced, viz. by the operation of insensible particles on our senses. For, it being manifest that there are bodies and good store of bodies, each whereof are so small, that we cannot by any of our senses discover either their bulk, figure, or motion, as is evident in the particles of the air and water, and others extremely smaller than those; perhaps as much smaller than the particles of air and water, as the particles of air and water are smaller than peas or hail-stones; let us suppose at present that the different motions and figures, bulk and number, of such particles, affecting the several organs of our senses, produce in us those different sensations which we have from the colours and smells of bodies; v.g. that a violet, by the impulse of such insensible particles of matter, of peculiar figures and bulks, and in different degrees and modifications of their motions, causes the ideas of the blue colour, and sweet scent of that flower to be produced in our minds. It being no more impossible to conceive that God should annex such ideas to such motions, with which they have no similitude, than that he should annex the idea of pain to the motion of a piece of steel dividing our flesh, with which that idea hath no resemblance.

§14   What I have said concerning colours and smells may be understood also of tastes and sounds, and other the like sensible qualities; which, whatever reality we by mistake attribute to them, are in truth nothing in the objects themselves, but powers to produce various sensations in us; and depend on those primary qualities, viz. bulk, figure, texture, and motion of parts as I have said.

§15   From whence I think it easy to draw this observation, that the ideas of primary qualities of bodies are resemblances of them, and their patterns do really exist in the bodies themselves, but the ideas produced in us by these secondary qualities have no resemblance of them at all. There is nothing like our ideas, existing in the bodies themselves. They are, in the bodies we denominate from them, only a power to produce those sensations in us: and what is sweet, blue, or warm in idea, is but the certain bulk, figure, and motion of the insensible parts, in the bodies themselves, which we call so.

§16   Flame is denominated hot and light; snow, white and cold; and manna, white and sweet, from the ideas they produce in us. Which qualities are commonly thought to be the same in those bodies that those ideas are in us, the one the perfect resemblance of the other, as they are in a mirror, and it would by most men be judged very extravagant if one should say otherwise. And yet he that will consider that the same fire that, at one distance produces in us the sensation of warmth, does, at a nearer approach, produce in us the far different sensation of pain, ought to be think himself what reason he has to say that this idea of warmth, which was produced in him by the fire, is actually in the fire; and his idea of pain, which the same fire produced in him the same way, is not in the fire. Why are whiteness and coldness in snow, and pain not, when it produces the one and the other idea in us; and can do neither, but by the bulk, figure, number, and motion of its solid parts?

§17   The particular bulk, number, figure, and motion of the parts of fire or snow are really in them, whether any one's senses perceive them or no: and therefore they may be called real qualities, because they really exist in those bodies. But light, heat, whiteness, or coldness, are no more really in them than sickness or pain is in manna. Take away the sensation of them; let not the eyes see light or colours, nor the ears hear sounds; let the palate not taste, nor the nose smell, and all colours, tastes, odours, and sounds, as they are such particular ideas, vanish and cease, and are reduced to their causes, i.e. bulk, figure, and motion of parts.

§18   A piece of manna of a sensible bulk is able to produce in us the idea of a round or square figure; and by being removed from one place to another, the idea of motion. This idea of motion represents it as it really is in manna moving: a circle or square are the same, whether in idea or existence, in the mind or in the manna. And this, both motion and figure, are really in the manna, whether we take notice of them or no: this everybody is ready to agree to. Besides, manna, by the bulk, figure, texture, and motion of its parts, has a power to produce the sensations of sickness, and sometimes of acute pains or gripings in us. That these ideas of sickness and pain are not in the manna, but effects of its operations on us, and are nowhere when we feel them not; this also every one readily agrees to. And yet men are hardly to be brought to think that sweetness and whiteness are not really in manna; which are but the effects of the operations of manna, by the motion, size, and figure of its particles, on the eyes and palate: as the pain and sickness caused by manna are confessedly nothing but the effects of its operations on the stomach and guts, by the size, motion, and figure of its insensible parts, (for by nothing else can a body operate, as has been proved): as if it could not operate on the eyes and palate, and thereby produce in the mind particular distinct ideas, which in itself it has not, as well as we allow it can operate on the guts and stomach, and thereby produce distinct ideas, which in itself it has not. These ideas, being all effects of the operations of manna on several parts of our bodies, by the size, figure number, and motion of its parts; why those produced by the eyes and palate should rather be thought to be really in the manna, than those produced by the stomach and guts; or why the pain and sickness, ideas that are the effect of manna, should be thought to be nowhere when they are not felt; and yet the sweetness and whiteness, effects of the same manna on other parts of the body, by ways equally as unknown, should be thought to exist in the manna, when they are not seen or tasted, would need some reason to explain.

§19   Let us consider the red and white colours in porphyry. Hinder light from striking on it, and its colours vanish; it no longer produces any such ideas in us: upon the return of light it produces these appearances on us again. Can any one think any real alterations are made in the porphyry by the presence or absence of light; and that those ideas of whiteness and redness are really in porphyry in the light, when it is plain it has no colour in the dark? It has, indeed, such a configuration of particles, both night and day, as are apt, by the rays of light rebounding from some parts of that hard stone, to produce in us the idea of redness, and from others the idea of whiteness; but whiteness or redness are not in it at any time, but such a texture that hath the power to produce such a sensation in us.

§20 Pound an almond, and the clear white colour will be altered into a dirty one, and the sweet taste into an oily one. What real alteration can the beating of the pestle make in any body, but an alteration of the texture of it?

§21 Ideas being thus distinguished and understood, we may be able to give an account how the same water, at the same time, may produce the idea of cold by one hand and of heat by the other: whereas it is impossible that the same water, if those ideas were really in it, should at the same time be both hot and cold. For, if we imagine warmth, as it is in our hands, to be nothing but a certain sort and degree of motion in the minute particles of our nerves or animal spirits, we may understand how it is possible that the same water may, at the same time, produce the sensations of heat in one hand and cold in the other; which yet figure never does, that never producing the idea of a square by one hand which has produced the idea of a globe by another. But if the sensation of heat and cold be nothing but the increase or diminution of the motion of the minute parts of our bodies, caused by the corpuscles of any other body, it is easy to be understood, that if that motion be greater in one hand than in the other; if a body be applied to the two hands, which has in its minute particles a greater motion than in those of one of the hands, and a less than in those of the other, it will increase the motion of the one hand and lessen it in the other; and so cause the different sensations of heat and cold that depend thereon.

§22 I have in what just goes before been engaged in physical inquiries a little further than perhaps I intended. But, it being necessary to make the nature of sensation a little understood; and to make the difference between the qualities in bodies, and the ideas produced by them in the mind, to be distinctly conceived, without which it were impossible to discourse intelligibly of them; I hope I shall be pardoned this little excursion into natural philosophy; it being necessary in our present inquiry to distinguish the primary and real qualities of bodies, which are always in them (viz. solidity, extension, figure, number, and motion, or rest, and are sometimes perceived by us, viz. when the bodies they are in are big enough singly to be discerned), from those secondary and imputed qualities, which are but the powers of several combinations of those primary ones, when they operate without being distinctly discerned; whereby we may also come to know what ideas are, and what are not, resemblances of something really existing in the bodies we denominate from them.

§23   The qualities, then, that are in bodies, rightly considered, are of three sorts:

First, The bulk, figure, number, situation, and motion or rest of their solid parts. Those are in them, whether we perceive them or not; and when they are of that size that we can discover them, we have by these an idea of the thing as it is in itself; as is plain in artificial things. These I call primary qualities.

Secondly, The power that is in any body, by reason of its insensible primary qualities, to operate after a peculiar manner on any of our senses, and thereby produce in us the different ideas of several colours, sounds, smells, tastes, &c. These are usually called sensible qualities.

Thirdly, The power that is in any body, by reason of the particular constitution of its primary qualities, to make such a change in the bulk, figure, texture, and motion of another body, as to make it operate on our senses differently from what it did before. Thus the sun has a power to make wax white, and fire to make lead fluid. These are usually called powers.

The first of these, as has been said, I think may be properly called real, original, or primary qualities; because they are in the things themselves, whether they are perceived or not: and upon their different modifications it is that the secondary qualities depend.

The other two are only powers to act differently upon other things: which powers result from the different modifications of those primary qualities.

§24   But, though the two latter sorts of qualities are powers barely, and nothing but powers, relating to several other bodies, and resulting from the different modifications of the original qualities, yet they are generally otherwise thought of. For the second sort, viz., the powers to produce several ideas in us, by our senses, are looked upon as real qualities in the things thus affecting us: but the third sort are called and esteemed barely powers. v.g. The idea of heat or light, which we receive by our eyes, or touch, from the sun, are commonly thought real qualities existing in the sun, and something more than mere powers in it. But when we consider the sun in reference to wax, which it melts or blanches, we look on the whiteness and softness produced in the wax, not as qualities in the sun, but effects produced by powers in it. Whereas, if rightly considered, these qualities of light and warmth, which are perceptions in me when I am warmed or enlightened by the sun, are no otherwise in the sun, than the changes made in the wax, when it is blanched or melted, are in the sun. They are all of them equally powers in the sun, depending on its primary qualities; whereby it is able, in the one case, so to alter the bulk, figure, texture, or motion of some of the insensible parts of my eyes or hands, as thereby to produce in me the idea of light or heat; and in the other, it is able so to alter the bulk, figure, texture, or motion of the insensible parts of the wax, as to make them fit to produce in me the distinct ideas of white and fluid.

§25   The reason why the one are ordinarily taken for real qualities, and the other only for bare powers, seems to be, because the ideas we have of distinct colours, sounds, &c., containing nothing at all in them of bulk, figure, or motion, we are not apt to think them the effects of these primary qualities; which appear not, to our senses, to operate in their production, and with which they have not any apparent congruity or conceivable connexion. Hence it is that we are so forward to imagine, that those ideas are the resemblances of something really existing in the objects themselves: since sensation discovers nothing of bulk, figure, or motion of parts in their production; nor can reason show how bodies, by their bulk, figure, and motion, should produce in the mind the ideas of blue or yellow, &c. But, in the other case, in the operations of bodies changing the qualities one of another, we plainly discover that the quality produced hath commonly no resemblance with anything in the thing producing it; wherefore we look on it as a bare effect of power. For, through receiving the idea of heat or light from the sun, we are apt to think it is a perception and resemblance of such a quality in the sun; yet when we see wax, or a fair face, receive change of colour from the sun, we cannot imagine that to be the reception or resemblance of anything in the sun, because we find not those different colours in the sun itself.

Commentary on Locke

You might be struck by how unargumentative much of this extract is. If one searches for conclusions and arguments carrying one to them, then one sometimes searches in vain. But while it is true that in the early paragraphs here Locke is simply setting out his view, in later paragraphs he takes trouble to try to persuade his reader of the doctrines he is advocating. He uses various argumentative strategies, two of which we shall draw attention to as we go through Locke's paragraphs.

In §8 Locke sets up his terminology of 'ideas' and 'qualities'. In Book I of the *Essay*, Locke announced that he uses the word 'idea' in a very general way 'to express whatever it is which the mind can be employed about in thinking'. He talks now of ideas as *immediate* objects of perception, produced in minds (he sometimes says 'understandings') by the qualities of things – such as snowballs – that we perceive. Like Boyle, whom we compared with Descartes above, Locke is working with a dualist account of perception. For Locke the mental aspect of perception consists of the presence of an idea in a mind. Locke uses the word 'sensation' for an idea that is in the mind on an occasion of perception.

Locke says that he is going to use the word 'qualities' for the powers in a material thing. He equates qualities with powers, because he takes them to work causally in perception. Like Boyle, Locke thinks that qualities of objects have effects upon our sense organs and in turn upon our minds: qualities are powers to produce ideas in our minds. Locke's use of 'power' is akin to today's philosophers' use of 'disposition' (see above, in 'Commentary on Boyle').

In §9 Locke says what he means by 'primary qualities': they are qualities which material things cannot lack. (Like Boyle, Locke uses the word 'bodies' for material things.) He provides the example of the grain of wheat to show that the smaller parts of a thing with primary qualities have primary qualities too.

Locke's point at $\boxed{a} \mapsto$, about primary qualities remaining when an object is divided, may remind you of Boyle. Re-read Boyle sections I, II and III. Say exactly what it is that you find that Boyle and Locke agree about.

Locke lists the primary qualities. By 'extension', Locke means size, and by 'figure' shape. 'Number' might not seem really to belong on Locke's list: you might not think that you attribute a quality to anything if you say that there are four chairs. But perhaps one can understand Locke's including 'number' among the primary qualities if one thinks of him as interested in what belongs in a description of the mechanistic world – the world of matter and motion portrayed by Boyle, or the world of the scientist we considered in the 'Introduction' to this chapter. Locke speaks below of 'the number of the particles' (at §13). At this point, as at various others, Locke is thinking of a thing's primary qualities at the microscopic level: the 'particles' here are the corpuscles of Boyle's corpuscularian hypothesis. (Locke rarely uses the word 'corpuscle': he says something later on which suggests that he wants to spare his reader the scientific details.)

In §10 Locke says what he means by 'secondary qualities'. Locke has called *all* perceivable qualities powers in §8, and now he wants to use the notion of a power to characterize secondary qualities specifically. The point about secondary qualities is that they are powers *to produce sensations in us*, and *that is all that they are* (they are 'nothing but' such powers). If so, primary qualities – or sensible primary qualities at any rate – can also be powers to produce sensations, but there is more to them than their being such powers.

Locke also mentions qualities of a third sort, which he thinks have the same sort of reality as the secondary qualities. On this third sort of quality he will have more to say later, at §23.

In §§11, 12 and 13 Locke tells us how bodies produce ideas in us – *via* motions external to us and motions inside us. And he tells us that secondary qualities produce their ideas in the same way as primary ones: particles that are 'insensible' (too small to be sensed) operate on our senses. Like Boyle, Locke thinks that the colour and sweet smell of a violet are not remotely like the qualities of the violet which are responsible for the complicated motions from which our ideas of its colour and smell result.

At b⟩ Locke follows Boyle in using the example of pain to help us to understand why there simply need not be any quality in an object which is 'like' (Locke says has 'similitude to') the idea that it produces in minds. Locke encourages us to think of God as having set up correspondences between kinds of motion and texture of corpuscles and kinds of idea produced in our minds (ideas which are produced by objects made up of corpuscles with such kinds of motion and texture).

In §14 we see that Locke also shares Boyle's view that people are apt to suppose mistakenly that secondary qualities have a different 'reality' from what they actually have. (Boyle was more explicit about this than Locke: he said that what people suppose is that secondary qualities have effects in the material world as well as upon our sense organs and minds.) It seems that Locke thinks that in so far as secondary qualities are real qualities, their reality is got from their depending upon the primary qualities of corpuscles.

Consider what Locke means at c⟩ when he says that secondary qualities are nothing 'in' objects. Look for other such uses of 'in' in earlier paragraphs of Locke, and in Boyle. What does Locke convey to you when he uses the word 'in' for the relation between objects and their qualities?

In §15 Locke makes out the distinction between primary and secondary qualities in a way that relies upon his initial separation of qualities from ideas. The primary/secondary distinction now shows up as a distinction between those qualities the ideas of which resemble the qualities (the primary ones) and those qualities the ideas of which do not resemble the qualities (the secondary ones). To understand this, one has to remember that Locke places qualities in material things and ideas in minds, so that the question can be raised: is the idea in the mind *like* the quality in the material thing that produced it? Do the quality and the idea *resemble* one another? Where the idea in the mind does not resemble any quality in the material thing – in the case of a secondary quality – *all* there is in the material thing is a power to produce such an idea in a mind, according to Locke.

In §16 Locke gives some examples. Recognizing that most people think it daft (Locke says 'extravagant') to deny that our ideas of secondary qualities resemble the qualities, he wants to show such people wrong. Again he trades on the fact that people don't think that the idea of pain resembles any quality in an object. When one gets very close to the fire, so that it is felt as painfully hot, one doesn't think that there is anything like one's pain in the fire. Why should one think differently about the warmth one feels when one is less close to the fire? Locke's suggestion is that those who accept that the idea of pain does not resemble any quality in objects will be inconsistent unless they also accept that the ideas of secondary qualities do not resemble qualities in objects.

In §17 Locke claims that only the primary qualities are really in objects, on the strength of the fact that if you take away the sensing of an object's primary qualities the qualities remain, but if you take away the sensing of the secondary qualities all you have left is the primary qualities of the small parts of the object.

In §18 Locke uses the example of manna, a sweet juice extracted from certain plants (and a substance miraculously supplied as food to the Israelites according to a Bible story). He thinks that it takes some explaining why we readily allow that manna's capacity to make us sick is dependent on its operations on our stomach and guts, but don't allow that manna's capacity to produce ideas of sweetness and whiteness is similarly dependent on its operations on our palates and our eyes.

In §19 Locke gives the first of two examples. Porphyry is a hard rock composed of red and white crystals. Locke points out that we don't think the porphyry itself is changed when light stops shining on it. So whatever ensures that the porphyry looks red when light shining on it is reflected on to a person's eyes doesn't need any light or any person. It must be something about the porphyry's texture.

In §20 we have Locke's second example, of the almond. Locke again wants to persuade us that the secondary qualities of something are the upshot of its primary quality texture. He says that the almond's secondary qualities (its colour and taste) change when it is pounded, and he wants us to think that you could only change the almond's secondary qualities by changing its primary quality texture. His question at ⬚d→ is evidently rhetorical: Locke's reader is meant to answer 'You can't really change anything except primary qualities by pounding.' It then seems as if Locke may have helped himself to what he is trying to prove itself, i.e. it seems as if Locke has begged the question.

Consider how you think §20 is meant to work. Do *you* think Locke begs the question?

In §21 Locke claims to have an explanation of how water felt as cold by one hand may be felt as warm by the other. The phenomenon in question is an example of what is called 'perceptual relativity': how things seem to be in experience – how hot they feel, what colour they look to have – is relative to the perceiver or to the conditions of perception.

If you have never encountered the phenomenon that Locke is relying on, then do an experiment! You will need three bowls of water, one nearly as hot as your hands can bear, one very cold, and one lukewarm. Put one hand each in the hot and cold bowls for a minute or two, and then simultaneously put both hands into the lukewarm bowl. The result is very striking.

At $\boxed{e} \mapsto$ Locke tells us how we can understand the water's being felt differently by the two hands. His explanation relies upon treating warmth (i.e. what is felt when something feels warm, as opposed to what a thermometer measures) as a secondary quality. By giving his explanation, he hopes to provide support for his account of perception. We can step back from Locke's argument, and characterize it in an abstract way, in order to bring out the sort of strategy he is using here. Thus:

If you have an explanation of a phenomenon that your opponents cannot explain, then you have an edge over them. Suppose you believe that p, and your opponents don't accept that p. By giving an explanation which relies on p, you can gain support for your belief that p.

Think of Locke as employing this argumentative strategy when he gives his explanation at $\boxed{e} \mapsto$. Say in your own words what belief Locke is attempting to gain support for. Exactly what explanation does Locke give of this particular example of perceptual relativity?

The 'natural philosophy' into which Locke tells us he has made a 'little excursion', in §22, is the corpuscularian theory of matter which we have seen expounded in Boyle.

In §§23 and 24 Locke sets out his distinction between *three* sorts of qualities in bodies. The first two are the primary and the secondary, and the third are powers, but, unlike the secondary qualities, they are not powers to produce sensations in us. Locke thinks that we will appreciate that secondary qualities are powers when we see examples of his third sort of quality, such as the power of fire to melt lead. Just as the fire affects the lead by causing it to become molten, so the snow can affect a person's mind by causing an idea of whiteness in it. He claims that people erroneously assimilate secondary qualities to perceptible primary qualities to qualities, which are real qualities in things. People ought rather to assimilate secondary qualities to qualities of his third sort – which everyone acknowledges are mere powers: 'they are allowed to be barely powers' as he put it at §10.

> Try to come up with some other examples which Locke would have agreed are examples of qualities of his third sort, i.e. 'bare powers' but not secondary qualities.

In §25 Locke explains why people fail to assimilate secondary qualities to qualities of his third sort, and why they actually assimilate them to primary qualities. Here we find another example of an argumentative strategy that we can characterize abstractly. Thus:

> Suppose that you are in a minority in thinking that p. And suppose that you can give a plausible explanation of why other people should think that not-p. Your explanation doesn't tend to show that they're right: it shows only why people should *think* that not-p. Then you can uphold p against the majority. The fact that nearly everyone else thinks the opposite to you makes no odds if you can explain this fact away.

> Think of Locke as employing the argumentative strategy just suggested in §25. Exactly what is it that Locke wants to explain away?

Locke appreciates that he needs to persuade his readers of his claim that secondary qualities do not really exist in objects. Presumably he realizes that he might face an objection similar to that which Boyle recognized when he 'foresaw a difficulty' – namely that it seems obvious that secondary qualities 'have an *absolute* being irrelative to *us*' (Boyle section VI, above). Like Boyle, Locke thinks of secondary qualities as 'relative'. He speaks now of all powers as 'relating' to other bodies; in the particular case of the secondary qualities, the powers in question are relative to *us*.

When Locke says that secondary qualities are 'mere powers' or 'powers barely', he apparently thinks of them rather as today's philosophers think of dispositions. If we recast today's philosophers' account to fit Locke's dualistic framework, then the idea will be that, where Q is any secondary quality, something's being Q is a matter of its being so disposed as normally to cause ideas of Q-ness in our minds. Example: something's being red is a matter of its being so disposed as normally to cause ideas of redness in our minds.

Ask yourself whether Locke accepts the account just suggested. To do this, you will need to re-read in a focused way what Locke has to say about the secondary qualities.

Introduction to Berkeley

The Irish philosopher George Berkeley (1685–1753) was an empiricist and an idealist. As an idealist, Berkeley thought that there are no 'unperceiving substances': he denied the existence of the material things in which Locke and Boyle believed.

In the course of his life, Berkeley lived in Dublin, London, Rhode Island, Inokelly and Oxford, and he travelled in France and Italy. Inokelly is in the diocese of Cloyne (in County Cork in the south of Ireland), where Berkeley was made bishop in 1734. After becoming bishop, his writings moved from philosophical questions to questions of social reform and of religion.

Berkeley was an undergraduate at Trinity College Dublin. During his student years, he kept a kind of scrapbook of thoughts – his *Philosophical Commentaries*, printed long after his death. The work shows the formative influence of Locke's *Essay* which was then a textbook at Trinity. Berkeley's idealism is already evident in the *Commentaries*, where he refers to his doctrine of 'the immaterial hypothesis': only God and persons exist; 'all other things are not so much existences as manners of the existence of persons'. The version of idealism now associated with Berkeley's name is defended in his *Treatise Concerning the Principles of Human Knowledge* (1710), and *Three Dialogues Between Hylas and Philonous* (1713). The passages from these two books extracted here are those in which Berkeley presents his disagreement with Locke over primary and secondary qualities.

Berkeley was very disappointed with the reaction that his *Principles* received when it was published: hardly anyone took him seriously. Thinking that he had not been properly understood, Berkeley wrote the *Three Dialogues* in which Philonous, representing Berkeley's views, patiently puts his case to Hylas who stands in for Locke. Philonous's name derives from the Greek for *lover of mind*, Hylas's from *materialist*. Hylas is the intelligent layman of Berkeley's time who has been imbued with the worldview upheld by Boyle and Locke: Hylas knows what 'the philosophers' think; but he represents naïve wisdom. When Philonous has persuaded Hylas to abandon his belief in matter, Hylas is won over to idealism, but (as Berkeley portrays him) he never gives up on common sense.

George Berkeley, *The Principles of Human Knowledge* and *Three Dialogues Between Hylas and Philonous* (extracts)

The Principles (extracts)

VIII But say you, though the ideas themselves do not exist without the mind, yet there may be things like them whereof they are copies or resemblances, which things exist without the mind, in an unthinking substance. I answer, an idea can be like nothing but an idea; a colour or figure can be like nothing but another colour or figure. If we look but ever so little into our thoughts, we shall find it impossible for us to conceive a likeness except only between our ideas. Again, I ask whether those supposed originals or external things, of which our ideas are the pictures or representations, be themselves perceivable or no? if they are, then they are ideas, and we have gained our point; but if you say they are not, I appeal to any one whether it be sense, to assert a colour is like something which is invisible; hard or soft, like something which is intangible; and so of the rest.

IX Some there are who make a distinction betwixt primary and secondary qualities: by the former, they mean extension, figure, motion, rest, solidity or impenetrability, and number: by the latter they denote all other sensible qualities, as colours, sounds, tastes, and so forth. The ideas we have of these they acknowledge not to be the resemblances of any thing existing without the mind or unperceived; but they will have our ideas of the primary qualities to be patterns or images of things which exist without the mind, in an unthinking substance which they call matter. By matter therefore we are to understand an inert, senseless substance, in which extension, figure and motion, do actually subsist. But it is evident from what we have already shown, that extension, figure, and motion, are only ideas existing in the mind, and that an idea can be like nothing but another idea, and that consequently neither they nor their archetypes can exist in an unperceiving substance. Hence it is plain, that the very notion of what is called matter, or corporeal substance, involves a contradiction in it.

X They who assert that figure, motion, and the rest of the primary or original qualities, do exist without the mind, in unthinking substances, do at the same time acknowledge that colours, sounds, heat, cold, and such like secondary qualities, do not, which they tell us are sensations existing in the mind alone, that depend on and are occasioned by the different size, texture, and motion of the minute particles of matter. This they take for an undoubted truth, which they can demonstrate beyond all exception. Now if it be certain, that those original qualities are inseparably united with the other sensible qualities, and not, even in thought, capable of being abstracted from them, it plainly follows that they exist only in the mind. But I desire any one to reflect and try, whether he can, by any abstraction of thought, conceive the extension and motion of a body, without all other sensible qualities. For my own part, I see evidently that it is not in my power to frame an idea of a body extended and moved, but I must withal give it some colour or other sensible quality which is acknowledged to exist only in the mind. In short, extension, figure, and motion, abstracted from all other qualities, are inconceivable. Where therefore the other sensible qualities are, there must these be also, to wit, in the mind and nowhere else.

XI   Again, great and small, swift and slow, are allowed to exist no where without the mind, being entirely relative, and changing as the frame or position of the organs of sense varies. The extension therefore which exists without the mind, is neither great nor small, the motion neither swift nor slow, that is, they are nothing at all. But, say you, they are extension in general, and motion in general: thus we see how much the tenet of extended, moveable substances existing without the mind, depends on that strange doctrine of abstract ideas. And here I cannot but remark, how nearly the vague and indeterminate description of matter or corporeal substance, which the modern philosophers are run into by their own principles, resembles that antiquated and so much ridiculed notion of materia prima, to be met with in Aristotle and his followers. Without extension solidity cannot be conceived; since therefore it has been shown that extension exists not in an unthinking substance, the same must also be true of solidity. [...]

XIV   I shall further add, that after the same manner as modern philosophers prove certain sensible qualities to have no existence in matter, or without the mind, the same thing may be likewise proved of all other sensible qualities whatsoever. Thus, for instance, it is said that heat and cold are affections only of the mind, and not at all patterns of real beings, existing in the corporeal substances which excite them, for that the same body which appears cold to one hand, seems warm to another. Now why may we not as well argue that figure and extension are not patterns or resemblances of qualities existing in matter, because to the same eye at different stations, or eyes of a different texture at the same station, they appear various, and cannot therefore be the images of any thing settled and determinate without the mind? Again, it is proved that sweetness is not really in the said thing, because, the thing remaining unaltered, the sweetness is changed into bitter, as in case of a fever or otherwise vitiated palate. Is it not as reasonable to say, that motion is not without the mind, since if the succession of ideas in the mind become swifter, the motion, it is acknowledged, shall appear slower without any alteration in any external object.

XV   In short, let any one consider those arguments which are thought manifestly to prove that colours and tastes exist only in the mind, and he shall find they may with equal force be brought to prove the same thing of extension, figure, and motion. [...]

The First Dialogue (extract)

Hyl.   I tell you, Philonous, external light is nothing but a thin fluid substance, whose minute particles being agitated with a brisk motion, and in various manners reflected from the different surfaces of outward objects to the eyes, communicate different motions to the optic nerves; which, being propagated to the brain, cause therein various impressions; and these are attended with the sensations of red, blue, yellow, &c.

Phil.   It seems then the light doth no more than shake the optic nerves.

Hyl.   Nothing else.

Phil.   And consequent to each particular motion of the nerves, the mind is affected with a sensation, which is some particular colour.

Hyl.   Right.

Phil.   And these sensations have no existence without the mind.

Hyl.   They have not.

Phil.   How then do you affirm that colours are in the light; since by *light* you understand a corporeal substance external to the mind?

Hyl.   Light and colours, as immediately perceived by us, I grant cannot exist without the mind. But in themselves they are only the motions and configurations of certain insensible particles of matter.

Phil.   Colours then, in the vulgar sense, or taken for the immediate objects of sight, cannot agree to any but a perceiving substance.

Hyl. That is what I say.

Phil. Well then, since you give up the point as to those sensible qualities which are alone thought colours by all mankind beside, you may hold what you please with regard to those invisible ones of the philosophers. It is not my business to dispute about *them*; only I would advise you to bethink yourself, whether, considering the inquiry we are upon, it be prudent for you to affirm – *the red and blue which we see are not real colours, but certain unknown motions and figures which no man ever did or can see are truly so.* Are not these shocking notions, and are not they subject to as many ridiculous inferences, as those you were obliged to renounce before in the case of sounds?

Hyl. I frankly own, Philonous, that it is in vain to stand out any longer. Colours, sounds, tastes, in a word all those termed *secondary qualities*, have certainly no existence without the mind. But by this acknowledgment I must not be supposed to derogate, the reality of Matter, or external objects; seeing it is no more than several philosophers maintain, who nevertheless are the farthest imaginable from denying Matter. For the clearer understanding of this, you must know sensible qualities are by philosophers divided into *Primary* and *Secondary*. The former are Extension, Figure, Solidity, Gravity, Motion, and Rest; and these they hold exist really in bodies. The latter are those above enumerated; or, briefly, *all sensible qualities beside the Primary*; which they assert are only so many sensations or ideas existing nowhere but in the mind. But all this, I doubt not, you are apprised of. For my part, I have been a long time sensible there was such an opinion current among philosophers, but was never thoroughly convinced of its truth until now.

Phil. You are still then of opinion that *extension* and *figures* are inherent in external unthinking substances?

Hyl. I am.

Phil. But what if the same arguments which are brought against Secondary Qualities will hold good against these also?

Hyl. Why then I shall be obliged to think, they too exist only in the mind.

Phil. Is it your opinion the very figure and extension which you perceive by sense exist in the outward object or material substance?

Hyl. It is.

Phil. Have all other animals as good grounds to think the same of the figure and extension which they see and feel?

Hyl. Without doubt, if they have any thought at all.

Phil. Answer me, Hylas. Think you the senses were bestowed upon all animals for their preservation and well-being in life? or were they given to men alone for this end?

Hyl. I make no question but they have the same use in all other animals.

Phil. If so, is it not necessary they should be enabled by them to perceive their own limbs, and those bodies which are capable of harming them?

Hyl. Certainly.

Phil. A mite therefore must be supposed to see his own foot, and things equal or even less than it, as bodies of some considerable dimension; though at the same time they appear to you scarce discernible, or at best as so many visible points?

Hyl. I cannot deny it.

Phil. And to creatures less than the mite they will seem yet larger?

Hyl. They will.

Phil. Insomuch that what you can hardly discern will to another extremely minute animal appear as some huge mountain?

Hyl. All this I grant.

Phil. Can one and the same thing be at the same time in itself of different dimensions?

Hyl. That were absurd to imagine.

Phil. But, from what you have laid down it follows that both the extension by you perceived, and that perceived by the mite itself, as likewise all those perceived by lesser animals, are each of them the true extension of the mite's foot; that is to say, by your own principles you are led into an absurdity.

Hyl. There seems to be some difficulty in the point.

Phil. Again, have you not acknowledged that no real inherent property of any object can be changed without some change in the thing itself?

Hyl. I have.

Phil. But, as we approach to or recede from an object, the visible extension varies, being at one distance ten or a hundred times greater than another. Doth it not therefore follow from hence likewise that it is not really inherent in the object?

Hyl. I own I am at a loss what to think.

Phil. Your judgment will soon be determined, if you will venture to think as freely concerning this quality as you have done concerning the rest. Was it not admitted as a good argument, that neither heat nor cold was in the water, because it seemed warm to one hand and cold to the other?

Hyl. It was.

Phil. Is it not the very same reasoning to conclude, there is no extension or figure in an object, because to one eye it shall seem little, smooth, and round, when at the same time it appears to the other, great, uneven, and regular?

Hyl. The very same. But does this latter fact ever happen?

Phil. You may at any time make the experiment, by looking with one eye bare, and with the other through a microscope. [...]

Commentary on Berkeley

When Berkeley sets out to attack Locke's distinction between primary and secondary qualities, he takes himself already to have established one plank of his idealism – that all ideas are dependent upon minds. As an idealist, Berkeley denies the existence of the material world of Locke and Boyle wherein there are 'unperceiving substances' as Berkeley sometimes calls the things that he rejects.

The Principles

'Some there are' says Berkeley at section IX, when he embarks on his attack. Although he doesn't name names here, Berkeley makes it clear that he has Locke in mind as his opponent. In section VIII, Locke's doctrine that ideas in the mind resemble qualities in objects outside the mind – a doctrine which Locke held to be true of the primary qualities, and which he took to separate the primary from the secondary – is evidently part of what Berkeley denounces.

At section VIII, Berkeley has his opponent saying that there may be things resembling ideas which exist outside the mind. He counters with the claim that 'an idea can be like nothing but an idea'. Berkeley challenges the opponent to say what sense can be made of the claim that there is something which is not an idea but which is like an idea. His argument poses a dilemma. Suppose there was such a something; then either it would be perceivable or it would not.

> State the steps by which Berkeley gets from his dilemma to his conclusion that 'an idea can be like nothing but an idea'.

The second step in Berkeley's argument from a dilemma might seem unfair on Locke. For Berkeley asks how a colour can be like something invisible. And Locke, who thinks that coloured things have 'insensible parts' whose 'bulk, figure, texture, and motion' are responsible for our ideas of colour, does not say that invisible qualities of insensible parts are like our ideas of colours. It

might seem that Berkeley would need one of Locke's primary qualities –
which Locke did think were like the ideas that they produced – if he wanted
to refute Locke at this point. But perhaps one can understand Berkeley's
general difficulty with the idea that something which is not an idea can be
like something which is an idea.

> Look at a book and think about what shape it is. Ask yourself whether you
> are able to compare the shape of the book with an idea of its shape you
> have in your mind. Presumably you need to be able to make such a
> comparison in order to understand what it means to say, as Locke did,
> that one is like the other.

Berkeley's argument in section IX comes to focus on the primary qualities.
His principle that an idea can be like nothing but an idea is applied to them.
He gives an argument against the idea of primary qualities residing in something that is not a mind. By 'archetypes' here Berkeley means things of which
ideas are supposedly copies or resemblances.

> Try to put the argument of section IX into your own words.

In section X Berkeley puts forward what has sometimes been called his
Inseparability Thesis, which says that we cannot prize secondary qualities
apart from primary ones – that it is impossible to 'conceive the extension and
motion of a body, without all other sensible [i.e. secondary] qualities'. The
Inseparability Thesis is introduced at $\boxed{a} \mapsto$, where Berkeley tells us that if it is
true, then original (primary) qualities 'exist only in the mind'. Berkeley invites
his reader to experiment, by trying to 'conceive' for themself that his thesis is
wrong.

> Are you persuaded that you cannot 'conceive' for yourself that Berkeley is
> wrong? Do you think that the only way to conceive of something is to form
> a picture of it?

In section XI Berkeley asserts that the primary qualities change 'as the
frame or position of the organs of sense varies'. This is an assertion of the
perceptual relativity of primary qualities. (For 'perceptual relativity', see
'Commentary on Locke' at §21. There will be more on the perceptual relativity of primary qualities in 'The First Dialogue' below.) Berkeley makes it
clear that he is opposed not only to Boyle and Locke, but also to the worldview inherited from Aristotle which Boyle wanted to supplant.

In sections XIV and XV Berkeley is very explicit that he accepts some of
what Locke says about the secondary qualities. He thinks that what Locke
was right about in the case of the secondary qualities – their subjectivity, or
mind-dependence – goes for the primary qualities too.

See whether you can formulate the disagreement between Locke and Berkeley precisely. Ask yourself what Locke says about the secondary qualities with which Berkeley does not agree.

The First Dialogue

There is no enumeration in this text; nor have any arrow markers been introduced. You are left to match up the text with this commentary. Note for yourself where one line of argument stops and another starts in Berkeley.

The characters Hylas and Philonous were introduced in the 'Introduction to Berkeley' above. The terms in which Hylas speaks at the start of this extract make it clear that he stands in for Locke until he has heard Philonous's arguments. Hylas's view of light and its reflection relies on Boyle's corpuscularian world of matter in motion. Philonous persuades Hylas that his conception of colours, which derives from this view of light, is at odds with his ordinary conception of colours – of colours 'in the vulgar sense'.

At the point at which Hylas gives in to Philonous and acknowledges that this only conception of colours is of something in his mind, he rehearses Locke's distinction between the primary and the secondary qualities, and says how very convinced he suddenly is of that distinction. When Hylas says 'I ... was never thoroughly convinced of its truth until now', Berkeley is using an argumentative strategy which the dialogue form helps him with.

Can you say what Berkeley's strategy (which the dialogue form helps him with) is? Ask yourself why Berkeley should represent Hylas as finding himself especially convinced of the primary/secondary quality distinction at this particular point. Why does Philonous start by persuading Hylas that secondary qualities are only within the mind?

Once Hylas has agreed with him about secondary qualities, Philonous has only to win him over to the idea that primary qualities are no different – they also exist in minds. Philonous convinces Hylas that his view that primary qualities – figure and extension (i.e. shape and size) – belong to mind-independent objects leads to absurdity.

What is the absurd conclusion to which Philonous claims Hylas is committed? What premises lead to this conclusion?

Philonous uses two different sets of considerations to convince Hylas of the perceptual relativity of size. He then reminds Hylas of one of Locke's examples of perceptual relativity – of warmth as experienced by two different hands. This is an example he has used earlier in this *Dialogue*. Philonous likens warmth as experienced by two different hands to size as experienced by two different eyes.

> How do you think Hylas ought to have reacted to Philonous's claim that 'as ... we recede [move away] from an object, the visible extension varies'? Assume that an object's visible extension is how big the object looks. Think about the phrase 'how big it looks'. Consider what it means to say that something looks two metres long.

At the end of the extracted passage, Philonous tells Hylas that the perceptual relativity of secondary qualities is assumed to supply 'a good argument' for the conclusion that secondary qualities are not in objects – that neither heat nor cold is in the water, for example. Philonous's point, then, is that primary qualities exhibit the same phenomenon of perceptual relativity as secondary ones: he uses as an example now the different primary qualities that something will seem to have according to whether it is looked at with a bare eye or through a microscope.

> Look back to the relevant passages in Locke and ask yourself what the phenomenon of perceptual relativity contributes to his arguments.

In thinking about this question, one needs to consider Locke's treatment not only of the example of cold and warm hands in water (§21), but also of the examples of the taste and colour of manna (§18), of porphyry in the dark (§19), and of pounding an almond (§20). It appears that Locke treats these examples in order to demonstrate that his view of secondary qualities enables us to understand the phenomena, and that Locke did not intend to ground the primary/secondary distinction in the fact of the perceptual relativity of secondary qualities. If this is right, then Berkeley cannot cast doubt on the distinction simply by pointing to the perceptual relativity of primary qualities. Even so, Berkeley himself will surely find a difficulty in thinking that any quality could both exhibit perceptual relativity and 'exist without the mind': look again at *Principle* XI. And it is far from obvious how the perceptual relativity of primary qualities might be supposed to fit with Locke's thesis that 'the ideas of primary qualities of bodies are resemblances of them'.

In his arguments against Locke, Berkeley relies on Locke's speaking of secondary qualities as not 'existing in' or 'inherent in' objects, and as not 'real' qualities. In Berkeley's view, this can only mean that secondary qualities do not 'exist without the mind'. For Berkeley, unlike Locke, never thinks that secondary qualities might be powers: Hylas doesn't have 'powers' in his vocabulary when he speaks on Locke's behalf.

> Ask yourself whether Hylas would have been better placed to defend himself against Philonous if he had helped himself to Locke's notion of a power.

Further Questions

Three problems were listed in the 'Introduction'. To these, two more can now be added.

Is the world mind-dependent?: realism v. idealism

You will have gathered from these readings that Locke and Berkeley disagreed with one another over very much more than the distinction between primary and secondary qualities. Berkeley, the idealist, took Locke's treatment of the primary qualities to be a part of the erroneous foundation of Lockean realism. In Berkeley's view, all ideas which have their origin in sense experience – and not only, as Locke thought, the ideas of secondary qualities – are mind-dependent. So whereas Locke held (at least according to Berkeley) that ideas of things' secondary qualities depend upon perception and that ideas of their primary qualities do not, Berkeley thought about *all* ideas that 'it is impossible that they should have any existence, out of the minds or thinking things which perceive them' (*Principles*, III). The question of whether a distinction between primary and secondary qualities is sustainable has thus come to seem pivotal to a very large philosophical debate about realism versus idealism.

Realists believe in the existence of material things; and they think that the material things we see and touch retain their qualities, or at least some of their qualities, when no one perceives them. The idealist Berkeley believes that there are in the world only minds and their ideas.

Do we perceive things directly?

There are two sorts of perceptual realist – direct realists and indirect realists. Direct realists hold that in sense perception we are directly aware of the existence and nature of objects in the surrounding material world. Indirect realists hold that we are never directly aware of a material object but can only be indirectly aware of one in virtue of a direct awareness of an intermediary object. Locke was an indirect realist. Ideas are Locke's intermediary objects: he talks of ideas as *immediate* objects of perception produced in us *by* the objects we perceive. Locke thought that we are directly aware only of our ideas, and that our perception of objects in the world and their qualities is indirect. His view about perception is sometimes known as the Representative Theory: our ideas (which we are directly aware of) represent to us objects and their qualities (which we perceive only indirectly).

Locke evidently relies on his being an *indirect* realist when he makes out his distinction between primary and secondary qualities. For he distinguishes between two ways in which the ideas in our minds relate to the (indirectly perceived) qualities of the objects outside our minds. They may be like them (ideas of primary qualities) or unlike them (ideas of secondary qualities).

Notice that the question 'Do we perceive things directly?' separates Locke not only from a direct realist but also from Berkeley. Locke answers this question *No*: we perceive things indirectly. A direct realist and Berkeley both answer *Yes*: both think that the only objects of awareness are direct objects. For the direct realist, the objects of direct awareness are material objects; for Berkeley, they are ideas.

We have just noticed that one doesn't have to be an idealist like Berkeley to take Berkeley's side against the *indirectness* of Lockean realism. One might be a direct realist, agreeing with Locke that there are material objects existing independently of our minds and agreeing with Berkeley that we have direct awareness of the objects we perceive. So it might be possible to reject Locke's indirect realism (as Berkeley did), and yet (like Locke) maintain that the distinction between primary and secondary qualities is significant.

The possibility that a primary/secondary quality distinction could be sustained outside the context of Locke's indirect realism is one that emerges now. Having read Berkeley's criticisms of Locke, you can consider whether one might accept *some* of the things that Locke says but agree with *some* of Berkeley's criticisms. Here it is useful to notice that one does not have to speak of ideas in Locke's sense (of things in the mind, not in the material world) in order to take Locke's view of secondary qualities as powers of a particular kind. When we first looked at the claim of some of today's philosophers that secondary qualities are dispositions (near the end of the 'Commentary on Boyle'), we didn't speak of ideas. We had to recast the claim and put it into a dualistic framework, in order to introduce Locke's 'ideas' (at the end of the 'Commentary on Locke'). Evidently one of the things that Berkeley dislikes in Locke is the dualistic account of perception (which we found back in Descartes). If one can preserve some of Locke's thinking without accepting that account, then one might be in a position to accept some of the things that Locke says but agree with some of Berkeley's criticisms.

Might someone take the view that Locke was right to think that there is a genuine distinction between primary and secondary qualities although Locke did not draw the distinction correctly himself? See whether you can elaborate such a view.

Final task
Consider what you want to say about each of the five problems in the light of your reading of the philosophers. Make some notes on each problem. See whether, using these notes, you can construct a plan for an essay answering the following question: 'Was Locke right to think that there is

a genuine and significant distinction between primary and secondary qualities?'

You will find that in order for your essay to be addressed to this question and to have a suitable structure, you will need to reorganize the material you have assembled in your notes. Some of the thoughts you have had, in reflecting on the five problems, won't belong in this particular essay. So start on your plan by going through your notes asking what is relevant to the question.

(There are some further Essay/Examination Questions, relating to this chapter and all the others, at the end of the book.)

Essay/Examination Questions

These questions cover all of the topics in this book. Some of them were set in the written examination for the London University External Diploma in Philosophy. In that examination, students have to answer three questions in three hours. Some readers may want practice with writing in examination conditions, and they could use these questions. But many readers may wish to pick one question at a time, and write an essay on it in their own time, using Further Reading as appropriate.

1   In his *First Meditation*, how does Descartes attempt to show that there is reason to doubt everything one believes?
2   In connection with the *Second Meditation*, Hobbes said that it was possible that something that thinks should be something corporeal. Do Descartes's arguments succeed in ruling this possibility out?
3   Strawson states the principle: 'If we are to talk coherently about individual consciousnesses or minds, . . . we must know the difference between one such item and two such items.' Is this principle acceptable? Does it make a problem for Descartes?
4   Is Hume right to think that tragedy is more enjoyable to an audience the more they suffer painful feelings? How successful is he in explaining why this might be so?
5   Do we, as Feagin alleges, take pleasure in our distress at the sufferings of tragic characters? Does this help us to understand the ethical significance of tragedy?
6   Williams distinguishes between two elements in the idea of equality: *equality of opportunity* and *equality of respect*? What is the difference

between these? Is there any reason to think that there could be a problem in practice of combining equality of opportunity with equality of respect?

7 What does Nozick mean to show using the example of Wilt Chamberlain? Does the example succeed in showing this?

8 What, according to Lemmon, differentiates the Platonic dilemma from the Sartrean one? Is this difference significant for our understanding of moral dilemma?

9 Does Mill's use of the principle of utility threaten the reality of moral dilemmas? In so far as there is a tension between Mill's theory and the reality of moral dilemmas, what is the best way of resolving it?

10 Outline and evaluate Locke's account of persons and their identity.

11 Is it really possible for one person to change bodies with another?

12 '[T]he will turns at once, like a weathervane on a well-oiled pivot in a changeable wind ... It turns successively to all the motives that lie before it as possible, and with each the human being thinks he can *will* it, and thus fix the weathervane at this point; but this is a mere deception' SCHOPENHAUER. What are Schopenhauer's reasons for saying 'this is a mere deception'? Are they good reasons?

13 Strawson doubts that the question whether determinism is true is a significant question for morality. What arguments does he give for doubting this?

14 Hume gives two definitions of 'cause' in the *Treatise*. Say how these definitions differ from one another. Do you think we could accept them both?

15 What are Anscombe's reasons for denying that causal relations are instances of exceptionless universal generalizations?

16 What distinction do Boyle and Locke make between primary and secondary qualities? Explain and assess two arguments, given by Boyle and/ or Locke, for making the distinction.

17 'An idea can be like nothing but an idea' BERKELEY. How does Berkeley argue for this claim? What conclusions does Berkeley draw using this claim?

Further Reading

1 Doubt

J. Cottingham, *Descartes* (Blackwell, 1986): an accessible account of Descartes's philosophy.

T. Nagel, *What Does it all Mean? A Very Short Introduction to Philosophy* (Oxford University Press, 1987), ch. 2: elementary introduction to possible solutions to the problem of knowledge of the world beyond our minds.

J. Dancy, *An Introduction to Contemporary Epistemology* (Blackwell, 1985): a clear introduction to the main topics of contemporary debate in the theory of knowledge. Chapter 1 is recommended for its discussion of scepticism.

P. F. Strawson, *Scepticism and Naturalism: Some Varieties* (Routledge, 1987): takes a wider look at scepticism in the modern period, and examines different strategies for resisting the sceptic. Quite accessibly written, in the form of lectures.

B. Stroud, *The Significance of Philosophical Scepticism* (Oxford University Press, 1984), ch. 1: introduces scepticism about the external world, and examines in detail a sceptical argument from the possibility that one is dreaming.

B. Williams, *Descartes: The Project of Pure Enquiry* (Penguin Books, 1978): an investigation of Descartes's philosophy in his *Meditations*. Written at a relatively demanding level.

2 Self

E. M. Curley, *Descartes against the Sceptics* (Harvard University Press, 1978; paperback edn, 1999), ch 7: concerned with the content of Descartes's doctrine of dualism, and with the arguments Descartes gives for it in the *Meditations*.

T. Nagel, *What Does it all Mean? A Very Short Introduction to Philosophy* (Oxford University Press, 1987), ch. 4: elementary introduction to possible solutions to the mind–body problem.

G. Strawson, 'The Self', *Journal of Consciousness Studies*, vol. 4 (1997), pp. 405–28 (available at http://www.imprint.co.uk/strawson.htm): introduces thinking about the self in philosophers subsequent to Descartes, and explores a prior sense we have, before we do philosophy, that there is such a thing as the self.

S. Guttenplan, *Mind's Landscape: An Introduction to the Philosophy of Mind* (Blackwell, 2000): introduces the philosophy of mind, covering, in an elementary way, questions beyond those broached in chapter 2.

T. Nagel, *The View from Nowhere* (Oxford University Press, 1986; paperback edn, 1989), chs 1, 2 and 3: concerned with the fact that we can view the world both from a detached point of view and also from a uniquely 'personal' point of view. Its early chapters concern problems about self, mind and body.

3 Tragedy

M. Budd, *Values of Art* (Penguin, 1995), pp. 110–23: these short sections of Budd's book give a succinct analysis of different approaches to the paradox of tragedy, including Hume's.

A. Neill, 'Tragedy', in B. Gaut and D. M. Lopes (eds), *The Routledge Companion to Aesthetics* (Routledge, 2001): a survey of ways in which tragedy has been treated in the history of philosophy.

F. Schier, 'The Claims of Tragedy: An Essay in Moral Psychology and Aesthetic Theory', *Philosophical Papers*, vol. 18 (1989), pp. 7–26: a sophisticated but accessible treatment of the value of tragedy, which the author links in part with the acquisition of knowledge of painful truths.

F. Schier, 'Tragedy and the Community of Sentiment', in P. Lamarque (ed.), *Philosophy and Fiction: Essays in Literary Aesthetics* (Aberdeen University Press, 1983), pp. 73–92: another well-argued and compelling discussion by Schier.

Aristotle, *Poetics*, translation and commentary by Stephen Halliwell (Duckworth, 1987): the classic text from Ancient Greece on the nature and value of tragedy. Still poses some of the most profound questions and is discussed in contemporary debates. Chs 1–15 are especially recommended.

F. Nietzsche, *The Birth of Tragedy*, translation by Shaun Whiteside, with an introduction by Michael Tanner (Penguin, 1994): an idiosyncratic and influential book which attempts to account for the artistic power of ancient tragedy as something that modern culture has lost. Sections 1–15 are most recommended.

A. D. Nuttall, *Why Does Tragedy Give Pleasure?* (Oxford University Press, 2001): a recent attempt to answer the question, drawing on a wide range of literary sources.

4 Equality

T. Nagel, *What Does it all Mean? A Very Short Introduction to Philosophy* (Oxford University Press, 1987), ch. 8: elementary introduction to a fundamental question about distributive justice/equality.

J. Baker, *Arguing for Equality* (Verso, 1987): this contains a clear and non-technical presentation of the arguments for equality.

T. Nagel, 'Equality', in his *Mortal Questions* (Cambridge University Press, 1979): among other things, this article considers arguments about equality in the context of utilitarianism.

R. Dworkin, 'What is Equality?', in his *Sovereign Virtue: The Theory and Practice of Equality* (Harvard University Press, 2000): a thoughtful account by one of the most important contemporary political philosophers.

G. A. Cohen, *If You're an Egalitarian, How Come You're so Rich?* (Harvard University Press, 2000), chs 6 and 10: demanding but rewarding discussions of various aspects of the arguments for egalitarianism.

H. Frankfurt, 'Equality as a Moral Idea', in his *The Importance of What We Care About: Philosophical Essays* (Cambridge University Press, 1988): offers a challenge to the egalitarian different from Nozick's.

5 Dilemma

C. Gowans (ed.), *Moral Dilemmas* (Oxford University Press, 1987): contains all of the articles that you need to take you further into the debates on moral dilemma. Especially recommended are the pieces by Foot, Williams, Nagel, Marcus, Hare, Kant, Bradley and Ross.

B. Williams, 'Conflicts of Values', in his *Moral Luck* (Cambridge University Press, 1981): this article will give you a slightly different perspective on the issue of dilemma.

R. Crisp, *Mill on Utilitarianism* (Routledge, 1997): a very readable book on Mill and his account of utilitarianism.

J. Skorupski, *Mill* (Routledge, 1989): another readable book on Mill and his account of utilitarianism.

6 Identity

H. Noonan, *Personal Identity* (Routledge, 1989): a survey of the history of the problem and the contemporary debate.

D. Parfit, 'Personal Identity', *Philosophical Review*, vol. 80 (1971), pp. 3–27. Also in Perry (see below): a seminal article for the position sometimes known as neo-Lockean. Despite its importance in current philosophical writing, it will not place great demands on the beginner in philosophy.

B. Garrett, *Personal Identity and Self-consciousness* (Routledge, 1998): a very readable account of the recent debate.

J. Perry (ed.), *Personal Identity* (University of California Press, 1975): a useful collection of articles, some of which are quite demanding.

M. Johnston, 'Human Beings' in *Journal of Philosophy*, vol. 84 (1987), pp. 59–83: demanding discussion of personal identity with special reference to the kinds of cases that Williams considered.

7 Freedom

T. Honderich, *How Free Are You? The Determinism Problem* (Oxford University Press, 1993, new edition, including paperback, 2002): a simple introduction to the 'determinism problem'. The author traces out the consequences both of the view that freedom and determinism are incompatible, and of the view that they are compatible.

T. Nagel, *What Does it all Mean? A Very Short Introduction to Philosophy* (Oxford University Press, 1987), ch. 6: elementary introduction to possible solutions to the problem of free will.

R. Kane (ed.) *Free Will* (Blackwell, 2002): a comprehensive collection of essays that is well organized to be helpful for the relative beginner.

G. Watson (ed.), *Free Will* (Oxford University Press, 1982): a collection of essays giving a variety of perspectives on free will, with a good general introduction.

C. Janaway, *Self and World in Schopenhauer's Philosophy* (Clarendon Press, 1989), ch. 9: contains an analysis of Schopenhauer's essay on Freedom.

8 Causality

T. Crane, 'Causation', in A. Grayling (ed.), *Philosophy: A Guide through the Subject* (Oxford University Press, 1995), pp. 184–194: an elementary introduction to the topic of causation, beginning from Hume's view.

G. Dicker, *Hume's Epistemology and Metaphysics: An Introduction* (Routledge, 1998): provides an introduction to Book I of Hume's *Treatise* and Hume's first *Enquiry*.

K. Clatterbaugh, *The Causation Debate in Modern Philosophy 1637–1739* (Routledge, 1999): provides an elementary treatment of writings on causality of Descartes, Hobbes, Gassendi, Le Grand, Malebranche, Spinoza, Leibniz, Boyle, Rohault, Newton, Locke, Berkeley and Hume.

D. Gasking, 'Causation and Recipes', *Mind*, vol. 64 (1955), pp. 479–87: introduces an approach to causation very different from Anscombe's, but one which, like Anscombe's, is opposed to Hume's.

E. Sosa and M. Tooley (eds), *Causation* (Oxford University Press, 1993): sets out some strands in a present-day debate about causation in the 'Introduction'. The collection as a whole contains some recent seminal papers, although many of these are difficult.

9　Qualities

M. R. Ayers, 'Introduction' to Everyman Library edition of *Berkeley's Philosophical Works including the Works on Vision* (J. M. Dent, 1975): useful for learning how the philosophies of Locke and Berkeley relate to one another.

J. L. Mackie, *Problems from Locke* (Oxford University Press, 1976), ch. 1: provides a view of the primary/secondary quality distinction arrived at through the interpretation of Locke.

R. S. Woolhouse, *John Locke* (Harvester, 1983, and Gregg Revivals, 1994), ch. 4: concerned with questions of Lockean interpretation connected with the primary/secondary quality distinction.

F. Jackson, *Perception: A Representative Theory* (Cambridge University Press, 1977), ch. 5: shows how a distinction between primary and secondary qualities turns out in the work of a present-day materialist.

H. Robinson, *Perception* (Routledge, 1994), pp. 59–74: shows how a distinction between primary and secondary qualities turns out in the work of a present-day idealist.

Index